Unfinished

Unfinished

The Anthropology of Becoming

JOÃO BIEHL & PETER LOCKE | EDITORS

DUKE UNIVERSITY PRESS
Durham & London 2017

© 2017 Duke University Press
All rights reserved
Printed in the United States of America on
acid-free paper ∞
Designed by Matthew Tauch
Typeset in Arno Pro by Westchester Publishing Services

Library of Congress Cataloging-in-Publication Data
Names: Biehl, João Guilherme, editor. | Locke, Peter Andrew, [date]– editor.
Title: Unfinished : the anthropology of becoming / João Biehl and Peter Locke, editors.
Description: Durham : Duke University Press, 2017. | Includes bibliographical references and index.
Identifiers: LCCN 2017024177 (print) | LCCN 2017040725 (ebook)
ISBN 9780822372455 (ebook)
ISBN 9780822369301 (hardcover : alk. paper)
ISBN 9780822369455 (pbk. : alk. paper)
Subjects: LCSH: Ethnology—Philosophy. | Anthropology—Philosophy. | Critical theory. | Ethnosociology.
Classification: LCC GN345 (ebook) | LCC GN345 .U545 2017 (print) | DDC 301.01—dc23
LC record available at https://lccn.loc.gov/2017024177

Duke University Press gratefully acknowledges the support of Princeton University's Committee on Research in the Humanities and Social Sciences, which provided funds toward the publication of this book.

Cover art: Francis Alÿs, *Reel-Unreel*, 2011. In collaboration with Julien Devaux and Ajmal Maiwandi; video documentation of an action; film still.

Contents

FOREWORD. *Unfinished*
João Biehl and Peter Locke   ix

INTRODUCTION | ETHNOGRAPHIC SENSORIUM
João Biehl and Peter Locke   1

I   **ONE | THE ANTHROPOLOGY OF BECOMING**
João Biehl and Peter Locke   41

II   **TWO | BECOMING AGGRIEVED**
Laurence Ralph   93

THREE | HEAVEN
Angela Garcia   111

III   **FOUR | REBELLIOUS MATTER**
Bridget Purcell   133

FIVE | WITNESS
Naisargi N. Dave   151

IV   **SIX | I WAS CANNIBALIZED BY AN ARTIST**
Lilia M. Schwarcz   173

SEVEN | ON NEGATIVE BECOMING
Lucas Bessire   197

V   **EIGHT | TIME MACHINES**
Elizabeth A. Davis   217

NINE | HORIZONING
Adriana Petryna   243

VI   **TEN | MEANTIME**
Peter Locke   269

ELEVEN | HEREAFTER
João Biehl   278

AFTERWORD. *Zen Exercises: Anthropological Discipline and Ethics*
Michael M. J. Fischer   293

ACKNOWLEDGMENTS   317

BIBLIOGRAPHY   319

CONTRIBUTORS   353

LIST OF ILLUSTRATIONS   357

INDEX   359

PLATE 0.1 Alice Neel, *James Hunter Black Draftee*, 1965

Foreword

UNFINISHED

JOÃO BIEHL AND PETER LOCKE

Alice Neel's 1965 oil painting *James Hunter Black Draftee* is an arresting portrait. Hunter's pensive face and supporting hand are richly filled in, while his ears and the rest of his body are only loosely sketched. The uncompleted image exposes how lifeworlds enter into the work of art: the artist had been inviting passersby on the New York City street into her studio to sit for her. Hunter, who said he had been drafted to fight in the war in Vietnam, never returned for a second sitting.

We don't know what happened to Hunter.[1] But we know who wanted war and what war did, and how old and new wars make plain the transience and value of all things. Outlined by Neel in the spur of the moment, the seemingly invisible body of this fleeting subject is now a powerful reminder of the perennial struggle of minorities in the United States and elsewhere for full political recognition of their personhood. Hunter's detailed, expressive face also evokes his singularity and the concerns that weigh on him, while revealing little of who he is. Yet it is Hunter who punctuates the representation. So the painting seems unfinished, and this transfixing unfinishedness—the worlds on edge and the open-endedness of people's becoming—is the very stuff of art.

With its receptiveness to and incorporation of the accidental and the unknown, Neel and Hunter's artwork (not possible without each other and the world's ongoingness) leaves us with a haunting, incomplete aesthetic and a challenge to further inquire into the multiplicity of lifeworlds and the plasticity of anthropological figures.

So, how can we ethnographically apprehend these worldly fabrications and the lives therein, constituted as they are by that which is unresolved, and bring this unfinishedness into our storytelling?

How are long-standing theoretical approaches able—or not—to illuminate emergent political, economic, and affective realities?

How can the becomings of our informants and collaborators, and the movements and counterknowledges they fashion, serve as alternative figures of thought that might animate comparative work, political critique, and anthropology to come?

Ethnographic creations are about the plasticity and unfinishedness of human subjects and lifeworlds. And the essays in this book are themselves unfinished views of people (including anthropologists, scientists, and artists) in the process of becoming through things, relations, stories, survival, destruction, and reinvention in the borrowed time of an invisible present.

The notion of becoming, which organizes our individual and collective efforts, emphasizes the plastic power of people and the intricate problematics of how to live alongside, through, and despite the profoundly constraining effects of social, structural, and material forces, which are themselves plastic. Unfinishedness is both precondition and product of becoming, and we chose our title—*Unfinished*—as a way to draw attention to this important feature of all of the book's characters and inquiries, its attempts at open thinking and experimental writing. Unfinishedness is a feature as generative to art and knowledge production as it is to living.

We work with an expansive definition of unfinishedness. Our ethnographic work always begins in the midst of social life, its rhythms, affects, surprises (from the trivial to the tragic), and urgencies. The categories and books we bring to our investigations are continually challenged by the figuring out, disfiguring, and refiguring of lifeworlds and subjects. Desire follows world-historical trajectories, and ethnographic subjects have their own ideas of and relationships to the constraints and unfinishedness of their lives and milieus. Becoming troubles and exceeds our ways of knowing and acting. It pushes us to think against the grain, to consider the uncertain and unexpected in the world, and to care for the as-yet-unthought that interrogates history and keeps modes of existence open to improvisation. We are tasked with the otherwise.

To attend to the unfinished, we need a conscientious empiricism wedded to a radical analytical openness to complexity and wonder. For critical analysis, writing, and social engagement, the rewards of staying with formations that exceed us and exploring the incomplete are far from trifling. We can better understand how political forces and capital expansions exhaust existing (not ideal) forms and absorb some of the qualities and textures of individual and collective experiments with relating and knowing—lived tensions between power and flight, mortality and vitality, history and invention, creation and ruination, care and disregard, and belonging and fugitivity. As we seek to articulate a human science of the uncertain and unknown, we can also restore movement and possibility to ethical thinking and political practice: a countertechnique, a continual capacity for recalibration that the ethnographic craft and theorizing enable.

Engaging a range of pressing contemporary problematics—including war and its aftermath, economic transformation, racial inequality, gun violence, religiosity, therapeutic markets, animal rights activism, and abrupt environmental change—the authors of *Unfinished* foreground the malleable nature of human-nonhuman interactions and demonstrate how people and social forms partake of and are shaped by multiple systems and forces, themselves contingent and shifting, all with variable degrees of agency.

We work at a granular level of ethnographic description and interpretation, following people and things—those deemed ex-human, canny artists and wounded animals, forest firefighters and climate scientists, embattled neighborhoods, inks and pharmakons, sites of prayer, the bones of missing war victims. We listen carefully and notice swerves, follow leads and trajectories, and translate these movements into thought and writing. Each essay in *Unfinished* finds its way to an arresting encounter, image, concept, or kernel that enters into a series, always midway, providing prismatic points of contact with assemblages of force and form in multiple worlds.

An anthropology of becoming demands more than the flat realism that comes with standard practices of contextualization and historicization, and it must not simply mimic or echo the dark determinisms that mark much of social theory. The authors of *Unfinished* insist on the indispensable moral and analytical value of the micro, the singular and partial, which requires a different, more fine-grained, and humble logic than that of a generality subsuming all things into aggregates, repetitions, and models. Thus we take a situated, cartographic (rather than archaeological) approach to self-world entanglements and leaking social fields.

Here, objects are milieus in themselves; worlds are at once material, social, and symbolic, simultaneously precarious and in motion; and individuals and collectives are constituted as much by affects and intensities as by structural forces. We trace people's trajectories as they grow out of themselves, fold in exteriorities, and become other. In attending to orientations, directions, entries, walls, and exits, our combined ethnographic essays produce a geography of becomings: maps of the microdynamics of living and the new configurations of thought, affect, solidarity, and resentment that create tears and exclusions—but also openings, however minor—in macro-level realities and scaling projects.

To grow closer to our anthropological subjects—and to build a form of critique concerned more with identifying crossroads and opening up possibilities than with making judgments and enforcing totalizing analytical schemes—each of the chapters in *Unfinished* embraces the literary expressivity and exploratory potentials of the essay genre. Our "Ethnographic Sensorium" introduces the book's main ethnographic characters and lifeworlds and articulates the methodological and analytical significance of an anthropology of becoming. Throughout *Unfinished*, the authors offer a rich spectrum of the ways that becoming emerges in specific lives and milieus and against the backdrop of world-historical forces—all experimenting with writing and grappling with the incompleteness and open-endedness of fieldwork and cultural theory. In the book's afterword, Michael M. J. Fischer lovingly rereads the essays, teasing out their generativity and what they reveal about the becoming of anthropology and the problematics of futures on the horizon.

We tell stories that are as much material and political-economic as personal and ethical. We are always working outward: pulling into line with our subjects, moving sideways to follow them, getting out of their way, returning and sitting with them, drawing out characters, probing philosophical questions, bringing certain concepts into focus, and letting others emerge only partially, but meaningfully so. Our storytelling destabilizes hierarchies of expertise and confuses the distinction between the finished and the unfinished, illuminating the ethnographic open systems in which anthropologists and subjects are entangled, folded into lives, transformations, and thinking across time and space.

Unfinished's ethnographic essaying is an invitation to readers to open their own thinking to the unpredictability, multiplicity, and incommensurability that animate lives and realities—and the ethnographic craft itself—and to find resonances, keeping critical thought engaged and multiplying.

NOTE

1 Alice Neel's painting *James Hunter Black Draftee* was shown in the 2016 exhibit *Unfinished: Thoughts Left Visible* at the Metropolitan Museum of Art in New York City. "We don't think [James Hunter] died because his name is not on the Vietnam Veterans Memorial, in D.C.," said Kelly Baum, one of the curators of the exhibit. "But we don't know what happened to him" (quoted in C. Swanson, "What Happened to 'James Hunter Black Draftee'? A Mystery at the Met Breuer"). See also Baum, Bayer, and Wagstaff, *Unfinished: Thoughts Left Visible*.

Introduction

Ethnographic Sensorium

JOÃO BIEHL AND PETER LOCKE

Hear the loud crack of gunfire, followed by Mrs. Lana's piercing scream. She has just seen her son fatally shot in their neighborhood in gangland Chicago. Mrs. Lana goes mad, and in the weeks and months that follow, she keeps screaming at passersby. As neighbors look after her and continue to hold her in high regard, they too reflect on the countless young black lives lost. With and through Mrs. Lana's unanswerable cry, the community itself becomes aggrieved and contemplates what form of life might be livable in the American city today.

Picture Catarina writing her dictionary, her ailing body struggling to inscribe the words that form her from within: "What I was in the past does not matter." Abandoned as a meaningless leftover in Vita, an asylum in southern Brazil, she invents a new name for herself—Catkine—from the drug Akineton, one of many that have mediated her social death and supposed madness. As Catkine tries to disentangle herself from the forces that led her to Vita's endpoint and holds onto what could have been—"mine is an illness of time"—she seeks vitality in an exhausted present. Years later, her daughter Andrea, who was given up for adoption by her father, reaches for ties to a lost mother. Andrea calls on the anthropologist, who has also become a part of his characters' metamorphoses.

A political demonstration in Mexico City: feel the crowd, the rage as thousands protest the devastating violence of the drug war and demand that the government find the forty-three students who have recently disappeared. As the demonstration unfolds, security forces are descending on *anexos* in the surrounding barrios—religiously inspired drug rehabilitation centers for the poor, where violence is inseparable from healing. What will come of their sudden takeover by the state?

In southeast Turkey, just across the border from Syria, where the threat of the Islamic State of Iraq and Syria (ISIS) looms: another crowd in another world on the edge. Notice the movement of thousands of pilgrims congregating at a mosque on the holiest night of the year. Look closer: you will see Özlem and Zuhal, young students of Islamic theology, growing agitated by the crowding, the noise, and the garbage strewn across the sidewalks, ill at ease with the supposed healing power of the site's sacred waters. Amid revivalist reforms and the upheaval of war and displacement, the faithful confront new challenges in relating to ritual space and practice—becoming, in the process, new kinds of religious subjects.

In a bright Rio de Janeiro studio, the artist Adriana Varejão is making ink for each of the more than one hundred skin color terms that Brazilians use to describe themselves and others. Collaborating on a project inspired by Brazil's complex history of race and racism, an anthropologist finds her own thinking on "the spectacle of the races" unpredictably cannibalized by the artist. Along the way, she comes to a new understanding of works of art as lively agents that combine, reconfigure, and reinterpret the materials and ideas that make up people and shape time's passage.

An encounter with a wounded horse on a crowded Indian road turns an onlooker into an animal rights activist, its bleeding eye sockets a call to witness and surrender. This meeting marks a rebirth of sorts for the witness and others, the surrender of the self to working against futility for a life of responsibility to nonhumans. It also propels movements: an opening of the social skin and a thickening of worldly relations. What becomes of both human and animal in these multispecies intimacies, these encounters with unfree suffering others? Does becoming animal subvert or reinforce our human-centric visions of ourselves and our worlds?

Elsewhere, there is waiting: a meantime haunted by unresolved legacies of violence and dispossession, by unimaginable loss, by longing for transformation.

Post-war Sarajevo, Bosnia-Herzegovina: pockmarked façades are smoothed over, and shopping centers rise in place of hollow ruins. Two hours to the east, world leaders speak of hope and regret as newly identified remains are interred on the twentieth anniversary of the genocide at Srebrenica. As thousands of desperate refugees from the Middle East make their way through the Balkans, Bosnians live with the unresolved legacies of their own violent conflict. Here Sarajevo's urban poor—and the civil society groups that support them—await a still uncertain transformation, finding ways to get on with life and change themselves amid a stagnating transition.

Peer over shoulders at the gloved hands of forensic anthropologists sorting and identifying human bones under the glare of laboratory lights—applying and tinkering with techniques pioneered in the aftermath of the Bosnian war. In Cyprus, the remains and belongings of the missing transform experiences of time and loss for families and scientists decades after the violence of conflict has subsided. Recovered and identified against a painful backdrop of paranoia, rumor, and unsettled grievances, these troubling objects trigger new personal and political struggles at the collapsing frontiers of past, present, and future.

Paraguay: in the dense forests and cleared pastures of South America's Gran Chaco, Tié and Cutai whisper stories by firelight. Aasi, once a warrior, became a peacemaker and later, after encounters with missionaries, a Christian. His nephew Pejei thrashes against the ropes binding him, gripped by *urusoi*, a madness wrought by the soul fleeing the body. They are Ayoreo, members of one of the last bands in the Chaco to be "contacted" and ushered violently into brutal interpersonal and regional economies. To endure world-ending violence and ravenous deforestation, many radically disavow their precontact ways of life— here self-negation is a technique for reproducing moral life in a world of death. The anthropologist is not immune; in his witnessing, he, too, is caught up in the delirium.

Time-lapse images, clear and breathtaking, show the rapid retreat of enormous Arctic glaciers over just a few years. Far away in the American Southwest, as megafires blaze, first responders grapple with the failure of predictive models in the face of new and frightening wildfire dynamics. As scientists struggle to anticipate forms of environmental calamity that elude prediction in the borrowed time of an invisible present, extinctions continue, and models for remediation must be continually rescaled. As we face dire tipping points, how can communities and policy makers prepare for the unknowable futures of our planet and maintain its ability to sustain life?

PLASTICITY

These moments and stories are incomplete views onto subjects and lifeworlds in the process of becoming. Taken together, they make up an ethnographic sensorium: a multifaceted and affective point of contact with worlds of inequality, hovering on the verge of exhaustion while also harboring the potential for things to be otherwise.

Indeed, the realities in which we are all entangled today, and in which the becomings of our characters unfold, are on the edge: of financial collapse, infrastructural breakdown, and environmental calamity; racial violence, right-wing populism, and alarming new regimes of security and surveillance; and chronic warfare, mass migration, and deadly health disparities. In the meantime, people may find ways to endure the intolerable and struggle to repair and heal, untangle themselves from the known and establish new relations (or not), negotiate threatening detours and the newly uncertain, and make use of these very realities to craft viable forms of life and project themselves into a future—or simply remain in suspension amid the collapse of messianic structures. Yet amid today's alarming global political shifts, it is also obvious that people's plasticity—shaped as much by fear and resentment as by hope and desire—carries destructive and violent potentials.

The anthropology of becoming is about the plastic power of people, worlds, and thought—that is, "the power of specifically growing out of one's self, of making the past and the strange one body with the near and present."[1] In this book, we are concerned with the ways in which our ethnographic subjects, their bodies, the material and symbolic worlds they inhabit, and the structural forces they must navigate all grow out of themselves, becoming other and unpredictably constructive or perilous in their entanglements and over time.

As ethnographers of the contemporary, we always begin our work in the midst of social life, within asymmetries and constraints of all kinds, traversed by myriad flows that are of indeterminate origin and destination, both vital and deadly. Above all concerned with plasticity and with the unfinishedness that emerges through intensive work with people and their trajectories, we break open totalizing abstractions; pursue lives that are bifurcated, stagnating, or in flux; chart the worlds and abrupt changes that our characters are caught up in; and record the granularities of the ongoing, shared episodes that shape life stories and horizons—our subjects' and our own. We are interested in the human subject as always under construction and in the unforeseeable concepts that can be generated through fieldwork. In attending to these processes, we find materials for a critique of today's evolving dynamics of knowledge production, political economies, and social control that are themselves plastic and have real human and material consequences.

This plasticity does not exist independently of contingency and death. Omnipresent materially and figuratively for the characters and scenarios in the essays that follow, resistance to destruction and death in all their forms—historical oblivion, social abandonment or political exclusion, accidents, sickness and the end of biological life, or the loss of an imagined future—is woven into all processes of becoming, activating and shaping people's trajectories. As Angela Garcia puts it in chapter 3, in considering the brutal toll of the War on Drugs in Mexico, "the darkness of the present moment is the very condition that might generate the possibility of moving beyond it. It is the site of hope and the precondition of becoming."

In contrast to judgments of intellectual stagnation and futures without anticipation, this book's ethnographic sensorium opens new channels of communication and conceptual work, calling attention to the plethora of existential struggles, improvisations, ideas, and landscapes that shape what life means and how it is experienced and imagined in splintering and pluralizing presents. People's becomings and their varying forms of dissent and flight are fundamental to both how ethnography unfolds and its own potentialities. They drive our craft's capacity to map alternative fields of immanence and to illuminate new ethical terrains and politics in the making.

In this way, ethnographic inquiry brings us closer to the world's matters of fact and people's simultaneous movements away from and toward material structures and relational fields, unsettling established forms of thought and invoking both alternative conceptual frameworks and figures of what is yet to come. "Like a bullet," Laurence Ralph writes in chapter 2, Mrs. Lana's voice "was an intrusion that ruptured the present. Symbolically reinstating the violence that had taken Jo Jo, she drew an audible line, every day, between life and death." And as Adriana Petryna reminds us in chapter 9, "tipping points—points that, if crossed, mean irreversible change—exist and require a countertechnique, a continual capacity for recalibration, a horizoning work" on the part of scientists, policymakers, and communities all over the world.

UNFINISHEDNESS

The anthropology of becoming can be understood through three distinct, though related, dimensions. First, it emphasizes the plastic nature of human-nonhuman interactions and acknowledges that people belong simultaneously to multiple systems that themselves are made up of people, things, and forces with varying degrees of agentive capacity.[2] Attuned to "the mutual constitution of entangled agencies" and the unstable nature and malleability of all social fields and subjectivities, the anthropology of becoming acknowledges how power and knowledge form bodies, identities, and meanings, and how inequalities disfigure living, while refusing to reduce people to the workings of such forces.[3]

Instead of viewing people in terms of core principles or as fully bounded by structure or form, the anthropology of becoming attends to people's transformations and varied agencies, and to the ways in which power itself is shifting and contingent—less a solid, stable entity than a product of manipulation, systematic falsehood, and ongoing struggle, and constantly punctured and put to flight by people's becomings. In this way, anthropology makes space for unfinishedness, and bodies, power, and things do not remain frozen in place.

The second dimension has to do with experiences of time, space, and desire. Lived time is not reducible to clock time, and people inhabit multiple temporalities at once. Becoming occupies its own kind of temporality that unfolds in the present: a dynamic interpenetration of past and future, actual and virtual. Distinct from potentiality and not reducible to causality or outcomes, becoming is characterized by the indeterminacies that keep history open, and it allows us to see what happens in the meantimes of human struggle and daily life. Becoming also attunes us differently to the shifting cultural and material particularities of the spaces our interlocutors must traverse: cartographic rather than archaeological, becomings "belong to geography, they are orientations, directions, entries and exits."[4] The very materialities of space affect and impinge on the subject, encouraging or constraining possibilities for movement and adding further texture to lived experiences.

These meantimes and interstitial spaces are not stagnant vacuums: they overflow with shifting aggregates of desire and power, the emerging sociopolitical fields and intersubjective entanglements produced as people imagine and attempt to make real what they need and long for. Desire does not seek a singular, decontextualized object, but a broader world or set of relations in which the object is embedded and becomes meaningful.[5] Attending to this aggregating capacity and the operative fields in and through which institutions and social processes combine and collapse, the anthropology of becoming approaches the interplay between the motions of becoming different and moments of impasse or plateaus of stabilization.

The third dimension involves an attentiveness to the unknown, both as a critical feature of people and material worlds and as a productive force in research and conceptual work. Through its relentless empiricism and radical analytical openness, anthropology creates the conditions of possibility for moments of surprise and the sustained, open-ended engagements that wonder, itself always historically and locally situated, precipitates. Whether through the classic anthropological realization that other systems and ideas organize life elsewhere, or the recognition that our own presuppositions often prove inadequate in describing the complex realities of the lives of others, fieldwork moves us away from entrenched categories and expands the perspectives—on other cultures, space-times, and species—from which we can perceive and understand the world (if only always partially). Ethnographic subjects are, in a sense, both life experimenters and figures of surprise—not knowable ahead of time, unpredictable, and capable of shifting something in our own thinking. Remaining open to the unfathomable complexity of layered entanglements of biology, environment, social life, and material forces of all kinds, and acknowledging—even embracing—the unknown can inspire scholars to produce a more humble, tentative social science, keeping our theory more multirealistic and sensible and our modes of expression less figurative and more readily available for swerves, breaks, and new paths.

Together, these three dimensions challenge the craft of anthropology to continue to cultivate forms of field research and expression that can bring us closer to the plasticity and virtuality, the transformations and dead ends, of our ethnographic subjects and their worlds within worlds and languages within languages—none of which can be known in the abstract or ahead of time. Such a commitment to ethnographic empiricism, we hope, can help illuminate how older dynamics of difference-making and violence are reinvigorated and the conditions under which something new might be produced.

BECOMINGS

In working toward an anthropology of becoming, we have drawn on the work of French philosopher Gilles Deleuze (in dialogue with his longtime collaborator Félix Guattari), whose particular empiricist sensibility and attentiveness to the constructedness of both subjects and power lends itself to ethnographic inquiry and to a more humble and creative form of critique and conceptual thinking. For us, Deleuze offers one opening into the multiple theoretical and disciplinary lineages that work with and from this plasticity and inventiveness of people, and he attunes us to ongoing, diverse exchanges between anthropology and philosophy.[6]

In Deleuze's writing we find approaches that seem refreshingly ethnographic and unabashedly open-ended—cartography as opposed to archaeology, rhizomes as opposed to deep structures, leaking social fields as opposed to enclosed systems, and lines of flight and deterritorialization forever breaking through the impasses imposed by totalizing forms of power and knowledge. The tension between empirical realities and theories is permanent and irresolvable, and these approaches allow theory to be always catching up to reality, always startled, making space for the incompleteness of understanding that is often a necessary condition for anthropological fieldwork and thinking.

One of the key terms of Deleuze's thought, *becoming* embodies such sensibilities and has been particularly productive in our own work. As deployed by theorists, the concept of becoming destabilizes the primacy of being and identity in the Western philosophical tradition in favor of attending to shifting sets of relations and the ongoing production of difference in the world. Becoming moves through every event, so that each is simultaneously the start, end, and midpoint of an ongoing cycle of production. In this Nietzschean eternal return of change and difference, the worlds and histories we traverse are both products and conditions of becoming, and the human subject is not an autonomous, rational individual or a stable self but an always unstable assemblage of organic, social, and structural forces and lines of flight that at once shape and are shaped by their milieus.[7] The nonlinear space-time and the extensive, contingent itineraries of becoming cannot be permanently closed, completely deciphered, or planned in advance.

In the essay "Many Politics," Deleuze articulates more precisely how becoming fits into his larger theory of individuation and the forming of social fields. "Whether we are individuals or groups, we are made up of lines," he says.[8] These lines fall into three main kinds.

The first kind of line is segmentary, defining and sorting people according to categories: "binary machines of social classes; of sexes, man-woman; of ages, child-adult; of races, black-white; of sectors, public-private; of subjectivations, ours-not ours."[9] If these ordering and classifying "molar"[10] lines are part of Foucauldian normalizing apparatuses of power,[11] then the second kind of line is "supple,"[12] charting the actual lives and social worlds that depend on the rigidity of forms, categories, and boundaries while never quite corresponding to them. Ever crossing thresholds, these molecular lines are the means and materials of meandering transformations that cannot be engineered by arts of governance. Many things happen on this second kind of line: "becomings, micro-becomings, which don't even have the same rhythm as our 'history.'"[13]

The third kind of line—the line of flight—is both distinct from and of a piece with the molecular lines that jostle with the molar lines, more radical and mysterious: "as if something carried us away, across our segments, but also across our thresholds, towards a destination which is unknown, not foreseeable, not preexistent."[14] Above all, the point is that "all these lines are tangled" as they make up concrete social fields; mutually constitutive and dependent, each type of line comes with its own openings, dangers, and dead ends.[15]

To write, says Deleuze, is "not to impose a form (or expression) on the matter of lived experience."[16] Literature (and ethnography tuned to becomings, we hope) instead moves "in the direction of the ill-formed or the incomplete ... it is inseparable from becoming."[17] Becoming, as theorized by Deleuze, always happens "in the middle": people moving along and amid multiple lines, pushing the boundaries of forms, escaping and inventing new forces, and combining with other fluxes.[18]

To become is "not to attain a form" but to find "a zone of proximity, indiscernibility, or indifferentiation where one can no longer be distinguished from *a* woman, *an* animal, or *a* molecule—neither imprecise nor general, but unforeseen and nonpreexistent, singularized out of a population rather than determined by a form."[19] Beyond mere resemblance or sentimental identification, one can enter into such a zone of deep proximity with anyone or anything—"I is an other," in Arthur Rimbaud's formulation[20]—"on the condition that one creates the literary means for doing so."[21]

Always singular yet ever producing multiplicity, the work of becoming is inherently a work of creation. It invokes the capacities of people to endure and live on as they reckon with the overdetermined constraints and resources of the worlds into which they are thrown, while also, crucially, calling on their ability to approach the open-ended, to imagine worlds and characters that do not—but may yet—exist. One of the guiding principles of Deleuze's conceptual work is that the real and the virtual are always coexisting, always complementary, two juxtaposable or superimposable parts of a single trajectory: "two faces that ceaselessly interchange with one another, a mobile mirror" that bears witness until the end to a new vision whose passage it remains open to.[22]

Training anthropology's focus on people's becomings across forms and scales and over time highlights the extent to which a bounded concept of society, culture, or politics does not neatly align with empirical realities. "For me, society is something that is constantly escaping in every direction," Deleuze said in a conversation with Paul Rabinow in the mid-1980s: "It flows monetarily, it flows ideologically. It is really made of lines of flight. So much so that the problem for a society is how to stop it from flowing. For me, the powers come later."[23]

To draw on this productive unmooring, we might need to let go of some venerable assumptions about the human condition and about where we locate political action, instead asking what life-forms, collectives, and new kinds of politics are on the horizon, brewing within the leaking excesses of existing force fields and imaginaries. Becoming, thus, is a style of noticing, thinking, and writing through which to capture the intricate relations, movements, and dynamics of power and flight that make up our social worlds.

The time of becoming is the real time in which life struggles are waged, in which stasis is sustained or transformation plays out, fragmented and uneven. As Deleuze argued in an interview late in his life, "becoming isn't a part of history; history amounts only to the set of preconditions, however recent, that one leaves behind in order to 'become,' that is, to create something new."[24] While ethnographic work bears out Deleuze's insight that becoming unfolds at a different tempo of change from the seemingly linear march of historical events, it also troubles the philosopher's sense that becoming unequivocally "leaves behind" the force of the past. Even as becoming cannot be reduced to history and our subjects often carve out unexpected paths, history remains folded into the present and the contingent, both imposing limits on and furnishing resources for people's social and material labor.[25] In Bridget Purcell's words in this volume, "layered histories persist—not only as material traces, but folded, also, into perception, practice and sensibility."

Indeed, if the concept of becoming provides important openings for anthropology with its emphasis on transformation and its attention to the constant reworking of lives and worlds, in its typical philosophical renderings and uptake it may be too distant from experience, missing something of the various constraints and conditions that shape how becomings actually unfold.[26] These conditions beg for a distinct perceptual capacity and critical understanding and are themselves rich starting points for alternative theorizing, holding off what the anthropologist Kathleen Stewart calls "the quick jump from concept to world—that precarious habit of academic thought."[27] Attending to life as it is lived and adjudicated by people produces a multiplicity of approaches, critical moves and countermoves, and an array of interpretive angles as various as the individuals drawn to practice anthropology. At stake is finding creative ways of not letting the ethnographic die in our accounts of the contemporary.

Ethnography is not just protophilosophy, but a way of staying connected to open-ended, even mysterious, social processes—a way of counterbalancing the generation of certainties and foreclosures by other disciplines.[28] Ethnographic subjects like Mrs. Lana and Catarina/Catkine, who open this sensorium, embody complex realities in unforeseeable ways, neither fully constrained by nor fully detached from the legacies of historical patterns and systemic violence. Mrs. Lana's mourning emerges from stubborn structures of inequality with deep roots, yet it also triggers new conversations and solidarities in her community. In Cyprus, the remains of the missing do not freeze the past in place but renew it, in all its uncertain tragedies and crimes, as a symbolic and material excess that lends political and social force to the intertwined grievances of the bereaved. Crowds in Mexico City protesting the enormous human toll of state and drug-related violence and turn the intense affect of personal loss into a fierce collective demand for accountability and will for political change, however fleeting.

The ethnographic sensorium, in other words, shows us social aggregates not as givens that must be embraced or resisted, but as temporary collectives that—whether they evaporate or congeal into lasting forms of change—reveal transformative visions and potentials emerging from unexpected corners. Indeed, ethnography has a knack for apprehending and mediating changes in people's lives that are not only political-economic and material but also ethical, interpersonal, and singular.

Like the Ayoreo in Paraguay, whose negative existence emerges through traumatic encounters with dominant forms, people in the field show us the extent to which becoming is always excessive and unruly. To be unformed is a kind of active (if unanticipated) resistance. The political subjects of ethnography are ambiguous, creative, and unpredictable, always pushing the boundaries of our abstractions. They act, borrowing Michael M. J. Fischer's apt phrasing, as "pebbles and labyrinths in the way of theory,"[29] calling on anthropologists to resist synthetic closure and totalizing explanation and to keep our focus on the interrelatedness and unfinishedness of all human life—indeed, of all life and of the planet itself—in the face of precarity and the unknown.[30]

Grounded in this candid empiricism and emancipatory openness, attentive to deadly impasses as well as to abrupt—even catastrophic—forms of change, ethnography can generate empowering social and political critique with our subjects rather than about them, illuminating the rationalities, interests, and moral issues of our times and the shifting horizons against which they unfold.[31] In the anthropology of becoming, "relationships with our subjects," as Lilia M. Schwarcz puts it in chapter 6, "transform, create, or suggest new forms of communication and perhaps understanding."

PEOPLING CRITICAL THEORY

Nearly a century of critical theory emanating from anthropology and related fields, including feminist and postcolonial critiques, has dislodged the sway of crude universals in favor of attending more closely to the specificity and world-historical significance of people's plasticity and everyday experiences.[32]

In the early twentieth century, Sigmund Freud wrote of the "allo-plastic" capacity of his neurotic patients to alter reality through fantasy,[33] while Bronislaw Malinowski argued for the "plasticity of instincts" under culture.[34] In the same era, Marcel Mauss articulated his famous concept of *l'homme total* to highlight the malleability of the human subject at the interface of psychology, social relations and modes of reciprocity, and culturally ingrained routines and "body techniques."[35] A few decades later, in his seminal exploration of mental health under the French colonial regime in Algeria, Frantz Fanon demonstrated that the "I" is a material of politics, the platform on which agonistic struggles over inequality, domination, and human dignity are waged. To the question facing the colonized subject—"In reality, who am I?"—Fanon's answer is one of deconstruction: which and whose reality is this?[36] More recently, Judith Butler has written incisively of the self-empowerment afforded to the subjected by ambiguity. She denaturalizes gender norms and highlights people's capacities to defy and rewrite cultural scripts, while exploring the specific forms of vulnerability and grievability that shape precarious lives.[37]

Since its emergence as a research methodology, ethnographic fieldwork has been essential to understanding how this plasticity of people and social fields unfolds in historically and culturally contingent worlds. In their classic work among the Tswana of southern Africa, for example, Jean and John Comaroff highlight how colonial encounters confronted Europeans with the possibility of other forms of personhood. For the Tswana, they explain, "the person was a constant work in progress," referring "not to a state of being but to a state of becoming. No living self could be static. Stasis meant social death."[38]

In its emphasis on understanding personhood in context and through field and archival research, the Comaroffs' work exemplifies how anthropology and critical theory can attend to processes of becoming as empirical realities of societies past and present: the labor of making oneself and one's life, always already in relation to others and to the values and imperatives of the social—and, in the Tswana case, against a background of colonial domination. In such contexts, anthropologists have also explored what Michael Taussig, drawing on the work of Frankfurt school thinkers such as Theodor Adorno and Walter Benjamin, calls the "mimetic faculty"—that human capacity to "copy, imitate, make models, explore difference, yield into and become Other."[39] Subjugated communities, Taussig shows, blur subject-object divides, instrumentalize misrecognitions, and sustain capacities for alternative becomings, even amid the violence of colonial power relations.[40]

Indeed, the notion of becoming—or some close analogue—has long been familiar and helpful to anthropologists, and innovative scholars have foregrounded kindred ideas as guides for peopling critical theory through fieldwork and ethnographic writing. For example, Michael M. J. Fischer has brought ethnographic groundedness to science studies through his attention to the "emergent forms of life" that arise through and in contrast to the technologies, networks, and infrastructures of contemporary bioscience, the media, and humanitarianism.[41] How, Fischer asks, can anthropology build new ethical terrains of decision making and new landscapes of political assemblages within, around, and beyond older frameworks? Fischer draws our attention to new and challenging "ethical plateaus" (a term that comes from the anthropologist Gregory Bateson, via Deleuze and Guattari) on which multiple technologies interact, showing that our ethical and analytical models are failing amid fast-paced revolutions in our technoscientific worlds ranging from big data to genetics.[42] Fischer argues that by carefully attending to what he calls "switching points"—moments when technoscientific innovations or political maneuvers make possible alternative forms of life and citizenship—and by staying close to how new technological and social infrastructures are lived with, ethnographic work helps ensure that our analyses keep pace with the times and remain able to imagine new institutions and forms of protection for the vulnerable, and to deflate dehumanizing theoretical abstractions and universals.

As the work of Fischer—and that of many other critical anthropologists of science, technology, and medicine—continually remind us, the categories of supposedly objective scientific nomenclature always carry real political, ethical, and bodily stakes.[43] Consider the ways in which the notion of a new "Anthropocene" geological era—the term was first coined by the Nobel Prize–winning chemist Paul Crutzen in 1995 and has been gaining popularity ever since—may continue to mystify the global workings of power and inequality even as it adds much-needed urgency to the work of recognizing human responsibility for environmental change. "The formal definition of the Anthropocene," as two earth scientists write in *Nature*, "makes scientists arbiters, to an extent, of the human-environment relationship, itself an act with consequences beyond geology."[44] The universal humanity of *anthropos* obscures the ways in which specific politics and ways of living have contributed to the climate crisis, painting as universal and somehow innate to our species the highly contingent—and devastatingly destructive—patterns of consumption and production that characterize the world's wealthiest capitalist societies. "Ours is the geological epoch not of humanity, but of capital," writes one ecologist.[45]

From vast planetary timescales and transformations to cells under the microscope, scholars are increasingly identifying power and inequality at work even in the most ostensibly natural—read "apolitical"—processes. In their book *Biosocial Becomings*, for example, the anthropologists Tim Ingold and Gisli Palsson draw on the work of heterodox biologists, the new field of epigenetics, and a post-Darwinian understanding of evolution to perceive a world not of discrete life-forms transforming through linear pathways of descent, but a "developmental unfolding of the entire matrix of relations"— inevitably conditioned by history, culture, and power—"within which forms of life (human and non-human) emerge and are held in place."[46]

Indeed, even at the molecular level, epigenetic researchers now find that specific politics and histories shape the intertwined becomings of people and ecosystems, both within the individual life course and across generations.[47] Such findings hold out the promise of lending broader legitimacy to existing social scientific concepts that emphasize entanglements between bodies and the worlds they live in—from the biosocial[48] and the ecosocial[49] to the mindful body[50] and local biologies.[51] Yet while epigenetics has the potential to make space for the social in conversations about the biological body, it might also, as Margaret Lock warns in her recent writings, serve as a new form of "somatic determinism" by reifying social determinants as static variables that can be clearly distinguished from biological processes.[52]

Ingold and Palsson draw on anthropology's long tradition of critiquing reductive nature-culture dichotomies to highlight how the biological and the social are always bound together in a process of mutual becoming and transformation—a process in which genes are exchanged between organisms, historical traumas alter what is inherited, and what might first appear as an individual organism (the human subject, for example) is in fact an aggregate of numerous life-forms existing in symbiotic cooperation and evolving together.[53] "Humans become human through relations with other becoming organisms and species and the environments within which they are embedded," writes Palsson,[54] evoking the fecundity of new work in the burgeoning area of "multispecies ethnography."[55] "Becoming," as Deleuze suggests, "is 'always 'between' or 'among.' "[56] The entanglement of the human, the animal, and the material produces the shifting matrix of relations through which one "becomes-woman, becomes-animal or vegetable, becomes-molecule to the point of becoming-imperceptible"[57]—this, in Deleuze's words, is what "makes a world."[58]

Building on this and related notions of becoming-animal, multispecies ethnographers are broadening the scope of their projects to study the "mutual ecologies" that develop between humans and other beings.[59] In a time of discouraged, apocalyptic theorizing about the accumulating consequences of man-made environmental transformation, Eben Kirskey finds that new and promising relations between people, environments, and other species are "flourishing in the aftermath of order-destroying disruptions."[60] Such "emergent ecologies"—crucially, perceived only through the nimble deployment of ethnographic fieldwork far from centers of ivory tower expertise—challenge both the social and natural sciences to attend to the ways in which "a multitude of tinkerers and thinkers are transforming feelings of futility into concrete action, cynicism into happiness and hope," even amid destruction and extinction.[61]

Here the promise of multispecies ethnography lies not in casting aside anthropology's strengths in learning from people in context as somehow obsolete; instead, it makes the tinkering of everyday eco-bricoleurs a source of insight and inspiration for imagining how alarming forms of environmental change may yet reveal new opportunities for the mutual becoming-other of human societies and the "swarming multitude" of nonhuman life forms with whom we share the planet.[62] Yet even as we consider emerging forms of hope, to understand the limits of life in local worlds and on our shared planet—and the kinds of politics and policy that are possible or desirable—it remains crucial to address questions of history, political economy, the theorizing of difference, and the uneven global distribution of risk and vulnerability.

As Anna L. Tsing notes, we are "surrounded by many world-making projects, human and not human."[63] The challenge, it seems, is to integrate interspecies relations and shifting ecological contexts into our understanding of "biosocial becomings" without obscuring[64]—in the pursuit of, for example, an "anthropology beyond the human"[65]—the unavoidable fact that the fields of our fieldwork are both peopled by human communities in their multiple engagements and perspectives[66] and shaped by the forces and flows of global capitalism.[67]

In *The Mushroom at the End of The World*, Tsing shows what it might look like to attend to the broad weave of life—human and nonhuman—in the increasingly precarious "blasted landscapes" of our "worldwide ruination" without losing sight of political economy (or assuming its totality).[68] Rejecting strongly held beliefs about progress (economic, scientific, or otherwise), the anthropologist calls on us to cultivate our "arts of noticing" and to "look around rather than ahead."[69] While highlighting the precarious yet vital "possibility of life in capitalist ruins," her capacious forms of attention bring nonhumans into the fold without hiding from capital or the state: "assemblages," she insists, "drag political economy inside them, and not just for humans."[70]

Shifting from living beings and ecosystems to material objects, how might an anthropology of becoming also address the vibrancy of matter without losing sight of the human? As Elizabeth A. Davis's work with the bones and belongings of missing war victims shows, objects work through and on us. They do not exist outside of sociohistorical worlds, and thus they come to be infused with multiple, sometimes contradictory, human meanings and signs. As Davis writes in chapter 8: "The force operated by the artifacts of the missing lies in their capacity not to exceed but to slip between semiotic captures, to condense multiple temporalities and thus to accommodate discrepant meanings. They are in the right place at the right time to make things happen." Or, as Schwarcz's reflections in chapter 6 on her collaboration with the artist Adriana Varejão demonstrate, things themselves—in this case, paintings and sculptures—are inscribed in multiple systems of meaning and reference that shape their production, their legibility, and their effects on us: "instead of using images as illustrations," Schwarcz suggests, "the idea [is] to understand how works of art can interfere in reality, creating and destroying customs, values, and symbols."

In *Vibrant Matter*, the political theorist Jane Bennett proposes a dual philosophical-political project that takes nonhuman things as its object of analysis.[71] Writing against the "idea of matter as passive stuff, as raw, brute, or inert" and the supposed "partition of the sensible" that divides "dull matter (it, things)" from "vibrant life (us, beings)," she argues that matter itself is vital, lively, and—in its own way—agentive.[72] Things, she argues, possess vital powers, serving "not only to impede or block the will and designs of humans but also to act as quasi agents or forces with trajectories, propensities, or tendencies of their own."[73] Yet if, as Arjun Appadurai has cautioned, the "new materialisms" of contemporary social theory sometimes leave little space for "questions of ethics, accountability, normativity, and political critique," focusing less on objects as givens and more on their trajectories and milieus allows us to see the crossroads and configurations that work on human subjects and the worlds they occupy.[74] In this way, as Davis's and Schwarcz's work shows, we might read things as lively not only ontologically or in themselves, but as material artifacts or "mediants" (to use Appadurai's word) that are entangled with larger social, political, and economic forces.[75]

While fieldwork among people and attention to the "imponderabilia of actual life" remains, for us, the indispensable foundation of anthropological thought and inquiry,[76] we are not out to reiterate a problematically anthropocentric humanism that cuts off people's becomings from those of other species and our living and material environments. Quite the contrary, the humanism that grounds the anthropology of becoming assumes that the very boundaries and meanings of "human being" are porous and changeable, made and remade through eco-bio-social relations within political economies.[77] As Naisargi Dave shows us in her exploration in chapter 5 of the ambivalent and often excruciating journeys of contemporary animal rights activists in India, her subjects' becomings happen precisely through a vulnerability to other beings that explodes rather than reinforces a bounded conception of the human or the self—a vulnerability that thickens relationality by painfully "exfoliat[ing] the social skin," in the words of the anthropologist Elizabeth Povinelli.[78] Can we, as Dave puts it, "become something other than the safely encased human self?" Citing Deleuze and Guattari,[79] the anthropologist reminds us that becoming turns the self "not into another kind of self, but only into a 'question-machine.'" This question-machine, in turn, is a part of social movements; they "are full of becomings: they are defined and made by them."

From social movements full of becomings to emergent ecologies in blasted landscapes, there is something about the concept of becoming that lends itself to snatching glimmers of hope from bleak horizons. Yet the anthropology of becoming may equally illuminate trajectories of loss and stagnation, grief and decay, and worlds on the verge of—or already enveloped in—ruin and disaster. Catarina/Catkine's writing, in the end, could not take her back home to the life she wanted. Postcontact Ayoreos' radical rejection of former ways of life, Lucas Bessire shows in chapter 7, might lead both to further destitution and misery and to "novel vital experiments and unsettling kinds of immanence." Becoming cannot be measured by outcome, nor is it necessarily about progress or even hope. In responding to unlivable conditions, experimentation with the limited resources of life is just as likely to lead to a deadly endpoint as to "actionable critique" and a liberating swerve. Understanding the fine nuances of these struggles, terms of transformation, and contradictions demands, above all, methods that immerse us in the worlds of our subjects over extended periods of time.

It is by holding onto close engagement with people that we cultivate new ways of understanding and relating to worlds and ecologies, social structures and biologies. In this way, ethnographic fieldwork can make visible the ideologies, maneuverings, and fabulations of power in which life chances are foreclosed and can highlight the ways desires can break open if not alternative pathways, then at least the possibility of imagining things otherwise as one lives on. As Deleuze so poignantly comments in an interview with Antonio Negri in the early 1990s: "What we most lack is a belief in the world, we've quite lost the world, it's been taken from us."[80] Fieldwork and the encounters, texts, and modes of expression it engenders offer us a way back into worldliness.

WORLDS ON THE EDGE

What are the worlds, then, that fieldwork attuned to becomings draws us into today?

Two decades ago, scholars were preoccupied with the post–Cold War "world in pieces," in which nation-states were fragmenting along resurgent ethnic divisions.[81] Clifford Geertz ended his classic essay on the topic with measured hope in the capacity of Western political liberalism to adapt to this "splintered world," suggesting that liberal principles were still "our best guides to law, government, and public deportment."[82]

Yet this faith in the politics of liberal democracy has been hard to maintain. After the turn of the millennium, the specter of terrorism in the United States propelled an unanticipated intersection of new technologies with the antidemocratic surveillance concerns of the post-9/11 security state.[83] Late liberal rearrangements of state and capital have both dismantled regulatory regimes and implemented new ones, as well as strengthened older power formations, and traditional democratic politics have become increasingly oligarchical and divorced from the needs of the governed, even as public infrastructures and services crumble.[84] With the rise and increasing electoral success of right-wing populist movements across the world—from the United Kingdom's Brexit vote to leave the European Union in June 2016, to the election of the xenophobic demagogue Donald J. Trump to the U.S. presidency a few months later—we see anxious, resentful electorates embracing a hauntingly familiar politics of chauvinism and scapegoating.

What science and critical thinking could have anticipated today's acute struggles over inclusion and exclusion; white supremacy, race, and policing; gender and sexuality; socioeconomic inequality; chronic warfare; data and surveillance; and abrupt environmental change, so often addressed in rhetorics of recovery even as conditions stagnate or worsen? What entanglements of wishful thinking, denial, and privilege have marginalized voices of warning and amplified fantasies of linear progress?

Uncannily, the late American pragmatist philosopher Richard Rorty seems to have anticipated the toxicity of today's growing backlash against progressive agendas of diversity and inclusion, entangled as they have been with neoliberal globalization. Writing in 1998 and drawing on the fears of socioeconomic analysts of the day, Rorty cautioned that "fascism may be the American future.... The nonsuburban electorate will decide that the system has failed and start looking around for a strongman to vote for—someone willing to assure them that, once he is elected, the smug bureaucrats, tricky lawyers, overpaid bond salesmen, and postmodernist professors will no longer be calling the shots.... One thing that is very likely to happen is that the gains made in the past forty years by black and brown Americans, and by homosexuals, will be wiped out. Jocular contempt for women will come back into fashion."[85]

The present moment profoundly defies teleologies of progress: if in the 1990s, the fall of the Soviet Union allowed some to judge Euro-American democracy and capitalism as "the end of history,"[86] today faith in these systems as eventual guarantors of a good life for all is faltering. Austerity-based approaches remain dominant despite ever-accumulating evidence of their failure to resolve states of crisis and their contribution to exacerbating inequality. Progressives in the United States continue to fight—and surely face a period of heightened adversity and struggle—for the basic rights of women and racial and sexual minorities, highlighting the unfinishedness and precarity of the civil rights achievements of the 1960s.[87] Rubrics such as religion, long assumed to be falling away, have reemerged in the public sphere as enduring sites of politics and identity.[88]

From increasing doubts about the viability and efficacy of the European Union to the World Health Organization's bungling of the initial response to the 2014–15 Ebola epidemic in West Africa, the innovations in international political cooperation and accountability that once seemed to embody the highest promises of a liberal democratic globalism have come to appear toothless and inept, simultaneously revealing the exclusionary interests that have driven them all along.[89] While the continuing failure of major world powers and institutions to adequately confront the realities of climate change grows ever more alarming, affluent societies themselves—comfortable in their established patterns of consumption and waste and cynical about the possibility of change—fail to extend their sense of empathy and imagination to the impoverished communities who will feel the effects of environmental shifts most acutely.[90]

The notion of crisis has been a tempting, if problematic, lens through which to understand today's historically rooted forms of precarity and reactionary politics of othering.[91] Scholarly diagnoses of the present moment often, and understandably, convey a sense of dwindling possibilities. In *Undoing the Demos*, for example, the political theorist Wendy Brown argues that the encroachment of neoliberalism into all spheres of life is destroying democracy and the broader political realm.[92] Her assessment is bleak: "neoliberalism is the rationality through which capitalism finally swallows humanity."[93]

The splash made by the French economist Thomas Piketty's ambitious work *Capital in the Twenty-First Century* is another sign of the times.[94] For Piketty, expanding inequality is inherent to the logic of an underregulated capitalism in which assets matter more than labor. Absent significant intervention, he argues, the ratio of wealth to income will continue to rise, steadily expanding gaps between rich and poor. Widely read and discussed in both academic and public spheres, the book has struck a chord in a post–financial crisis, post-Occupy America where income inequality remains a central fact of lived experience and, increasingly, a critical feature in public discourse.[95] If the American dream was premised on equal opportunity for class advancement through hard work, Piketty's demonstration that returns on capital matter far more than earned income from labor highlights the extent to which the system itself was rigged from the beginning.

The failure of this system is experienced both materially and affectively. In *Cruel Optimism*, Lauren Berlant explores the textures of fantasy and attachment in contemporary Euro-American capitalism. Concerned with the fraying of the so-called normative good life that promises upward mobility, stability, intimacy, and equality, she discusses the various ways in which these aspirations are simultaneously life-sustaining and self-defeating. This is the double bind that Berlant calls "cruel optimism": a relation in which the very object you desire is, in her words, "an obstacle to your flourishing" and "actively impedes the aim that brought you to it initially."[96] These attachments represent the very possibility of happiness even as they render happiness impossible; yet because they sustain us and anchor us to the world in ways that seem livable, losing them or letting them go is as much a threat as the destruction that holding onto them precipitates.

In Berlant's account, desire and the possibility of imagining alternative futures are somehow already in the service of—or only thinkable within—the logics of failed social systems. Yet might even the cruelest of optimisms open out onto something else? Is there also a kind of power in fabulation that tethers us to life in ways that are not only self-defeating but also generative, in small and often unexpected ways—through new configurations of thoughts, affective states, and solidarities, even in the face of futility? For Brown, we are "only and everywhere *homo oeconomicus*," and democratic citizenship has been thoroughly "hollowed out,"[97] but perhaps there is something too totalizing in this account that begs for deeper specificity about what social life is becoming in present-day capitalism. What kinds of counterideologies and counterconduct might be at work that do not rest on an imaginary outside of capital? How can we make sense of the ways people are mobilizing in the present, making demands on the streets or online for equality and workable infrastructures, and forging tenuous and often subversive links between themselves, the state, and the marketplace?[98]

By engaging the granularity of these "dramas of adjustment"[99] and "public appearances"[100] in messy social worlds and particular lives, what might come into view within and beyond the impasse? In other words, how might close-up ethnographic attention restore our capacity to perceive the becomings of our subjects, even amid dire situations and against darkening political horizons, and how might it enlarge our sense of ethics and politics in crucial ways?

Where Brown, Piketty, and Berlant all rightfully highlight the very real ways in which our systems—and the hopes we invested in them—have failed us, attentiveness to becomings helps us see what else is emerging in everyday struggles, foregrounding the microdynamics of people's lives in a way that illuminates rifts, dangers, and possibilities, however minor, in macrolevel social and political realities.[101] While these openings may ultimately lead nowhere, and futurity always struggles with futility and a sense of the inevitable, people can simultaneously be stuck and do things, and this is not nothing.

The work of the French philosopher Jacques Rancière offers a helpful perspective. He defines a political sphere that resonates with the realities anthropologists encounter in the field: worlds peopled by the uncounted and the excluded, ambiguous political subjects who, as they "assert dissensus," doggedly resist the total triumph of any form of governmentality and sustain opportunities for change.[102] As João Biehl shows in his work on right-to-health litigation in Brazil, for example, low-income people are using available legal mechanisms to claim access to medical technologies and care and, in the process, turning the judiciary into a critical site of politics and state accountability.[103] In chapter 4, Bridget Purcell tracks the "overlapping normative orders that constitute people's lives" in Turkey, attentive to how "bodies, spaces, and subjects seem not to submit to the linear trajectory of discipline." A mother mourns on the over-policed streets of Chicago's inner city, and in chapter 2 Ralph learns how people in low-income communities "invert popular expectations of mourning, thereby developing a concept of 'becoming aggrieved' that does not merely lament death but also affirms life." Unlike Brown's *homo oeconomicus*, who has lost even the barest capacity for democratic dreams, or Berlant's duped optimists, doomed by the pursuit of middle-class stability, these ethnographers of becomings perceive subjects who continue to resist normative regimes and to imagine alternative possibilities, performing dissensus and affirming the value of their chosen social worlds.

Politics and antipolitics continue to play out in the present in a range of vital forms, and the ups and downs of recent social movements (from the Arab Spring, Occupy Wall Street, and Black Lives Matter to their conservative counterparts) highlight the deeply felt tensions of the moment and point to the ongoing, creative ways that people mobilize against inequalities of all kinds and for the conditions of a livable life.[104] As economic injustice, racial violence, and the failed promises of democracy push people to precarious limits—including under the thrall of charismatic demagoguery—attending to the ethics of their exhausted bodies along with the processes of mobilization and the diverse kinds of politics being enacted in different forms of assembly, time frames, and scales helps us identify the edges where contemporary societies find themselves.[105]

While it is easy to write off failed social movements for their perceived lack of revolutionary outcomes, such denunciations miss something crucial, ignoring the vitality and experimentalism of new collectives as they assemble and disperse or transform themselves. Long-standing social grievances suddenly fuel mass protests and hopes for a "Bosnian Spring" of sorts, and then dissipate, though not without revealing possibilities for a more democratic and accountable political process; ongoing investigations of the missing in Cyprus both freeze time and restructure it, generating politically potent solidarities around grief and loss. Such plural embodied actions engender shifts for people and local worlds, if not in obvious ways, building new critical perspectives and understandings of the broader political-economic realities and scaling projects that they challenge.

The ethnographic sensorium produced by attention to becomings illuminates not only the plasticity of our subjects, but also the ways in which systems and forces that appear intractable were not always inevitable. Although capitalism has an inherent tendency toward spiraling inequality, the abstract, unimpeded free-market economy is a fantasy, and the system as it exists has been propelled and shored up by intermediate processes, ideologies, and political choices linked to particular values and interests. Restoring this intermediate analytic zone allows us to demystify the workings of capital and power, attending to destructive plasticities without assuming the machines and abstractions to be natural or self-evident. This analytical move simultaneously brings us closer to worlds in flux, sheds light on what sustains entrenched systems, and maintains space for political engagement.

A HUMAN SCIENCE OF THE UNCERTAIN

In the early 1990s, Deleuze proposed that we were witnessing a shift to what he called "control societies."[106] Where Michel Foucault had famously illustrated a transition from sovereign to disciplinary societies,[107] Deleuze predicted a collapse of emblematic sites of confinement and biopolitical governance—prisons, hospitals, and factories—and foresaw the emergence of a new, dispersive, modulatory form of power. In this vision of the future in formation, the centralized panoptic gaze and the spatial confinement of bodies give way to flexible yet omnipresent tracking, normalized surveillance, and increased technological, digital, and market involvement in the regulation of life and labor. This breakdown of older institutions and familiar disciplinary modes heralds not liberation but another transformation in their hold on us: "it's not a question of asking whether the old or new system is harsher or more bearable, because there's a conflict in each between the ways they free and enslave us."[108] Subjects are no longer individuals but "have become 'dividuals.'"[109] The walls, so to speak, have fallen away, and discipline itself is no longer confined to its former institutional homes.

A quarter of a century later, Deleuze's brief account feels remarkably prescient in many ways. The explosion of the Internet—not yet a major social force in the early 1990s—and the wide range of new technologies, markets, and data it has generated have become crucial features in contemporary consumption, production, and sociality, enabling unprecedented tracking of both individual behavior and macrolevel patterns. The ongoing flexibilization and growing contingency of labor (itself linked to the decay of employee rights, benefits, and job security) and our increasing imbrication in diffuse, invisible systems of tracking (through our smart phones, online activity, and the no-longer-futuristic presence of wearable devices and facial-recognition technologies) have indeed left us subject to new, dispersed modes of control within and beyond virtual spaces. Analysts and policy makers have staked their hopes on the predictive capacities of quantitative and positivist sciences, even as these methods so often fail to anticipate coming challenges and to render the indeterminacies of our invisible presents and ever-shifting horizons knowable or manipulable. Meanwhile, Edward Snowden's revelations remind us of the dark side of "big data," highlighting its mobilization as an instrument of control and surveillance underpinned by rhetorics of security.[110]

Critical for anthropology today is Deleuze's alertness to the canny workings of techno-capitalism and the plasticity of power, as well as his acknowledgment of the existence of counterknowledge—that is, understanding and critique that grows with being governed in a particular way, which has the potential to turn into an act of resistance or of making things otherwise.[111] Yet while much of Deleuze's description rings true, his brief sketch of a society to come does not answer the question of how social transformation happens; how people reckon with it; and what kinds of social spheres, sensibilities, and forms of self-fashioning come into being as changes take hold and forms of governance rework themselves.

An anthropology attuned to becomings asks how people engage with this modulation of their desires, this tracking of their behaviors and consumptions, and this imperative to continually craft and recraft their digital selves.[112] From clinics and courtrooms in Brazil where medical technologies and shifting legal configurations offer new possibilities for gender-affirming care,[113] to online platforms where new forms of community and solidarity emerge for those previously excluded from the mainstream public sphere, technology is never only controlling.[114] Recent work by Faye Ginsburg and Rayna Rapp in the anthropology of disability,[115] for example, highlights how digital technologies create "counterdiscursive sites of representation" for marginalized subjects, providing unexpected opportunities for "people with disabilities to engage in a first-person discussion of their world and experiences."[116]

In other words, people are actively deploying new technologies for their own ends, waging politics and challenging entrenched assumptions. Gabriella Coleman's work on the hacker collective Anonymous highlights a different form of counterdiscursivity playing out in contemporary digital worlds. "Their political tools," she writes, "emerge from the concrete experiences of their craft."[117] Coleman characterizes these "radical tech warriors," who are armed with technological savvy and computing skills, as revolutionary rogues,[118] simultaneously subversive and principled—a new kind of political subject facing the machineries of power in the twenty-first century.[119] More broadly, the corporate capture and commodification of the expansive data exhaust produced by social media activity raises questions for activists and social scientists alike about what unforeseen potentials—beyond surveillance, security, and personalized marketing—all these data might have.

If Deleuze's vision for the dawning control society overlooked the possibility that new digital media might become tools for social mobilization as well as for the management of criminality and political dissent, it also did not anticipate how old sites of confinement and punishment would not truly disappear.[120] Spaces of abandonment like Vita emerged as part and parcel of the dismantling and transformation of more centralized institutions of control and care in Brazil, and deinstitutionalization of the mentally ill engendered similar translocations from the asylum to streets and jails in the United States. Public hospitals, prisons, and schools have become private, profit-generating institutions that increasingly are embedded in other social domains and the domestic sphere and, as Garcia's work on Mexican *anexos* shows (see chapter 3), violence and religion are increasingly folded together in new regimes of care and security.

Such reconfigurations of power, discipline, and profit are apparent across domains. After the era of so-called white flight, for example, gentrification, housing and foreclosure crises, and debates over policing are all reshaping cities and their neighborhoods, both spatially and socially. In education, shady online universities and degree programs proliferate to mine profits and personal data by delivering the classroom to the laptop. In the United States, the enormous expansion of standardized testing in primary and secondary education—supported by a booming industry of for-profit exam production—monitors and modulates, ever more intensively and intrusively, the learning of new generations, conditioning young people for new forms of anxiety-driven self-governance. The privatization of prisons and the development of new technologies for monitoring offenders beyond the jail cell all seem to consolidate rather than disperse the brutal edifice of American mass incarceration,[121] still the default tool for containing the excesses and resistances produced by systemic racism and socioeconomic inequality; and in the meantime, new communities of grievance take root where the families of the incarcerated settle in to wait and hope.[122] In health care, the faltering or collapse of public systems in the era of neoliberalism has made way for worlds in which families become proxies for biomedical power and triage, nongovernmental organizations make up patchwork landscapes of care delivery, and patients must create new and agonistic forms of citizenship and medical self-management to live with the biosocial illnesses and vulnerabilities generated by severe inequality and toxic environments.[123]

If disciplinary society in the past was characterized by bodies known and governed by nation-states, today, as public infrastructures and institutions falter, it is an assemblage of clandestine security agencies and multinational corporations that track (and profit from) our bodies and labor. In ways of which we are only dimly aware, our digital activity constantly produces value for corporations as they become ever more integrated with larger virtual systems that extract from us a new kind of alienated labor. All the while, new forms of high-tech profiling risk exacerbating disparities along lines of race, class, and gender. Yet the question of who can participate in this new form of society is intimately linked to the production of value. As Deleuze noted, "capitalism still keeps three quarters of humanity in extreme poverty, too poor to have debts and too numerous to be confined."[124]

What can be learned about social order and the political moment by closely attending to this impoverished "three quarters"? In contexts shaped by arbitrary neoliberal economic policies, myopic cultural politics, and unforgiving humanitarianisms, people like the Ayoreo of the Gran Chaco live in the dizzying, fraught spaces of postcolonial and neocolonial violence, overwhelming our assumptions of what counts as indigeneity and what modes of existence and transformation are conjured up in the ruptures of contact. How are today's poor entangled in the opaque and alarming realignments of governance, market, security, and citizenship, driven along altered trajectories of hypermarginality and survival that, in turn, may generate new dangers, sensibilities, and landscapes of possibility?[125] "Hunger, nothing, void," Garcia writes in chapter 3: "these are the negative forces that have the potential to move one forward, and to be able to find in chains something else." Broadening our view of contemporary society draws us into shifting dynamics of market inclusion, indebtedness, and dissensus. Such dynamics are linked to both emerging consumer desires and the "dreams and schemes"[126] of development and redistribution projects,[127] affecting ideas of equality, solidarity, and circuit-breaking and world-making capacities.

Deleuze's almost casual aside that the astonishing scope and severity of global poverty is connected to the shape and futures of evolving modes of control is an essential insight that calls for granular, daring, cross-disciplinary work. As ever, in exploring processes of social transformation we find power, interests, and domination. Only by insisting on a space where precarity is actually a mobilizing force and where those of no account are counted can we restore the place of the poor and most vulnerable in the political community.[128] Yet the metastories flowing from centers of thought and research today are often depoliticizing. From game theory, mathematical modeling, and randomization to the hype of big data's predictive potential, quantitative approaches all too often treat societies like deterministic machines and assume that all we lack to anticipate their vulnerabilities and implement solutions are the right methods for generating and interpreting data—methods imagined to be just around the corner.[129]

Yet the very possibility of politics depends on scrutinizing the boundaries of inclusion and exclusion in preposterous social orders, examining shared uncertainties about how best to confront looming challenges, and creating space for collective actions.[130] Perfectly predictive quantitative approaches would cast political action as the inevitable outcome of calculation (and therefore not really political at all), rather than a product of debate, discernment, and ethical reasoning informed by partial knowledges, mediated by plural acts of resistance, and oriented toward futures not yet anticipated. What would it take, as Petryna puts it in chapter 9, "to open up a conversation about what it means when we look into the future and say we don't know?" Exploring "the disconnects and ambiguities that characterize abrupt ecosystem dynamics for scientists and the rest of us," she shows how the making of imperfect scientific knowledge in contexts of radical uncertainty and "inexorable threat" is part of a "new kind of intellectual labor." As we grapple with "a complex future that is right at hand," Petryna asks, "how do temporal horizons themselves become political, or how do they demarcate (or dissolve) a space of political action?"

If we are reluctant to offer here a pithy name to label the transformed workings of power and inequality after "control societies,"[131] this hesitance to hurriedly abstract and simplify carries its own epistemic force insofar as it challenges—or altogether dismantles—the blinders imposed by more rigid, technical, or philosophical methods of knowledge production. Rather than establishing a final paradigm of knowing, the anthropology of becoming helps us track how the social itself is unmoored, and the shape of collectives and the right course of action remain undetermined. As Petryna suggests, the current moment seems to call less for the all-knowing hubris of totalizing analytical schemes than for a human science (and politics) of the uncertain and the unknown.

In the meantime, however, the dominant voices of economists and quantitative modelers acquire power, scientific authority, and resources by claiming to represent empirical reality with their opaque measurements and faulty predictions.[132] They alter social dynamics and political possibilities as they put communities in the service of evidence production—rather than the other way around.[133] Where in these calculations, polls, models, randomized trials, and projections is there room for the contingent political decision or policy swerve, the unexpected social movement or upheaval that sets events on an unforeseen course? What algorithms and predictions generate insight about the moral and political dimensions of coming challenges or help navigate questions of accountability and responsibility—or, as Donna Haraway might put it, our ethical "response-ability"?[134]

FIELDWORK AND STORYTELLING

Exploring tangles of microdynamics and macroforces in the present day, the anthropology of becoming resists the binaries of inner/outer, individual/collective, human/nonhuman, and local/global, instead choosing to look at how lives, rationalities, social fields, and power relations are inflected in one another and in the enclosures, impasses, thresholds, and breakthroughs that are the materials of lifeworld and subject construction. The precariousness of our lives is not merely happy or sad happenstance; it is part and parcel of small- and large-scale assemblages and shifts that color our every experience. Yet desire is immersed in and shaped by world-historical trajectories; in facing the arbitrary and the contingent, people carve out footholds and surprising escapes, and we must find ways of attending to them.

Ethnographically attuned to the interdependence and plasticity of live forms across scales,[135] we can weave together the affective trajectories of singular lives and "tiny solidarities" with planetary-level political-economic, technological, and environmental dynamics.[136] As Judith Butler poignantly puts it, "perhaps the human is the name we give to this very negotiation that emerges from a living creature among creatures and in the midst of forms of living that exceed us."[137]

Tracking such negotiations is never only the prerogative of the anthropologist. Attuned to asymmetries of all kinds, we remain committed to speaking and writing with people and their worlds, learning how they understand and conceptualize their conditions and do the work of scaling and invention in their everyday lives. As Bridget Purcell shows in the attention she pays in chapter 4 to the "tentative, nonlinear ways that individuals orient themselves in a ritual landscape that exceeds their full control," people inhabit and negotiate "multiple, overlapping" realities in their material and moral lives. Open to wonder and to the various derailments that come with fieldwork, the anthropology of becoming is marked by this animated, worldly multiplicity "even in the person that speaks or acts."[138]

People and the worlds they navigate and the outlooks they articulate are more confounding, incomplete, and multiplying than dominant analytical schemes tend to account for. Drawn to the unsettling of rationalities and ingrained commonsense, the anthropology of becoming thus eschews a sense of theory as a totalizing enterprise or as the privileged domain of elite knowledge makers self-appointed to speak for or on behalf of benighted populations. Upholding an equality of intelligences and rejecting the division between those who "truly" or "critically" know the world and those who merely possess the pragmatic know-how needed to survive in it, this book's ethnographic essays chronicle lived tensions between theory and practice. They invoke both alternative conceptual frameworks and new kinds of imagination, in the spirit of what the political economist Albert Hirschman might call "a little less straitjacketing of the future."[139]

Like our subjects, we tell stories to grapple with the world, and to understand and intervene in it.[140] While philosophers tell stories with concepts, the stories we tell in this book are crafted from instances of becomings.

In Ralph's inner-city Eastwood (see chapter 2), Mrs. Lana's screams are at once the shattering thrum of death and a means of creating "a public sphere in which oppositional voices are not feared, degraded, or dismissed but valued for the productive reflections they inspire." Affirmed by the anthropologist, these unforeseen "collective practices of care" speak to "locally salient ways of interpreting the human condition," evincing the worldliness and creativity of ethnographic theory. Such inventiveness also occurs at the level of the self. As Naisargi Dave illustrates in chapter 5 regarding animal activism in India, bearing witness to the suffering of others (in this case, animals) "might best be understood as a radical interpenetration of life and death" that "opens up a death" and "then compels a new kind of responsible life in a previously unimaginable skin." Fieldwork, theorizing, and writing thus emerge from and in conversation with this hard-to-pin-down multiplicity—practical and theoretical, real and virtual, and in bits and pieces—that places people, worlds, and thinking in motion.

The subjects of our ethnographies are themselves concept makers and creators. From Petryna's climate scientists, who navigate imperfect knowledge and an inexorable threat, to Schwarcz's cannibalizing artist, they actively interfere in reality, crafting ways of knowing and translating across scales and domains.[141] Petryna tells us in chapter 9 that scientists grappling with uncertainty carve "a space of decision making out of a line of inevitability," creating "new projective possibilities" while "sustaining space for action even in dire conditions." Such open-ended concept work grows out of the demands of the times and, as Schwarcz writes of Varejão's artistic reworking of the racial classification schemas she uncovered, may be "a tribute to the different possibilities of discourse, the multiplicity that is a kind of common foundation of depiction in art"—and in world making.

Theories play a part in the realities they describe and imagine. They have traction in the world, becoming integrated into (for better or for worse) people's bodies, values, relationships, and the possibilities they envision for themselves and others. Ethnography can capture this active embroiling of reason, life, and ethics, and the anthropologist can learn to think with circulating theories, however fully articulated, that concern both large-scale social dynamics and people's immediate conditions, travails, and anticipations. It can also offer entry points into the plasticity of systems, theorizers, and norm makers themselves, making it possible to pursue new forms of anthropological thought and research.

As Catarina/Catkine told Biehl in Vita, "I began to disentangle the facts with you.... I began to disentangle the science and the wisdom. It is good to disentangle oneself, and thought as well." Through Biehl's work with Catarina, various forms of reason (psychiatric, familial, gendered, economic, and pharmaceutical) came into view, complicating the very concept of the human: "They want my body, my body as medication... Catkine rots." Still, Catarina crafted her own lines of flight: "When men throw me into the air, I am already far away" (see chapter 1). This work of detaching oneself from what is accepted as true is "philosophy in activity," as Foucault would have said: "the displacement and transformation of frameworks of thinking, the changing of received values and all the work that has been done to think otherwise, to do something else, to become other than what one is—that, too, is philosophy."[142]

Meanwhile, as Sarajevans confront the effects of the neoliberal rationalities implemented by international institutions of aid and governance—theories of reconciliation and democracy, market economics and the public good, trauma and humanitarianism, and dealing with the past and building anew—they work to craft their own temporalities of change and ways of navigating the vicissitudes of politics, both local and global. As the short-lived but explosive experiments in direct democracy that spread across Bosnia-Herzegovina in 2014 seem to attest, people often perceive both the forces that constrain them and the ways things might (or should) be otherwise. Amid the making and remaking of a divided postwar country, their becomings—narrated by Peter Locke in chapter 10—suggest alternative possibilities for living with difficult pasts and the uncertainties of rapid social transformation.

It is not only the ideas of political scientists, economists, biologists, and psychiatrists that shape the becomings of individuals and collectives in this book's geography of becomings; anthropology's own key terms and theories travel and are taken up in unpredictable ways. In this regard, Bessire's critical approach to indigeneity in chapter 7 highlights the deep—and even deadly—afterlives of anthropological concepts as they become part of larger exclusionary and violent projects: "a politics whereby cultural legitimacy is increasingly used to distinguish who is worthy of exceptional protection and who is allowed to die." In contrast, he argues, the anthropology of indigenous becomings "challenges the sense of inevitability implied by many analytic tools and allows indigenous subjects to reappear not as ideal types known in advance but as always unfinished, incomplete, and open-ended."

Certainly, to carry out our analyses, we need models, types, and theories—abstractions of various kinds—and there is a rich and important history of engagement between anthropology and philosophy.[143] Yet can philosophy really transform the characters and realities we engage with and the stories we tell into figures of thought?

Our engagements with texts, theories, and philosophies occur in particular times and spaces, woven into our experiences in the field and in the world at large, and find their ways into our thinking and writing in a relationship that might be productively seen as one of creative tension and cross-pollination.

The authors in this book draw from and participate in multiple intellectual lineages, opening up ways in which we might, in Davis's words in chapter 8, both "coexist and fruitfully interact with other dispositions to knowledge." "In step with the intensifying violence in Mexico," Garcia writes in chapter 3 that she "found [herself] turning to [Ernst] Bloch's mystical and revolutionary writings," while for Davis, William Connolly's vision of complex time in a world of becoming offered "a vitalizing complement to the paranoid hermeneutics in which the violent history of Cyprus seems so deeply entrenched." Similarly, in making sense of the Ayoreos' senseless expenditure amid world-ending violence, Bessire draws from the work of Georges Bataille to highlight the subversive powers of life beyond utility. Meanings and concepts flow freely across fuzzy academic boundaries and change in the process, and these ethnographers further displace becoming from its philosophical origins and uptake.

Ethnographic theory emerges from and in conversation with unfinished subjects and lifeworlds, as well as books and various ways of knowing and relating. It is a way of staying connected to open-ended, even mysterious, social processes and uncertainties—a way of counterbalancing the generation of certainties and foreclosures by other disciplines. Keeping interrelatedness, uncertainty, and curiosity in focus, our theorizing is never detached from praxis but instead directly shapes and channels anthropology's entanglements in processes of transformation. In this way, theory is multiple and multiplies, a "tool box" that can be actionable, in the world and in our writing: "it has to be used, it has to work."[144]

Marked by returns, ongoingness, and the meantimes that unfold while the anthropologist is in the field and afterward, ethnography also brings subjects into contact with each other in lasting, unpredictable, and transformative ways.[145] Through fieldwork, we become a part of ethnographic open systems and are folded into lives, relationships, and swerves across time and space.[146] These systems hold us in a kind of unfinished proximity with one another, retreating and reemerging, engendering unanticipated connections and reconfigurations, never definitively closed off nor decisively transformational. Ethnographic open systems tether us to other selves and worlds and destabilize the temporal and spatial boundaries of an imagined field we leave behind.

Like art, ethnographic theorizing and writing can push the limits of language and imagination as it seeks to bear witness to life in a manner that does not bound, reduce, or make caricatures of people and their lifeworlds but liberates, if always only partially, some of the epistemological, political, and aesthetic force of their circuitous paths, interactions, and stories.

Becomings create holes in dominant theories and interventions and unleash a vital plurality: being in motion, ambiguous, and contradictory; not reducible to a single narrative; projected into the future; transformed by recognition; and thus the very fabric of alternative world making. "We try to write about what is missing," as Schwarcz notes in chapter 6, "but in so doing we create new possibilities." The life stories we compose do not simply begin and end. They are stories of transformation: they link the present to the past and to a possible or impossible future, creating unexpected ties among subject, scribe, and reader.

For indeed the reader, too, is always implicated. And there is much at stake in different forms of reading. If one takes a book "as a box with something inside"—an ultimate meaning or truth—one's task is to interrogate and deconstruct what it contains.[147] In our times, criticism has largely been naturalized as an act of judgment and indictment—a habit of faultfinding, of reading as jaded consumers of knowledge—in a way that reifies ideologies, ultimately stifling curiosity and obscuring the realities we wish to better understand.[148] But there are also other modes of reading, less audit-like or prosecutorial.

"To have done with judgment,"[149] as Deleuze puts it, allows us to move away from criticism as condemnation toward more interesting, constructive questions: How do the stories and ideas and becomings that unfold in these pages work for you, reader? What do they produce, open up, or foreclose? What possibilities—intellectual, relational, or political—do they illuminate and make available?

This form of engagement is "like plugging into an electric circuit.... It relates a book directly to what's Outside." A book, after all, "is a little cog in much more complicated external machinery."[150] What if we resisted the tendency to know too much in advance, and the drab and deadly power to condemn and exclude, and instead engaged in forms of reading that were productive and enlivening, multiplying instead of stifling?

This active form of reading—"reading with love"[151]—frees us from critique as combat in favor of critique as care: care of the self and others, of aspirations for less violent and more just ways of inhabiting and sharing the planet, and of the imagination and thought itself. It makes it possible to engage in what texts unleash, the forms of understanding that they open up, and the larger external machineries of which they are part.

There is an ethos of unfinishedness and an invitational quality to the ethnographic writings that compose this book: an openness to the knowledge and mystery of others, a curiosity toward how human ways of living are entwined with nonhuman modes of life, a desire to bring us closer to people rather than creating distance, a humility in relation to our own thinking. It is in this spirit of open inquiry and wonder, of not being governed too much, of creating relations and always probing their very natures and stakes, of becoming a mobilizing force in this world, that *Unfinished* ends with blank pages—after all, readers and the distinct publics they make up are also part of the writing and of how the story continues . . .

NOTES

1. Nietzsche, *The Use and Abuse of History*, 10.
2. Connolly, *A World of Becoming*.
3. Barad, *Meeting the Universe Halfway*, 33.
4. Deleuze, *Two Regimes of Madness*, 2.
5. Deleuze and Parnet, *Gilles Deleuze from A to Z*.
6. See Bataille, *The Unfinished System of Nonknowledge*; Das et al., *The Ground Between*; Geertz, *The Interpretation of Cultures*; Lambek et al., *Four Lectures on Ethics*; Malinowski, *Argonauts of the Western Pacific*; Rabinow, *Marking Time*; Wolf, *Europe and the People without History*.
7. See Nietzsche, *Thus Spoke Zarathustra* and *The Will to Power*; Deleuze, *Nietzsche and Philosophy*.

8   Deleuze, *Two Regimes of Madness*, 124.
9   Deleuze, *Two Regimes of Madness*, 128.
10 Deleuze, *Two Regimes of Madness*, 124.
11 Foucault, *Discipline and Punish*, and *The History of Sexuality*.
12 Deleuze, *Two Regimes of Madness*, 124.
13 Deleuze, *Two Regimes of Madness*, 124.
14 Deleuze, *Two Regimes of Madness*, 125.
15 Deleuze, *Two Regimes of Madness*, 128.
16 Deleuze, *Essays Critical and Clinical*, 1.
17 Deleuze, *Essays Critical and Clinical*, 1.
18 Deleuze, *Essays Critical and Clinical*, 1.
19 Deleuze, *Essays Critical and Clinical*, 1.
20 Rimbaud, *Complete Works*, 101.
21 Rimbaud, quoted in Deleuze, *Essays Critical and Clinical*, 29.
22 Deleuze, *Essays Critical and Clinical*, 63.
23 Deleuze, *Two Regimes of Madness*, 280.
24 Deleuze, *Negotiations, 1972–1990*, 170.
25 See Comaroff and Comaroff, *Ethnography and the Historical Imagination*; Das, *Life and Words*; Fassin, *When Bodies Remember*; Mbembe, *On the Postcolony*; Stoler, *Along the Archival Grain* and *Carnal Knowledge and Imperial Power*; Trouillot, *Silencing the Past*.
26 See M. Jackson, *Life within Limits*, and *Lifeworlds*; Malabou, *The Ontology of the Accident*.
27 Stewart, "Precarity's Form," 8.
28 Biehl, "Ethnography in the Way of Theory."
29 M. Fischer, Comment on João Biehl and Peter Locke's article "Deleuze and the Anthropology of Becoming," 338.
30 See Allison, *Precarious Japan*; Berlant, *Cruel Optimism*; Bessire, *Behold the Black Caiman*; Butler, *Precarious Life*; Davis, *Bad Souls*; Ralph, *Renegade Dreams*.
31 Haraway, *Staying with the Trouble*.
32 See Berlant, *Cruel Optimism*; Bhabha, *The Location of Culture*; Malabou, *The Ontology of the Accident*; Morris, *Can the Subaltern Speak?*; Scott, "To Be a Wonder"; Spivak, "Can the Subaltern Speak?"; Stewart, *Ordinary Affects*; Strathern, "Negative Strategies."
33 Freud, *Collected Papers*, vol. 2, 279.
34 Malinowski, *Sex and Repression in Savage Society*, 126.
35 Mauss, "The Notion of Body Techniques." See also Garces and Jones, "Mauss Redux"; Mauss, "L'expression obligatoire des sentiments (rituels oraux funéraires australiens)."
36 Fanon, *The Wretched of the Earth*, 250.
37 Butler, *Excitable Speech*, *Frames of War*, and *Precarious Life*.
38 Comaroff and Comaroff, *Theory from the South*, 56.
39 Taussig, *Mimesis and Alterity*, xiii.
40 See Good, DelVecchio Good, Hyde, and Pinto, "Postcolonial Disorders: Reflections on Subjectivity in the Contemporary World," 8.
41 M. Fischer, *Emergent Forms of Life and the Anthropological Voice*. See also Inhorn, *Cosmopolitan Conceptions*; Malkki, *The Need to Help*; Sharp, *The Transplant Imaginary*.

42 M. Fischer, *Emergent Forms of Life and the Anthropological Voice*, 30.
43 See Briggs and Mantini-Briggs, *Tell Me Why My Children Died*; Dumit, *Drugs for Life* and *Picturing Personhood*; K. Fortun, *Advocacy after Bhopal*; Gusterson, *Nuclear Rites*; Haydn, *When Nature Goes Public*; Helmreich, *Alien Ocean*; Kaufman, *Ordinary Medicine*; Jain, *Malignant*; Lakoff, *Pharmaceutical Reason*; Lakoff and Collier, *Biosecurity Interventions*; Livingston, *Improvising Medicine*; Lock and Nguyen, "Local Biologies and Human Difference"; Martin, *The Woman in the Body*, and *Bipolar Expeditions*; Petryna, *When Experiments Travel*, and *Life Exposed*; Prentice, *Bodies in Formation*; Rabinow, *The Accompaniment* and *Marking Time*; Sharp, *The Transplant Imaginary*.
44 Lewis and Maslin, "Defining the Anthropocene."
45 Malm, "The Anthropocene Myth."
46 Ingold and Palsson, *Biosocial Becomings*, 20.
47 Landecker and Panofsky, "From Social Structure to Gene Regulation and Back."
48 For a discussion of biosocial approaches, see Farmer, *Infections and Inequalities* and *Pathologies of Power*.
49 For a discussion of ecosocial approaches, see Krieger, "Theories for Social Epidemiology in the 21st Century."
50 Lock and Scheper-Hughes, "The Mindful Body."
51 Lock and Nguyen, "Local Biologies and Human Difference."
52 Lock, "The Epigenome and Nature/Nurture Reunification," 292. See also Lock, "Comprehending the Body in the Era of the Epigenome."
53 Ingold and Palsson, *Biosocial Becomings*.
54 Palsson, "Retrospect," *Biosocial Becomings*, 244.
55 Kirskey and Helmreich, "The Emergence of Multispecies Ethnography." See also Deane-Drummond and Fuentes, "Human Being and Becoming"; Haraway, *When Species Meet*; Raffles, *Insectopedia*; Tsing, *The Mushroom at the End of the World*.
56 Deleuze, *Essays Critical and Clinical*, 2.
57 Deleuze, *Essays Critical and Clinical*, 2.
58 Deleuze and Parnet, *Gilles Deleuze from A to Z*.
59 Kirksey and Helmreich, "The Emergence of Multispecies Ethnography," 545.
60 Kirskey, *Emergent Ecologies*, 217.
61 Kirskey, *Emergent Ecologies*, 217, 219.
62 Kirskey, *Emergent Ecologies*, 5. See also Povinelli, *Geontologies*; Connolly, *Facing the Planetary*.
63 Tsing, *The Mushroom at the End of the World*, 22.
64 Ingold and Palsson, *Biosocial Becomings*.
65 Kohn, *How Forests Think*.
66 Viveiros de Castro, "Cosmological Deixis and Amerindian Perspectivism."
67 See Cadena, *Earth Beings*; Gordillo, *Rubble*; Li, *Land's End*; West, *From Modern Coffee Production to Imagined Primitive*.
68 Tsing, *The Mushroom at the End of the World*, 19. See also Stoler, *Imperial Debris*.
69 Tsing, *The Mushroom at the End of the World*, 22.
70 Tsing, *The Mushroom at the End of the World*, 23.

71. Bennett, *Vibrant Matter*.
72. Bennett, *Vibrant Matter*, vi.
73. Bennett, *Vibrant Matter*, vii.
74. Appadurai, "Mediants, Materiality, Normativity," 221.
75. Appadurai, "Mediants, Materiality, Normativity," 221.
76. Malinowski, *Argonauts of the Western Pacific*, 16.
77. See Cadena, *Earth Beings*; Kelly and Lezaun, "Urban Mosquitoes, Situational Publics, and the Pursuit of Interspecies Separation in Dar es Salaam"; Nading, *Mosquito Trails*; Povinelli, *Geontologies*.
78. Povinelli, *The Empire of Love*, 179.
79. Deleuze and Guattari, *A Thousand Plateaus*, 259.
80. Deleuze, *Negotiations, 1972–1990*, 176.
81. Geertz, *Available Light*.
82. Geertz, *Available Light*, 221, 246.
83. Masco, *The Theater of Operations*.
84. Fennell, *Last Project Standing*.
85. Rorty, *Achieving Our Country*, 89–90. This passage circulated widely on social media in the days following the 2016 U.S. presidential election. Other seemingly prophetic perspectives, in and beyond the academy, are sure to be recognized as critical thinkers and activists reckon with the election's significance.
86. Fukuyama, "The End of History?"
87. See Glaude, *Democracy in Black*; John Jackson, *Harlemworld* and *Real Black*. See also Dave, "Indian and Lesbian and What Came Next"; Greenhouse, *The Paradox of Relevance*; and D. Thomas, *Exceptional Violence*.
88. See Fernando, *The Republic Unsettled*; Hirschkind, *The Ethical Soundscape*; Luhrmann, *When God Talks Back*; Mahmood, *Politics of Piety* and *Religious Difference in a Secular Age*; Sullivan et al., *Politics of Religious Freedom*. See also M. Fischer, "Receptions in the Revolution" and *Emergent Forms of Life and the Anthropological Voice*.
89. See Biehl and Petryna, *When People Come First*; Farrar and Piot, "The Ebola Emergency"; Lakoff, Collier, and Kelty, "Ebola's Ecologies."
90. See Nixon, *Slow Violence and the Environmentalism of the Poor*; Sheikh and Weizman, *The Conflict Shoreline*.
91. Roitman, *Anti-Crisis*. See also Fassin and Pandolfi, *Contemporary States of Emergency*; Redfield, *Life in Crisis*.
92. W. Brown, *Undoing the Demos*.
93. W. Brown, *Undoing the Demos*, 44.
94. Piketty, *Capital in the Twenty-First Century*.
95. Graeber, *The Democracy Project* and "Occupy Wall Street Rediscovers the Radical Imagination."
96. Berlant, *Cruel Optimism*, 1.
97. W. Brown, *Undoing the Demos*, 10 and 35.
98. Biehl, "The Judicialization of Biopolitics."
99. Berlant, *Cruel Optimism*, 3.

100 Butler, *Notes Toward a Performative Theory of Assembly*, 41.
101 See M. Fischer, Comment on João Biehl and Peter Locke's Article "Deleuze and the Anthropology of Becoming"; Livingston, *Improvising Medicine*; Mattingly, *Moral Laboratories*.
102 Rancière, *Moments Politiques*, 75.
103 Biehl, "The Judicialization of Biopolitics: Claiming the Right to Pharmaceuticals in Brazilian Courts" and "Patient-Citizen-Consumers: The Judicialization of Health and the Metamorphosis of Biopolitics."
104 See Graeber, *Debt*; Simpson, *Mohawk Interruptus*; Stevenson, *Life Beside Itself*; Taylor, *From #BlackLivesMatter to Black Liberation*.
105 See Biehl, "The Postneoliberal Fabulation of Power"; Kleinman, *What Really Matters*; Kleinman and Wilkinson, *A Passion for Society*; Povinelli, *Economies of Abandonment* and *Geontologies*.
106 Deleuze, *Negotiations, 1972–1990*, 177.
107 Foucault, *Discipline and Punish* and *The History of Sexuality*.
108 Deleuze, *Negotiations, 1972–1990*, 178.
109 Deleuze, *Negotiations, 1972–1990*, 180.
110 See Borneman and Masco, "Anthropology and the Security State"; Poitras, *Citizen Four*.
111 Povinelli, "The Will to be Otherwise/The Effort of Endurance."
112 Turkle, *Reclaiming Conversation*.
113 Biehl, "Patient-Citizen-Consumers."
114 See Winslow, "Living Life Forward."
115 Ginsburg and Rapp, "Disability Worlds."
116 Ginsburg, "Disability in the Digital Age," 102–3.
117 Coleman, *Hacker, Hoaxer, Whistleblower, Spy*, 280.
118 Coleman, *Hacker, Hoaxer, Whistleblower, Spy*, 280.
119 Biehl and Zucker, "The Masked Anthropologist."
120 See Fassin, *Enforcing Order* and *L'ombre du monde*; Knight, *addicted.pregnant.poor*; O'Neill, *Secure the Soul*; Rios, *Punished*.
121 See Alexander, *The New Jim Crow*; Murakawa, *The First Civil Right*.
122 H. Pearson, "The Prickly Skin of White Supremacy."
123 See Han, *Life in Debt*; James, *Democratic Insecurities*; Raikhel and Garriott, *Addiction Trajectories*; Rouse, *Uncertain Suffering*; Scheper-Hughes, "Parts Unknown"; Shapiro, "Attuning to the Chemosphere"; Ticktin, *Casualties of Care*.
124 Deleuze, *Negotiations, 1972–1990*, 181.
125 See Bessire, *Behold the Black Caiman*; De Leon, *The Land of Open Graves*.
126 Tsing, *Friction*, 1.
127 See A. Escobar, *Encountering Development*; Ferguson, *Give a Man a Fish*; Piot, *Remotely Global* and *Nostalgia for the Future*.
128 See Agier, *On the Margins of the World*; Butler, *Notes Toward a Performative Theory of Assembly*; Das, *Affliction*; Nelson, *Who Counts?*; Rancière, *The Emancipated Spectator*; L. Segal, *No Place for Grief*; Singh, *Poverty and the Quest for Life*; Walley, *Exit Zero*.
129 See Cartwright and Hardie, *Evidence-Based Policy*; Deaton, "Instruments of Development."

130 See Butler, *Notes Toward a Performative Theory of Assembly*; Rancière, *Moments Politiques*.
131 Deleuze, *Negotiations, 1972–1990*, 177.
132 See Deaton, *The Great Escape*; Easterly, *The Tyranny of Experts*.
133 Adams, "Evidence-Based Global Public Health: Subjects, Profits, Erasures" and *Metrics*.
134 Haraway, *When Species Meet*, 89.
135 Stewart, "Precarity's Form."
136 Lévi-Strauss, *The View from Afar*, 287.
137 Butler, *Notes Toward a Performative Theory of Assembly*, 43.
138 Deleuze, *Desert Islands and Other Texts 1953–1974*, 207.
139 Hirschman, *Exit, Voice and Loyalty*, 338.
140 Geertz, *Works and Lives*.
141 See Pandian, *Reel World*.
142 Foucault, *Ethics*, 327.
143 Das et al., *The Ground Between*.
144 Deleuze, *Desert Islands and Other Texts 1953–1974*, 210.
145 See K. Fortun, "Ethnography in/of/as open systems."
146 See Biehl, "Ethnography in the Way of Theory"; De Leon, *The Land of Open Graves*; Desjarlais, *Subject to Death*; M. Jackson, *In Sierra Leone*.
147 Deleuze, *Negotiations, 1972–1990*, 7.
148 Felski, *The Limits of Critique*.
149 Deleuze, *Essays Critical and Clinical*, 126.
150 Deleuze, *Negotiations, 1972–1990*, 8.
151 Deleuze, *Negotiations, 1972–1990*, 9.

I

1

The Anthropology of Becoming

JOÃO BIEHL AND PETER LOCKE

The pen between my fingers is my work
I am convicted to death
I never convicted anyone and I have the power to
This is the major sin
A sentence without remedy
The minor sin
Is to want to separate
My body from my spirit
— CATARINA INÊS GOMES MORAES, quoted in João Biehl, *Vita*, 2000

For how long will we have to live like it's still the war? When will we start to live?
—Marija (Maja) Šarič, Executive Director, *Krila Nade/Wings of Hope*

The ultimate aim of literature is to set free, in the delirium, this creation of a health or this invention of a people, that is, a possibility of life.
— GILLES DELEUZE, *Essays Critical and Clinical*

AN EMPIRICAL LANTERN

In the settings in which we work—Brazil and Bosnia-Herzegovina—people are at the mercy of volatile economies and faltering infrastructures. As individuals and communities scavenge for resources and care from broken public institutions, they find themselves entangled in novel biomedical and pharmaceutical rationalities and in altered forms of common sense. We find Gilles

Deleuze's empiricist reflections on the person as a provisional outcome of processes of subjectivation and his attention to the inventiveness of becoming both provocative and helpful as we address lives in such contexts of political-economic, material, and clinical precariousness.

For Deleuze, the subject is not a fixed entity, but an assemblage of multiple heterogeneous elements; not a given, but always under construction; not a product of an imagined interiority, but a folding and bending of outside forces: "it is a being-multiple, instead of being-one."[1] In asserting this "logic of multiplications," Deleuze upholds an allegiance to empiricism that strikes us as deeply ethnographic.[2] Subjects anticipate and invent—and anticipate because they invent—in concrete circumstances, navigating between things and relations.[3] In this way, the constitution of subjects is imbricated in world and place making, and subjectivity is far more active and uncertain than the search for an inside would assume.[4]

Together with his close collaborator Félix Guattari, Deleuze was particularly concerned with the idea of becoming: those individual and collective struggles to come to terms with matters of fact, contingencies, and intolerable conditions and to shake loose, to whatever degree possible, from determinants and definitions—"to grow both young and old [in them] at once."[5] In becoming, according to Deleuze, one can achieve an ultimate existential stage in which life is simply immanent and open to new relations—camaraderies—and trajectories without predetermined telos or outcome.

In our ethnographic work, we are drawn to human efforts to live with, subvert, or elude knowledge and power, and to express desires that might be world altering. Our interlocutors in the field are more complex, strategic, and inventive than hegemonic forces and philosophical theories of the subject are able to capture. People are not stable or fixed entities, unidirectionally determined by history, power, and language, nor are they only cultural and social. How can anthropology methodologically and conceptually engage people's becomings? And how could such work challenge dominant ethical and political frameworks and technocratic or medical modes of intervention? It is time to attribute to the people we study the kinds of ambiguities and complexities we acknowledge in ourselves, and to bring these dimensions into the critical knowledge we craft and circulate.

We have no grand philosophical aspirations, and we wish neither to reduce Deleuze's enormously complicated venture to a theoretical system or set of practices to be applied normatively to anthropology, nor to suggest a new dominant analytic or coin a new buzzword. In this essay, we limit ourselves to thinking through Deleuze's insights on the relationships between power, desire, and the virtual and his cartographic approach to lives, social fields, and the unconscious. These insights help us grasp what is at stake for individuals, affects, and relations in the context of new rational-technical interventions, and vis-à-vis ingrained inequalities of all kinds.[6]

Exploring Deleuze's ideas in light of the ethnographic realities we study—mental illness, poverty, and the long aftermaths of war—might offer openings to particular kinds of thinking, writing, and theorizing. It can, for example, highlight the limits of psychiatric models of symptoms, recovery, and human agency.[7] It can also provide a helpful supplement to prevailing applications of Michel Foucault's concepts of biopower and governmentality in anthropology[8] and to neo-Marxist theories of structural violence.[9] We aim to honor and contribute to anthropology's long and productive history of exploring human matters that dominant epistemologies do not routinely account for, keeping theory unsettled and in motion.[10] As Gregory Bateson put it over half a century ago in his classic *Naven*, "my fieldwork was scrappy and disconnected ... my own theoretical approaches proved too vague to be of any use in the field."[11]

In emphasizing the potentials of desire (both creative and destructive), the ways in which social fields leak and transform (power and knowledge notwithstanding), and the in-between, plastic, and ever-unfinished nature of lives, much of Deleuze's writing can inspire ethnographic efforts to illuminate the dynamism of the everyday and the literality and singularity of human becomings. By paying close attention to concrete circumstances, and with careful observation always complicating the a priori assumptions of universalizing theory, ethnographic work can explore both the modes of power that constrain life chances and the ways people's desires reveal alternative possibilities. In learning to know people, with care and an "empirical lantern,"[12] we have a responsibility to think of life in terms of both limits and crossroads—where new intersections of technology, interpersonal relations, desire, and imagination can sometimes, against all odds, result in surprising swerves and futures, even when our liberal projects of the good life writ large have turned into "cruel optimism."[13]

This is not to recommend giving up on attempts to discern relationships of causality and affinity in social and medical phenomena, or to deny the often deadly force of social realities and inequalities. Rather, it is to urge increased focus on our receptivity to others, the kinds of evidence we assemble and use—the voices we listen to, the silences we notice, and the experiences and turns we account for—and how we craft our explanations. Our analytics must remain attuned to the intricacy, uncertainty, and unfinishedness of individual and collective lives. Just as medical know-how, international political dynamics, and social realities change, people's lives (biological and political) are in flux.

Remaining open to surprise and the deployment of categories important to human experience can make anthropological work more realistic and, we hope, better. As the political economist Albert Hirschman, an ethnographer at heart, put it, "I like to understand how things happen, how change actually takes place."[14] People's everyday struggles for survival, belonging, and imagination exceed the categories informing experimental and statistical approaches and demand in-depth listening, dynamic mutual attunement, and a readiness to make bold analytical swerves. Ethnographic work engaged with becomings thus takes on conceptual force by building multidimensional figures of thought from the stories and trajectories of the people we engage with in the field. Tracking the intertwining of shifting material structures, uncharted social territories, and the formed and deformed bodies and senses of our field sites helps us empirically grasp what is actually happening in our radically unequal worlds and how power relations are being newly reinforced, always with an eye to how bodies also escape their figurations and forge unanticipated space-times.

PROBLEMATICS OF LIVING

In our reflections, we draw from Biehl's work with Catarina Inês Gomes Moraes, a young woman abandoned by her family and left to die in an asylum called Vita in the southern Brazilian city of Porto Alegre.[15] Largely incapacitated and said to be mad, Catarina spent her days in Vita assembling words in what she called "my dictionary." She wrote: "The characters in this notebook turn and un-turn. This is my world after all."

Catarina's puzzling language required intense listening, suspending diagnosis, and an open reading. Since Biehl first encountered her, he thought of her not as someone who was mentally ill but as an abandoned person who was claiming existence on her own terms. Catarina knew what had made her a "maimed statue" and a void in the social sphere—"I am like this because of life"—and she organized this knowledge for herself and her anthropologist, thus bringing the public into Vita. "I give you what is missing." Her family, she claimed, thought of her as a failed medication regimen. "Why is it only me who has to be medicated?" The family used this explanation as an excuse for abandoning her. Her condition highlighted the pharmaceuticalization of mental health care in Brazil and the social side effects that come with the encroachment of new medical technologies in urban-poor settings.

Catarina's life tells a larger story about shifting human values and the fate of social bonds in today's dominant mode of subjectivation in the service of science and capitalism. She suggests that one can become a medical or scientific thing and an ex-human for the convenience of others. At the merciless interface of capitalist and scientific discourses, we are all part of a new kind of proletariat: hyperindividualized psychobiologies doomed to consume diagnostics and treatments (for ourselves and for others) as we seek fast success in economies without empathy.[16] But Catarina fought the disconnections that psychiatric drugs introduced in her life and clung to her desires. She worked through the many layers of (mis)treatment and chemical changes that now composed her body, knowing all too well that "people forgot me."

Catarina wrote to sublimate not only her own desires for reconnection and recognition but also the social forces—familial, medical and scientific, and economic—aligned against her. While she integrated her experience with drugs into writing and a new self-perception (the drug biperiden, sold under brand names including Akineton, is literally part of the new name Catarina gives herself in the dictionary: Catkine), she kept seeking camaraderie and another chance at life. Biehl discusses Catarina's creative capacity for living through things in dialogue with Deleuze's idea of "a delicate and incomplete health that stems from efforts to carve out life chances from things too big, strong and suffocating."[17] In anticipating and imagining the possibility of an exit from Vita, Catkine's minor literature thus grounds an ethnographic ethics and gives us a sense of becoming and a style of reasoning that other analytic approaches might foreclose.

We also draw on Locke's fieldwork in Sarajevo, Bosnia-Herzegovina (hereafter, following the standard local abbreviation, BiH), to consider collective processes of becoming and to highlight Deleuze's intriguing suggestion that one should write for the benefit of a "missing people."[18] The collaborative nature of this coauthored chapter serves as a method of thought and an experiment in grappling with patterns across cases and scales. In the two decades since Yugoslavia's collapse and the long siege of Sarajevo, the symptoms and consequences—individual, social, and political—of the city's ordeals have been apparent. Wartime and postwar projects of humanitarian psychiatry and psychosocial support have made psychiatric diagnostics (specifically, collective depression and post-traumatic stress disorder) available for use in interpreting frustrating and persistent social ills. Such clinical-sounding assessments have the effect of emphasizing damage over possibility, painting the city primarily in terms of its wounds (which are indeed deep and still bleeding) while disregarding the hopes and desires—and resistances to neoliberal economic forms—that suffering also communicates.

Just as psychiatry helps silence Catarina's struggle to understand and reclaim her experience, in BiH, the psychologization of war's aftermath can sometimes "vitiate the moral and political meaning of subjective complaints and protests."[19] In this way, each of our cases addresses a struggle (individual and collective, respectively) to navigate public and private imperatives that have been remade by intersecting scientific and economic rationalities. In each case, a void is engineered in place of older modes of self-assessment—which nevertheless, and by circuitous paths, continue to thrive.

The strict application of a Foucauldian theoretical sensibility—seeking out, for example, the ways that fear-mongering nationalist politics, neoliberal market reforms and concomitant corruption, and years of humanitarian services and international supervision have newly disciplined bodies and normalized subjectivity and social relations—would miss the anxious uncertainty and open-endedness that inflect life in Sarajevo. Symptoms are, at times, a necessary condition or resource for the afflicted to articulate a new relationship to the world and to others. Catarina's family used her supposed madness to excuse themselves for her abandonment—even as she assimilated her experience of psychiatric treatment into a new identity in her struggle to anticipate a more livable reality. By the same token, Locke's work in Sarajevo suggests how the availability of psychiatric drugs and psychosocial services has enabled hybrid ways of remaking lives, families, and social roles.

Psychiatric rationality is enmeshed, to varying degrees, in the worlds we engage with, and it alters people's lives and desires—sometimes deleteriously, cementing foreclosures, and at other times allowing for new openings and forms of care. Anthropological work is well qualified to understand this tension, bringing us closer to the politics and ethics involved in the on-the-ground deployment of psychiatric categories and treatments—which increasingly takes place outside the clinic, in homes and people's solitary relationships to technology.[20]

Both anguish and vitality simmer beneath Sarajevo's scarred—but slowly brightening, rejuvenating—surfaces, and the work of Deleuze is helpful in finding an analytic approach that can illuminate the interdependence of these twin intensities: the ways symptoms may simultaneously index darknesses and dominations past and present and the minor voices of a "missing people" that speak within alternative "universes of reference," capable, perhaps, of one day unleashing unforeseen social transformations in BiH.[21] While aspirations for a better life and widespread frustrations with the status quo harbor the kinds of destructive potentials unleashed in the 1990s—the ethnic fear and violence, politics of scapegoating, and paranoia that come with chronic economic insecurity—they may also fuel unexpected solidarities and reveal alternative political pathways.

Sarajevo's "missing people" is composed of layers, each with its own intertwined violence, grief, and aspiration. The wartime dead (thousands of whom remain literally missing) continue to inhabit political claims and keenly felt grievances.[22] Who one was before the war (what one believed and whom one loved) no longer has the same value in new economies and forms of governance, but persists in people's anger and hope. And lived experience continually escapes the social categories—competing ethnic and/or victim identities—that dominate the public sphere.[23] In such a context of routinized urgency, the social sciences are challenged to respect and incorporate, without reduction, the ambiguity of political subjects, the uncertain roots and productivities of violence, and the passion for the possible that life holds in its passages through and beyond technical assessments. Performing this task is what ethnography does best.

MOVING IN THE DIRECTION OF THE UNFINISHED

We read Deleuze together with our ethnographic cases to reassert the symbiotic relationship between close empirical engagement with people and their worlds and theoretical inventiveness in anthropology. We recognize that "nobody needs philosophy for reflecting," as Deleuze himself noted, and are certainly not advocating for another philosophical scheme to be confirmed by the figures encountered in the field.[24] As John Borneman and Abdellah Hammoudi argue, the "tendency for anthropologists to deploy their work only as illustrative cases for philosophical trends or concepts threatens to make anthropology into a sterile intellectual exercise."[25] The point is well taken. In their relentless drive to theorize, anthropologists run the danger of caricaturing complex realities; neglecting key realms of experience; and missing lived figurations, ironies, and singularities that might complicate and enrich their analyses.

We thus return to ethnographic encounters and episodes not only to address their specificities, but also to make a case for allowing our engagements with others to determine the course of our thinking about them, and to reflect more broadly on the agonistic and reflexive relations between anthropology and philosophy.[26] We do so to suggest that through ethnographic rendering, people's own theorizing of their conditions may challenge present-day regimes of veridiction, including philosophical universals and anthropology's subjugation to philosophy. This is not to naively assume the ethnographic to be metonymic with a bounded ethnos, but rather to consider what is at stake in the ways that anthropologists chronicle and write about the knowledge emerging from our work with people.

Long-term engagement with people is a vital antidote to what Hirschman identifies as "compulsive and mindless theorizing."[27] The quick theoretical fix has taken its place in contemporary culture alongside the quick technical fix. For Hirschman, as for us, people in all their multiplicity must come first.[28] This respect for people and this attention both to how political discourses are manufactured and to the sheer materiality of life's necessities make a great deal of difference in the kind of knowledge anthropologists produce. Throughout this chapter, we are concerned with the conceptual fecundity of people's own practical theorizing. All too readily disqualified by both scholars and policy makers, this knowledge may well yield new or countertheories of human agency and of the shifting nature of social formations and resistance, for example, as well as new approaches to politics and more effective policy solutions.[29]

In an assessment of anthropology's intellectual health in the first decade of the new millennium, George Marcus worried that since the publication of the path-breaking *Writing Culture*, which he edited with James Clifford,[30] the discipline had been "suspended": "There are no new ideas and none on the horizon."[31] Marcus looked to innovations in the anthropology of science and science studies as possible inspirations.[32] Such scholarly attention to how knowledges and technologies are fabricated, and how they affect people and their worlds, has been productive.[33] Yet much of this field has given a privileged place to the official makers of expertise, technology, and policy.[34] While this side of the story is undoubtedly essential, it cannot encompass the full range of subjects, approaches, and methods with which anthropologists have continued to productively and innovatively engage. Marcus acknowledged that since the 1980s, anthropologists have played a useful role in studying emerging global political economies, but he did not think that was enough for "anthropologists to stimulate themselves intellectually."[35] Investment in and enthusiasm for public anthropology, for example, is in Marcus's view a "symptom" of a "weak center" and disciplinary disorganization, rather than an indicator of professional vitality and theoretical innovation.[36]

For Marcus, "what's left to do" while anthropology awaits the renewal or transformation of the "ideas that move and stimulate it . . . is to follow events, to engage ethnographically with history unfolding in the present, or to anticipate what is emerging."[37] Marcus seems to designate the core work of anthropology as a remainder: a matter of record building and knowledge accumulation that (at least) can occupy us productively as we await the development of a new guiding theory to "motivate" research or anticipate the future.[38] It seems to us, however, that anthropology has (and has always had) a theoretical force as it charts and engages the generativity of people navigating contemporary political, economic, and technological configurations, and that it is stronger for the multiplicity of philosophical ideas with which it engages in any given period. As Paul Rabinow puts it, "the problem for an anthropology of the contemporary is to inquire into what is taking place without deducing it beforehand. And that requires sustained research, patience, and new concepts, or modified old ones."[39]

What if we broadened our sense of what counts as theoretical innovation and let go of the need for central discursive engines—the modus operandi that shaped much of anthropology in the twentieth century? Epistemological breakthroughs do not belong only to analysts. The cumulative experiences of "the unpredictability of the political and social effects of technological inventions"—borne by people traversing contemporary entanglements of power and knowledge—are also epistemological breaks that demand anthropological recognition.[40] Simply engaging with the complexity of lives and desires—that is, people's intensities, constraints, subjectivities, things, relationships, and projects—in changing material and social worlds constantly necessitates the rethinking of our theoretical apparatuses. What would it mean for our research methodologies and ways of writing if we consistently embraced this unfinishedness, seeking ways to analyze the general, structural, and processual while maintaining an acute awareness of the inevitable incompleteness of our theories?

Paying attention to the sociology and politics of knowledge production helps contextualize current explorations at the frontiers of anthropological theory: ontological and multispecies approaches, posthumanisms and new materialisms, and postsuffering slot anthropologies of the good.[41] These explorations are doing important work in interrogating taken-for-granted objects of inquiry and categories of analysis; mobilizing new generations of scholars; and opening up new possibilities for fieldwork, collaboration, and expression. Yet their reception and deployment as so-called turns might be read as symptomatic of a continued longing for comprehensive paradigms, orthodoxies, or the next big thing for our academic vanguard theaters, in which more and more seems to be said, while increasingly less is truly heard or read. Meanwhile, the attention to everyday human social life and the diversity of approaches that, for many of us, make anthropology so exciting in the first place are passed over, and theorizing becomes experience-distant and ultimately impaired.[42]

New and useful ideas do not have to look like overarching paradigms, nor do we have to attribute unconditional authority to them. It is important to be mindful of the moral and political stakes of widespread criticisms of human exceptionalism in anthropology: it is clear that the inequities of human societies—and their different valuation of human lives and the differential impacts of their classificatory systems—still matter enormously. We need not brush aside our discipline's great strengths in working with people to consider the mutual becomings of humans, other species, and our shared environments.

Ethnographic realities are never fully explained by the books and theories we bring to the field. What does it take for the "life in things"—the minor voices, missing peoples, and "ill-formed" and tentative "collective enunciations" that seem to Deleuze to carry so much transformative potential—to attain recognition and political purchase?[43] What role can anthropology play in this process, and how can we write in a way that unleashes something of this "plastic power" instead of containing, reducing, or simplifying it?[44] In what follows, we begin to explore these questions and their implications for ethnographic research and writing.

It is often a nemesis that compels us to work, a politics of writing against. From Bronislaw Malinowski's critique of the universalizing claims of Western psychoanalytic and economic theories[45] to Clifford Geertz's suspicion of functionalist and structuralist approaches,[46] anthropologists have always fought against reductionist and hegemonic analytical frames, even as we struggle to articulate and theorize the conditions of our subjects' ways and forms of life. Yet academic debates can become suffocatingly polarizing. In writing against, do we not risk being consumed by our nemeses, producing ever more monstrous abstractions?

In this chapter, we are more interested in writing for a certain ethnographic multirealism, and for the anthropologist's relationship to people and their worlds, than we are in writing against a set of simplified foils. This is one of the reasons that we work through two ethnographic cases. Where Biehl's work with Catarina focuses on the literary force of an individual life in her disfigured domesticity, Locke's discussion of Sarajevo considers collective and political dimensions of becoming. In this way, we attempt to provide complementary angles from which to think with Deleuze's ideas and expand contemporary configurations of the human. Individual biography is replete with collective inflections and implications, just as collective categories and alternative solidarities are suffused by individual lives and stories. Thus, actual people and their lives, words, materialities, and affects are at the core of both cases.

There is an improvisatory quality to our collaboration as we shift between individual narrators and a unified voice. Throughout, we hope to convey the messiness of the social world and the real struggles in which our informants and their loved ones are involved. In the field and at each juncture, a new valence of meaning is added, and a new incident illuminates each of the lives and assemblages in play. In addition to indicating the institutional and clinical processes that bear on our interlocutors, we try to evoke the domestic, counterpublic, and provisional spaces in which lives are also shaped, turbulent affects are borne and shared, and difficult circumstances are imbued with partial meanings. Details reveal nuanced fabrics of singularities and the institutional, political-economic, and scientific logics that, in their own provisionality, keep inequality in place and problematic situations from dissolving or improving. The ethnographic ethos of curiosity, ambiguity, and openness to relationality inflects our own sensibilities in how we try to portray our characters: as living people, with their own mediated subjectivities, whose actions are partly overdetermined without being inevitable, and who are caught in a constricted universe of choices that remains the only source from which they can craft their lives.

HUMAN BODY?

I (Biehl) first met Catarina in March 1997, and I saw her again when I returned to Vita in January 2000. Vita had been founded in 1987 as a rehabilitation center for drug addicts and alcoholics. Soon its mission was enlarged. An increasing number of people who had been cut off from social life were left there by relatives, neighbors, hospitals, and the police. Vita's team then opened an infirmary where the abandoned, like Catarina, waited with death. Catarina was in her midthirties, and her health had deteriorated considerably. Seated in a wheelchair, she insisted that she suffered from "rheumatism." Catarina seemed dazed and spoke with great difficulty. But she was adamant: "I speak my mind. I have no gates in my mouth."

Although her external functions were almost dead, she retained a puzzling life within her body. Her "dictionary" was a sea of words, references to all kinds of illness, places and roles she no longer inhabited, and people she once knew and lived for: "Documents, reality, tiresomeness, truth, saliva, voracious, consumer, saving, economics, Catarina, spirit, pills, marriage, cancer, Catholic church, separation of bodies, division of the state, the couple's children." Her seemingly disaggregated words were in many ways an extension of the abject figure she had become in family life, medicine, and Brazil. "Medical records, ready to go to heaven," she wrote. "Dollars, Real, Brazil is bankrupted, I am not to be blamed, without a future. Things out of justice. Human body?"

Some fifty million Brazilians (more than a quarter of the population) live far below the poverty line, and twenty-five million more are considered indigent. Although Vita was in many ways a microcosm of such misery, it was distinctive in some respects. A number of its residents came from working- and middle-class families and had once been workers with their own households. Others had lived in medical or state institutions. As I learned from health officials and human rights activists, despite appearing to be a no-man's-land cut adrift, Vita was in fact entangled with several public institutions through its history and maintenance. Porto Alegre contained more than two hundred such institutions, most of them euphemistically referred to as geriatric houses. Some 70 percent of them operated as unlicensed businesses. These precarious places housed the unwanted in exchange for their welfare pensions; a good number of them also received state funds or philanthropic donations and were used as platforms for clientelistic politics. Ethnographic work with Catarina helped me to break open the totalizing frames of thought that made Vita and other zones of abandonment into a common sense that ultimately left no one accountable for the abandoned.

These are some of the things Catarina told me during our conversations in early 2000: "Maybe my family still remembers me, but they don't miss me.... My ex-husband sent me to the psychiatric hospital.... The doctors said that they wanted to heal me, but how could they if they did not know the illness?... My sister-in-law went to the public clinic to get the medication for me.... My brothers want to see production, progress. They brought me here.... They say that it is better to place us here so that we don't have to be left alone, at home, in solitude . . . that there are more people like us here. And all of us together, we form a society, a society of bodies."

Caregivers at Vita told me that Catarina was *louca* (mad) and *fora da casinha* (out of her mind; literally, "out of her little home"). They gave her tranquilizers and said that they knew nothing about her life outside of Vita. As for her growing paralysis, they reasoned that "it must have been from giving birth." I was fascinated by what she said and by the proliferation of her writing. Her words did not seem otherworldly to me. They carried the force of literality.

"Even if it is a tragedy? A tragedy generated in life?" Those were Catarina's words when I asked her for the details of her story one day. "I remember it all. My ex-husband and I lived together and we had the children. We lived as a man and a woman. I worked in the shoe factory, but he said that I didn't need to work. He worked in the city hall. He used to drink a bit after work when he played billiards in a bar. I had nothing against that. One day, however, we had a silly fight because he thought that I should be complaining about his habits and I wasn't. That fight led to nothing. Afterward, he picked another topic to fight about. Finally, one day he said that he had gotten another woman and moved in with her. Her name was Rosa. What could I do?"

I remembered the phrase "the separation of bodies" in Catarina's dictionary, and it seemed to me that her pathology resided in that split and in her struggles to reestablish social ties. In Vita, out of that lived fragmentation, the house and the family were remembered: "I behaved like a woman. Since I was a housewife, I did all my duties, like any other woman. I cooked, and I did the laundry. My ex-husband and his family got suspicious of me because sometimes I left the house and attended to other callings. They were not in agreement with what I thought. My ex-husband thought that I had a nightmare in my head. He wanted to take that out of me, to make me a normal person. They wanted to lock me in the hospital. I escaped so as not to go to the hospital. I hid myself; I went far. But the police and my ex-husband found me. They took my children."

She was constantly recalling the domestic events that led to her abandonment: "When my thoughts agreed with my ex-husband and his family, everything was fine. But when I disagreed with them, I was mad. It was like a side of me had to be forgotten. The side of wisdom. They wouldn't dialogue, and the science of the illness was forgotten. Science is our consciousness, heavy at times, burdened by a knot that you cannot untie."

"After my ex-husband left me, he came back to the house and told me he needed me. He threw me onto the bed saying, 'I will eat you now.' I told him that that was the last time. . . . I did not feel pleasure, though. I only felt desire. Desire to be talked to, to be gently talked to."

In abandonment, Catarina recalled sex. There was no love, simply a male body enjoying itself. No more social links, no more speaking beings. Out of the world of the living, her desire was for language, to be talked to. I reminded Catarina that she had once told me that the worst part of Vita was the nighttime, when she was left alone with her desire.

She kept silent for a while and then made it clear that seduction was not at stake in our conversation: "I am not asking a finger from you." She was not asking me for sex, she meant. Catarina looked exhausted, though she claimed not to be tired. At any rate, it seemed that she had brought the conversation to a fecund point, and I also felt like I could no longer listen. No countertransference, no sexual attraction, I thought, but enough of all these things. The anthropologist is not immune. I promised to return the next day to continue, and I suggested that she begin to write again.

My resistance did not deter her from recalling her earliest memory, and I marveled at the power of what I heard—an image that in its simplicity appeared to concentrate the entire psyche:

> I remember something that happened when I was three years old. I was at home with my brother Altamir. We were very poor. We were living in a little house in the plantation. Then a big animal came into the house—it was a black lion. The animal rubbed itself against my body. I ran and hugged my brother. Mother had gone to get water from the well. That's when I became afraid. Fear of the animal. When mother came back, I told her what had happened. But she said that there was no fear, that there was no animal. Mother said nothing.

This could have been incest, sexual abuse, a first psychotic episode, the memory of maternal and paternal abandonment, or simply a play of shadows and imagination—we will never know.

The image of the house, wrote Gaston Bachelard, "would appear to have become the topography of our intimate being. A house constitutes a body of images that give mankind proofs or illusions of stability."[47] In this earliest of Catarina's recollections, nothing is protecting the I. It is in Vita that she recalled the insecure household and the animal so close to the I. This story speaks to her abandonment as a valueless animal as well as to the work the animal performs in human life. In this last sense, the animal is not a negation of the human, I thought—it is a figure through which Catarina learned to produce affect and that marks her singularity. When I told her it was time for me to leave, Catarina replied, "You are the one who marks time."

GEOGRAPHIES OF BECOMING

It was not enough to deconstruct Catarina's classification as mad or her confinement in institutions of control. Claiming language and agency, she was not reducible to "bare life," and her knowledge revealed complicated realities and the noninstitutionalized spaces in which life chances were crystallized or foreclosed.[48]

Deleuze, who did not share Foucault's confidence in the determining force of power, is helpful here. In a 1976 article called "Desire and Pleasure,"[49] Deleuze reviewed Foucault's then recently published *History of Sexuality*.[50] In that book, Foucault took a new step with regard to his earlier work in *Discipline and Punish*:[51] now power arrangements were no longer simply normalizing, they were also constituents of sexuality. Attentive to historical preconditions and singular efforts of becoming, Deleuze instead "emphasize[d] the primacy of desire over power" and pursued "lines of flight."[52] For him "all organizations, all the systems Michel [Foucault] calls biopower, in effect reterritorialize the body."[53] But a social field, first and foremost, "leaks out on all sides."[54] "Desire," he wrote, "comes first and seems to be the element of a micro-analysis."[55]

According to Deleuze, desire is constantly undoing, or at least opening up, forms of subjectivity and power. It is at the core of the concept of assemblage, used by Aihwa Ong and Stephen Collier to name emerging global configurations of science, capital, and governance.[56] For Deleuze and Guattari, assemblages are contingent and shifting interrelations among "segments"— that is, institutions, powers, practices, and desires—that constantly and simultaneously construct, entrench, and disaggregate their own constraints and oppressions.[57] An assemblage, they write, is "a concretization of power, of desire, of territoriality or reterritorialization, regulated by the abstraction of a transcendental law. But we must declare as well that an assemblage has points of deterritorialization; or that it always has a line of escape by which it ... makes the segments melt and ... liberates desire from all its concretizations in order to dissolve them."[58]

This emphasis on desire and the ways—humble, marginal, minor—that it cracks through "the concretization of power" and apparently rigid social fields and serves as the engine of becoming figures centrally in Deleuze's divergences from both Foucault and Sigmund Freud. In Deleuze's view, Freud and his followers offer a philosophy of top-down penetration of depths—of memory and memorialization—that digs through the past for the core, defining truths of a person's being encapsulated in childhood mother-father oedipal dynamics.[59] This is an archaeological conception of psychoanalysis, according to Deleuze. His use of this term also evokes his critique of Foucault, whose archaeology of the subject traces the ways in which he or she is constituted and confined by, for example, the top-down categories of expert discourses.[60] Freud and Foucault each define the subject through dependencies and determinants—by past traumas and unconscious complexes, and by entangled regimes of power and knowledge, respectively.

In the essay "What Children Say,"[61] Deleuze revisits Freud's seminal case study of Little Hans[62] to develop the idea of cartography as an alternative to oedipal archaeology. The objects of cartography, what the analyst maps, are milieus (contexts that are at once material and social and are infused with affects and intensities) and trajectories (the journeys people take through milieus to address needs, pursue desires and curiosities, or to simply try to find room to breathe under constraint): "The trajectory merges not only with the subjectivity of those who travel through a milieu, but also with the subjectivity of the milieu itself, insofar as it is reflected in those who travel through it."[63]

For Deleuze, the analytical challenge is to illuminate desire and possibility, not only structural determinants. Rather than focusing on origins or the weight of memory, our analyses must reveal mobilization and flight. "From one map to the next," Deleuze suggests, "it is not a matter of searching for an origin, but of evaluating displacements. Every map is a redistribution of impasses and breakthroughs, of thresholds and enclosures, which necessarily go from bottom to top."[64] In other words, it is "no longer an unconscious of commemoration but one of mobilization."[65]

Defining subjects in terms of the archaeology of their dependencies may be less revealing than mapping out their movements through space, time, and social fields: people's lines of flight as well as their blocked passages, moments when the libido is stuck or pushed backward. Done right, hints Deleuze, such maps can show the Dionysian force of the libido as it breaks down forms and constraints by investing the indefinite, which, he argues, "lacks nothing": "It is the determination of a becoming, its characteristic power, the power of an impersonal that is not a generality but a singularity at its highest point."[66]

This cartographic approach makes space for possibility (the otherwise, or what could be) as a crucial dimension of what is or what was. It brings crossroads—places where other choices might be made or other paths taken—out of the shadow of deterministic analytics. It brings alternatives within closer reach. Ethnography, at its best, strives for the same achievements.

As Michael M. J. Fischer argues, subjectivities are now "raucous *terrae incognitae*" for anthropological inquiry: "landscapes of explosions, noise, alienating silences, disconnects and dissociations, fears, terror machineries, pleasure principles, illusions, fantasies, displacements, and secondary revisions, mixed with reason, rationalizations, and paralogics—all of which have powerful sociopolitical dimensions and effects."[67] In Fischer's view, we need to attend to more than the "enunciative function" of the subject: subjectivity does not merely speak as resistance, nor is it simply spoken to or silenced by power.[68] It continually forms and reappears in the complex play of bodily, linguistic, political, and psychological dimensions of human experience; and within and in contrast to new infrastructures, value systems, and transforming injustices and insecurities. Ethnography can help us chart paths across larger structures and forces of repetition, technologies at play, and "the slippery slopes of unforeseeable consequences of action."[69] It can help us account for people, experiences, and voices and silences that remain unaddressed and raise calls for new ethics and politics. Ethnography matters.

THE PSYCHIATRIC AURA OF REALITY

Catarina's speech and writing captured the messiness of what her world had turned into—filled with knots that she could not untie, although she desperately wanted to because "if we don't study it, the illness in the body worsens." Her words described real struggles, the ordinary world from which she had been banished, and the multiple therapeutic itineraries that had altered her body and become the life of her mind. With the on-the-ground study of a single other comes an immense parceling out of the specific ways communities, families, and personal lives are assembled and valued, and how they are embedded in larger entrepreneurial processes and institutional rearrangements. But Catarina was not simply trying to find a place for herself in history. By going through the components and singularities of events, she was resuming her place in them as in a becoming: "To make peace with time, the hours, minutes, and seconds, with the clock and the calendar, to be well with all, but mainly with the pen."

Writing helped her draw out the best of herself and make it all endurable and somehow open: "From the letters I form words, and from the words I form sentences, and from the sentences I form a story." Catarina created a new letter character that resembled a *K*, as well as new names for herself such as CATAKINA, CATKINA, CATIEKI, and CATKINE. She explained that "*K* is open on both sides. If I wouldn't open the character, my head would explode." She continued: "One needs to preserve oneself. I also know that pleasure in life is very important, the body of the other. I think that people fear their bodies.... I have desire, I have desire." As Catarina rethought the literal realities that had led to her exclusion, she demanded one more chance in life. There was something in the way she moved from one register to the other—past life, Vita, and desire—that eluded anthropological understanding. This movement was her own language of abandonment.

From 2000 to 2003, I took numerous trips to southern Brazil to work with Catarina. I studied all twenty-one volumes of the dictionary she was composing and discussed the words and associations with her. In her recollections and writing, I found clues to the people, sites, and interactions that constituted her destiny. As an anthropologist, I was challenged to reconstruct the world of her words, to illuminate self-world entanglements. I wanted to directly address the various circuits in which her intractability and silence or voice gained form, circuits that seemed independent of both laws and norms—the in-betweenness through which social life and ethics are empirically worked out. With Catarina's consent, I retrieved her records from psychiatric hospitals and local branches of the country's universal health-care system. On a detective-like journey, I also located her family members in the nearby city of Novo Hamburgo. Everything she had told me about the familial and medical pathways that had led her to Vita was consistent with the information I found in the archives and in the field—a field that was not self-evident, but that became manifest through ethnographic returns, diligence, and care.

Catarina was born in 1966 and grew up in the very poor western region of the state of Rio Grande do Sul. After finishing fourth grade, she was taken out of school and became the housekeeper, while her youngest siblings aided their mother in agricultural work. The father had abandoned the family. In the mid-1980s, two of her brothers migrated to find jobs in the booming shoe industry in Novo Hamburgo. At the age of eighteen, Catarina married Nilson Moraes, and a year later she gave birth to her first child. Shady deals, persistent bad harvests, and indebtedness to local vendors forced Nilson and Catarina to sell the land they had inherited to take care of Catarina's ailing mother, and in the mid-1980s, the young couple decided to join her brothers in Novo Hamburgo and the shoe industry. In the coming years, Catarina had two more children. As her illness progressed and her marriage disintegrated, her older son and daughter went to her husband's family, and her younger daughter was given up for adoption.

Catarina had become too much of a burden for her family; caught up in webs of disease, poverty, and fear, she was frequently hospitalized and overmedicated with powerful antipsychotics. Yet exploring her medical records, I uncovered something more. Catarina suffered from a rare neurodegenerative disorder called Machado-Joseph Disease, which caused her to lose her ability to walk and, over time, shut her body down almost entirely.[70] It was an illness that had afflicted Catarina's mother, and in both of their cases it presented itself after childbirth. Reaching this diagnosis took me through a maze of medical hoops, and as the picture of her illness became clearer, I took her to a geneticist and neurologist who finally made the correct diagnosis and provided the best possible care.

In many ways, Catarina was caught in a period of political and cultural transition: politicians were implementing a state reform to make Brazil viable within a supposedly inescapable economic globalization and fostering alternative partnerships with civil society to maximize the public interest within the state.[71] In *Vita*, I show how such large-scale change and redistribution of resources, power, and responsibility take place locally, as overburdened families and individuals are left to negotiate these processes alone.[72] In this context, the family is increasingly the medical agent of the state (providing and at times triaging care), and pharmaceuticals become a tool for such deliberate action.

Free distribution of drugs is a central component of Brazil's universal health-care system, a democratic success of the late 1980s. Increasing calls for the decentralization of services and the individualization of treatment, exemplified by the mental health movement, coincided with dramatic cuts in funding for health-care infrastructure and with the proliferation of pharmaceutical treatments. Data from the government's database for health resource use in the period 1995–2005 show that the country's reform of psychiatric care was accompanied by a significant fall in the percentage of resources dedicated to that care.[73] Meanwhile, there has been a dramatic increase in resource allocation for community services and medicines, particularly second-generation antipsychotic drugs. The increased allocation of funds for pharmaceuticals was followed by a relative decrease in the number of public psychiatrists hired, with psychiatrists replaced in large part by social workers and psychologists.

In engaging with this new regime of public health and in allocating their own overstretched and meager resources, families become proxy psychiatrists. They can dispose of unwanted and unproductive members, sometimes without sanction, on the basis of individuals' noncompliance with their treatment regimens. Psychopharmaceuticals are thus central to how personal lives are recast in this particular moment of socioeconomic change, and to how people create life chances vis-à-vis what is bureaucratically and medically available to them.[74] Such negotiations are entangled with market exploitation, gender domination, and a managerial-style state that is increasingly distant from the people it governs. The fabric of this domestic activity of evaluating which life is worth living remains largely unexamined, not only in everyday life but also in the literature of transforming economies, states, and civil societies in contexts of democratization and social inequality. As this study unfolded, I was challenged to devise ways to approach this unconsidered infrastructure of decision making that operates, in Catarina's own words, "out of justice," or outside the bounds of the judiciary and the public ministry—that is, close to home. "I know," she said, "because I passed through it. I learned the truth and I try to divulge what reality is."

Ethnography makes visible the intermingling of colloquial practices and relations, institutional histories, and discursive structures that—in categories of madness, pharmaceuticals, migrant households, and disintegrating state services—have defined normalcy and displaced Catarina onto the register of social death, where her condition appears to have been "self-generated." Catarina knew that the verb "to kill" was being conjugated—"dead alive, dead outside, alive inside"—and I was challenged to chart this process and to reflect on what made it not only possible, but ordinary. This is also, then, a story of the methodological, ethical, and conceptual limits of anthropology and its own becoming as the ethnographer goes to the field to verify the sources of a life excluded from family and society and to capture the density of a locality without leaving the individual person and her subjectivity behind.

TO LIVE IS EXPENSIVE

As I listened to what had made Catarina's voice posthumous, a life force emerged that reworked ideas of the person and the value of social ties. While trying to speak, Catarina was overwhelmed by the chemical alterations of drugs: layers of chemical compounds and the side effects that were her body and identity now. To speak the unspeakable, she resorted to metaphors and writing. In the following dictionary entry, for example, she tried to break open the reader's blindness, bringing a Greek tragic figure together with her brothers, children, and renamed self: "Look at Catarina without blindness, pray, prayer, Jocastka, there is no tonic for CATKINE, there is no doctor for any one, Altamir, Ademar, Armando, Anderson, Alessandra, Ana."

Marked by paradoxes and impossibilities, she continued: "I need to change my blood with a tonic. Medication from the pharmacy costs money, to live is expensive." Medical science was indeed part and parcel of Catarina's existence—the truths, half-truths, and misunderstandings that brought her to die in Vita, and on which she nonetheless subsisted. "Pharmacy, laboratory, marriage, identity, army, rheumatism, complication of labor, loss of physical equilibrium, total loss of control, govern, goalkeeper, evil eye, spasm, nerves. . . . In the United States, not here in Brazil, there is a cure, for half of the disease."

In writing, as in speech, Catarina often referred to her condition as "rheumatism": "People think that they have the right to put their hands in the mangled threads and to mess with it. Rheumatism. They use my name for good and for evil. They use it because of the rheumatism." A possible reading is that her rheumatism tied various life threads together. It is an untidy knot, a real matter that makes social exchange possible. It gives the body its stature and is the conduit of a morality. Catarina's bodily affection, not her name, is exchanged in that world: "What I was in the past does not matter." Catarina disappears, and a religious image stands in her place: "Rheumatism, spasm, crucified Jesus." In another fragment, she writes: "Acute spasm, secret spasm. Rheumatic woman. The word of the rheumatic is of no value."

Catarina knew that there is a rationality and a bureaucracy to symptom management: "Chronic spasm, rheumatism, must be stamped, registered." All of this happens in a democratic context, "vote by vote." We must consider side by side the acute pain Catarina described and the authoritative story she became in medicine and in common sense—as being mad and ultimately of no value. The antipsychotic drugs Haldol and Neozine are also words in Catarina's dictionary. In a fragment, she defiantly writes that her pain reveals the experimental ways science is embodied: "The dance of science. Pain broadcasts sick science, the sick study. Brain, illness. Buscopan, Haldol, Neozine. Invoked spirit."

An individual history of science is being written here. Catarina's lived experience and ailments are the pathos of a certain science, a science that is itself sick. The goods of psychiatric science have become as ordinary as Buscopan (hyoscine, an over-the-counter antispasmodic medication) and have become a part of familial practices. As her experience shows, the use of such drugs produces mental and physical effects apart from those related to her illness.

In Catarina's thinking and writing, global pharmaceuticals are not simply taken as new material for old patterns of self-fashioning but are entangled in and act as vectors for new mechanisms of sociomedical and subjective control that have both a deadly and a generative force. Seen from the perspective of Vita, the illnesses Catarina experienced were the outcome of events and practices that annulled the person she had learned to become. Abandoned in Vita to die, Catarina nonetheless has ties to pharmakons, which also work as kernels of a fugitive lifeworld. Her desire, she writes, is now a pharmaceutical thing with no human exchange value: "Catarina cries and wants to leave. Desire, watered, prayed, wept. Tearful feeling, fearful, diabolic, betrayed. My desire is of no value. Desire is pharmaceutical. It is not good for the circus."

LITERATURE AND HEALTH

Catarina also writes to remain alive, I thought. In the dictionary, she constantly places her new names in relation to those of others she meets in Vita, such as Clóvis and Luis Carlos, or people she knew in the past, such as Valmir. She creatively redirects disciplinary clinical elements into a literary and therapeutic line of flight and contact.

Deleuze says that writing is "a question of becoming, always incomplete, always in the midst of being formed, and goes beyond the matter of any livable or lived experience. It is a process, that is, a passage of Life that traverses both the livable and the lived."[75] He thinks of language as a system that can be disturbed, attacked, and reconstructed: the very gate through which limits of all kinds are crossed and the energy of the "delirium" unleashed.[76]

The delirium suggests alternative visions of existence and of a future that clinical definitions tend to foreclose. Language in its clinical state has already attained a form, says Deleuze: "We don't write with our neuroses. Neuroses or psychoses are not passages of life, but states into which we fall when the process is interrupted, blocked, or plugged up. Illness is not a process but a stopping of the process."[77] The radical work of literature, however, moves away from truths and forms (because truth itself is a form) and toward intermediate, processual, even virtual stages. Writing, he insists, is inseparable from becoming.

While I tried to cartographize her lived experience of abandonment, Catarina was herself producing, in her dictionary, an ethnographic theory of the leftover subject, the *it* she had become. Consider this stanza:

Catarina is subjected
To be a nation in poverty
Porto Alegre

Without an heir
Enough
I end

Catarina places the individual and the collective in the same space of analysis, just as the country and the city collide in Vita. Subjection has to do with having no money and being part of a nation gone awry. The subject is a body left in Vita without ties to her life with the man who, as she states, now "rules the city" from which she is banished. With nothing to leave behind and no one to leave it to, Catarina still has her subjectivity—the medium through which a collectivity is ordered in terms of lack, and in which she finds a way to disentangle herself from the mess the world has become. In her writing, she faces the concrete limits of what a human being can bear and makes polysemy out of those limits—"I, who am where I go, am who am so." In her words, real and imaginary voyages compose a set of intertwined routes: "I am a free woman, to fly, bionic woman, separated. . . . When men throw me into the air, I am already far away." These trajectories are inseparable from becoming: "I will leave the door of the cage open. You can fly wherever you want to."

Actualized by literature is the power of an impersonal that, says Deleuze, "is not a generality but singularity at the highest point: a man, a woman, a beast, a child. . . . It is not the first two persons that function as the condition for literary enunciation; literature begins only when a third person is born in us that strips us of the power to say 'I.'"[78] The shift to the indefinite—from *I* to *a* or *it*—leads to the ultimate existential stage in which life is simply immanent, a transcendental field where man and woman and other men and women or animals or landscapes can achieve a web of variable relations and situated connectedness, call it camaraderie.

"There, in Novo Hamburgo it is Catarina. Here it is CATKINE," she told me when I asked her why she invented this name: "I will be called this now. For I don't want to be a tool for men to use, for men to cut. A tool is innocent. You dig, you cut, you do whatever you want with it. . . . It doesn't know if it hurts or doesn't. But the man who uses it to cut the other knows what he is doing." She continued with the most forceful words: "I don't want to be a tool. Because Catarina is not the name of a person . . . truly not. It is the name of a tool, of an object. A person is an other."

Psychopharmaceuticals mediated Catarina's expulsion from the world of exchanges and were now the means through which she recounted bodily fragmentation and withering. This was what she was left with—"enjoyment enjoying itself" (*se goza gozo*), as she wrote in the dictionary: "Pleasure and desire are not sold, cannot be bought. But have choice."

The opportunity to "restart" and a human choice were all she wanted. This was what Catarina affirmed in her love stories in Vita. "I dated a man who volunteered as a security guard here," she told me. "He bought me a ring and a bracelet, shampoo, many things. We met at night and had sex in the bathroom. But people were trying to separate us. Vera began to say that he was her boyfriend, too. So I gave him the ring back. He refused to take it back. I said, 'I will not throw this into the garbage,' so I put it in my suitcase. After we split, he had other women here.... But as far as I am concerned, I was not his prey. I didn't fall to him. I wanted it. I have desire, I have desire. I am with Clóvis now."

Catarina refused to depict herself as a victim. Along with hunger, spasms, and pain, her body experienced uncontrollable desires, an overflow unthinkable in terms of common sense. While exposing Vita as a place of total annihilation, she also spoke of the vitality of sexuality and affirmed her agency. She spoke openly of having sex "in the bathroom and in the pharmacy" with Clóvis, a man who, after passing through the rehabilitation areas, became the infirmary's "nurse" and "pharmacist." For Catarina, desire and pleasure were gratifying, "a gift that one feels." During sex, she said, "I don't lose my head, and I don't let my partner lose his head. If it is good for me, I want to make it good for him, too." She was, in her own words, "a true woman" (*mulher de verdade*): "Female reproducer, reproduces, lubrification, anonymous reproducer, to fondle the aggressive lust, and manias. Scientific decadence, kiss, electricity, wet, mouth kiss, dry kiss, kiss in the neck, to start from zero, it is always time, to begin again, for me it is time to convert, this is salvation day, Clóvis Gama, CATKINE, Catakina Gama, Ikeni Gama, Alessandra Gomes, Ana G., to restart a home, a family, the spirit of love, the spirit of God, the spirit becomes flesh inside."

Catarina remarked that other people might be curious about her words, but she added that their meaning was ultimately part of her living: "There is so much that comes with time ... the words ... and the signification, you will not find in the book. It is only in my memory that I have the signification. And this is for me to untie." Catarina refused to be merely an object of understanding for others, yet she challenges us to inquire into the benefits that can come from ethnographic knowledge making, especially in the ways care can be redirected: "Nobody will decipher the words for me. With the pen, only I can do it.... In the ink, I decipher.... I am writing for myself to understand, but, of course, if you all understand I will be very content." And she anticipated an exit from Vita. It was as difficult as it was important to sustain this anticipation: to find ways to support Catarina's search for ties to things, people, and the world and her demand for continuity, or at least its possibility.

TO WRITE FOR THE PEOPLE WHO ARE MISSING

Where Biehl's work with Catarina probes the significance of Deleuze's thought in understanding *a* life, I (Locke) explore Deleuze's insights for understanding collective becomings in Sarajevo. Here, what is held in common (who one cares for, identifies with, supports, or is supported by in the course of the fraught unfolding of a postwar everyday) does not always correspond to official divisions and categories—that is, ethnoreligious divisions (Croat, Serb, and Bosniac) and competing victim identifications (veteran, widow, camp survivor, rape victim, displaced person, and returnee, e.g.).[79] The collective is an open space of ambivalence and contestation, where there is room for difference to be affirmed, tentative bonds to be formed, and shared frustrations to cross entrenched boundaries and mark out new ones.

Although the specificities of the cases are different in crucial ways, my Sarajevan interlocutors, like Catarina, negotiate an evolving interface of psychiatric and neoliberal economic rationalities. Here clinical diagnoses applied to whole populations can obscure the many political, economic, and social discontents behind their shared symptoms. Sustained ethnographic engagement produces a counterinterpretation that, by taking seriously local desires, struggles, and dissent, evokes the potential for alternative solidarities and political life in the region—"a people to come."[80]

On a hot morning in July 2007, I took a taxi to Sarajevo's Koševo Hospital to visit Senadin Ljubović. A psychiatrist with decades of experience, he had worked extensively with traumatized ex-soldiers and rape victims since the war. On my way into his office, I passed a gaunt, expressionless woman on her way out. Ljubović told me, without prompting, that she was from Srebrenica; that she had spent months in a concentration camp where she had been subjected to sexual violence; and that many of her male family members were killed in the July 1995 genocide. She had no job, no friends, and no family in Sarajevo. She received only meager assistance from the government and was about to be evicted from her apartment.

Calm and resigned in his white coat, Ljubović asked me what a psychiatrist could do for someone like her. Her problems were social: the extreme violence of the early 1990s had shattered her networks of support, and in a city still resentful of villagers and refugees, she had found little in the way of new human warmth and connection. And her problems were financial: more than a decade after the war, the Bosnian economy remained (and remains today) weak, and there were few prospects for formal employment or further education. The trauma of her terrible losses and violations was evident, Ljubović said, in her crippled capacity to trust, connect, and hope. But Ljubović—one of Bosnia-Herzegovina's relatively few mental health professionals[81]—hardly had the time or resources to address this particularly bitter facet of her predicament. He could only prescribe medication, offer a few words of advice, and let her go, admitting the next client in line.

A few months earlier, I sat at the long table in the common area of the offices of Wings of Hope (often referred to by those in its orbit simply as "Wings"), a local psychosocial support nongovernmental organization (NGO) focused on services for children and their families. Three mothers waited in a cloud of cigarette smoke, while elsewhere in the office staff members worked with their children. The mothers were angry and frustrated. Their husbands were gone (some lost in the war) or unemployed; their children were struggling in school; and government was doing little to help them. Neighbors and friends were too preoccupied with their own daily struggles to take much interest. NGOs such as Wings of Hope, limited in capacity because of donor fatigue and the declining interest of the international community, fill in where they can in the absence of government services. "Politicians do not care about us," the women agreed. One said: "They just use their positions to get rich.... My husband died in the war and I live off his soldier's pension. But it is not enough! And there are no jobs for me." As they exchanged bitter complaints, the mothers began remembering together what the system was like before the war they did not want, when material security, employment, and health care were all (ostensibly) guaranteed by the state: "Everything was better before. The war was for nothing." They were grateful for the assistance they had found at Wings, but they resented the fact that it was their only apparent option.

Ljubović and the mothers at Wings of Hope both criticized painful failures of postwar governance (local and international) and an absence of services and assistance; and they expressed a general sense of social dysfunction, stagnancy, and disconnection. Despite bloated, redundant layers of bureaucracy that at the time drained an estimated 70 percent of Bosnia's yearly gross domestic product, government felt to my interlocutors in Sarajevo less like a weight than a lack of care, support, and opportunity. Local politics—dominated by zero-sum, angry, fear-inducing debates between ethnic nationalists on all sides—

unfolded in a bubble of compulsive repetition disconnected from concrete socioeconomic problems.

People were left to fend for themselves. What care and opportunities they could obtain often required personal or political connections or bribery. Students, I was often told, were paying to pass exams; graduates were paying to be employed; a patient needing stitches would hand the nurse a little extra to receive local anesthetic. And with the steady withdrawal of international aid projects, leaving local NGOs scrambling for meager resources, the limited services provided by civil society (including those addressing mental health) could only scratch the surface of actual need.

During the war in BiH (whose population was roughly four million), approximately a hundred thousand people were killed, and at least two million were displaced.[82] Legacies of the conflict continue to compromise Bosnia's infrastructure, economy, and civic institutions. The Dayton Accords, which ended hostilities in 1995, brought to BiH an enormous international apparatus of governance, monitoring, peacekeeping, and humanitarian aid—what the anthropologist Mariella Pandolfi, in the context of Kosovo, has called a kind of "migrant sovereignty."[83] Renewed warfare has been held at bay, but major reforms have been spotty and fitful. Nationalist politicians who depend on the electorate's fear and insecurity frequently stymie the efforts of both international authorities and local activist movements to stimulate political change. It does not help that the Dayton Accords entrenched the role of divisive ethnic identifications in the political process.[84] Since 1995 BiH has remained a kind of international protectorate, and the high representative (an unelected political appointee who jointly represents the United Nations and the European Union, and whose mandate was originally intended to last only one year) retains the capacity to exercise significant political authority, though this rarely happens. In economic domains, international organizations' neoliberal market ideology and structural adjustment policies have led to by now familiar outcomes—corrupt privatization, the auctioning off of once-public assets, and the dismantling of social welfare services.[85]

"It was international intervention in former Yugoslavia, especially Bosnia," argues the political scientist Vanessa Pupavac, "that heralded 'the triumph of the therapeutic.'"[86] Borrowing the quoted expression from Philip Rieff's[87] study of the integration of Freudian thought into modern culture, Pupavac argues that over the course of the 1990s, international policy in postcrisis situations created a form of power she calls "therapeutic governance."[88] Humanitarian organizations in the Balkans conducted psychosocial projects—by some accounts, thousands of such projects were implemented in the region during and just after the war, collectively costing millions of dollars—to address the trauma and mental health of war survivors.[89] The psychosocial approach emphasizes the link between trauma and recurring cycles of violence. And, as Fassin and Rechtman show in *The Empire of Trauma*, the emergent field of humanitarian psychiatry has generally cast war survivors as psychologically damaged and therefore in danger of repeating the atrocities they have witnessed or to which they have been subjected.[90] According to Pupavac, this set of assumptions has helped to justify the continuing supervision of BiH by foreign overseers. Contemporary therapeutic governance presumes that postwar citizens can be trusted with neither their political rights nor their own emotional well-being. Symbolic justice is emphasized, while "substantive social justice" is all but ignored.[91]

As my fieldwork began, I expected to watch the "triumph of the therapeutic" in postwar remediation efforts play out in everyday life in Sarajevo.[92] However, I quickly discovered that, notwithstanding the millions of aid dollars that had been spent, the structural effect of international psychosocial projects in Bosnia-Herzegovina has been relatively narrow. While various international programs—the once-common seminars, workshops, trainings, and conferences on themes such as conflict resolution, nonviolence, communication skills, and trauma—did shift the way a number of local civil society workers understood the psychological effects of war, most people do not tend to see any form of psychotherapy as a possible remedy for their woes. Even if they did, mental health care services in BiH, and public understanding of them, are limited.

While strong mental health care infrastructures and treatment-seeking cultures have not fully taken root in BiH, psychological language has seeped into local common sense, confounding the way people understand the country's social-structural and political-economic problems. Interpretation of the features of life in contemporary BiH often takes place in a clinical-sounding register, through which Bosnian voices seem to emit only signs of lives blocked by collective illness. What if we listened to Bosnian lives on a literary rather than a clinical register, paying attention to a different kind of agency that pulses in a language of despair and refusal, of anger and abiding, a syntax of mournful waiting? Might we hear, between the lines, a tentative "collective enunciation" that points to alternatives for social solidarity and mobilization for public accountability?[93]

DIAGNOSING A CITY

The postwar flurry of international psychosocial work in BiH was short-lived, leaving behind a handful of small locally run NGOs, whose staff members were more often than not trained by international mental health professionals during and just after the war. These NGOs try to adapt their sense of Western mental health science to what they perceive to be local problems and needs, often creating a disjuncture between mission statements and grant applications (couched in psychological terminology) and actual practices (which are more eclectic, weaving a range of therapeutic modalities together with social work and community organizing). The organizations' beneficiaries are often seeking material assistance as much as some form of emotional support; NGO workers regularly told me stories of people appearing at psychosocial activities to ask for money or materials to rebuild damaged homes or buy food for a few days. This is the sort of assistance that citizens might have reasonably expected of their prewar communist government, suggesting an important microhistory of the kinds of values and expectations that linger as philosophies and infrastructures of governance transform.[94]

At Wings of Hope, what is billed as "psychodetraumatization" for children has evolved into academic tutoring for young people struggling in school; assistance in transitions from education to work; and pragmatic problem solving, counseling, and general support for families. On balance, it seemed that such efforts address the effects of contemporary socioeconomic pressures as much as—or even more than—those of extreme wartime experiences. Yet staff members, volunteers, and beneficiaries talk in psychological terms, attributing poor grades to transgenerational trauma, and children are usually selected for the program based on a checklist of traumatic indicators developed for Wings several years ago by a psychologist from the University of Sarajevo. Marija Šarić (hereafter Maja, at her request), the executive director of Wings, often told me that Sarajevo is in the grip of "collective depression" and "mass trauma"—although when I interviewed staff members, some were less certain about such blanket diagnoses. If ideas about trauma only loosely guide NGO activities, they nevertheless seem to inflect, to differing degrees, the explanations people at Wings give about what they are doing.

There is something here akin to processes of medicalization—the tendency to obscure the social etiology of affliction and reduce it to a biological reality amenable to medical intervention.[95] Yet without the presence of a powerful medical or psychiatric infrastructure, this form of objectification works along other lines: diagnostics from the private clinical encounter come to operate, fluidly and ambivalently, in domestic and public spheres and collectively constructed narratives about postwar life. People do not simply become the diagnostic categories applied to them—they inhabit them to greater or lesser degrees, refuse them, redefine and redeploy them, or ignore them entirely. Medical anthropologists including Margaret Lock have insisted on the limits of philosophical categories and the indispensability of ethnographic methods of research and writing for understanding such complex appropriations and redirections of medical rationality.[96] As Ian Hacking acknowledged in his essay on how new kinds of people can be "made up" by medical diagnostics, "my concern is philosophical and abstract . . . and [I] reflect too little on the ordinary dynamics of human interaction."[97]

The legacy of therapeutic governance and humanitarian psychiatry in BiH is mixed in many senses. In the same breath, Sarajevans can talk about psychiatric trauma as the source of socioeconomic challenges—for example, saying that when people are depressed, they lack the kind of individual initiative required to make capitalism work—and then reverse the formula, pointing to economic problems as the true traumatic experience. In late July 2008—a few days after Radovan Karadžić, the wartime Bosnian Serb leader, was finally captured (he had been practicing as a new age healer under a false identity in Belgrade)—I took a taxi to the city's central bus station. The driver talked about how difficult it was for him to see Karadžić in the media again—the erstwhile psychiatrist and poet was a key architect of the long siege of Sarajevo—then he asked what I was doing there. "I'm most interested in how people are thinking about and dealing with trauma," I told him. He replied: "That is very difficult. What you are looking for is hidden."

The driver explained that at first glance, everything looks relatively "normal" in Sarajevo: people socialize, work, spend time in cafes with their friends, study at the university, and take buses to the Adriatic coast in July. Under the surface, though, "something is not right." People are "explosive" and "temperamental," he said, flying into a rage at the little irritations of daily life, in a way that they had not done before the war. But war trauma is not the only reason for this half-buried malaise: "There are no jobs." He began to recite a familiar litany of social ills—unemployment, corruption, poor social services, a country seemingly emptied of compassion and solidarity. "This is not a normal society," he told me. "This is not what I fought for."[98] He had served in the militias that defended Sarajevo during the siege.

In 2003, Slobodan Loga, a psychiatrist then working at the University of Sarajevo, told a reporter for Britain's *Daily Telegraph* that everyone in Sarajevo had posttraumatic stress disorder (PTSD), and I heard him make similar pronouncements at two separate conferences during my fieldwork in 2007. In the *Telegraph* article (tellingly titled "The War Is Over but Sarajevans Cannot Find the Peace They Seek"), he rattled off the symptoms gripping the city: "violent mood swings, excitability, flashbacks, nightmares, emotional numbness, depression, anxiety attacks and trying to find someone else to blame."[99] Suicide has gone up by 40 percent, he said: "PTSD is part of our lives."[100] One of Loga's colleagues, a psychiatrist who has worked extensively with war veterans, similarly suggested to me in an interview that "trauma here is so widespread that it is banal." And Alma Delić (a pseudonym), a psychiatrist turned homeopath and a veteran of Médecins Sans Frontières' psychosocial programs, told me that "you can't talk about mental health for people who suffered during the war. They have no mental health. They are just human animals surviving day-to-day with these horrible memories."

However, Delić soon left the war behind, and designated the transition to capitalism—and the "passive" way Bosnians have responded to it—as the true catastrophe. "Some of those who managed well during war just broke to pieces at the end," she said. "Lots of psychiatrists figured out that the more challenging experience was the shift from socialism to some sort of capitalism. That proved to be an even bigger source of stress than the war."

As a matter of fact, she went on, people often said that they preferred life during the siege to life under the new postwar economy: "Life then [in the war] was more straightforward—just stay alive, day to day." Moreover, Sarajevans were connected by a shared sense of struggle and of persecution by a common enemy, and, in Delić's words, "took better care of each other." She meant that they expressed sympathy and solidarity in common suffering and shared supplies and survival strategies. Getting by in postwar Sarajevo, and getting along with others, feels to many people like a different, lonelier, and more pointless kind of struggle. They always knew the war had to end some day, even as it dragged on well past expectations. But an end to poisoned postwar politics and the infuriating inequalities of the new economy is harder to perceive.

Seen from Delić's perspective, Sarajevans are longing for lost collectivities and solidarities—not only those of prewar Yugoslavia, but also those of wartime. The social ties that they desire are not addressed in contemporary Bosnian politics. People recall connections anchored less by ethnicity than by a shared, against the odds "will to live"[101] and the need to preserve a familiar humanity amid dire circumstances.[102]

THE SUBJECTIVITY OF A MILIEU

As reminders of a difficult past jostle with people's efforts to make the best of things, Sarajevo can produce contradictory impressions. During my fieldwork, the city landscape featured largely gray, shrapnel-scarred, and bullet-holed Austro-Hungarian and communist-era façades under perpetual restoration—leading a *New York Times* travel writer to remark wryly that "the predominant color of Sarajevo is spackle"[103]—but was increasingly punctuated by gleaming new modern structures, such as the recently rebuilt Council of Ministers building or the striking, if jarringly out-of-place, Avaz tower, now the highest building in the Balkans. Small reminders of grief stood out to me in the urban scenery: underfoot were the Sarajevo roses, mortar impact craters filled in with red paint; and on trees, walls, and bus stop shelters were short obituaries (*smrtovnice*), posted both at the time of the person's passing and at repeated intervals in subsequent years, printed on standard A4 paper, with pictures of the deceased and short poems or expressions of loss.[104]

The everyday gestures of hospitality I observed were warm and enthusiastic, and social relations always struck me as no more or less affable or strained than anywhere else. Yet Sarajevans often complained to me about the inconsiderateness of others, recalling better manners and more gentle dispositions before the war, and they worried about what they saw as people's increasingly limited patience with daily irritations and rudeness. Tempers everywhere seemed short. In February 2008, three teenagers stabbed a fourth to death on a tram for (apparently) looking at them the wrong way, prompting thousands of citizens to take to the streets in a rare display of coordinated outrage against city officials.

The anger expressed by psychosocial service providers like Maja and Delić drove them to action, and they were upset with people whose frustration led to apparent immobility or self-indulgence. Delić railed about the "inertia" of her fellow Sarajevans—many of the unemployed spent much of their time in cafes venting their anger about the state of things in their world. Delić mocked their supposed dependence: "The world should help us, give us this, no one is taking care of us. . . . I say no, cut the crap, go and clean the street and do whatever, you can't just sit back and wait. . . . This whole inertia . . . it was always there, it's just that now it has emerged as the mode of living."

Delić suggested that "people who lived in [Josip Broz] Tito's time" were the most guilty of this kind of passive inertia. In light of the hardships and horrors of the intervening years, many people in Sarajevo—especially those in middle or advanced age—express longings for prewar life under communism. This is a phenomenon known (affectionately or dismissively, depending on who is speaking) as "Yugo-nostalgia."[105] The complaints of older generations thus emerge in part from the values and dreams of Tito-era Yugoslavia, when many saw neighborliness, tolerance, the Yugoslav ideal of brotherhood and unity, and a strong welfare state as key ideals guiding individual and collective striving. After diagnosing all of Sarajevo with PTSD, Loga pinned the blame not on war trauma but on "economic and social problems."[106] His further comments are revealing. "We had a good life before the war," he said. "Why can't we go back to that? Our communism wasn't like Russia or Hungary. I don't mind democracy but this privatization is just a mafia. I don't know why the international community wants us to be in this mess."[107]

Tito's stated ideals were only imperfectly achieved.[108] Zlatko Hurtić, the former director of BiH's poverty reduction strategy and a one-time World Bank employee, complained a few years ago that Bosnians "expect to live like they used to before the war—going abroad, buying Italian clothes. But it wasn't real; the economy was funded by Tito's foreign borrowing, and they won't believe that."[109] But whether or not the prewar economy rested on a "real" base—Yugoslavia had foreign debts of nearly $20 billion by the early 1980s, and other systemic problems suggest that its economy was wobbly at best[110]—the values, ethics, and expectations of the time were not illusions. The fact that after the war many Sarajevans were still holding onto them in private and invoking them as they struggled to make sense of their milieu indicates the potential for alternative political hopes and subjectivities that run counter to the visions of both local and international elites.

Observers like Hurtić and Delić, as well as Western policy makers heavily enculturated into ideologies of individual initiative and capitalist risk taking, have often condemned these Yugoslav yearnings as another kind of pathology of memory parallel to or part of the complex of mass PTSD. In this view, Bosnians—rendered passive, entitled, and dependent by decades of socialism and humanitarian handouts, and traumatized by the violent disintegration of Yugoslav-era dreams—are unable to accept their losses and move on. It is a clinical-sounding diagnosis (for example, a United Nations Development Program report diagnosed Bosnia-Herzegovina as having "a huge dependency syndrome"),[111] blaming social problems on the accumulated individual psychological injuries of the past fifty years of Balkan history. Such perspectives empty Sarajevo's affects and intensities—what Deleuze[112] might call its subjectivity as a milieu, the set of trajectories, landscapes, and socialities that comprise its own painful becoming as a community—of content, meaning, and context. They obscure the locatedness of people's complaints and frustrations by calling them indicators of a universal psychiatric disorder and, in the process, fail to perceive the haunted generativity of living amid and through destruction.

THE INTERPRETATION OF SYMPTOMS

Deleuze's distinction[113] between language in a clinical state and language as literature suggests intriguing possibilities for listening. My interlocutors were navigating both the continuing force and legacy of a shattered world and the partial unfolding of new powers and knowledges. I came to see the care and labor of Wings of Hope staff members and their beneficiaries as a way of opening up spaces between the Yugoslav past and neoliberal imperatives, where creative survival, desire, and grief could intersect to illuminate alternative futures. Inertia and waiting, as well as anger and nostalgia, may carry meanings other than collective illness.[114] What possibilities does seeing the language of refusal, waiting, or nostalgia as a "collective depression" foreclose, for analyst and interlocutor alike? If I posit that in this refusal there is an agency, in this "Yugo-nostalgia" the seeds of an alternative future, in this waiting a set of becomings, will my listening attune me to something else—a nascent "life in things," as Deleuze would put it, growing in the "necessary detours" of syntax?[115]

Deleuze articulates a key divergence with psychoanalysis in how to approach and interpret symptoms. He quotes Guattari, who argued that "lapses, parapraxes and symptoms are like birds that strike their beaks against the window. It is not a question of interpreting them.... It is a question instead of identifying their trajectory to see if they can serve as indicators of new universes of reference capable of acquiring a consistency sufficient for turning a situation upside down."[116] In other words, a symptom is not necessarily or only an indicator of pathology structured by a memorializing unconscious. It is also, as in Guattari's haunting image, a bird beating its beak against the window; it is a potentiality for becoming, breaking free of forms, and sublimating the violence of both everyday and world-historical forces. In this vision, symptoms express a desire or life force trapped at an impasse, waiting for a chance to break through.

Sarajevans are not just waiting for "someone to come fix their lives," as Delić and many others put it. They have much more specific expectations, as a range of ethnographic work in Bosnia-Herzegovina continues to show.[117] They wait for politics to improve, to move beyond nationalist fear mongering and deadlock and again provide the kind of social protections and safety nets they recall from the communist era. They wait for people to become kinder, warmer, more neighborly—the way they were before the war shattered trust.[118] They wait for new industries to provide jobs and an economic base. They wait in Sarajevo's abundant cafes, endlessly drinking coffee with friends and complaining about the government, about the fecklessness of Bosnia's foreign supervisors, and about unemployment. They wait for war criminals to be brought to justice.

Their waiting is something other than a passive depression: it is a holding pattern, an abiding of barely tolerable circumstances, a new kind of day-to-day survival that echoes the remarkable ways Sarajevans survived the siege, when they waited more than three brutal years for foreign intervention.[119] It connects them with each other in an unnamed, unrecognized collectivity, a "tissue of shifting relations" woven by the shared experience of a meantime (between destruction and renewal) of grieving, anger, and anticipation.[120] And it is a kind of politics, a refusal to take on a social form—capitalism as a privatization mafia; government as corrupt and heartless bureaucracy; and neighborliness as competition, mutual suspicion, and carelessness—that bears little resemblance to the prewar values they continue to hold in reserve for better days.

People are not just the sum of the forces—however overwhelming—that construct and constrain them. To trace the trajectories, the ever-deferred desires and expectations, and the symptoms of Sarajevans is to map a shared desperation for flight: anger and inertia have evolved from so many failed escape attempts and disappointed dreams. Where obstacles block passages of life, some trajectories dead-end: the war veteran, unable to find steady employment after many years, finally only travels a daily path between home and a neighborhood bar; and the university student, unable to afford the cost of passing grades, takes the same exams over and over into her late twenties, caught in a limbo of extended adolescence. But just as often, people move around impasses or push through them, carving out small life chances against the odds.

A SARAJEVO BECOMING

Claude Lévi-Strauss suggested that bricolage, the kind of thinking characteristic of the "untamed mind," works via a swerve away from defined and conventional paths: "a ball rebounding, a dog straying or a horse swerving from its direct course."[121] Maja, the executive director of Wings of Hope, has made a life out of such swerves. She survived the sieges of both Mostar and Sarajevo, working where and when she could to support humanitarian efforts. Coming from an ethnically mixed background, as many Bosnians do,[122] and compelled to choose a Croat identity as the war broke out, she now picks none of the official choices available—Croat, Bosniac (Muslim), or Serb—and is one of a minority in BiH to choose a civic Bosnian identity. Director of a psychosocial organization, she is neither psychologist nor psychiatrist; during my fieldwork she was studying philosophy and sociology, and before the war pursued degrees in mechanical engineering and economics.

Maja relied on diagnoses including collective depression and PTSD to interpret the needs of her beneficiaries and life in postwar Sarajevo in general, and she considered the young people at Wings to have at least partly absorbed the trauma of their parents. Yet in her work she fought against feelings of futility, militantly communicating a sense of power and possibility to her clients. She considered herself as effective as psychologists in helping children because, as she would tell them, she is a "professional friend" and not a therapist. She tutored them in math and took a consistent, active interest in the details of their day-to-day lives. For a week each January, she and her colleagues still lead about twenty children to a snowboarding camp on Mount Igman (a former Olympic ski slope just above Sarajevo) where, in learning to master an extremely difficult sport, they develop a greater sense of possibility and confidence.

Maja was just as angry, disappointed, and discouraged as any other Sarajevan—if not more so. One of the first things she said to me was, "I am always angry." Her struggle to overcome feelings of overwhelming frustration was obvious, and she tried to channel her anger into providing the small, practical forms of social assistance offered by Wings. She may have tended to speak of Bosnia in clinical terms, but her trajectory tells a more complicated story, evoking the possibilities of what Deleuze calls "missing" people[123] and the unexpected futures that remain latent and minor, sidelined by dominant political patterns and compulsive repetition. Maja's frustration and short temper are more than symptoms of trauma: they are the flip side of a set of positive aspirations and values—ever-thwarted but never-extinguished desires for a different world, the parameters of "a people to come still ensconced in its betrayals and repudiations."[124]

Maja's agency radiates across social and institutional domains and through kinship ties. She has a young cousin named Milan, born in September 1992—

just after the war began—in the town of Prijedor in northwestern Bosnia, now part of the Republika Srpska. I met him for the first time at Wings of Hope's snowboarding camp in early January 2007. Maja brought Milan down from Prijedor every year and paid his way at the camp.

Milan has had a very difficult life, though you would not know it from his charismatic and positive demeanor. His mother is a Catholic, and his father is a Serb who fought for the Republika Srpska during the war. Milan's maternal grandmother helped take care of him for a while, but she died when he was eight; after that, he stayed with his parents. His mother is intellectually disabled and makes very little money as a seamstress for a company in nearby Banja Luka. His father struggles with alcoholism. At the time of my fieldwork, Maja's mother was sending Milan money regularly: the cash went directly to him instead of to his parents, whom Maja did not trust to manage it. Milan's misshapen nose is the result of having been hit by a car while crossing the street. He is uninsured, and no one in his family could afford the operation to repair the broken bones, so Maja was saving up to pay for it, and for the braces Milan needed to straighten his jumbled mouthful of teeth. The only way that Milan could get independent health insurance at his age was by dropping out of school and registering at the unemployment bureau, and Maja would not allow this.

Milan took care of himself and his parents. He cooked and cleaned the family apartment in Prijedor. After school each day, he went from apartment to apartment in his neighborhood, offering to do small errands or chores; he earned more in a day than his father did through his meager veteran's pension. Milan had amazing survival skills, but at least initially he was not a great student. He was naturally curious about how things work, but Maja was the only person in his life who seemed to take the time to engage him and encourage his interests, mostly over the phone.

Milan did not seem to harbor any resentment about his circumstances. At the snowboarding camp, he was unfailingly sunny and kept an eye out for his friends. He told me that "everything will be fine," in spite of so much evidence to the contrary. Many of the young people I met in Sarajevo told stories about having taken on adult responsibilities too early, having had to become the grown-ups in families mired in hardship, depression, and drunkenness. It was Milan's optimism that seemed rare. I wondered whether it would last, and how much it depended on his relationship with Maja. Most of my young Sarajevan friends had become cynical about their prospects in BiH and just wanted to leave the country.

There was no money or insurance to repair Milan's nose; in a way, he embodied the constraints of postwar household economies. Yet as a figure in Maja's economy and redirection of therapeutic governance, he remained oriented toward future possibilities. Milan had no direct experience of any world other than the postwar society into which he was born, and he made the best he could of it. Parents and grandparents whom I interviewed at Wings, on the other hand, regularly resorted to the past to evaluate their present.

"Yugo-nostalgia," as I came to understand it over time, is something other than a pathological burden, a symptom of depression or mass PTSD. Here, memory is not only about obsessive commemoration of, or unfinished mourning for, a lost era. Older generations perform acts of remembering that are as much about the present and the future as the past. These acts of memory play a role in mobilizations for alternative trajectories. The invocation of Yugoslav-era dreams and values by my informants in Sarajevo—whether or not the past to which they refer actually existed in the shape in which they currently cast it—participates in the construction of postwar solidarities, minor becomings[125] on the margins of Bosnian society.

Wings of Hope, though inevitably limited in capacity and, like its beneficiaries, often forced to survive month to month by patching together short-term sources of funding, tries to weave social relationships on different terms than those that seem to prevail in Bosnian politics. The organization's work implicitly draws on Yugoslav-era political ideals to renegotiate the terms of solidarity and the common good: the community its staff members strive for is not one of individual entrepreneurship and the pulling up of bootstraps, of strict ethnic segregation, or of clientelism and corruption, but of institutionalized, free social support that disregards ethnic divisions and social status and attempts, in some small way, to compensate for the state's abandonment of the vulnerable. Wings is one of the few places Sarajevans can go for help where a bribe or personal connection is not required, and where assistance comes without months of trying to overcome bewildering bureaucratic obstacles. For staff members and their beneficiaries, healing the wounds of war is sociopolitical rather than simply individual and is accomplished less through personal therapeutics than through a small-scale, tentative restoration of ties of trust and support.

The force of the past is evident not only in backward-looking nostalgia but also in critical comparisons allowing a reimagining of the possible and the posing of an alternative ethics of postwar social life. The mothers first connected with each other around the meeting table at Wings by exchanging bitter grievances about the lack of social services or any apparent sense of compassion and responsibility from the state, but then their conversation shifted. They began to build a shared understanding—still frustrated and bitter, but tinged with longing—of how things should be, firmly rooted in what they recalled of the Yugoslav-era social contract and the feeling of communal life and support that it produced. Now and again at Wings, in other words, connections based on an angry sense of victimization turned into (or at least gestured toward) solidarity based on shared values, aspirations, and morally weighted memories of prewar national life and politics.

We can find in Sarajevan lives and words a frozen form and call it collective depression; see their waiting and lack of initiative as a blocked passage of life; or see them as stuck, mired in nostalgia and dysfunctional politics, as many observers do. But even in seemingly backward-looking melancholy and longings for times past, there is a component of flight that escapes this form by stubbornly alluding to and sometimes living, in seedling stage, hope for something different. They yearn for a reality beyond nationalism and competing victimhood claims, beyond corrupt and compassionless capitalism, and beyond trauma—a sociality that might reassemble, together with lessons learned in the crucible of war, fragments of prewar Sarajevan and Yugoslav values.

Such a sociality might correspond to a different—and for Sarajevans, more legitimate—configuration of governance and economic policies, a different relationship to foreign powers and humanitarian organizations, and a broader understanding of the effects of trauma and loss and concomitant processes of healing. Careful and open listening, via sustained ethnography, can allow us to hear the voice of this people to come, this possibility of another lifeworld.[126] It can reveal Bosnia-Herzegovina as an assemblage of places, peoples, desires, hopes, and grievances, situated at a crossroads of alternative pathways rather than trapped in a dead end of collective psychiatric disorder or doomed to the anomie and inequality of unchecked capitalism.

Anthropology attuned to becomings—to people's aspirations, however frustrated or futile, and to what they make of the world and themselves in pursuing those aspirations—is critical for illuminating these crossroads and the agonistic, everyday struggles waged to keep alternative routes open. At stake, broadly speaking, is how anthropology can contribute to opening up opportunities for progressive transformation in forms of care, politics, and economy, and whether it takes the additional step beyond explaining dark realities to the work of imagining, in collaboration with its interlocutors, concrete ways in which things could be otherwise.

A PEOPLE TO COME

In their study of Franz Kafka, Deleuze and Guattari suggest that "the expressions of the solitary researcher tend toward the assemblage of a collective enunciation ... even if this collectivity is no longer or not yet given. There is not a subject; there are only collective assemblages of enunciation, and literature expresses these acts insofar ... as they exist only as diabolical powers to come or revolutionary forces to be constructed."[127] This vision for literature can also inspire ethnography: when we listen as readers and cocreators, rather than clinicians, our own sensibility and openness become instrumental in spurring social recognition of the ways ordinary people think through their conditions.

In the ethnographic cases discussed in this essay, people struggle to survive and belong through and against the intersecting psychiatric, humanitarian, and neoliberal rationalities that diagnose and depoliticize their projects and desires as forms of nonsense or madness, either individual or collective. Anthropologists can render publicly intelligible the value of what people, amid new rational-technical and political-economic machineries, are left to resolve alone. People's practices of inquiry and searches for symbolic authority challenge the analytic approaches we bring to the field, forcing us to articulate more immediately relevant and experience-near conceptual work. Theory is embattled and unfinished on both sides of the conversation and the text.

Ultimately, it is the subjects of fieldwork who, through and beyond their relationships with us, are the true creative wellsprings of anthropological thinking. The point is not to move our interlocutors in the field up to our (or the European white male philosopher's) level in the hierarchy of epistemological authority, but to argue for an "equality of intelligences," and to find novel public and scholarly ways to harness the creative conceptual and relational work activated amid the unfathomably complex and layered entanglements of the field.[128]

Large-scale processes are not abstract machines that overdetermine the whole social field. Personal actions and social mobilization have a key role in the stories we tell here. Neither can the microarrangements of individual and collective existence be described solely in terms of power or rational choice. Both Catarina's writings and people's struggles to get by in postwar Sarajevo evince an everyday life force seeking to break through forms and foreclosures and to define a kind of subjectivity that is as much about swerves and escapes as about determinants. Freud's oedipal theorizing, contemporary psychiatric common sense, and even Foucault-inspired anthropological analytics all tend to disregard this plasticity. Such a disavowal, we believe, has significant real-world consequences for ideas and forms of care and for social intervention ("a tragedy generated in life," as Catarina put it).

By reading our cases in dialogue with some of Deleuze's ideas, we attempt to strongly reaffirm the value of ethnographic microanalysis, bringing into view the immanent fields that people, in all their ambiguity, invent and live by. Such fields of action and significance are porous and mediated by power and knowledge, but they are also animated by desires and claims to basic rights. In making public a nuanced understanding of these fields—which are always at risk of disappearing—anthropologists can help make larger structural and institutional processes visible and their true influence known.

In our research, we have seen novel subjectivities and sociological phenomena emerge: unanticipated relationships to medical technology and discourse outside clinical settings, forms of transcendence woven into everyday labor and community, and the making of agency via psychopharmaceuticals and of political sensibilities via a reconfigured language of psychiatric diagnostics. Lines between public and private, and between institutions and other more fluid and open-ended social milieus, routinely blur and transform. Actual political subjects are ambivalent about public institutions and infrastructures. Traversing worlds of danger and inequality, constrained without being totally overdetermined, they create small and fleeting spaces through and beyond apparatuses of governance and control in which to perform a kind of life bricolage with the limited choices and materials at hand. Such becomings, we believe, are a fundamental entry point to the work of capturing the fabric of the times and people's everyday inventiveness and resolve. Placing becomings at the center of ethnographic thought can help circumvent agonizing over academic fads and allow us to linger, more creatively, with the agonistic and uncertain dimensions of our field engagements.

From an ethnographic perspective, both social theory and politics can appear limited and often impoverished, restricted in imagination, and out of touch with intricate and shifting realities that carry the potential to become vital and/or deadly. People have an understanding of their worlds, the social problems they must circumvent or transcend, and the kind of politics that would actually serve their aspirations that is not taken into account in policy discussions and decisions. This is not a subjugated social knowledge, constituted as a reaction to power, but something personal that bears traces of singularity not easily framed or contained. Even when institutionally ignored, it persists, and it merits more attention in the public sphere. By more actively cultivating this kind of recognition, ethnography has the potential to trouble the inequality that has, in Didier Fassin's words, "insinuated itself into the humanitarian politics of life . . . there are those who can tell stories and those whose stories can only be told by others."[129] In the meantime, however, interventions of governance—in postwar and resource-poor settings alike—remain epistemologically myopic and are not systematically structured to work with people, notice how they belong in varying degrees to multiple systems, and incorporate the insights of their real-world knowledge into policy and care.

The process of communicating and disseminating evidence of becomings to other disciplines, and to public debates more generally, can reveal the limits of dominant or currently operational concepts of justice, social welfare, ethics, and crisis intervention (among others). Anthropology retains and can continue to build on its capacity to challenge orthodoxies. Take human rights, for example: typically conceptualized as primarily political, involving mainly democratic rights to free speech and voting, the human rights our interlocutors the world over consistently seek—to social, economic, and health security—are largely neglected.[130] Or consider what evidence of becomings might do to orthodoxies of care, social work, and postcrisis remediation: interventions are often individualized, biomedical, and psychotherapeutic or pharmaceutical, neglecting the need to rebuild relations of trust and support or even to ensure basic requirements for health and day-to-day survival, not to mention social mobility. Our field cases compel a return to the enduring question of what the complicated and empirical grit of ethnographic evidence can and should do to the contemporary nature of politics and policy. How can we find ways to bring our material to technocrats, policy makers, and caregivers in a way that truly challenges their evidence-making practices and assumptions?

We work to understand people in a different kind of temporality—"the time is out of joint"[131]—as they endure and try to escape constraints and articulate new systems of perception and action. Attentive to what could have been and dwelling in the meantime of individual lives and social worlds, we strive to produce a knowledge that is not obsolete in the moment of its formulation. In this regard, the time of anthropological knowing runs counter to that of political and economic rationalities and to the reason of policy and governance, which makes people the objects of technical fixes with specific, temporally limited stages of progress and measurement.[132] Our knowledge, in contrast, has a tentativeness and an open-endedness that can make it simultaneously historically attuned and untimely,[133] defying historical circumstances and constraints in the service of the unexpected and in defense of "the right to a nonprojected future as one of the truly inalienable rights of every person and nation."[134]

This tentativeness and receptivity to different temporalities is not always easily borne: with an eye to the possibilities and noninevitability of people's lives, social scientists must also recognize the thresholds where liberating flights and creative actions can become deadly rather than vital forms of experimentation, opening up not to new webs of care and empathy but to systematic disconnection. In our work, we have become mindful of the dangers of romantically projecting agency and hope onto desperate situations. Biehl recalls how startled he was when on one occasion Catarina became enraged and threw her dictionary to the ground. She had just heard that Biehl had been unable to convince her family to schedule a visit. Writing, in the end, could not take her back home—which is what she wanted most.

Becoming is not always heroic. Solidarities formed in reaction to the alienations of capitalism can become exclusionary, founded less on expanded empathy than on shared rage and competitive claims to victimhood; dreams of the past can turn reactionary; new institutions of care can be co-opted and twisted into instruments of power, violence, or abandonment; and mobilization for rights can culminate in atomized and highly privatized political subjectivities. In all this, market ideologies and practices may work as a hidden engine, reconfiguring and relocating social and administrative functions, as if behind the scenes: social work shifts from government to civil society, medication from clinic to family, and diagnosis from medical practice to the public sphere. How can we empirically pinpoint and hold accountable the workings of the market? How do we disentangle our agencies and modes of thought from those workings?

Finally, our anthropological engagements challenge us to maintain a sense of where assemblages—complicated new configurations of global, political, technical, biological, and other segments—touch ground, how they take on institutional grip and individual, human valence. It is not enough to simply observe that assemblages exist; we must pay attention to the ways that they are constantly constructed, undone, and redone by the desires and becomings of actual people who are caught up in the messiness, desperation, and aspirations of life in idiosyncratic milieus. Nor is ours necessarily a choice between global assemblages[135] and local "splinters" of a "world in pieces."[136] At the horizon of local dramas; in the course of each event; and in the ups, downs, and arounds of each individual life, we can see the reflection of larger systems in the making (or unmaking).

Engaging people's plasticity and becomings may be key to anticipating, and thereby making available for assessment and transformation, the modes of existence and futures of emerging communities. Both ethnography and the becomings it explores can have the power of art—to invoke neglected human potentials and expand the limits of understanding, imagination, and empathy— and we believe that it is not just literary giants like Franz Kafka, James Joyce, and Marcel Proust who can "invent a new language within language."[137] "There is no work of art," as Deleuze wrote, "that does not call on a people who does not yet exist."[138] This project includes the active participation of readers. Thus also at stake is our capacity to generate a we, an engaged audience and political community that has not previously existed: our craft's potential to become a mobilizing force in this world.

Moving away from the overdetermined and toward the unfinished, human becomings intrude into reality, enlarging our sense of what is socially possible and desirable. Any endeavor to engage with this mobile dimension of human experience is, by its very nature, fraught, and will undoubtedly require increasing professional freedom and bold experiments in anthropological expression. But even if the outcomes are limited and incomplete, it would be a moral and intellectual failure not to try to represent people's in-betweenness and multiplicity and sustain their sense of anticipation, even in the darkest of circumstances. These tensions should not paralyze our storytelling but should find expression so that the reader can grow closer to people.

NOTES

1 Deleuze and Parnet, *Dialogues II*, viii.
2 Deleuze and Parnet, *Dialogues II*, viii.
3 See Boundas, *Gilles Deleuze*; Connolly, *A World of Becoming*; Massumi, *Parables for the Virtual*.
4 See Bessire, *Behold the Black Caiman*; Biehl, Good, and Kleinman, *Subjectivity*; Garcia, *The Pastoral Clinic*; Han, *Life in Debt*; Navaro-Yashin, *The Make-Believe Space*; Stoler, *Along the Archival Grain* and *Race and the Education of Desire*.
5 Deleuze, *Negotiations, 1972–1990*, 170. See also Deleuze, *Pure Immanence*.
6 See Allison, *Precarious Japan*; Berlant, *Cruel Optimism*; Livingston, *Improvising Medicine*; Povinelli, *Economies of Abandonment*; Ralph, *Renegade Dreams*; Stewart, *Ordinary Affects*.

7   See Abramowitz, *Searching for Normal in the Wake of the Liberian War*; Biehl and Moran-Thomas, "Symptom"; Davis, *Bad Souls*; DelVecchio Good et al., *Postcolonial Disorders*; Jenkins, *Extraordinary Conditions*; Jenkins and Barrett, *Schizophrenia, Culture, and Subjectivity*.
8   See Fassin, *When Bodies Remember*; Ferguson, *Global Shadows*; Foucault, *Security, Territory, Population*; Lovell, "Addiction Markets"; Ong and Collier, *Global Assemblages*; Rabinow and Rose, "Biopower Today."
9   See Bourgois, *In Search of Respect*; Bourgois and Schonberg, *Righteous Dopefiend*; Farmer, *Infections and Inequalities* and *Pathologies of Power*; Holmes, *Fresh Fruit, Broken Bodies*; Scheper-Hughes, *Death without Weeping*.
10 See Bateson, *Steps to an Ecology of Mind*; Benedict, *Patterns of Culture*; Boaz, *Race, Language and Culture*; Clastres, *Society Against the State*; Geertz, *The Interpretation of Cultures*; Trouillot, *Global Transformations*.
11 Bateson, *Naven*, 257.
12 Hirschman, *Crossing Boundaries*, 88.
13 Berlant, *Cruel Optimism*.
14 Hirschman, *Crossing Boundaries*, 67.
15 Biehl, *Vita*.
16 See Martin, *Bipolar Expeditions*.
17 Deleuze, *Essays Critical and Clinical*, 3.
18 Deleuze, *Essays Critical and Clinical*, 4.
19 Biehl, Good, and Kleinman, "Introduction: Rethinking Subjectivity," 3.
20 See Biehl and Moran-Thomas, "Symptom"; Sanal, *New Organs within Us*.
21 Deleuze, *Essays Critical and Clinical*, 64.
22 See Nettelfield and Wagner, *Srebrenica in the Aftermath of Genocide*; Wagner, *To Know Where He Lies*.
23 See Bougarel, Helms, and Duijzings, *The New Bosnian Mosaic*.
24 Deleuze, "Having an Idea in Cinema," 4.
25 Borneman and Hammoudi, "The Fieldwork Encounter, Experience, and the Making of Truth: An Introduction," 17.
26 See Das et al., *The Ground Between*; M. Jackson, "Where Thought Belongs."
27 Hirschman, *Exit, Voice and Loyalty*, 329.
28 Biehl and Petryna, *When People Come First*.
29 See Ortner, "Dark Anthropology and Its Others."
30 Clifford and Marcus, *Writing Culture*.
31 Marcus, "The End(s) of Ethnography," 3.
32 See Haraway, *Simians, Cyborgs, and Women*; Rabinow, *Making PCR*.
33 See M. Fischer, *Anthropological Futures* and *Emergent Forms of Life and the Anthropological Voice*; K. Fortun, *Advocacy after Bhopal*; M. Fortun, *Promising Genomics*; Martin, *Bipolar Expeditions*; Rapp, *Testing Women, Testing the Fetus*.
34 See Jasanoff, *The Fifth Branch*; Lakoff, *Pharmaceutical Reason*; Latour and Woolgar, *Laboratory Life*.

35 Marcus, "The End(s) of Ethnography," 2–3.
36 Marcus, "The End(s) of Ethnography," 1.
37 Marcus, "The End(s) of Ethnography," 3.
38 Marcus, "The End(s) of Ethnography," 3.
39 Rabinow, *Marking Time*, xxiii.
40 Canguilhem, "The Decline of the Idea of Progress," 318.
41 See Descola, *Beyond Nature and Culture*; Kirskey and Helmreich, "The Emergence of Multispecies Ethnography"; Kohn, *How Forests Think*; Mol, *The Body Multiple*; Pederson, *Not Quite Shamans*; Robbins, "Beyond the Suffering Subject"; Viveiros de Castro, *Métaphysiques cannibales*.
42 See Bessire and Bond, "Ontological Anthropology and the Deferral of Critique"; M. Fischer, "The Lightness of Existence and the Origami of 'French' Anthropology."
43 Deleuze, *Essays Critical and Clinical*, 1–4.
44 Nietzsche, *The Use and Abuse of History*, 10.
45 Malinowski, *Sex and Repression in Savage Society*.
46 Geertz, *After the Fact*, *Available Light*, and *Local Knowledge*.
47 Bachelard, *The Poetics of Space*, xxxvi.
48 Agamben, *Homo Sacer: Sovereign Power and Bare Life*.
49 Deleuze, *Two Regimes of Madness*, 122–34.
50 Foucault, *The History of Sexuality*.
51 Foucault, *Discipline and Punish*.
52 Deleuze, *Two Regimes of Madness*, 126.
53 Deleuze, *Two Regimes of Madness*, 131.
54 Deleuze, *Two Regimes of Madness*, 127.
55 Deleuze, *Two Regimes of Madness*, 126.
56 Ong and Collier, *Global Assemblages*.
57 Deleuze and Guattari, *Kafka*, 86.
58 Deleuze and Guattari, *Kafka*, 86.
59 Deleuze and Guattari, *Kafka*, 86. See also Freud, *Five Lectures on Psycho-Analysis*.
60 Foucault, *The History of Sexuality*.
61 Deleuze, *Essays Critical and Clinical*, 61–67.
62 Freud, *Complete Psychological Works of Sigmund Freud, Volume 10: Two Case Histories (Little Hans and The Rat Man)*.
63 Deleuze, *Essays Critical and Clinical*, 61.
64 Deleuze, *Essays Critical and Clinical*, 61.
65 Deleuze, *Essays Critical and Clinical*, 61.
66 Deleuze, *Essays Critical and Clinical*, 65.
67 M. Fischer, "To Live with What Would Otherwise Be Unendurable," 442.
68 M. Fischer, "To Live with What Would Otherwise Be Unendurable," 436.
69 M. Fischer, "To Live with What Would Otherwise Be Unendurable," 426.
70 Jardim et al., "Machado-Joseph Disease in South Brazil."
71 See Biehl, *Will to Live*; Cardoso, "Notas Sobre a Reforma do Estado."
72 Biehl, *Vita*.

73 Andreoli et al., "Is Psychiatric Reform a Strategy for Reducing the Mental Health Budget?"
74 Petryna, Lakoff, and Kleinman, *Global Pharmaceuticals*.
75 Deleuze, *Essays Critical and Clinical*, 1.
76 Deleuze, *Essays Critical and Clinical*, 1. See also Deleuze, *Pure Immanence*; Didion, *The Year of Magical Thinking*.
77 Deleuze, *Essays Critical and Clinical*, 3.
78 Deleuze, *Essays Critical and Clinical*, 3.
79 Bougarel, Helms, and Duijzings, *The New Bosnian Mosaic*; Jansen, "On Not Moving Well Enough"; M. Markowitz, *Sarajevo: A Bosnian Kaleidoscope*; Hayden, "Moral Vision and Impaired Insight."
80 Deleuze, *Essays Critical and Clinical*, 4. See also Rasza, *Bastards of Utopia*.
81 World Health Organization, *Mental Health Atlas 2011*.
82 See Bougarel, Helms, and Duijzings, *The New Bosnian Mosaic*.
83 Pandolfi, "Contract of Mutual (In)difference," 369. See also Fassin and Pandolfi, *Contemporary States of Emergency*; Good et al., *A Reader in Medical Anthropology*.
84 See Chandler, *Bosnia*; Hayden, *Blueprints for a House Divided: The Constitutional Logic of the Yugoslav Conflicts*.
85 Donais, *The Political Economy of Peacebuilding in Post-Dayton Bosnia*.
86 Pupavac, "International Therapeutic Peace and Justice in Bosnia," 377.
87 Rieff, *The Triumph of the Therapeutic*.
88 Pupavac, "International Therapeutic Peace and Justice in Bosnia."
89 See Pupavac, "Securing the Community?," 163; Summerfield, "A Critique of Seven Assumptions behind Psychological Trauma Programmes in War-Affected Areas," 1452.
90 See Fassin and Rechtman, *The Empire of Trauma*. A comprehensive survey of the rich and growing literature on the politics of psychological trauma in medicine, humanitarianism, and global health is beyond the scope of this essay. See, for example, Abramowitz, *Searching for Normal in the Wake of the Liberian War*; James, *Democratic Insecurities*; Kienzler, "The Social Life of Psychiatric Practice"; and Kirmayer et al., "Trauma and Disasters in Social and Cultural Context."
91 Pupavac, "International Therapeutic Peace and Justice in Bosnia," 392.
92 Rieff, *The Triumph of the Therapeutic*.
93 Deleuze, *Essays Critical and Clinical*, 4.
94 Jansen, *Yearnings in the Meantime*.
95 See Kleinman, *The Illness Narratives*; Kleinman and Good, *Culture and Depression*; Lock, *Encounters with Aging*; Scheper-Hughes, *Death without Weeping*; Young, *The Harmony of Illusions*.
96 Margaret Lock, in reviewing the literature on medicalization across disciplines, concludes with a call for an understanding of the process as less deterministic and more open-ended and context dependent: "Medicalization, understood as enforced surveillance, is misleading. So too is an argument that emphasizes the social construction of disease at the expense of recognizing the very real, debilitating condition of individuals who seek out medical help. Rather, an investigation of the forms taken by political

economies, technological complexes, and the values embedded in biomedical discourse and practice and in popular knowledge about the body, health, and illness that situate various states and conditions as residing within the purview of medicine better indicates the complexity at work" ("Medicalization and the Naturalization of Social Control," 123). See also Biehl and Petryna, *When People Come First*; Lock, "Medicalization and the Naturalization of Social Control"; Nguyen, *The Republic of Therapy*; Whyte, *Second Chances*.

97   Hacking, "Making Up People," 162.
98   On the importance of notions of "normality" in the cultures of Bosnia-Herzegovina and in relation to the war and its aftermaths, see Jansen, *Yearnings in the Meantime*; Maček, *Sarajevo under Siege*.
99   Quoted in Eager, "The War Is Over but Sarajevans Cannot Find the Peace They Seek." This passage was also quoted by Pupavac ("International Therapeutic Peace and Justice in Bosnia," 392).
100 Quoted in Eager, "The War Is Over but Sarajevans Cannot Find the Peace They Seek."
101 Biehl, *Will to Live*.
102 See Maček, *Sarajevo under Siege*; Jansen, *Yearnings in the Meantime*; Sorabji, "Managing Memories in Post-War Sarajevo."
103 Solomon, "Emerging from the Shadow of War, Sarajevo Slowly Reclaims Its Lost Innocence."
104 See Karaboeva, "Death and Memory in the Context of the Contemporary Bulgarian Street Posted Obituary"; Savić, "Diskursne osobine citulja."
105 See Buric, "Dwelling on the Ruins of Socialist Yugoslavia"; Jansen, *Yearnings in the Meantime*; Lindstrom, "Yugonostalgia"; Volcic, "Yugo-Nostalgia."
106 Quoted in Eager, "The War Is Over but Sarajevans Cannot Find the Peace They Seek."
107 Quoted in Eager, "The War Is Over but Sarajevans Cannot Find the Peace They Seek."
108 See Ramet, *Balkan Babel*.
109 Quoted in Eager, "The War Is Over but Sarajevans Cannot Find the Peace They Seek."
110 Donais, *The Political Economy of Peacebuilding in Post-Dayton Bosnia*, 6.
111 United Nations Development Program, *Social Inclusion in Bosnia and Herzegovina*, 2.
112 Deleuze, *Essays Critical and Clinical*, 64.
113 Deleuze, *Essays Critical and Clinical*, 1–6.
114 M. Fischer, *Anthropological Futures*.
115 Deleuze, *Essays Critical and Clinical*, 2.
116 Quoted in Deleuze, *Essays Critical and Clinical*, 63.
117 See Helms, *Innocence and Victimhood*; Hromadžić, "Bathroom Mixing" and "Once We Had a House"; Jansen, "The Privatisation of Home and Hope" and "Troubled Locations."
118 See Sorabji, "Bosnian Neighborhoods Revisited: Tolerance, Commitment, and *Komšiluk* in Sarajevo."
119 See Maček, *Sarajevo under Siege*.
120 Deleuze, *Essays Critical and Clinical*, 59. See also Jansen, *Yearnings in the Meantime*.
121 Lévi-Strauss, *The Savage Mind*, 16.
122 Burić, "Becoming Mixed."

123 Deleuze, *Essays Critical and Clinical*, 4.
124 Deleuze, *Essays Critical and Clinical*, 4.
125 Deleuze and Guattari, *Kafka*, 19.
126 See Borneman, "Reconciliation after Ethnic Cleansing"; A. Gilbert et al., "Reconsidering Postsocialism from the Margins of Europe."
127 Deleuze and Guattari, *Kafka*, 18.
128 Ranciére, *The Emancipated Spectator*, 1.
129 Fassin, "Humanitarianism as a Politics of Life," 518.
130 Farmer, "Challenging Orthodoxies."
131 This line is spoken by Hamlet to Horatio: "The time is out of joint; O cursed spite!/ That ever I was born to set it right!" (Shakespeare, *Hamlet*, 1.5.189–90).
132 See Connolly, *A World of Becoming*; Greenhouse, *A Moment's Notice*.
133 Rabinow, *Marking Time*.
134 Hirschman, *A Bias for Hope*, 37.
135 Ong and Collier, *Global Assemblages*.
136 Geertz, *Available Light*, 221, 218.
137 Deleuze, *Essays Critical and Clinical*, lv.
138 Deleuze, *Two Regimes of Madness*, 329.

II

2

Becoming Aggrieved

An Alternative Framework of Care in Black Chicago

LAURENCE RALPH

"Man, every other block in Chicago has a crazy lady," a friend, Justin, once told me when we heard the piercing screams of our neighbor, Mrs. Lana. According to Justin, Mrs. Lana had been addicted to drugs and he reasoned: "that's why she followed people down the street and yelled at them from her porch." But when I met Mrs. Lana's daughter, a young woman named Marla, she complicated Justin's characterization. Marla never knew her mother as an addict but did confirm that heroin had once been her main vice. Still, she offered another explanation for Mrs. Lana's behavior: "My mother's just mad."

"Mad," in Marla's usage, refers to an aspect of mental illness that had as much to do with anger as apparitions. According to Marla, her mother could see people walking down the street, minding their own business, and before they knew it an invisible but deadly bullet was lodged in their skull. If she could just get your attention, if she could just warn you, then maybe you had a chance to survive. If not, you were done for.

Jo Jo Thomas didn't get the warning. One afternoon he was eating in a restaurant with Marla while waiting for their mother to give them a ride home. Mrs. Lana called Jo Jo on his cell phone to say that she was outside in her car and Marla, still eating, asked her brother to go out to the car and return with an umbrella—it was raining, and she didn't want to get wet. Ever chivalric, Jo

Jo agreed. But when he stepped outside, gunfire rang out, and Jo Jo was in the midst of it. From the driver's seat, Mrs. Lana screamed so loud and long that Marla swears she heard it from inside the restaurant. Jo Jo might have heard it too, Marla says, because he turned around and took two steps toward his mother's car before collapsing. Mrs. Lana bolted from the car, dove onto the ground, and cradled the back of her son's head. Blood and brains spilled out, mixing with rainwater and then swirling into the gutter.

After Jo Jo's death, Mrs. Lana kept screaming.

When it comes to the relationship between race and mental illness, social scientists are often more concerned with explaining the lack of access to medical resources in poor, urban communities than with exploring the indigenous strategies that people in underresourced communities develop to cope with mental illness.[1] In Black Chicago, for example, one common way of understanding the relationship between mourning and mental illness is a contemporary version of a very old psychological theory. It was, of course, Sigmund Freud who famously distinguished between "mourning and melancholia" in his 1917 essay of that name.[2] For Freud, the loss in mourning relates to literal death. Accordingly, expressions of sadness in the mourner are viewed as appropriate and healthy, maybe even cathartic. Still, the expectation is that the mourner will overcome her grief over time. Melancholia, on the other hand, is indistinguishable from mourning when the sadness begins, but the aggrieved person never overcomes her loss. In fact, she may refuse to concede that the object of her affection has been lost at all. She subsequently retreats within herself, disregarding the norms and expectations of the outside world. If in mourning her son a mother is keenly aware of her loss, in melancholia she may also be aware, but she remains uncertain about what this loss means in a larger existential sense.

In Chicago, the way doctors treat Mrs. Lana is based on this Freudian distinction. Even though mourning is considered normal, what makes Mrs. Lana "mad" is a specific interpretation of her actions in relation to her loss—particularly the fact that she is deeply invested in Jo Jo's death. However, what I want to make clear is that, in contrast to doctors, people in Mrs. Lana's neighborhood, Eastwood, have come to view this woman's madness (in all its glorious aggression) as normal. They shun the societal expectation that her madness should diminish after some time, and they seek to pin down the political (rather than existential) meaning of Mrs. Lana's screams.

My argument is that Eastwoodians add a layer of depth to the common medicalized interpretation of mental illness because, in this community, a mother's madness is not merely her own. It signifies the grief that all residents may express for the many devalued black lives that have also been prematurely extinguished. I should say that, in this chapter, grief is a superordinate category that contains both a temporary sadness that can be overcome (mourning) and a perpetual condition that cannot (madness). Thus, I will show that a collective framework of care is constituted in the reaffirmation of humanity on behalf of the dead, and that by attending to her needs, residents grieve their own losses alongside Mrs. Lana's. That is, in occasioning people to reflect on the countless young black people who have perished too soon, Mrs. Lana enlists members of a community in becoming aggrieved.

Before we can fully grasp how an Eastwoodian understanding of the human condition undermines the distinction between mourning and madness, we must first examine how black life becomes devalued and thus dehumanized in the American city. This dehumanization, we will see, has implications for how grief is understood and expressed. In *Precarious Life*, Judith Butler turns grief into a political resource by demonstrating that the failure to understand the capacity to mourn amounts to a failure to understand the value of life itself.[3] Drawing on Butler's thesis, we can examine Mrs. Lana's screams in light of how the medical establishment continuously pushes the diagnostic reach of illness outward to capture more and more of the population. Anthropologists like Arthur Frank and Arthur Kleinman have regarded this capture as a form of censorship that silences certain people's voices underneath the heavy weight of a medicalized understanding of life.[4] But at the same time that it silences that which contradicts the medical perspective, the exclusion of the dissenting voice also establishes the boundaries of the public. This is how "normal" people understand themselves as those who do not yell and scream irately, even in the face of the violence they experience on an everyday basis. And this is why communities that face a disproportionate amount of violence must mask their grief. Just as their lives and communities are devalued, their grief is likewise illegitimated.

Focusing on "Eastwood,"[5] a low-income, African American community in which I have conducted ethnographic research for the past decade, I will examine the coping mechanisms residents develop after Mrs. Lana suffers her psychotic breakdown. Here, I build on Butler's theory of grief to reconceptualize madness as a sometimes productive force that allows scholars to see how certain populations are systematically dehumanized. After presenting a brief history of Mrs. Lana's community, in which I discuss how it came to have the socioeconomic markers of poverty it is known for today, I explore in further detail the circumstances surrounding Mrs. Lana's mental illness.[6] Ultimately, I argue that the story of Mrs. Lana's madness is productive because it gives us valuable insight into the ways in which blacks, especially those living in low-income communities with a dearth of institutional resources, invert popular expectations of mourning, thereby developing a concept of "becoming aggrieved" that does not merely lament death but also affirms life.[7]

A CITY OF SCARS: THE DEHUMANIZATION OF BLACK LIVES

I lived in Eastwood from 2006 to 2010, and have returned countless times since. When I first moved to Eastwood, I learned that back in the 1970s, the community was known by another name: Sacred City. In those Black Power days, this place became sacred in the same way that "black" became proud and "nigger" became a term of endearment. Local gangs still insist on the sacredness of this place. But in Eastwood, people outside of the gangs believe that all the talk of sanctity is nothing more than a pretext masking the profane. The statistics seem to bolster this point. Eastwood is a community in which 42 percent of the nearly 42,000 residents lived below the poverty line, and, as crime is heavily implicated in this climate of poverty, 57 percent of all Eastwoodians were in some way involved in the criminal justice system—in jail, on parole, or under house arrest. Months after moving into Eastwood, with my boxes still unpacked, I heard an unfunny joke (at least, from the perspective of community residents) that points to how black lives are dehumanized in Chicago.

When I was attending a community policing meeting, taking field notes, a police officer named Thompson said: "We're doing our best to stop the violence. We feel terrible that you all have to live here." Then, referring to the local gang members, he continued, "They call it Sacred City. You know what we call it?" He wrote "Sacred" in chalk and then, using his palm to wipe away a few letters, he said, "We just call it Scarred."

A few of the other officers present chuckled, including the precinct captain. Meanwhile, the residents gave them blank stares. In an effort to diffuse the tension (which had become palpable at this point), another cop, named Kearns, stood up and told everyone in the room his family's story. Generations ago, his great-grandparents had immigrated from Poland and settled in Eastwood. "This neighborhood has a special place in my heart," Kearns said. "I could show you old pictures we have at home. You wouldn't believe how beautiful it was."

Ironically, immigrant families like his are implicated in Eastwood's inglorious history. The community's wounds first began to fester in the 1970s, after the local tractor company closed. Then the major department store moved its headquarters, causing 80 percent of the manufacturing jobs to vanish. Other companies closed, taking with them 44 percent of the area's retail jobs. This process of deindustrialization was in full swing even before the assassination of Martin Luther King Jr. sparked uprisings in Eastwood. After the fires had been extinguished, many storeowners left the neighborhood when insurance companies canceled their policies or prohibitively increased premiums, making it difficult to rebuild businesses in their previous locations. Disinvestment peaked after King's murder, but it had been steadily increasing since the 1950s. These economic woes plagued all of Eastwood's retailers. By 1970, 75 percent of the businesses that had buoyed the community just two decades earlier were boarded up and abandoned. There has not been a significant migration of jobs or people into Eastwood since World War II.

Although Kearns did not mention these factors to explain why, eventually, immigrants from places like Poland, Ireland, Russia, and Germany packed their belongings and moved out of Eastwood, the lack of business opportunities was certainly a factor—not to mention the unbridled racism that led many of them to fear living alongside blacks. Ever since the early 1940s, when African Americans began migrating to Chicago in droves, the city has been deeply segregated, and this segregation has implications for how black lives are devalued today. Twenty-two of Chicago's seventy neighborhoods account for 82 percent of the city's homicides. Indeed, statistics like these are what motivated Eastwoodians to attend community policing meetings in the first place. Citing homicide rates and contextualizing them through a history of deindustrialization may be a circuitous way of saying that the reason why the police officer's joke fell flat for the Eastwoodians in the room was that they did not need an expert to tell them that their community was plagued with problems.

They were fully aware of their scars. Yet they asserted their humanity, nevertheless.

Mrs. Lana is a case in point. The fact that she is a mother who has been driven mad after witnessing the shooting death of her son exemplifies the reaffirmation of life in a context of death. I do not mean to suggest that this contention is not controversial. On many occasions, I have shared her story with police officers and doctors in Chicago as a way to talk about the relationship between race, mental illness, and grinding poverty. When I have done so, my discussion of Jo Jo's death (and Mrs. Lana's reaction to it) is often met with the following questions: How was Jo Jo raised? What did Jo Jo do? Was he a gang member? I can only assume that, by way of these inquiries, these experts are attempting to assess the amount of empathy they should feel for this family.

In the past I have replied that Jo Jo was, in fact, affiliated with a gang—but not in the way the experts might think. In Eastwood, even a teenager like Jo Jo, who opts not to join a gang, will be cognizant of who belongs with which group, as well as each group's jurisdictional boundaries. These boundaries are mapped onto neighborhoods, so that if a person is confronted by a member of a rival gang and asked where he or she lives, the street name the person provides will signal a gang affiliation (whether or not the person is a gang member) and can result in injury. (Many teenagers join gangs for protection after suffering injuries from rival gangs.) In Jo Jo's case, it is not clear whether he was mistaken for someone else, or if the people who shot him were operating under the logic that anyone who lived in proximity to the rival gang had an allegiance with them and therefore deserved to die. For our purposes, what is more important than whether or not Jo Jo officially belonged to the gang is how the logic of rivalry between gangs mirrors attitudes toward black Americans in the larger society.

The social movement #BlackLivesMatter demonstrates this point. #BlackLivesMatter began as a provocation on Twitter in 2013, after George Zimmerman, a self-appointed neighborhood watchman in Samford, Florida, shot and killed an unarmed black teenager, Trayvon Martin. The movement grew even more popular in 2014 after the civil unrest in Ferguson, Missouri, sparked by the shooting of Michael Brown, and the killing of Eric Garner, another unarmed African American who was choked to death by a New York City police officer. There are currently twenty-three #BlackLivesMatter chapters in the United States, Canada, and Ghana. Collectively, they have organized at least 672 demonstrations so far.

Contemporary movements like #BlackLivesMatter take as a point of departure the premise that certain people's lives—in this case, black lives—are devalued in American society. Because of this, the group focuses on the effort to make black lives count as those of normal human beings. Group members' protests speak against the notion that someone can be legitimately killed because his or her body was deemed threatening (regardless of whether the person committed an act of violence). The logic of a "justifiable homicide," they say, operates to produce and maintain an exclusionary idea of who is fully human and who is not. The public is to believe that the black person (for example, Trayvon Martin, Michael Brown, Rekia Boyd, Sandra Bland, or Jo Jo Thomas) deserved to die because of his or her criminal associations. This premise suggests that the alleged black criminal is less human than the upright citizen, and therefore the black person's killing is legitimate.

Mrs. Lana didn't agree that her son deserved such a fate. In fact, in her early days of grief, she was riddled with survivors' guilt, believing herself to be more deserving of death than her son. Before Jo Jo's shooting, Mrs. Lana had a relatively well-paying job as a postal worker. When she battled drug addiction, she found religion and transformed her life, and she remained a devout Christian. According to her neighbors, the only things she enjoyed talking about more than her spiritual transformation were the activities of her three children: Jo Jo, Marla, and Travis. In the eyes of many Eastwoodians, Mrs. Lana's psychotic breakdown marked her transition from a well-respected community member to an outcast—albeit an outcast whom people eventually came to admire greatly. What concerns us most is why Eastwoodians were drawn to her. This was not merely because they recognized what she had experienced; more specifically, they saw her screams as an attempt to create a public sphere in which oppositional voices are not feared, degraded, or dismissed but valued for the productive reflections they inspire.

In the next section of the chapter, I discuss how becoming aggrieved can be a productive force, since I see it as a kind of communal care that harbors political potential.

A MOTHER'S SCREAMS: THE POTENTIAL HIDDEN IN MADNESS

Drawing on black urban life from a different historical moment, Jonathan Metzl attaches the same crucial importance to the political potentiality embedded in mental illness as I do in this chapter.[8] In *The Protest Psychosis*, he shows that in the 1960s and 1970s, the diagnosis of schizophrenia underwent a striking shift in the United States. While the disease was originally associated with white middle-class women (such as those who were so bold as to commit the offense of chastising their husbands in public), over time this particular brand of madness became linked to black males, and the hostility, anger, and aggression that seemed to characterize their lives during the civil rights movement. Citing examples such as these, Metzl argues that treatments for mental illnesses are intrinsically political. For him, pointing to the political is not a way to dismiss schizophrenia by undermining its biological roots. Rather, these roots are given fertile soil in the social climate of the day.

The large body of literature suggesting that experiences of racism and poverty seem to increase a person's risk for mental illness is bolstered by Metzl's account, in which the emphasis is on how the social and political climate inflect the ways illness is interpreted, understood, and enacted. In the hindsight of history, it may seem strange that aggressive protests can be diagnosed as a form of madness. But Metzl's work attunes us to the fact that, although there are many institutional mechanisms for determining what illness looks like, it is much harder to say what should not be counted as part of the diagnosis. My work fills this void by describing locally salient ways of understanding death in which mourning (a loss that a person eventually overcomes) is not privileged over madness (a refusal to overcome loss that consumes one's existence). In this regard, each of the ethnographic scenes I describe contain hidden potentialities embedded within symbolic representations of grief—of which dice games, footwear, uncovered heads, and most importantly Mrs. Lana's screams are the most striking examples.

I learned about the local significance of symbols of grief while conducting fieldwork in Eastwood, where I often began structured interviews with the same three words: "Describe your neighborhood."

Young or old, most people stated that Eastwood could be desolate for hours on end and then, just as suddenly, bubble over with block parties, laughter, and life. But on "unfortunate nights," as one resident called them, the block could erupt with screaming and stampedes away from the unmistakable sound that too often rang out: a dreadful alarm. The threat of that untimely alarm—otherwise known as a gun blast—made one of my collaborators, Justin, insist on a prerequisite for helping me with my research: he said if I wanted his help, I couldn't stand on the "drug" corner. I could, however, stand on the less dangerous "lunch money" corner, where the teenagers shoot dice.

The "lunch money" corner was a recreational space more than anything else, a recess carved from concrete, where girls jumped rope and boys rode bikes. Surrounded by low-stakes games and laughter, this corner was a perch where, on ordinary days, young people practiced a modern jitterbug called "footworkin." They would bring iPods with portable speakers to mask the hollow sound of dice. Everyone's eyes would grow big with anticipation of the dots that would either win or lose them some pocket change. When those dots revealed themselves in front of us on the pavement, the winners would slap their knees and point their fingers at the others, now frowning, before snatching up wrinkled dollar bills and swearing that they'd mastered a special technique for tossing the plastic cubes against concrete and brick.

On this corner, it wasn't merely about the money. (Most days, the winners bought everyone a large bag of chips and soda, or even a stuffed slice of deep-dish pizza from the nearby restaurant, Big Al's.) It was about something far graver. The roll of the dice came to represent the fragility of life—the fact that, at even at so tender an age, you could never tell when your number was up.[9]

It would be easy for a passerby to see young people posted on the corner and not notice how the symbols of mourning could possess someone's body. On a winter day in 2008, for example, I watched as the dice rolled past the feet of a teenager named Danny. I then noticed that Danny was wearing a pair of boots that once belonged to Cook—his best friend, who had been murdered weeks before. Next, I realized something even more significant: Danny had not taken off those boots since his best friend passed away.

If one compares Danny's inherited boots to Mrs. Lana's screams, there are crucial differences. The boots might be a symbol of grief, but they do not necessarily signal mental illness. The grief that took place on street corners was subtle—and had to be—since even seemingly harmless scenes of mourning tended to be viewed by older residents with caution. Were a black male teenager to adopt Mrs. Lana's method of grievance (following people down the street while screaming), he would likely be seen as enacting the very forms of violence against which he was protesting. It was, in part, her role as a mother that made it more difficult to turn a blind eye and deaf ear to Mrs. Lana's screams. This is at least part of the reason that people were willing to make room for her madness.

Some contextual information about the nature of Mrs. Lana's screams will clarify this point.

Marla tells me, when driving past that intersection where Jo Jo was shot, she sometimes pictures her mother as she was before her son died: beautiful and not yet ravaged, wearing lipstick and a breezy dress, her head full of flowing locks. Marla chronicles her mother's life the same way Christians do Christ's, only in Mrs. Lana's case A.D. referred to Jo Jo's death, not the crucifixion.

Unlike the doctors and her Eastwood neighbors, at first Marla didn't think her mother's condition was permanent. Her theory was that one day, Mrs. Lana would not need to scream at people or follow them around, telling them to keep their heads covered. One day, Marla thought, her mother would finally accept Jo Jo's demise. It took at least a year for Marla to abandon this expectation.

A year after Jo Jo's shooting, Mrs. Lana could be seen standing on her porch, yelling at passersby in a high-pitched shrill. But this behavior started, Marla told me, when Mrs. Lana stared at her youngest child, Travis, then nine years old. Her glance at first was cautious. "What's wrong?" Marla remembers asking.

"Oh, nothing, baby," Mrs. Lana said, her eyes fixed on the back of her young boy's head.

This scene began to occur daily. Mrs. Lana would call Travis over and inspect him from head to toe. Once finished with her youngest, she would inspect her daughter, too. Though Marla was twelve years older than Travis, Mrs. Lana found special comfort in giving her hair a reassuring stroke.

I asked Marla when she first began to worry about her mother's safety.

In response she told me the drugstore story.

At the drugstore one day, Mrs. Lana knocked over the contents of shelves in a search for duct tape. When an employee finally handed her some tape, hoping that the unruly customer might leave, Mrs. Lana ripped the packaging open with her teeth and tried to use it right there in the store. And by "use it," I mean that Mrs. Lana attempted to apply the tape to strangers' heads.

Marla handed me a copy of the police report. After looking it over, I asked her how she made sense of the official description.

Marla's interpretation of this event was this: Her mother could not bear to see all those vulnerable bodies. Her mother "grew frightened" of the patrons fleeing from her—the unprotected who were rejecting her efforts to save their lives.

According to the report, Mrs. Lana's head was already covered with duct tape. She tried explaining to an employee the need for protective taping. The employee notified the store manager, and Mrs. Lana tried to cover his head as well. Finally, the manager called the police. "And I was happy to see them, too," Mrs. Lana later told her daughter. "At least they had the good sense to keep their hats on."

Unlike most patrons in the store, the manager reportedly told the police that he didn't believe Mrs. Lana was on drugs. As Eastwood is nationally known for heroin distribution, he claimed he could recognize an addict—usually, they were subdued and docile. In contrast, Mrs. Lana was frantic. She was mad. Still, when the police officers checked her record, they found that she had been arrested for possession of drugs. Even though that arrest had occurred more than twenty years earlier, it was all the evidence they needed to put her away.

Stapled to the report Marla handed me was another report. This second document came from the county jail where Mrs. Lana was held and contained the findings of a doctor's visit during her incarceration. She was examined in preparation for a hearing at the Mental Health Court.[10] There, her refusal to accept her son's death was codified into a diagnosis.

While incarcerated, Mrs. Lana's picture of Jo Jo was taken from her. She had carried it in an inside pocket ever since his death.

"That's when she lost herself," Marla said. The picture was a reminder to Mrs. Lana of who she was, and without it, Marla explained, her mother's urge to yell and scream and warn people to cover their heads became even harder to control.

This is what Marla learned about her mother's three-day stint in jail from the two reports and eventual hearing at the Mental Health Court. In jail, Mrs. Lana was subdued with sedatives and eventually placed in a cell by herself. It's impossible to say whether or not Mrs. Lana, lying on her bunk with drugs coursing through her veins, realized that her thoughts had become fragmented. Was she curious about when or if her mind, now scrambled, would ever be put to rights? She might have feared that if things could come undone like this, almost instantaneously, she could never hold everything in. Marla's theory is that this, her newfound reality, began to irritate her. And then that irritation transformed itself into rage, prompting Mrs. Lana to scream. "Screaming is the only rational thing she could think of to do," Marla said.

In contrast to Marla's acceptance of her mother's screams, Mrs. Lana's outbursts while incarcerated confirmed a doctor's determination that she had a "delusional disorder, with obsessional features." The court recommended that she be released, and Mrs. Lana was prescribed drugs that would block the neurotransmitter involved in developing her delusions. Additionally, family therapy was encouraged. That's where Marla decided that she would not fight her mother's madness. She would go with the tide.

Months after Mrs. Lana was released from jail, I asked Marla if her mother seemed to be a changed person.

Marla explained that at first, being outside was simply too much for her mother to bear. Mrs. Lana stayed indoors, her family accommodating her accordingly. Travis, who didn't like hats, wore his football helmet in the house. He learned that when his mother's eyes got big, he needed to buckle his chinstrap. Marla wore silk scarves on her head. "People in the neighborhood thought I had converted to Islam," she joked.

I asked her what the biggest challenge had been.

"Mother grew tired of such a confined lifestyle," Marla answered. "She wanted to at least feel the sun on her skin." But even sitting on the porch made her uneasy, as we know from her therapy. During her sessions, Mrs. Lana wondered how the Beverly twins across the street could jump rope like that, so carefree. And where was Mrs. Beverly, anyway? Mrs. Lana fought the urge to run across the road and grab those lighthearted children.

Mrs. Lana revealed other observations: She could see that the children and teenagers and grown folks around had parts or sometimes all of their heads missing. The human sounds emanating from their necks disturbed her. She wondered when these deformed people would fall to their knees, and when their headless bodies would collapse in the street. With visions such as these, it stands to reason that simply keeping her eyes open on the porch left Mrs. Lana weak. She would shuffle her feet, shake her head, look again, and finally close her eyes. Sometimes with her eyes still closed, she would cry soundlessly. Exhausted by her overloaded mind, she must have fought to tamp down the rage she had felt in jail. In my reading, this anxiety was about more than remembering who she was and how she used to live. It was born from a heartfelt need to warn her neighbors about death, which required that she dwell in a perpetual madness, a timeless space, where the urgency of the need to protect people from violence could never be forgotten, assuaged, or overcome.

BECOMING AGGRIEVED: THE ALTERNATIVE FRAMEWORK OF CARE

So far we have seen Marla struggle to place her mother's grief within a coherent frame. The primary way she attempts to do so is by positioning mourning and madness on an even social plane, so that the former is not deemed normal or the latter branded pathological. Rather, in refusing to overcome loss, Mrs. Lana is seen by her daughter as displaying a justifiable anger. In this section we will see that Marla's interpretation of her mother's pain as reasonable provides insights into the process by which Eastwoodians become aggrieved.

But before I describe a final ethnographic scene, which bolsters this point, a brief digression is warranted.

I mentioned from the outset that in my analysis grief connotes mourning as well as madness. It is now time to distinguish grief from the process of becoming aggrieved, which cannot merely be defined in terms of mourning the past: it is also about developing a communal framework for care. I realize that this relationship between becoming aggrieved and practicing care may strike some readers as strange, or at least counterintuitive. If the term *care* connotes safekeeping, consideration, and support, the term *aggrieved* connotes mistreatment, resentfulness, and injury. The words are not quite antonyms, but they are certainly distinct. Still, in what follows, I link the practice of care to the process of becoming aggrieved because to care for someone in an underresourced community is precisely about keeping loved ones safe, considering their needs and supporting them, while holding out hope that one's injuries and resentments may somehow prove productive in the end.

In the fall of 2009, Marla began to complain that whenever she had to leave the house—for school or work, or to go to the grocery store—Mrs. Lana would open her front door and walk through Eastwood with newspaper and duct tape, warning people to cover their heads. In the block club meetings I attended during this time, I noted that some of her neighbors initially expressed fear of Mrs. Lana. At the same time, knowing what she had been through, they felt remorse. Mrs. Lana's voice was so dreadfully sincere that they believed her shrill cries spoke to a breathtaking trauma. Indeed, the first time I heard Mrs. Lana scream I was as startled as if I had heard a gun blast. Like a bullet, her voice was an intrusion that ruptured the present. Symbolically repeating the violence that had taken Jo Jo, she drew an audible line, every day, between life and death.

After several worrisome confrontations, word began to spread about the nature of Mrs. Lana's madness. Soon Marla reluctantly confided in neighbors, telling them that since Jo Jo's death, her mother had been harboring a disquieting worry that either she or they were not real. At first Marla was ashamed to share this private information. The young boys who identified with the local gang might try to antagonize her mother, Marla feared. But she underestimated the respect they had for Jo Jo, and the love they had for Travis. Marla failed to recognize, in other words, that Jo Jo's peers may have been coping with their own grief through the care they expressed for Mrs. Lana.

Eventually, Marla invited her neighbors over. As they entered her home, Marla observed that her mother kept her eyes down, directly at their feet, then slowly scanned up to see their faces. In Marla's words, her mother was attempting to verify that they had a "head on their shoulders." When she saw their familiar faces and covered heads, their warm presence was as undeniable as it was reassuring, and this was the first step of a communal commitment to see Mrs. Lana strip madness of its stigma.

Pastor Scott was the first neighbor to come over in the winter of 2009. He kept his fedora on in the house, although it was mandatory for all men in his congregation to take their hats off when entering the sanctuary. A month later, it was Mrs. Beverly with her cashmere cowl and her twins with their pink hoodies. Marla monitored who came and went and learned to scrutinize their bare heads as closely as her mother did. "You can't step foot in this house unless you cover your head," she told everyone. Only weeks later, Mr. Gregory visited. He told me, "If you had to take your shirt off and fashion it into a makeshift turban when visiting Mrs. Lana, that's what you did." Marla's concerns were finally assuaged when, in early December, Travis's football team had a pizza party, and everyone ate slices at her mother's table through their helmets.

Flipping through her journal, Marla recounted her description of that day with a smile. She told me that the night of the pizza party, she watched from her mother's bedroom doorway as Mrs. Lana fell into a still, deep sleep that didn't require the aid of drugs—a sleep that began and ended in Mrs. Lana's own bed rather than Travis's, as had become the custom. Looking on as her mother slept, a yellow bandana affixed to her head, Marla came to realize that the struggle to order and focus experience was not just her mother's. It was a collective fight that would have to elevate madness so that it was not a devalued liminal state, but simply another response to violence. In this way, elevating madness—making room for it, even valuing it—was an effort to develop an alternate framework of care that searched for therapy through accommodation. It meant that people might be mad, but they were still human.[11]

Once her neighbors began to accommodate Mrs. Lana's voice, they could understand their own lives and losses—their own grief—in relation to it. Eastwoodians stopped trying to hurry past Mrs. Lana's porch or divert their eyes when they saw her sitting unstill. This is not to say that as time went on they took less notice of Mrs. Lana's madness. Quite the opposite: everyone took a little more care. Passersby looked for Mrs. Lana on her porch, gang members called her name and touched the brim of their caps (a personal salute), and women took their babies out of their strollers to show off their bonnets.

Toward the end of 2009, I began jotting down passing references to Mrs. Lana in my notebook. On the lunch money corner, adjacent to Mrs. Lana's house, idle talk about her was plentiful. Tiko, ready to leave the dice game, putting his sweater back over his R.I.P. T-shirt, said to Danny: "You sure did take a long time going to the store. I thought you were coming right back?"

Danny, brushing off his inherited boots, answered: "I had to walk the long way past Mrs. Lana's. I forgot my hat."

Or when Justin said to his wife, Tina, "We should feed that baby before we go to church." Tina agreed: "If we don't, she'll be screaming louder than Mrs. Lana in a barber shop."

And then Mrs. Pearl lent her grandson, Pete, some money, and there he was, standing on the corner with the hat he purchased, a suede cap with a snakeskin brim.

"You wasted my hard-earned money on that thing," Mrs. Pearl said. "That hat is so ugly that even Mrs. Lana would tell you to take it off."

Even Pastor Scott mentioned her in a sermon. "Mrs. Lana," he said, "has got more sense than any of the so-called 'antiviolence' activists I know. She doesn't hold a rally and then feel good about herself. She warns everybody, every day, about the consequences of the bullet." How many in the congregation, the pastor wanted to know, could claim they did the same?

In this way, Eastwoodians promoted Mrs. Lana's madness to the ranks of respectability. And her scars gained a status that was no less than sacred for people in Eastwood.

———

Throughout this chapter, we have witnessed residents creating a space to express grief in many different places (for example, on the corner where a teenage boy dons an R.I.P. T-shirt, wearing the boots his best friend has left behind, and inside Mrs. Lana's home, where people cover their heads). What I mean to point out is that in this context, the disproportionate likelihood that an Eastwoodian might suffer from mental illness or fall victim to gun violence shapes the ways in which grief is understood. Moreover, I have shown that many people who grapple with grief contribute to, and draw from, a critical reserve cultivated from their own vulnerabilities.[12] It follows that by donating their time, energy, and emotions to this reserve, Eastwoodians create what I refer to here as an alternative framework of care. From Marla we learned what the chief element in such a framework is: an elevation of madness, so that it is not denigrated or devalued but given the same respectability as mourning. My point here is that by cleansing madness of its stigma and shame, Eastwoodians become aggrieved through collective practices of care.

Metaphorically speaking, care in a context of structural violence includes the discontentment of a baby wailing in church, a woman whose grandson spends her hard-earned money on something frivolous, and the annoyance of having to walk the long way home even when there is a shorter path. Likewise, feeling irritated when your mother constantly leaves the house and yells at people, yet nevertheless exercising concern for her well-being, shows how anger and resentment might serve a greater good. Toward this end, the pastor's words (that Mrs. Lana "warns everybody, every day, about the consequences of the bullet") crystallize the common Eastwoodian contention that one's anger can be a critical asset when it is directed at the social problems that exacerbate mourning, madness, and all other manner of grief.

CONCLUSION

In crafting a concept of grief that accounts for both mourning and madness, it is crucial to distinguish the grief that many Eastwoodians express from the ways people become aggrieved—a process through which an alternative framework of care can be developed. This framework seeks to balance the scales of judgment and ridicule between the ephemeral sadness associated with mourning and the permanent sorrow that plagues the mad. By doing so, it challenges traditional and still common understandings of mourning, which rely on a model of the human subject that is wedded to a strict sense of the individual. In the Freudian scheme, mourning ceases when a mother ends her debilitating everyday preoccupation with her loss and finds a way to function as she had before the death of her child, thus reestablishing her own autonomy through sorrow. My analysis, in contrast, moves beyond the individual to examine collective grief. Like the Eastwoodians who visited Mrs. Lana at her home, I do not pathologize madness even as I compare it to mourning. Instead, placing mourning and madness on a spectrum of the same social plane makes grief more about the affirmation of life than merely coping with death. In this regard, I see Mrs. Lana's screams as an attempt to create a public sphere in which oppositional voices are not feared, degraded, or dismissed, but valued for the productive reflections they can occasion.

What I mean to make clear, in closing, is that insofar as it clues us in to the basic needs and desires of a dehumanized collective, examining the strategies for caregiving in black Chicago—as well as the premises behind them—can help scholars, researchers, and medical experts understand locally salient ways of interpreting the human condition. I urge researchers to begin their analyses by seeking to understand the local responses to trauma that are generated from within the communities they study because, as I see it, the framework of care that Eastwoodians developed is a therapeutic method of accommodating trauma that does not criminalize people. There, practices of care are rooted in the idea that, when it comes to managing the mad, there can be another world of regulation that has more to do with integration than with quarantine. Crucially, this alternative framework is at odds with the reliance on pharmaceutical drugs alone to treat trauma patients. Screaming is not an indication that someone should simply be institutionalized or merely be prescribed medication. People can scream, and it's okay.

Above all else, this is why I've gone into such details about the hidden potential embedded in a mad woman's screams. Her anger helps us reimagine grief by contemplating how life can be made livable on Chicago's West Side.

NOTES

1. Metzl, *The Protest Psychosis*.
2. Freud, "Mourning and Melancholia."
3. Butler, *Precarious Life*.
4. See Frank, *The Wounded Storyteller*; Kleinman, "From Illness to Caregiving as Moral Experience."
5. Please note that "Eastwood" is a pseudonym for the neighborhood where I conducted fieldwork. To protect the identities of my collaborators who are heavily criminalized, I do not identify the actual name of this neighborhood in my academic writing.
6. See Erikson and Erickson, *Crime, Punishment, and Mental Illness*; Pfeiffer, *Crazy in America*.
7. Here, I am referring to the "anthropology of becoming" that is rooted in Gilles Deleuze's philosophical theories (see "Deleuze and the Anthropology of Becoming"). João Biehl and Peter Locke argue that "Deleuze's ideas... uphold the rights of microanalysis, [while] bringing into view the immanent fields that people, in all their ambiguity, invent and live by." They continue: "Such fields of action and significance—leaking out on all sides—are mediated by power and knowledge, but they are also animated by claims to basic rights and desires" ("Deleuze and the Anthropology of Becoming," 335). Biehl and Locke's idea of "becoming" is meant to challenge accepted theories of social domination and popular modes of medical and political intervention. Drawing on this intervention, I seek to demonstrate the ways in which large structural and institutional processes are made visible through an ethnographic engagement with "neglected human potentials"

("Deleuze and the Anthropology Becoming," 317) such as a dialogue with, and a search for insight from, someone who, like Mrs. Lana, is considered mentally unstable.
8. Metzl, *The Protest Psychosis*.
9. Dice were among the local gang's most cherished symbols. "It represents that every day is a gamble," one member told me.
10. This court is located inside the jail.
11. See Bambara, *The Salt Eaters*; Morrison, *Sula*.
12. See Vargas, "Black Radical Becoming."

3

Heaven

ANGELA GARCIA

In this in-between, chaos becomes rhythm, not inexorably, but it has a chance to.
— GILLES DELEUZE AND FÉLIX GUATTARI, *A Thousand Plateaus*

There is no hope without anxiety and no anxiety without hope.
— ERNST BLOCH, *The Principle of Hope*

On a gray morning in November 2014, thousands of people gathered around Mexico City's golden-winged Angel of Independence. Simultaneous gatherings occurred at the Monument to the Revolution and the Plaza of the Three Cultures, sites that point to the intensities of state repression and opposition. As time passed the crowd swelled, as did its capacity to perceive and feel its expansion.

The point of convergence for the three groups was the desire to turn disappearance into presence, and presence into a process of transformation. The basic method was the reconnecting of people in space and time. In the afternoon the crowds flowed through Mexico City's broad avenues and cobblestone streets. As they moved, they chanted, "*Vivos se los llevaron, vivos los queremos!*" (You took them alive, return them alive!). They were referring, of course, to the disappearance of forty-three students from Ayotzinapa Normal School in Guerrero State, but also to Mexico's Dirty War and the Drug War, continuously recomposing 2014, 1968, and 2006. It was raining lightly and the aroma of marijuana mixed with that of copal.

The three groups converged in the Zócalo, Mexico City's immense public square. Black-and-white images of the dead and disappeared accompanied the living. At night an effigy of the Mexican president was set afire, casting light into the vast darkness. The fire suggested memory (this is how they perished),[1] collectivity, and new figurations of the political. The people gained courage through their connection, although they knew it might not last. But the burning of the fire nurtured their hope, and in its turbulent flames they caught a glimpse of their becoming.

Something else was happening. A group of demonstrators confronted police standing guard in front of the National Palace. The demonstrators threw Molotov cocktails, stones, and even rockets and set fire to the palace's ancient front doors. The demonstrators were quickly cast as infiltrators, but what criteria can we use to know the difference? The riot police moved forward—shields in one hand, weapons in the other. They sprayed tear gas and water and struck demonstrators indiscriminately with steel batons. People screamed "No violence, no violence!" but the police wouldn't stop until they cleared the Zócalo. The demonstrators resisted, and as they were pushed back and beaten up, they chanted the numbers one through forty-three.

The repetition of those numbers sent a melancholy tremor through the chaotic night, becoming its interior rhythm. It was a reminder and a challenge to the demonstrators that the movement must survive, even as it was being shattered.

I arrived back at my hotel that night to find two armed men guarding its heavy glass doors from the inside. Still and expressionless, they looked like creatures in an exhibit. "I am a guest!" I yelled at them, pulling on the locked doors. Throngs of demonstrators continued to run down the street, away from the besieged Zócalo. Some held their heads as if they were being struck from above, while others looked nervously over their shoulders. "Show us your key," the guards answered me. Feeling torn, I pressed my room key against the glass and was allowed to slip inside the hotel's quiet lobby.

The tall shuttered windows in my room opened onto the Zócalo. There were still thousands of demonstrators below. Some confronted the police, their bodies surging and retreating in furious waves. But most had already been rounded up and sat with their hands cuffed behind their backs. The rhythmic counting from one to forty-three continued, bouncing off the imposing buildings that framed the ancient plaza, ricocheting in multiple directions. For several hours I took comfort in those echoing sounds, until they were replaced by the morning call of church bells and street vendors passing by. But a sonic memory resounds, and it cannot be erased.

What does it mean to become at moments indistinguishable from erasure? Can violence be a vitalizing factor in the construction of a more livable future? In the darkness of our times, are we still able to see something else, to trust that there is something better to come?

This chapter probes these questions and their articulation in specific cultural forms. It draws on research I conducted in Mexico City to explore how people endure crushing destruction and injustice, while trying to maintain hope and the capacity for change. My ethnographic focus is two movements: a spectrum of generational experiences with social activism and a modality of coercive addiction treatment that is prevalent among the urban poor. While distinct, both movements embody a politically charged view of existence and incite creative responses that seek to transform what is seemingly hopeless into something hopeful. At stake are the movements' entanglements with violence, which seem to function as a condition and practice for becoming. In this sense, becoming involves a basic tension—or perhaps alchemy— between destruction and creation. I try to comprehend the logic and relation of these abstractions by studying their concrete expression in Mexico's social and therapeutic movements.

Ethnographically, this involves tracing the multiple crises that shape the immediacy of Mexico's present (for example, extreme inequality, systemic violence, femicide, and narcoviolence) in relation to broader political and structural durations. It also means revealing how these crises are transformed into a constant element in everyday life, with profound implications on human agency, subjectivity, and relationality. However, by studying the empirical reality of unrelenting negativity, I hope to offer more than a portrait of an apocalyptic Mexico, which seems to be a trend in scholarly and artistic productions alike.[2] Instead, I try to comprehend how the prevailing darkness in Mexico also operates in a rethinking of violence and becoming. This means paying close attention to the latent possibilities in Mexico's existing darkness, as well as the moments of rupture that express the presence of something different in the making.

Several theoretical lineages have helped shape my thinking in this essay— from Gilles Deleuze and Félix Guattari's formulation of the minority,[3] to Catherine Keller's apophatic theology,[4] and Benjamin Noy's thinking about negativity as a revelatory practice.[5] A more crucial influence is the philosophy of Ernst Bloch.[6] Indeed, in the past few years, and in step with the intensifying violence in Mexico, I have found myself turning to Bloch's mystical and revolutionary writings. At the heart of his work lies a tension between the darkness of human existence and the longing for a better world. This tension also expresses a key dynamic in the movements that are the focus of this essay. Let me offer an initial orientation to some of Bloch's key concepts, which guide my ethnographic analysis.

Darkness is fundamental to Bloch's thought, and he sees in it both annihilation and illumination. He describes humanity as being "enfolded," "missing," and "wandering" in what he calls "the darkness of the lived moment," a constant motif in his writing.[7] The ravages of the world wars, anti-Semitism, economic exploitation, and unjust material conditions characterize the darkness of Bloch's day, and it is from this specific historical context that his philosophy of hope emerges. The only thing that is transcendent about humanity, Bloch says, is our desire to "venture beyond" the present darkness.[8] Philosophy shares this desire, leading him to cast his discourse as a work of speculation.

While Bloch's philosophy is oriented toward the future, it is also firmly grounded in the present. Indeed, it is the "darkness of the present moment" that drives us forward, toward a future in which life might become something other than what it currently is.[9] According to Bloch, such a possibility depends on "flashes of hope" or "preilluminations" of things that exist in the present's latent potential.[10] He writes that "alone, novel and profound, the function of hope also flashes . . . itself nothing but *our expanded darkness, our darkness in the issue of its own womb, in the expansion of its latency.*"[11] Thus, a contradictory dynamic exists within Bloch's conception of darkness, for it is what limits and threatens our existence, as well as where our hope stirs and expands. Simply put, the darkness of the present moment is the very condition that might generate the possibility of moving beyond it. It is the site of hope and the precondition of becoming.

Like Deleuze, Bloch emphasizes unfinished processes of becoming over the fixity of being.[12] Bloch's interest in becoming is guided by a fundamental belief that "the world is full of disposition to something that does not yet exist."[13] For him, this disposition is firmly rooted in historical and material context and the search for the missing something (such as equality or freedom) is what drives us to become.

In addition to darkness, hope is central to Bloch's thinking on becoming. He calls hope "the most human of all mental feelings" and characterizes it in terms that we don't often associate it with today—hope is an "excessive" and "explosive" force often interchangeable with anxiety and hunger.[14] He views these dynamic qualities as necessary for motivating human efforts to "venture beyond" the "negative aspects" of the present.[15] Whether repression or exploitation, this negativity must be thought and ultimately negated through the anxious hope for a "not yet" reality he calls utopia. This orientation of hope toward the not-yet resonates with what Deleuze[16] and Deleuze and Guattari[17] call desire—that is, those unconscious drives that are shaped within concrete circumstances, and which are fundamental to the creation of new possibilities.

For Bloch, utopia is not separate from the historical present, nor is it an ideal place. Instead, it is a means of critiquing what is and it motivates hope and hunger for a different future. The hopeful quest for utopia requires that people "throw themselves actively into what is becoming, to which they themselves belong."[18] In this sense, darkness, hope, and utopia return one to what Bloch calls "the work" of becoming—work that is not only metaphorical or philosophical, but that also depends on the actual labor of the individual.[19] According to Bloch, there is an ethical imperative to share in this work for the good of the community, even if that good can never be known. In this sense, he conceives of becoming as a social process, not an individual one. There are shades of Deleuze and Guattari's collaborative writings here, which place a similar emphasis on the social, political, and technological dimensions of becoming.[20]

Dreams, visions, wishes, and the religious imagination figure prominently in Bloch's philosophy, and he views these not as naive, but as concrete expressions of the potential to become. These expressions operate as forms of dialectical critique through which the "not yet" is imagined and shaped. "Let the daydreams grow even fuller," Bloch writes, so that they may become "more familiar, more clearly understood and more mediated with the course of things."[21] This recalls Deleuze's thoughts on art and literature as offering forms of thought and feeling that can respond to, and potentially address, the problems of our times. Indeed, for both Bloch and Deleuze, becoming depends at once on concrete limits and struggles, affective and psychic investments, and the effort to understand and creatively expand their potential.

RECOLLECTIONS OF THINGS TO COME

"Mexico is becoming a hell," the writer Elena Poniatowska commented, after forty-three students from the Ayotzinapa Rural Teachers' College were disappeared.[22] Indeed, when considering Mexico today compared to during the Dirty War, which Poniatowska chronicled, one is struck by how much darker the present seems to be.[23] The darkness of Mexico is manifest in the mass deaths and disappearances of women and youths, unprecedented levels of criminal violence and impunity, worsening economic inequality and insecurity, and the corrosion of democracy and trust. But to conclude from these horrors nothing more than a hopeless descent into hell would mean assuming an existence without dreams or the possibility of change. Such an existence is inconceivable to Mexicans today who seek to endure, escape, and transform the darkness of the present. The question we are faced with, then, is how to articulate and expand these efforts while maintaining contact with the dangers and uncertainties that pervade Mexico today.

I began this chapter with the story of a demonstration because it is a clear expression of a movement seeking to sustain hope for change in the face of brutal, ongoing repression. Drawing people from all parts of Mexican society, the movement is a continuation of a long history of social mobilization by many groups challenging state authoritarianism and pursuing a better life.[24] Throughout the demonstration, references to past tragedies and mobilizations combined seamlessly with the messages of the present. *Todos Somos Ayotzinapa! EZLN! YoSoy132! Fue el Estado! 1968! Nunca Mas! Paz, Justicia y Dignidad! La Revolución no ha terminado!* Far from detracting from the crisis at hand, the force of past tragedies and ongoing struggles helped provide the energy for the movement on that November day, highlighting the unfinished process of social becoming.

In his memoir of the October 1968 massacre of student demonstrators in Tlatelolco, Mexico City, and the tumultuous decade that preceded it, Paco Ignacio Taibo addresses the difficulties presented by the very notion of the movement. "We didn't know what the movement was," he writes, "but it was growing . . . a tidal wave that just kept growing and growing."[25] Taibo recalls the relationships, ideas, affects, and actions—some from the past, others from the present—that gave expression to the desire for liberation, which was met with increasing levels of state repression in Mexico. He writes: "All we knew was that there was a Movement and that it had to be defended against those who sought to destroy it with clubs and bazooka fire, and protected from those who wanted to suffocate it with words, slow it down, halt it. We knew that we had to make it grow, nourish it, and take it beyond itself."[26]

The book's title, '68, delineates these efforts in relation to the darkness of a particular historical juncture. At the same time, Taibo carries '68 forward, like a pre-illumination of things still in the making. The book recalls Bloch's ontology of the "not yet" of utopia, which is organized around not a specific destination, but the gradual growing together of affect and action that posits a quest for a more positive future. In the context of the mass protests in '68, Taibo says that such a quest "meant violence, repression, fear, prison, assassination."²⁷ However, it also meant "the reengagement of a generation of students with their own society, their investment in neighborhoods hitherto unknown to them, discussions on the bus, a breaking down of barriers, a discovery of solidarity among the people."²⁸

This emphasis on producing arts of political opposition, and consequently modes of human connection, resembles Bloch's discussion of the importance of forms of social engagement that may open up new realizations of the future. For Bloch, these modes of engagement can manifest themselves as dreams and actions amid the darkness of the lived moment. Hence, the positive trajectory of hope is intrinsically linked to negativity. Likewise, when Taibo writes of "the tremendous force of our four hundred dead ... images of the wounded being dragged off by their hair ... memory of blood on the wet ground," he speaks of the generative force of darkness.²⁹

In Mexico, then as now, this force is embodied by an image of the dead and disappeared. It is an image that enables and challenges hope. And it shapes the movement that has again returned to the streets, confronting the darkness that surrounds us, finding within it sparks of light that enable us, as Bloch says, "to see around the corner, where a different, unfamiliar life may be going on."³⁰

A DARK CORRIDOR

Grupo Centro is located in a working-class area of downtown Mexico City, on a street crowded with traffic, pedestrians, vendors, and beggars. It occupies two small rooms in a building constructed when there was an explicit attempt to remake Mexico City in the image of European cities. Over the decades, the building's few spacious apartments were subdivided into smaller and smaller dwellings, many without kitchens or bathrooms. The ornate figural elements on the building's exterior are now chipped beyond recognition, and ivy climbs up its deep cracks. Yet the building endures, having survived the Mexican Revolution and the massive earthquake of 1985, which devastated Mexico City's historic downtown. Today, the building is home to dozens of families and street-level shops that specialize in miscellanea—plastic containers, hair accessories, cleaning supplies, and the like.

At the back of one of these shops is a shower curtain that covers a bolted metal door. Beyond the door lies a narrow flight of stairs that leads to Grupo Centro's own heavily bolted entrance. At all hours of the day, a man stands guard in the grim stairwell, monitoring traffic between Grupo Centro and the world outside.

Grupo Centro is an *anexo* (literally, an annex), the name given to informal, coercive residential treatment centers for addiction. It is one of the many thousands of anexos in Mexico City, many of which are unmarked and set deep within other structures, like apartment buildings, commercial warehouses, churches, and even parking garages. Every week the media tell stories of "slaves" being rescued from the invisible yet omnipresent hell that anexos are made to represent.[31] They are described as filthy and dark, teeming with people deprived of their liberty and subjected to horrific violence. Yet this identification of the anexo as an immutable netherworld remains unstable, for as a domain that exists connected to something else, as its name denotes, the anexo operates within, not beyond, the present.

Anexos are endlessly complex and so numerous—the Ministry of Health estimates that there are 1,500–4,000 in Mexico City alone, and thousands of others throughout the country—that I can't account for them in their entirety. But Grupo Centro is typical of the twenty or so anexos I have studied in the past five years. I want to offer a basic understanding of their structure and practices. This account is by no means exhaustive, but merely indicative of the myriad concerns that anexos raise and respond to.

Grupo Centro was run and utilized by the so-called informal working poor, who make up more than half of Mexico's population and often lack access to basic public services, including health care. Most of Grupo Centro's residents were taken there by force, usually via arrangements made by families, who paid the anexo 250–500 pesos a month (equivalent to US $20–$40) for their relative's treatment. Once confined, these individuals were called *anexados* and were subjected to a mix of interventions—from 12-step meetings and religious rituals to physical and psychological violence—all of which are employed in the anexo as treatment for addiction. Usually, the anexados remained confined until they were claimed by relatives or deemed successfully rehabilitated, a period that ranged from months to years. At any given time, the anexos I studied usually interned 10–50 anexados, although larger ones reportedly house over 100 anexados.

Being anexado means being annexed. It means having to sleep, eat, exercise, cook, clean, pray, confess, and be physically and psychologically disciplined in the same place, at the same time, with the same people day after day. Typically, these activities take place in one room, which is usually the only one that anexados have access to. Such rooms are typically without a view, are cramped, and feel too hot or too cold. Yet this restricted space is where life is lived and produced in ways that emphasize the tensions between life and death in the darkness of Mexico's present moment.

Consider forced testimonies (*testimonios*), which represent the foundation of anexos' therapeutic program. During these testimonies, anexados recount harrowing experiences of family, sexual, and criminal violence and identify themselves as victims, perpetrators, or witnesses. Offered multiple times a day, day after day, the relentless unfolding of testimonies doesn't just express life beyond the anexo, it becomes life within it. But this life also implies release, the possibility of which can occur only negatively, as the forces of coercion are part of the attempt to overcome. This is perhaps more readily apparent in the anexos' use of other intensive or direct therapeutic practices (*terapia directa*), which include things like hitting and kicking and verbal humiliation. Other common forms of corporal mortification and penance directly refer to Christ's atonement and redemption. The question that accompanies these practices is whether they will weaken, rather than increase, the potential for recovery, and whether and how they are constitutive of becoming.

While many anexos had names that tended toward spirituality, Grupo Centro was named after its location in the city's old historic center, known as the Centro. It consisted of two rooms, taller than they were wide, and a water closet with a toilet that rarely functioned. Both rooms had arched, wood-framed windows that faced the street below, with missing glass panes plugged up with cardboard. Each weekend, the street would fill with people from the area's surrounding working-class neighborhoods, who had gathered in the Centro to shop and stroll. The loud hum of activity penetrated the anexo, creating a kind of passage between the inside and out. Sometimes a single voice from the street would break through, eliciting an anexado's response. "That sounds like so-and-so," someone would say. "Is he calling me?" or "What did she say?"

The founder of Grupo Centro was a recovering drug addict named Padrino Rafa, *padrino* (godfather or sponsor) being the name given to founders and leaders of anexos. Two live-in counselors, former anexados of Grupo Centro, supported him in the anexo's daily operation, and they planned to open their own anexo one day.

Padrino Rafa retired to his apartment each night, which was located a few blocks away. Divorced and without children, Rafa spent the majority of his time at Grupo Centro: he considered it his "real home," and the individuals within it his real family. Like many padrinos I came to know, he had left primary school to work and help support his family. That was during the 1980s, a period of democratic transition and economic collapse for Mexico, as well as the growth of the transnational drug economy.[32] To eke out a living, dislocated rural farmers increasingly turned to the illegal production of marijuana and opium poppies, while young men in the city went into small-scale drug dealing. These income-generating strategies were also correlated with rising rates of addiction and death in poor communities and have fueled the proliferation of anexos since the 1980s.[33]

Over the years, Rafa developed an addiction to the same drugs he trafficked. Before getting clean and opening Grupo Centro in 2006, he was interned in at least twenty different anexos. His mother or ex-wife arranged and paid for some of these stints, and the drug trafficking organization he worked for was responsible for others. With each internment his treatment became more intensive, which he interpreted as a measure of how "fucked up" he had become. In one interview with me, Rafa recalled being chained to a wall for several days in an effort to subdue his rage and have him face his suffering. He said he felt like he was "starving," emptied of even his own intestines, and thus unable to eat the food the anexo eventually offered him. When his then wife saw his wasted body after four weeks in the anexo, she was worried and wanted to bring him home. But he didn't want to return, he said, because he "wasn't ready," although he didn't know for what.

Today, black chains are tattooed around Rafa's thick wrists, a constant reminder of his imprisoned existence as well as a provocation to "live better" (*vivir mejor*). In the shift from shackles to release, he seemed to pass from self-destructive insatiability to a kind of fulfilling hunger. Of course, the inability to fulfill hunger can be explained by oppression or sickness, and the desire to stay in the anexo—whether because of fear or madness. But the image on Rafa's skin suggests something more. It recalls Bloch's thoughts on the necessity of "something missing" for the process of becoming. Hunger, nothing, void—these are the negative forces that have the potential to move one forward, and to be able to find in chains something else—a "corridor with a door at the far end."[34]

Whether that door will ever be reached and where it leads remain uncertain. But it is an image that introduces the possibility of movement and change. This is what the restricted space of the anexo and its excessive practices also seeks to provide.

FACES IN THE CROWD

Twelve anexados lived in Grupo Centro when I first began observing it in 2011. They were mostly young people from the neighborhood, sometimes from the same block or apartment building, and they often knew each other. Addicted to alcohol, solvents, or crack cocaine, they usually stayed for three to six months, depending on their families' ability to pay.

The anexados spent their days together in a single room, except for one-on-one counseling sessions, Rafa's business meetings, and anexados' occasional visits with relatives, all of which took place in the second room. Sometimes a *curandera* (spiritual healer) would be called in to perform a *limpia* (cleansing) on an anexado, an activity that also took place in the second room. And every night the two or three female anexados were moved in there in an effort to provide them with safety.

The delivery of testimonies filled most of the day. Those with longer periods of sobriety and good behavior were permitted to sit on folding metal chairs, while others sat cross-legged on the uneven floor. Counselors continuously circled the perimeter of the cramped room, scrutinizing the seated residents and reprimanding those who slouched or dozed off. Speakers stood at a wooden podium at the front of the room. Rafa often interrupted the speaker's narrative, ordering them to "be honest," "go deeper" or "give in" to their suffering. These testimonies did not ascend from despair to hope to transformation, as recovery narratives typically do—ostensibly constructing a nonaddict identity and better future with each step. Instead, anexados were pressed to sink into and dwell, in both content and form, in the misery of their lives, which was also the misery of their time.

During one such testimony, a young man who was called Cabrito (literally, "young goat") recalled an afternoon when gunmen drove into his grandmother's small town in the state of Michoacán. He was with his mother, who had wanted to see her own ailing mother and convince her to leave her war-torn town and move to the capital, where it was safer. In a rhetorical form common among anexados, Cabrito spoke in the present tense and took on the identities and perspectives of his mother and grandmother.[35] In this sense, it can be seen as an attempt to occupy and understand multiple perspectives at once, constituting a system of thinking through human hopes and fears.

"Come home with us, Mama."
"No, no, I stay here."
"There's nothing here for you, Mama, nothing."
"Don't be stupid, everything is here for me."

In the end, Cabrito's grandmother refused to leave for reasons that seemed to revolve around birth and death. She had been born in that small town and had eight children there. Her husband and two of her children were buried there, and she would be, too. Cabrito saw that his mother's pleading was pointless, so he went outside to take a walk. His grandfather had been a barber and run the local shop where men used to gather to talk and primp. He wanted to see if the shop was still there and buy some snacks for the long bus ride home.

It was the middle of the day and very hot. Cabrito recalled the sight of kids, not much older than him, dressed in school uniforms. There wasn't much else to see. His grandfather's barbershop was now the town's *tiendita*, and he described its poorly stocked shelves—a few vegetables, soft drinks, potato chips, and random toys. His mother was right, he thought, there was nothing here. Cabrito said he couldn't wait to get home and see his girlfriend, smoke some marijuana and have sex, drawing laughter from a few of the anexados and a couple of lewd comments. "Shut up and pay attention!," the counselors yelled.

"*Había un mal*" (something was wrong). Cabrito said he noticed the SUV right away because it looked "out of place," but before he could respond with his feet, the shooting started: "*Pppppppppppp*. It sounded like that. *Pppppppppppp*. You hear? *Pppppppppppppp*." Cabrito kept making the sound of bullets spraying into the air, like he was caught inside of it and couldn't get out. Eventually, he collapsed onto the podium and started to cry, "I'm hit, I'm hit, fuck, I'm hit!" He wasn't the only one. When it was over, five people had been killed, including three schoolchildren.

"Numbers do not speak for themselves," Judith Butler writes, but they may help correct "the radical inequality that characterizes the difference between grievable and ungrievable lives."[36] With this goal in mind, I offer some numbers here. Since 2006, at least 120,000 Mexicans have been killed in the drug war, another 26,000 have been disappeared, and over 250,000 more have been displaced.[37] Submerged in a vortex of violence and impunity, the abstracted vision of these deaths and disappearances requires a mirror to reveal the faces in the existing darkness. And as the faces become clearer, so does the darkness.

Grupo Centro offers a terrain from which to discern both faces and darkness, and to take seriously the efforts of people as they try to perceive a way forward. This is admittedly difficult to discern in every circumstance, and the content of what lies ahead is also uncertain. But what *can* be seen in the anexo and testimonies such as the one Cabrito offered are attempts to provide a bridge between past and existing social conditions and possibilities for something else to occur. Thus, what appear to be deadly manifestations of the present in Cabrito's testimony become indications of life's destructive and creative potential.

HEAVEN

At the start of the drug war, there was a sense that living in Mexico City was like living in a bubble, at least for the solidly middle and upper classes. But this feeling of invulnerability to the violence that afflicted the rest of the country had completely shattered by 2013. A palpable sense of *inseguridad* was spreading throughout the capital, fueled in part by the increase in kidnappings. Most of these were express kidnappings, a crime in which an individual is abducted and held in a safe house while the person and his or her family members are drained of money. State officials posited that the source of danger to the people of the capital was youth gangs from Mexico City's fringes, a claim that became the rationalization for repressive policing of poor neighborhoods. Meanwhile, gentrified areas of the city saw a rise in fortified apartment complexes, surveillance cameras, and private security forces.

On a Sunday morning in May 2013, a mass kidnapping or *levantón* (literally, "a lifting") occurred in an after-hours bar called Bar Heavens. The bar was located in the touristy Zona Rosa district, designated by the government as a safe neighborhood (*barrio seguro*) where such things were not supposed to happen. The missing were thirteen youths, most between the ages of sixteen and twenty-six. Twelve were from Tepito, a poor neighborhood crowded with tenement apartments and a massive open-air market known for its pirated merchandise. Many of Grupo Centro's anexados hailed from Tepito, and some of them had tattoos or prayer amulets dedicated to Nuestra Señora de la Santa Muerte (the Death Saint). Santa Muerte is the patron saint of prisoners, drug dealers and users, sex workers, victimized women, and Mexico's underclass. Appearing as the female personification of the grim reaper, she bridges death with life, promising deliverance from violence and a safe delivery to the afterlife.[38] Tepito is her home.

Within hours of the mass kidnapping, the families of the missing reported the crime to the Ministry of Public Security, which was located only two blocks from Bar Heavens. They had an eyewitness, another boy from Tepito who saw the abduction take place in broad daylight. Yet despite multiple reports and the eyewitness, the crime was not investigated for a week. During that period, the families staged public protests against the authorities' indifference. Each day they marched from Tepito carrying images of the missing and placards announcing that the authorities did not care about them: "Ya es mucho tiempo y nada ayuda! Ayudanos a encontrarlos!" [So much time has passed and you haven't helped! Help us find them!]

Meanwhile in Tepito large banners that read "Les has visto?" [Have you seen them?] were draped across market stalls and apartment buildings. The banners described the identifying physical characteristics of the missing: a round face, mole, or cracked tooth; thin lips; pierced ears; black hair; light skin; tattoos of names in Hebrew; tattoos of Santa Muerte and the Virgin of Guadalupe; tattoos of hearts and diamonds; tattoos of tears.

Mexico City's prosecutor and mayor referred to the youth as absent, not disappeared. They said the crime was an act of retaliation between rival gangs based in Tepito and was not related to drug cartels, concluding that the incident at Heavens was not a cause of concern for citizens or visitors to Mexico City. Their comments made the residents of Tepito furious, and they staged even larger protests in response. I observed several marches and vigils, in which generations of relatives, mostly women, participated.

Within weeks of the kidnapping at Heavens, the number of anexados at Grupo Centro had doubled.

I was there the afternoon Magi arrived. The men who transported her to Grupo Centro immediately took her into the second room, where Rafa and the counselors were waiting. Everyone else was in the other room, with a more senior anexado named Mario left in charge. Mario had been in and out of anexos for more than a decade and had spent seven months at Grupo Centro. He couldn't imagine life beyond anexos, but was determined to change his position within them—first by acting as an *encargado* (the one in charge), then by becoming a counselor and eventually a padrino of his own anexo. Part of his training involved repeating the commands of Grupo Centro's counselors, and Mario carefully raised his voice an octave above theirs to signal his lesser status. On this particular occasion, he led the group in its daily reading of recovery literature.

I heard Magi before I saw her. She screamed obscenities and demanded to go home. Some of the anexados chuckled and wondered who the new girl was and whether she was attractive. Eventually, her screams broke into sobs. When I left the anexo that evening she was still crying in the second room, alone.

I finally met Magi when I returned to Grupo Centro the following week. She was small and thin, with long black hair that she tied on top of her head, only to let it loose and tie it up again. She was dressed like a typical teenager, in tight jeans, tennis shoes, and a T-shirt that read "The Ramones." To my surprise, the counselors didn't call her offensive names, as they did other newcomers, and she was permitted to sit in a chair, not on the floor. I figured that she must have been one of Rafa's relatives or the child of someone important. In fact, she was a cousin of one of the people abducted from Heavens and a close friend of several others.

It was July, and hope that the missing would be found alive was fading. Cut off from the news, Magi asked me for updates. I hesitated to say anything because I worried it might upset her. But the truth was that there wasn't much to report, which was also upsetting. Sometimes, after seeing Magi at Grupo Centro, I walked by Heavens. The walls were still plastered with images of the disappeared and handwritten messages to them. Scrawled in block print, the messages assured the disappeared that they weren't forgotten, that their children were still waiting for them, and that their families would keep looking for them and fighting for justice.

Anexos also engage in kidnapping. While their kidnappings are similar to violent acts of forced disappearance, and the sociohistorical context is the same, they should not be subsumed under the same category, be it criminal or narco. That is, the anexos' practice of kidnapping fosters a different experiential understanding—one that locates the significance of the negative practice in the search for a better future, although this cannot be guaranteed.

In an interview, Magi described the day she was "lifted" and taken to Grupo Centro. She had been working at her family's market stall in Tepito, calling out to potential customers. Typically her mother or aunt worked with her, but on that particular day she was alone. She recalled,

> It happened so fast. I was working and then I was in the dark. . . . I was hot. I could barely breathe. . . . No. . . . I couldn't move. . . .
>
> I heard laughing . . . doors opening and closing. . . . My heart pounded so hard it hurt me. . . .
>
> I thought, "My god, this is it. I am going to die. This is it, . . ."
>
> I kept thinking, "Is this is what happened to him [her kidnapped cousin]? Will anyone find me? Are they taking me to the same place?"
>
> But I landed here. I landed here. . . . I'm here.

In full view of neighboring vendors, customers, and passersby, Magi was kidnapped, wrapped in a blanket, and transported to Grupo Centro against her knowledge and will. Her terrifying experience was similar to those of many other (but not all) anexados, and it filled her with complex emotions, including rage. How could her parents have agreed to this, given the circumstances? She didn't even have a drug problem. But her rage was tinged with sadness, as she knew that her parents feared losing her to the terrible darkness that had befallen Mexico. During Magi's interment, several national and international agencies declared a femicide pandemic in Mexico, identifying the most dangerous place for women as the State of Mexico, which surrounds Mexico City.

Magi's account of being kidnapped conjures up one of the defining images of the drug war: the image of the *encobijado*, a murdered body (usually a woman's) literally "enfolded in a blanket" and disposed of in a vacant lot, a muddy canal, a dusty road. While anexos' modified engagements with encobijado joins the symbolic violence of the drug war, the usual story line doesn't apply.[39] For in this context, kidnapping and enfolding are figurative modes in which ideas of care and protection mix with the tangible criminal violence that pervades everyday life. And it is within the anexos' hybrid of violence and care that a process of becoming emerges, one that begins with being unfurled and leads to the revelation of survival. As Magi put it, "I landed here. I'm here."

Such awareness is achieved negatively, through the concrete threat of being enfolded within the terrifying conditions of the present reality. Experiencing darkness in such immediate terms, Magi's unfurling from the blanket can also be thought of as unveiling a horizon of life. In this sense, it echoes the kinds of contradictory experiences Bloch considers so necessary for becoming: experiences so "full of ambiguities" and tension that they point to the presence or possibility of something else.[40]

Three months after they were abducted from Heavens, the bodies of twelve of the missing were found in a concealed grave on the outskirts of Mexico City. Nine had been decapitated. As news of the discovery spread, so did the narrative that the victims must have been criminals, as if that justified their brutal deaths. Their families angrily rejected this idea. In the days that followed, they spoke to television reporters, describing their murdered relatives as young, dedicated parents or students—good, hard-working people, not involved in crime or drugs, people who were loved and missed.

Magi learned of the fate of her cousin and friends while she was at Grupo Centro. Many anexados tried to console her and often repeated the phrase "it could have been any one of us." Others seemed frustrated by all of the attention she received and pointed out that they had suffered similar tragedies but had not been fussed over. A shrine was created and a memorial service held, during which anexados offered prayers, expressed their feelings, and threatened revenge. In the weeks that followed, the anexados were made to continuously engage with the darkness of the moment, the precarious conditions of their own existence, and the possibility of release.

Magi remained at Grupo Centro for almost nine months—long enough for her family to feel that she was, somehow, out of harm's way. Or perhaps her internment had become too costly. Indeed, the mass kidnapping seemed to be taking a toll on Tepito's economy. Rafa measured the downturn by late and partial payments for his services, and by mounting requests to accept goods and services instead of money in exchange for a loved one's treatment.

Magi returned to Tepito and worked at her family's market stall. I saw her at the demonstration on November 2014. She wore a T-shirt that bore an image of her cousin's face, making his death a precondition of Mexico's movement to live.

THE POSSIBILITY WITHIN HEAVENS

Like the tides of demonstrators drawn together in the Zócalo, anexos represent a notion of futurity that is related to the historically situated darkness. Far from conceptualizing utopia as an impossibility, anexos suggest that the potential of a brighter future is present in its very absence.

Violence is a fundamental reality in both the activist movements and anexos, and this essay has tried to show how violence works both as a force for annihilation and as a summons to live. If Heavens presents the reality of annihilation, it also represents a longing that motivates collective political movement—movement that at once negates what is and points to what could be. For Bloch, this is the central function of utopia.

"Our space," Bloch writes, is "always life, or something more."[41] Answering the questions of what that something more is and how it can ever be known, remains life's difficult task. The anthropology of becoming takes on this task, following the horizon of life as it moves, even in the narrowest of spaces.

NOTES

1. The Mexican government claims that the forty-three students were incinerated in a remote trash dump in Guerrero State, but that claim has been dismissed by the Inter-American Commission on Human Rights.
2. Cultural production is obsessed with apocalyptic visions of Mexico related to problems in urban ecology, labor exploitation, and especially the drug war. These visions generally do not attempt to figure out what came before the apocalypse, or what might emerge from it.
3. Deleuze and Guattari, *Kafka*.
4. Keller, *Face of the Deep*.

5   Noy, *The Persistence of the Negative*.
6   I am not alone in this regard. See, for example, Thompson and Žižek, *The Privatization of Hope*.
7   Bloch, *The Spirit of Utopia*. These concepts are found throughout Bloch's writings, but I refer here to this text.
8   Bloch, *The Principle of Hope*, 4.
9   Bloch, *The Principle of Hope*, 4.
10 Bloch, *The Principle of Hope*, 4.
11 Bloch, *The Spirit of Utopia*, 200–201 (emphasis in the original).
12 Due to space constraints, I can mention only briefly some of the common aspects in Bloch's and Deleuze's work.
13 Bloch, *The Principle of Hope*, 76.
14 Bloch, *The Principle of Hope*, 74.
15 Bloch writes: "Hunger cannot help continually renewing itself. But if it increases uninterrupted, satisfied by no certain bread, then it suddenly changes. The body-ego then becomes rebellious, does not go out in search for food merely within the old framework. It seeks to change the situation that has caused its empty stomach, its handing head. The No to the bad situation, which exists, the Yes to the better life that hovers ahead, is incorporated by the deprived into a revolutionary interest. This interest always begins with hunger, hunger transforms itself, having been taught, into an explosive force against the prison of deprivation. Thus the self seeks not only to preserve itself, it becomes explosive" (*The Principle of Hope*, 76).
16 Deleuze, *The Logic of Sense*.
17 Deleuze and Guattari, *Anti-Oedipus*.
18 Bloch, *The Principle of Hope*, 4.
19 Bloch, *The Principle of Hope*, 198.
20 Deleuze and Guattari, *Anti-Oedipus*, and *A Thousand Plateaus: Capitalism and Schizophrenia*.
21 Bloch, *The Principle of Hope*, 43.
22 See, for example, "México se está convirtiendo en un infierno," Univision, November 16, 2014, http://www.univision.com/noticias/noticias-de-mexico/mexico-se-esta-convirtiendo-en-un-infierno-denuncia-la-escritora-elena-poniatowska.
23 The Dirty War (*Guerra Sucia*) refers to the period between the late 1960s and the early 1980s when thousands of university students, leftist activists, and political opponents of the government were killed, tortured, or disappeared by government forces. The most notable event was the 1968 student massacre in Tlatelolco, Mexico City. In April 2015, historical documents related to this period were reclassified "confidential" and removed from public view in Mexico's National Archives, adding to the growing distrust of the government.
24 See, for example, Becker, *Setting the Virgin on Fire*; Joseph and Nugent, *Everyday Forms of State Formation*.
25 Taibo, *'68*, 33–34.
26 Taibo, *'68*, 35–36.
27 Taibo, *'68*, 50.

28 Taibo, '68, 50.
29 Taibo, '68, 108.
30 Bloch, *The Principle of Hope*, 1193.
31 See, for example, Gutierrez, "Epidemias de Violencia."
32 A growing body of research demonstrates that the democratic transition and neoliberal policies and practices exacerbated long-standing socioeconomic inequalities and fueled the promotion of Mexico's illegal drug trade. See Astorga, *El siglo de las drogas*; González, "Neoliberalismo y crimen organizado en Mexico: El surgimiento del Estado narco."
33 Zamudio, *Las redes del narcomenudeo*.
34 Bloch, *The Spirit of Utopia*, 9.
35 In this way, his testimony expanded the limits of personal experience into a collective narrative of struggle, reflecting the genre of Latin American testimonio more broadly.
36 Butler, *Frames of War: When Is Life Grievable?*, xxii.
37 Heinle, Molzahn, and Shirk, *Drug Violence in Mexico*.
38 Lomnitz, *Death and the Idea of Mexico*.
39 Reguillo, "The Narco-Machine and the Work of Violence."
40 Bloch, *The Principle of Hope*, 948.
41 Bloch, *Traces*, 30.

III

4

Rebellious Matter

The Poetics of Ritual Space in a Turko-Syrian Border Town

BRIDGET PURCELL

In the hours before dawn on August 27, 2011, some thirty thousand men, women, and children had gathered at Balıklıgöl, the ritual complex at the heart of the city of Urfa in southeastern Turkey. This was Kadir Gecesi (in Arabic, Leylat al-Qadr; in English, Night of Power), the night commemorating the Quran's revelation to the Prophet Muhammad.[1] It is the holiest night of the year—"better than a thousand months"[2]—when prayers are heard and forgiveness is extended, and it is customary for Muslims to gather at mosques and spend the night awake in communal worship. That so many had chosen to do so at Balıklıgöl points to the site's dense significance: each of the mosques, graves, and carp pools in this centuries-old ritual complex is mythically tied to the prophet Abraham. This is where, according to local belief, Abraham was born; where he opposed the pagan king Nimrod and destroyed his idols; and where he was saved from a fiery death by the grace of God. For many people, these associations place Balıklıgöl in special relation to the divine—for instance, the carp are known as *kutsal balıklar* (sacred fish), and the spring water is believed to have healing powers.

On ordinary days, Balıklıgöl is clean, spacious, and organized. A multimillion-dollar restoration project carried out in the 1990s had refashioned the complex as a three-dimensional postcard, with its mosques standing serene and monumental amid manicured gardens and paved walkways. The effort had entailed cleansing the space of its noisy vernacular elements: gone were the houses that had crowded in around the mosques, the oddly spaced trees and crab grass, and sundry social activities like picnicking and swimming, so that what remained were clean lines and broad vistas. On this night, however, it was as though all of the efforts to preen and organize the site had been undone. The density of the crowds made the paths difficult to walk, and the grassy areas were covered with families seated or reclining on blankets. Though disorderly, the scene was also intimate, almost domestic: children slept at their mothers' sides, among simmering teapots and the remnants of *iftar* dinners.

I was accompanied that night by two friends, Özlem and Zuhal, students of Islamic theology who were visiting from a nearby Kurdish village. The two women usually came to Urfa's city center only on the formal errands of grocery shopping or visiting relatives, and for them the chance to spend a night amid the bustle of the crowd was a novel and exciting prospect. Later, back in the village, they would describe the evening over and over, recounting each detail. Yet on the night itself, I watched as my companions grew agitated by the crowding, the heat, and the garbage strewn across the sidewalks. "*Kalabalık*," they repeated—a word meaning uneasy-making crowdedness. And when I took out my camera to photograph the scene, the two seemed embarrassed, exchanging nervous glances and hastening to divert my attention. It struck me then that what I had first taken to be mere physical discomfort with this rite also involved for them a degree of moral discomfort.

In the months of my fieldwork that followed, I would learn that for many of my interlocutors, this ritual—and more precisely, this ritual setting—had indeed come to seem morally ambiguous. In recent years, a revivalist movement in Urfa had promoted a purified, text-based version of Islamic practice, casting doubt on Balıklıgöl and its panoply of folk practices. My friends' hesitation thus marked a wider cultural fault line, in Urfa and beyond, between those who are at home among saints' tombs and sacred fish, and a growing constituency who insist that such things have no place in Islam. Elsewhere, this issue has exploded into politics: the Islamic State's recent destruction of ancient ritual sites in northern Iraq is a dramatic example. But in Urfa, the shift was incipient, and for most people not precisely ascribable. Hence my impression of a ritual landscape in flux—a landscape where old practices were subject to new forms of doubt and uncertainty, and where it was possible to be an immersed participant one moment and an outsider the next.

Such experiences of dissonance have received little attention in the anthropology of Islam, notwithstanding the rich volume of scholarship on revivalist movements and their effects in reshaping religious landscapes and subjectivities.[3] For more than a decade, scholarly accounts of Islamic revival (and arguably of Islam writ large) have been dominated by a Foucauldian emphasis on discipline and subject formation.[4] One result of this shift has been a renewed interest in the materiality of religious life, including its spatial settings. But in many anthropological accounts of Islamic practice, materiality tends to be subordinated to a mandatory vision of ethical self-perfection—a disciplinary telos whose end point is the pious subject. Saba Mahmood, for instance, emphasizes those iterative, embodied practices whereby participants in revivalist movements—women like Özlem and Zuhal—progressively bring their religious subjectivities into line with authorized models of Islamic practice.[5] As some scholars have begun to note, this analytic leaves little room for experiences of doubt, ambivalence, and distanciation within religious experience.[6] What conceptual or ethnographic figures might illuminate moments like the one above, when bodies, spaces, and subjects seem not to submit to the linear trajectory of discipline?

I find an intriguing (if unlikely) figure of thought in Lewis Carroll's *Alice*—a character who struggles to orient herself in a complex landscape whose rules of engagement keep changing.[7] Like the pious subjects of recent ethnographies, Alice is concerned above all with the rules of proper conduct, and she struggles to comport herself accordingly.[8] But in Carroll's story, the subject is decentered with respect to the landscape: Alice is in Wonderland, Wonderland is not in Alice. As the milieu changes, Alice's strategies for engaging it must also change. She must be big enough to reach the key on the table, but small enough to pass through the door that leads to the garden. Availing herself of potions and cakes marked "eat me" and "drink me," she grows bigger and smaller, continually altering her relationship to her surroundings. Unfortunately for Alice, this is not a story of progressive mastery through iterative practice: her methods are always ad hoc and provisional, and she must begin again and again. Her shape-shifting is a matter not of discipline, but of becoming.

In this chapter, I explore the tentative, nonlinear ways that individuals orient themselves in a ritual landscape that exceeds their full control. In doing so, I draw on recent anthropological and feminist approaches to space and place that, inspired in part by Gilles Deleuze, insist on a vital materiality that at times exceeds and unsettles the subjects who encounter it.[9] I will argue that such a space demands much of the people who inhabit it, asking them to adopt multiple experiential and interpretive viewpoints in a single instant. Take, for instance, my friends' participation in the rite, but their discomfort with my photographing it—how they were at once open to the moment and reluctant to have it cast as an enduring emblem. While such dissonant moments might seem insignificant in themselves, they may point us toward tectonic shifts at the level of power, politics, and theology. Paying attention to them may help us understand how people apprehend large-scale processes of change and, in the process, change themselves.

SPACE AND POWER IN SOUTHEAST TURKEY

Urfa is a bustling city of 900,000 in the southeast of Turkey. Located just north of the Syrian border, it lies where the Anatolian plateau meets both the Kurdish highlands (to the east) and the Syrian desert (to the south). This border location is reflected in the city's population—a blend of Turks, Kurds, and Arabs who, until the early twentieth century, lived alongside autochthonous populations of Jews, Yezidis, and Christians (both Syriac and Armenian). Travelers to Urfa have long chronicled the shock of crossing the Euphrates and finding themselves in a Turkey that they no longer recognize. In "mystical and pious" Urfa, a popular English-language guidebook observes, "you begin to feel you've reached the Middle East."[10] This description condenses the various ways in which Urfa plays other to the west of the country—the purportedly modern, secular Turkey of the Turks, the one that could almost pass for Europe. Those "Middle Eastern" qualities touted as exotic touches in the guidebook—"women cloaked in black chadors" and "the call to prayer as an essential soundtrack"—are precisely those which, in the wider national imaginary, have singled Urfa out as both an object of cultural condescension and a target of state intervention.[11]

The province of Urfa was formally annexed to Turkey in 1939, yet in many ways its relationship to the state has remained unsettled and contested.[12] Throughout the remainder of the twentieth century, the state has engaged in aggressive spatial interventions in Urfa, attempting to fend off efforts (both real and imagined) to draw it into alternative geopolitical entities. There have been consistent serial efforts to "Turkify" the province, although the specific strategies have changed over time. For instance, in the early twentieth century, following the massacre and expulsion of ethnic and religious minorities from Urfa, these efforts entailed erasing the architectural traces of Armenians and other Christians, changing polyglot Ottoman place-names to Turkish toponyms, and so on.[13] During the second half of the twentieth century, these efforts entailed undermining Kurdish movements via decades of land expropriation, village destruction, and forced migration. Other spatial strategies included broadcasting nationalist symbols in restive areas—one still finds the Kemalist slogan "Happy is he who calls himself a Turk" emblazoned on mountainsides in predominantly Kurdish and Arab regions of the southeast.

Today, such aggressive, top-down displays of state power have largely given way to a softer approach grounded in economic development and modernization (though many scholars and activists view this approach as consistent with earlier assimilationist aims).[14] In recent decades, spatial interventions in the region have included land reform, village-to-urban migration, investments in tourism infrastructure, and, notably, the restoration of ritual sites like Balıklıgöl. Given the Turkish state's history of aggressive secularism, this contemporary investment in ritual space warrants some comment.[15] Much like the French *laïcité* on which it is based, Turkish secularism (*laiklik*) has always entailed substantial state involvement in regulating religious life. For instance, the state defines orthodox practice through an official ministry, which oversees everything from religious education to Friday sermons. Over the past twenty-five years, major shifts in national politics have resulted in a state less intent on suppressing religiosity than on promoting a specific version of it.[16] In brief, the version of Sunni Islam espoused by the contemporary Turkish state is characterized by a "modernist" or rationalist outlook that embraces adherence to the texts of the Islamic tradition and opposes charismatic practices such as saint worship—which are espoused both by other Islamic sects *and* by many Sunnis at the level of popular or folk religiosity.[17]

In Urfa and elsewhere, spatial interventions have been a key means whereby local religious cultures have been brought into line with a state-sanctioned, orthodox version of Sunni Islam.[18] Scholars have often understood this "orthodoxization" of local religiosity in a top-down fashion: the state promulgates an official or orthodox version of Islam, which is then disseminated locally through institutions (mosques and religious schools) and personages (imams and religious instructors), and eventually it comes to reshape religious practices and sensibilities at a local or neighborhood level. Space, here, is principally a site of collective discipline that molds the posture, sensibilities, and subjectivities of those who inhabit it. This disciplinary analytic applies both to the discipline that the state applies to its citizens (what Michel Foucault calls "power") and to the discipline that individuals intentionally apply to themselves (what

Foucault calls "ethics," including "technologies of the self").[19] In both cases, norms are progressively habituated or sedimented so that they become unconscious orientations.

This analytic illuminates much about revivalism as it is unfolding in Urfa—principally by drawing our attention to space and the body as sites for the functioning of disciplinary power, and vectors whereby authoritative or officialized standards of Islam are learned and put into practice. But discipline is only part of the story. As I describe below, space in Urfa is multiple, reflecting not a single religiopolitical regime, but transitions and overlaps among many. The site thus calls to mind what Foucault, in a short, exploratory essay, called a "heterotopia"—a space that condenses a range of exogenous institutions and practices, some of which are internally incongruous. He writes: "The heterotopia is capable of juxtaposing in a single real place several spaces, several sites that are in themselves incompatible."[20] Yet Foucault does not address *how* people inhabit heterotopias—that is, how they navigate uneven transitions among regimes of knowledge and power.

This is a question that Urfa raises with particularly clarity and urgency. As I write, the city has become an uneasy buffer zone, crisscrossed by Islamic State fighters, Kurdish militants, and Turkish armed forces, each representing distinct normative visions of religious and political life. In these circumstances, a focus on the continuity of tradition and the sedimentation of subjectivities will take us only so far. We must also pay attention to the multiple, overlapping normative orders that constitute people's lives and ask how people navigate their sometimes discrepant demands. This is a challenge that calls for an ethnographic approach attuned to both the complexities of space and the temporalities of becoming.

THE POETIC DENSITY OF RITUAL SPACE

The mosque complex of Balıklıgöl is Urfa's beating heart, the city's ritual and symbolic center. On any given day, the site teems with groups of villagers from the surrounding districts; Arabic-speaking families from Syria or Iraq; groups of Iranians, seventy or a hundred at a time, identifiable by their distinct dress; and the occasional tourist from Europe or Western Turkey. These visitors move among the site's various *ziyaret yerleri* (visitation places): mosques, gravesites, fountains, and—most significantly—the cave where Abraham is believed to have been born. These are dense sites of ritual activity. The cave's low, pockmarked ceiling bears evidence of stones chipped away as souvenirs or relics, and supplications are written directly on the walls, or scrawled on scraps of paper that are then tucked into crevices. Water flows up through an interior spring, and women press in around it, filling plastic bottles with its healing water.

One cannot miss here the significance of space—its affective density, its embodied draw—but its import exceeds the unconscious inscription emphasized in Foucauldian approaches. For Urfa's inhabitants are explicitly preoccupied with ritual space, and with spatial forms more broadly. Young people express their aspirations for upward mobility by describing the type of dwelling and neighborhood they hope to someday occupy. Men and women in their fifties and sixties describe the sights and sounds of the old city streets where they grew up. And on the shelves of the municipal library, one finds an immense volume of locally produced writing and photography devoted to Urfa's urban space, religious sites, and domestic architecture. Thus for the people of Urfa, urban form is the principal idiom for narrating processes of change—a medium that registers the effects of large-scale, often exogenous processes (migration and shifts in governance) on personal and communal life. Space here is marked by what Rupert Stasch calls "poetic density"—a capacity to condense or "make present" large-scale, exogenous processes that have shaped and reshaped social life.[21] A brief historical overview of Balıklıgöl reveals it to be a palimpsest or catalogue of these processes—one that bears witness to the always incomplete nature of transitions among religio-political regimes.

The earliest mentions of Urfa call it "Orhay," a Syriac name most likely derived from the Greek Orrha ("the city of beautiful flowing water") or the Semitic root r-w-' ("to bring water").[22] These names evoke a river that ran through the city's center—a tributary of the Euphrates aptly called Daisan ("leaping river") for its tendency to flood capriciously. In the third century CE, under the Seleucid Empire, the Daisan's waters were harnessed through underground channels, and diverted to springs and pools within the city walls. These pools—known today as the sacred carp pools of Abraham—became foci of healing and sacrifice for regional pagan cults, touching off an efflorescence of architecture, poetry, art, and ceremonial in honor of the fish goddess Atargatis.[23] Urfa's cultic center was widely known in the ancient world, taking its place alongside cities like Palmyra and Hieropolis, with which it was linked by a north-south caravan route that extended from what is now Diyarbakır through Mesopotamia.

When Urfa adopted Christianity—in the second century CE, it was one of the first cities to do so—the ritual center found new uses. Edessa, as the city was known in late antiquity, was a major center for the development of Syriac Christianity. New ritual sites like the Mother Mary Church (built in 363) were constructed on top of Urfa's old cultic centers, incorporating them materially while displacing their significance.[24] Yet the displacement was only partial. The Syriac chronicler Bar Daisan reports that as late as the third century, the men of Urfa would castrate themselves in honor of Atargatis. The practice was popular enough to elicit a rebuke from the Christian king, Abgar, who "commanded that anyone who emasculated himself should have a hand cut off."[25] This makes it clear that, despite the admonitions of the elite, popular Christianity in Urfa remained thoroughly suffused with the practices and sensibilities of the cults that preceded it. This influence was manifest, too, in the Eastern Christian "cult of the saints"—one major example of which was the cult of St. Thomas the Apostle, whose martyry was located at Balıklıgöl.[26]

As mythic and material schemes succeeded one another over the centuries, some of Balıklıgöl's meanings and materials were displaced, while others were resignified or incorporated into new ritual constellations—at times, uneasily. Around the fourteenth century, when Urfa was ruled by the Muslim Zengid dynasty, the site came to be associated with Abraham, and his famed confrontation with the pagan king Nimrod. As the story goes, Nimrod ruled over Urfa from the citadel that overlooks Balıklıgöl. When Abraham came of age, he confronted Nimrod and destroyed his idols. Infuriated, Nimrod made a catapult of the castle's twin pillars, from which he cast Abraham into a pit of fire below. But where Abraham landed, the flames turned into water, and the firewood turned into carp. Thus did the sacred fish of Atargatis and the healing waters of Edessa find their way into the city's Islamic myths and practices.

Ritual space in Urfa is layered, reflecting transitions and overlaps among successive schemes of power and governance. These disparate pasts are never entirely quelled but are continually "made present" in quotidian spatial forms. Today, Syriac inscriptions remain throughout Urfa's ritual site; neighborhoods are still informally called by their Armenian names; and one local church that was long ago converted to a mosque is sometimes referred to, curiously, as the Mosque of the Twelve Apostles. This mixed or syncretic character is not only a feature of Balıklıgöl's space; it is also a feature of people's experiences *in* that space. Consider Kadir Gecesi, the Islamic holy day discussed in the opening scene, which at Balıklıgöl is celebrated in a way that exceeds prescribed observance. People spend the hours from dusk to dawn at Balıklıgöl, camped out on blankets that are particularly concentrated around the cave of Abraham—a practice that some have traced to rites of "incubation" (sleeping at holy sites) practiced in Christian Edessa.²⁷ Kadır Gecesi also provides visitors a rare chance to glimpse the beard of the Prophet Muhammad (Sakal-ı Şerif), since the city's *müftü* (mufti) displays the beard here annually, wrapped in fabric and encased in glass. The scene is noisy and chaotic, as hundreds of people line up to view the beard each day, pressing in to touch the glass case and ideally to kiss it. According to one local belief—mentioned only in the absence of imams or scholars—spending Kadır Gecesi at Balıklıgöl three years in a row is equivalent to one visit to Mecca. Most of the time, the heterogeneity of such practices goes unremarked upon. But, it can—and recently *has*—become a reflexive focus.

THE POLITICS OF PURIFICATION

Today, the heterogeneity of Urfa's ritual space has become a point of moral and theological concern for many of the city's residents. This is largely due to the growing local influence of revivalist currents in Islam. Revivalism (also known as reform, purification, modernization, orthodoxization, and so on) refers to a range of transnational movements whereby the wide variety of local Islamic cultures are evaluated and revised in light of the canonical texts of the Islamic tradition. These processes, which are intimately linked to modernization, globalization, and the spread of literacy, have reshaped Islamic cultures throughout Turkey and the wider Muslim world. At the local level, revivalism proceeds by promoting the practices and values of Islam or religion (*din*), while differentiating them from (and devaluing) the practices of folk tradition (*gelenek*)—or, more pejoratively, superstition (*batıl inanç*). In practice, such distinctions have often been fought out around spatial forms, as ritual landscapes once marked by folk and pre-Islamic elements have been cleansed or purified.²⁸

In Urfa, the rise of Islamic revival was inseparable from the operation of state power and, specifically, processes of state-led modernization. In the last quarter of the twentieth century, a series of land-based interventions (including land reform, economic restructuring, and mass village-to-urban migration) rapidly transformed the province. These modernization efforts had a number of aims. The explicitly stated one was to integrate Urfa into Turkey's wider political economy by transforming it into an agro-industrial export basin. Another aim was undoubtedly to assimilate the province's Arab and (especially) Kurdish residents, whose complicated relationship to the Turkish state has ranged from strategic alliance to open conflict.²⁹ The resultant changes included shifts in labor and production, shifts in the size and structure of families, and rapid increases in literacy, formal education, and knowledge of Turkish. Although these decades of modernization were by no means motivated by revivalist concerns, they nonetheless laid the groundwork necessary for revivalism to emerge and flourish. For instance, it was the increase in rates of literacy and education in Urfa that enabled the rise of a generation of formally educated, textually trained men and women, who acted as local catalysts for religious reform.

Trained and licensed by the Ministry of Religious Affairs (Diyanet), and serving as imams, radio hosts, and *hocas* (religious instructors), local reformers acted as intermediaries between Urfa's inhabitants and a state-sanctioned Sunni Islam. In recent years, they have succeeded in raising questions about central and enduring features of Urfa's ritual landscape—including, for instance, the visitation of special places (such as shrines, tells, and the birthplace of Abraham) and the ritual use of objects (for example, strings, beads, and the beard of the Prophet). From a theological perspective, the salient question concerns mediation (*tawassul*)—that is, whether anyone or anything can mediate between a believer and God. The revivalist answer is unequivocally no. "The Prophet gave us the Quran as his trace, not his beard, or his coat," one imam told me. The latter could only be considered innovations (*bidat*) without textual foundation in Islam. Perhaps as important as these theological concerns are issues of social capital. Visiting a saint's tomb, for instance, is marked as not only theologically suspect, but also as rural and lower class—which in Urfa simultaneously carries an ethnic valence, an association with "backward" Kurds and Arabs as opposed to "modern" Turks.[30]

It is against this shifting backdrop that we must understand the transformation of Balıklıgöl in the late 1990s, courtesy of the multimillion-dollar, state-backed restoration project mentioned above. Today, Balıklıgöl is a gleaming monument to modernist religiosity. But prior to the restorations, the mosques were run-down, not to say derelict, with moss growing along the outer walls and caper bushes pushing out through cracks in the façades. Makeshift houses crowded in around the mosques and climbed to the edge of the citadel. The site was largely given over to folk religiosity—to the informal and charismatic practices that constitute religious life in southeastern Turkey. Ostensibly, the restorations were intended to transform the site into an open-air museum—a cultural heritage site and a tourist attraction. The restorations entailed the expropriation and demolition of the housing surrounding the site, which was deemed an eyesore and a safety hazard (for example, in its violation of building codes). All of the major mosques and monuments were restored and outfitted with plaques. The religious site was formalized, and set off from the ordinary residential life of the city in a new way.

Although the state-led restoration of Balıklıgöl was not an overtly theological project, it nonetheless imposed new constraints on how people could interact with ritual space, curtailing a wide range of traditional practices. Henceforth there would be no sacrificing of animals, no ritual ablutions in the spring water, no candles, no writing on the walls. Official signs posted throughout the ritual site designate such activities as both *haram* and *yasak* (that is, "forbidden" in both religious and secular language). The purification of Islam and the state-led renovation of Urfa's ritual space are thus resonant processes, working to advance a religious culture that is at once theologically sound, state-sanctioned, modern, middle class, and sanitized.

Yet Urfa's layered histories persist—not only as material traces, but also folded into perceptions, practices, and sensibilities. Despite the impressive conjunction of state-sanctioned religious reform with projects of spatial purification, people nonetheless inhabit and encounter space obliquely (with its intensities, memories, and virtualities). The opening scene dramatizes this point on a large scale: on that night, it was as though years of effort to purify the space had been undone—the folk past breaking into the reformist present, destabilizing it, and denying its taken-for-grantedness. In the final section of the chapter, I turn to the story of one woman to explore how an individual might orient herself in these shifting, and often contradictory, landscapes.

SUBJECTIVITY BEYOND SEDIMENTATION

On an uncharacteristically drizzly Saturday in September 2011, I strolled with Zehra among the fountains and monuments of Balıklıgöl. A Quran instructor and religious reformer, Zehra was among my most trusted interlocutors, and it was largely through our conversations that I learned the story of Islamic reform as it had unfolded in Urfa. This was a story that she had experienced firsthand. Born in the 1970s in a Kurdish village outside of Urfa, Zehra's life had unfolded against the backdrop of Urfa's rapid modernization. She not only experienced but helped bring about the transition from rural to urban religiosity, from folk practice to Islam proper. One might expect Zehra to narrate this reformist trajectory in linear terms—and at times she did. But this was a day of leisure, and we allowed our steps and our conversation to wander. As we walked among the ritual sites, Zehra shared with me memories and stories elicited by different loci, her narration tacking between past and present. "*Her adımda bir anı var*" (a memory with every step), she mused.

We bowed our heads low, entering the cave of Abraham. Zehra ran her fingers along the uneven surface of the walls, tracing the lines of supplication scrawled there, pausing on a talismanic charm made of dried chickpeas and string. Such objects constitute the tangible stuff of popular religiosity in Urfa: for example, the keeping of talismanic objects (like stones chipped from holy sites), healing practices that involve the tying of strings and drinking of curative water, prohibitions against bathing on Wednesdays, and common speech forms like maledictions. If these practices sound odd or unrelated in list form, it is precisely because they are nonsystematized, part of daily life, the mostly unremarkable stuff of habit. But not for Zehra, or not any longer. "When we learned to read the Quran," she told me, "we realized that such things had no religious basis." She learned, that is, that God alone has power, and that no person or object can mediate between a believer and God. She came to recognize such practices as mere superstitions or innovations, and left them behind. In adopting other practices (like prayer, attending mosque, and reading the Quran), she remade herself as a modern Islamic subject.

Describing Zehra's trajectory in this way implies that how people change themselves is a linear process. And indeed this is how scholars of Islam have tended to conceptualize religious change at the level of the subject. Through external actions, people progressively cultivate internal states. But, thinking back to Alice, we might develop a more nuanced notion of the relationship between practice and subjectivity. Consider that, with revival, people like Zehra were challenged to revise their habitual relationships with ritual space and ritual practice. Those relationships are not only cognitive, but affective, embodied, memorial. And if we look in a fine-grained way at how people go about changing these relationships, a different image emerges of time and of subjectivity.

I find a revealing instance in a short video clip taken by one of Zehra's students. The video shows a picnic, with some twenty women gathered in a circle, singing a devotional song. Immediately after the song ends, there is a moment's pause, when a few people clap but most hold back. Then everyone claps. Several of the girls begin discussing whether or not it is forbidden (*yasak*) to clap after a song that mentions the name of God. All of them were familiar with such a prohibition, but there was confusion among them as to whether the prohibition was *dini* (religious) or whether it was one of the *eski* or *batıl* ("old" or "false") beliefs (it turned out to be the latter). For Zehra, and now her students, habits like this one no longer passed below the threshold of attention; instead, they presented themselves as moments of doubt, minor disruptions in the ongoing flow of life. In the video clip, for instance, one can actually see that hiatus between the inclination to clap and the decision to do so, the hesitation that spread through the group before resolving itself in the fullness of applause.

I noticed such dissonant moments often during my time with Zehra—and more broadly during my time in Urfa, as the opening scene highlighted. When cultural logics are changing, one can expect to encounter such dissonances—for instance, between old cultural logics and new ones; or between entrenched habits at the level of the body and new judgments at the level of thought. These disjunctive presents call us to imagine the temporality of religious reform not as linear (the time of discipline), but as punctuated by breaks, revisions, and redirections (the time of becoming). This image of time helps us notice an element of creativity and unpredictability in processes of social and religious change. And it helps us imagine Zehra's story as more than an ethnographic illustration of a historical transition from folk tradition to Islam. Zehra was the first in her family to speak Turkish fluently, to read and write, to leave the village for the city, and to abandon folk practice in favor of something different. She narrates her biography not as a straightforward trajectory, but as a series of rifts—and, often enough, risks: choices between village and city life, between marrying her betrothed or the imam she'd fallen in love with, and between speaking to her students (and her children) in Kurdish or Turkish.[31]

But these alternative paths did not simply disappear—they are "made present" in the landscape and so in social life—and Zehra encountered them continually. Another brief vignette will help clarify this point—this one drawn from a meal that I shared with Zehra's extended family in the village where she'd grown up. During the meal, Zehra's uncle had cursed his wife, saying "May you go to the blue lake." Zehra, who had been immersed in the flow of conversation, paused and turned to me. She repeated the comment in Turkish (it had initially escaped me because it was in Kurdish). The phrase, she explained, was a *bedua* (a curse or malediction)—a fairly common speech form, but one she now refrained from using. This particular phrase ("May you go to the blue lake") had caught her ear. She asked her uncle the meaning, and he shrugged, saying it was just an expression and he didn't really think it meant anything. But for Zehra, who had developed a reflexive orientation to such habits, the phrase stood out. She wondered aloud whether it might refer to Lake Van in eastern Turkey, which is widely considered the ancestral home of Yezidis—a once widespread religious group for whom the color blue is prohibited. That is, Zehra interpreted her uncle's phrase as a survival from an earlier period of the region's religious history. I find remarkable in this conversation the layering of histories and languages, and the complex orientation that this demands of participants (the disruption of the conversational flow, the play of immersion and distanciation). It seems that when otherness is a quotidian feature of social and spatial life,[32] one's relationship to the present moment may be marked by multiple temporalities and spatialities.

This complex positionality is more than an annoyance or an obstacle to overcome. It is also, I would suggest, generative of a certain ethos of openness and receptivity to perspectives that differ from one's own. How might this inflect religious sensibilities? Consider Zehra's religious life, which appears to be marked by a certain playfulness or experimentalism. For instance, when I asked Zehra and her husband (an imam) about the annual showing of the beard of the Prophet she revealed that she had once gone to see it. When her husband expressed surprise (she had evidently never mentioned this before), Zehra shrugged: "I was curious." Thus even as individuals like Zehra work to purify the landscape, the landscape "recoils back" on individual desires and sensibilities—injecting an element of uncertainty or openness into personal trajectories that we might otherwise deem linear.[33] Zehra's receptivity to difference was also evident in the way that she related to people in her capacity as a religious instructor. One afternoon at Zehra's home, a young boy and his mother came to ask Zehra's help in treating a wart on the boy's back. Zehra agreed and proceeded to tie a string around the wart and read a verse of the Quran before sending the child home. Later, when I inquired about the string, she cited a popular belief that a wart will fall off if one ties a string around it and says a prayer. The string part was a superstition, she assured me, but the boy and his mother believed it, and she couldn't see any harm in trying it. "Responsibility to the other demands disjointing our time in order to allow the presenting of others," philosopher Tamsin Lorraine writes, "even when such presenting violates our own sense of 'the proper.' "[34]

Perhaps for those who, like Zehra, inhabit shifting, heterogeneous landscapes, the contingency and historicity of being may be closer to consciousness. It certainly suffused Zehra's sensibilities as a religious reformer, inflecting a potentially purist project with a sense of contingency and even reversibility—an attentiveness to how things were (and might still be) otherwise. As we walked through the ritual site that day, Zehra spoke nostalgically of times when, as a child, she would visit the site with her mother. "We used to chip stones from the cave walls, and bring them home, and put them in water and drink it to cure illness," she recalled. It was long before the restorations, she said, and the site was dirty and disorganized, so that by the end of the day the hem of one's skirt would be crusted in dust. Yet, she reflected, "this place was more beautiful then, people had more of a connection to religion." But then—as if coming to the present, or coming to her senses—she continued: "One must be careful, though, not to put one's faith in anything other than God." In other words, I take it, one must resist the occasional pull of old saints and old stones. She paused a moment, then said, "One has to always be vigilant."

CONCLUSION

This chapter has suggested that in Urfa, the landscape registers or "makes present" a range of large-scale religious and political formations into which the city has been drawn over the years, one of which is the current reformist project. These layered histories continue to resonate and disrupt the present—so that people like the three women I introduced here effectively find themselves amid shifting strata, the textures of which are tactile, as they walk the streets and encounter material worlds that are at once familiar and strange. For me, the key question is: How do they (and others) orient themselves in relation to these felt shifts among normative orders? How do people navigate landscapes in flux?[35]

Addressing this question calls us to connect the question of historical change (often glossed as the "large-scale") to the question of phenomenological experience (the "small-scale"). I have tried to show that moving among scales is not only a scholarly imperative, but something that people do in their daily lives. Zehra turns from the intimate flow of familial conversation, suddenly reframing it with reference to the region's Yezidi past. Or, in the opening scene, my friends grow large with the crowd, only to shrink back from it—perhaps imagining how they might appear in a photograph, in the future, through other eyes. In doing so, they grow bigger still, with reference to a larger religious imaginary thought to transcend the local. This is all to say that our actions are oriented toward wider scales of significance—which are themselves multiple, overlapping, and contested.

By highlighting the complex spatiotemporal orientations of my interlocutors, I hope to have raised some doubts about an approach that imagines religious practice as a straightforward trajectory, a telos. Like Alice, Zehra must continually alter her dimensions, growing bigger and smaller, changing along with—and sometimes in contrast to—the ritual landscape. It is precisely this double direction that, for Deleuze, makes Carroll's Alice a model for becoming.[36] Discipline moves in one direction, with the past building gradually toward the present. But becoming "moves in both directions at once. It always eludes the present, causing future and past, more and less, too much and not enough to coincide in the simultaneity of a rebellious matter."[37] I have suggested that the matter of Urfa's ritual landscape is "rebellious" in just this sense. It is a medium through which people open themselves to the overlaps and disjunctions of history, and strive to heed its contradictory calls.

NOTES

1. The night falls during one of the odd-numbered days in the last ten days of Ramadan. Although no one knows the exact date of the original event, it is conventionally celebrated on the twenty-seventh day of Ramadan.
2. Quran 97:3.
3. See Deeb, *An Enchanted Modern*; Hirschkind, *The Ethical Soundscape*; Schultz, "(Re)Turning to Proper Muslim Practice"; Silverstein, "Islamist Critique in Modern Turkey."
4. Largely following Asad, *Formations of the Secular*, and *Genealogies of Religion*.
5. Mahmood, *Politics of Piety*.
6. See Hammoudi, "Textualism and Anthropology"; Mittermaier, "Dreams from Elsewhere"; Schielke, "Being Good in Ramadan."
7. Carroll, *Alice's Adventures in Wonderland*. See also Deleuze, *Essays Critical and Clinical*, 21–22.
8. See, for example, Hart, *And Then We Work for God*; Mahmood, *Politics of Piety*.
9. See Bachelard, *The Poetics of Space*; Connolly, *A World of Becoming*; Coole and Frost, *New Materialisms*; Grosz, *Architecture from the Outside*; Ingold, *Being Alive*.
10. Bainbridge, *Turkey*, 607.
11. Bainbridge, *Turkey*, 607, 609.
12. In 1939 the region's independent Kurdish militias chose to fight with Turkish armed forces rather than the would-be French occupiers, and thereby helped deliver Urfa to the Turkish state instead of what was then the French protectorate of Syria.
13. Öktem, "Incorporating the Time and Space of the Ethnic 'Other.'"
14. It should be noted that the region's major development project, Güneydoğu Anadolu Projesi (GAP) got under way in the mid-1990s, which also marked the beginning of the Kurdish uprising. This is surely not a coincidence, and one Turkish academic in conversation with me dismissed GAP as little more than "an effort to rebrand Kurdistan."
15. See Bozdoğan and Kasaba, *Rethinking Modernity and National Identity in Turkey*.

16　See Hart, *And Then We Work for God*; Tuğal, *Passive Revolution*.
17　This version of state-sanctioned Islam is clearly not the only version of Islamic practice in Turkey, nor is it universally espoused. Yet it can reasonably be considered hegemonic, in part because it has supplanted or absorbed more radical Sunni movements in Turkey that had historically operated in opposition to the state (Tuğal, *Passive Revolution*).
18　Hart, *And Then We Work for God*; Tuğal, "The Urban Dynamism of Islamic Hegemony."
19　See Foucault, *Ethics*. The paradigmatic example of space in the former sense is the panopticon: by inhabiting the panopticon one internalizes the gaze of the authority and becomes a self-governing subject. The paradigmatic example of the latter is the skilled pianist: through iterative practice at the piano, one internalizes or habituates rules, so that they become unconscious orientations. For the difference between "power" and "ethics," see especially 223–28.
20　Foucault, *Of Other Spaces*, 6.
21　Stasch, "The Poetics of Village Space When Villages Are New," 556.
22　J. Segal, *Edessa*.
23　J. Segal, *Edessa*.
24　See Guidetti and Getti, "The Byzantine Heritage in the Dār al-Islām: Churches and Mosques in al-Ruha between the Sixth and Twelfth Centuries"; Guscin, *The Image of Edessa*.
25　Quoted in J. Segal, *Edessa*, 56.
26　P. Brown, *The Cult of the Saints*.
27　When the historian Judah Segal visited Urfa in the 1960s, he witnessed Muslims sleeping at Balıklıgöl, which he interpreted as a continuation of ancient rites of "incubation" practiced in Christian Edessa. The city "was celebrated for a well of healing waters that was . . . a holy place in the Christian period and later," he writes. "Rites of incubation are performed there, indeed, to the present day" (*Edessa*, 54). Several religious teachers whom I spoke with in Urfa considered this suggestion interesting and plausible, but they did not comment further on it. It should also be mentioned that there is a practice like "incubation" in Islam called *istikhara*. See Edgar, *The Dream in Islam*, chapter 3.
28　See Elias, *Aisha's Cushion*; Hammoudi, *A Season in Mecca*; Ho, *The Graves of Tarim*; Tuğal, "The Urban Dynamism of Islamic Hegemony"; Walton, "Practices of Neo-Ottomanism."
29　See Üngör, *The Making of Modern Turkey*; Van Bruinessen, *Agha, Shaikh, and State*.
30　See Hart, *And Then We Work for God*, and "The Orthodoxization of Ritual Practice in Western Anatolia."
31　Zehra describes her decision to teach religion in Turkish rather than Kurdish as a pragmatic but conflicted choice: "For me, Turkish is the language of learning, the intellectual language. When I am explaining the *hadith* [a collection of Mohammed's sayings] or *sunnet* [the tradition of ceremonial male circumcision], I find I am unable to express their meaning in Kurdish. Sometimes people say to me, 'We don't understand, explain it to us in Kurdish,' but I honestly can't. Unfortunately, Kurdish has been lost to me as an intellectual language. In this way, we [Kurds] have been assimilated a bit."
32　Stasch, "The Poetics of Village Space When Villages Are New."

33 Connolly, *Neuropolitics*, 18.
34 Lorraine, "Living a Time out of Joint," 45.
35 Biehl and Locke, "Deleuze and the Anthropology of Becoming."
36 Deleuze, *The Logic of Sense*.
37 Deleuze, *The Logic of Sense*, 2.

5

Witness

Humans, Animals, and the Politics of Becoming

NAISARGI N. DAVE

Maneka Gandhi, a member of India's famed political dynasty, the Nehru-Gandhis, is India's best-known animal rights activist. In the introduction to one of her books she explains what brought her to her activism.[1] She refers to the memoir of one of India's first animal welfare activists, Crystal Rogers, a British woman born in 1906 who found herself called by the sight of a dying animal in 1959 to stay and work in India. The passage Gandhi quotes from Rogers's memoir, *Mad Dogs and an Englishwoman*, reads as follows:[2]

> I was on my way to New Zealand when I saw a horse which caused me to remain in India. It was standing at the side of a very busy road, with the crows tearing the flesh off its back. As I ran towards it, it turned its head towards me and to my horror I saw that it had bleeding sockets from which the crows had already pecked out its eyes. I rang up the SPCA [Society for the Prevention of Cruelty to Animals] but there was little that could be done and the horse had to be shot. If any passerby had done something earlier the horse might have been saved. I cancelled my journey to New Zealand and stayed in India to see what I could do for animal suffering. We need to fight on every front. If we run away and hide our heads to avoid seeing the sight which horrifies us, we are unworthy of the compassion that has been granted us by the Almighty.[3]

After citing this passage, Gandhi writes: "Crystal is one of the people who opened my eyes twenty years ago and showed me how to work for what I believed in instead of merely showing concern."[4]

I want to begin this chapter by considering the variety of ways that both Rogers and Gandhi invoke sight and the eyes. Rogers sees a horse that compels her to stay; Rogers sees, but the horse, its eyes pecked out by crows, cannot see; we are told we must see the sight that horrifies us; and Gandhi's eyes are opened by a story about sight, its willful absence, and its graphic, pitiable loss. This centrality of sight and of human witnessing of acts of violence against animals is a standard trope in activist narratives. The trope is similar to a coming-out story, and animal rights activists in India (and perhaps elsewhere) stake their commitment to a way of life based on one critical moment after which nothing can ever be the same. I argue in this chapter that animal rights activists describe this critical moment as an intimate event in which the sight of a suffering animal, and the locking of eyes between human and nonhuman, inaugurates a bond demanding from the person a life of responsibility. That event is uniquely intimate because it occurs between two singular beings—because based on the locking of eyes, the human's knowledge is not of all animals in general, but of this animal at this moment. The moment is uniquely intimate, too, because it expands ordinary understandings of the self and its possible social relations. As Elizabeth Povinelli puts it, an intimate event "exfoliates the social skin."[5]

This chapter has two main objectives. First, I address how people come to act on behalf of animals in India. In doing so, I sketch moral biographies of action and inaction. These biographies connect with my second objective, to examine the sensorium of political engagement between humans and animals. Why this emphasis on sight, and the valorization of the witness? While I suggest that the event of intimacy between human and animal has the potential to blow the conceit of humanity apart, another reading is possible: that the act of intimacy, insofar as it relies on the witnessing human subject, constructs the animal as theoretical, as a mere object in the autobiography of the woman who sees and consequently acts.[6] Does animal activism thus reproduce the supposed value of human being—a valuation that underlies the mass exploitation of animals in the first place—a reproduction of what Giorgio Agamben calls "the lethal and bloody logic" of the anthropological machine, which requires the perpetual differentiation of human and its other to function?[7] Or is that reading itself a sign of humanism's triumph—is seeing humanism everywhere only a capitulation to its colonization of imagination and thought?[8]

If so, what would it mean to believe that in the ethical encounter between human and animal a woman can indeed become an animal, not theoretically but carnally, morally, spiritually? This chapter engages with the sensorium of animal activism and its life inside and outside the anthropological machine. But first, some context.

MORAL BIOGRAPHIES, AFFECTIVE HISTORIES

Animal activism in India is inseparable from a larger affective history of liberalism, a history that, in turn, is deeply entwined with the history and politics of empire.[9] If we were to simply replace *horse* or *animal* in Rogers's recollections with *female child* or *Hindu woman*, her memoir would read no differently, for example, than Katherine Mayo's 1927 anti-India polemic, *Mother India*—a book that, in its stark portrayal of everyday acts of astonishing violence against women and girls, served as a powerful tool of empire, arguing that the British needed to remain in India to protect its most vulnerable from barbarity and neglect.[10] Indeed, animal welfare in contemporary India (like pro-women reform in colonial India) is largely driven by foreigners. The biggest animal shelters and nongovernmental organizations (NGOs), except for Maneka Gandhi's, were founded by foreigners who came to India on vacation or for work and found themselves, like Rogers, compelled by the sight of suffering to stay there—or at least to try and transform the place from afar. People for the Ethical Treatment of Animals (PETA) has an office in Bombay, and the Humane Society International has a hub in Hyderabad.

Of course, a homegrown animal welfare politics exists, too: cow protection (*gauseva*). But even this is only superficially homegrown. Cow protection was conceived as an anticolonial endeavor and thus emerged in an unequal encounter with the foreign.[11] And in any case, cow protection does not really constitute a politics of animal welfare: it exclusively concerns the cow, and the cow as a symbol separating people who eat or slaughter them (Christians, Muslims, and lower-caste Hindus) from those who do not (higher-caste Hindus).[12] Because of this deep cultural association of animal protection with caste violence and Hindu nationalism, people (including the human rights activists I have worked with)[13] express their cosmopolitanism and progressive politics in part by deliberately and ostentatiously eating meat, a performance in the "aggressively visible public theater" that is eating in colonial and postcolonial India.[14] In their eyes animal activists are, at best, elite and out of touch with important human issues and, at worst, harbor high-caste, anti-Muslim sentiments. Try as some animal activists do to disassociate their work from right-wing politics, rumblings about Muslim butchers, the slaughterhouse's stench of death (reminiscent of language about Dalit leatherworkers), and beef-eating Christians continue to sound from within animal rights organizations.[15]

Animal rights activism faces challenges from India's changing economy as well. The conspicuous consumption of animal products, from leather to meats, has increased among elite and upwardly mobile groups during India's global economic rise. In part, this rise has been accomplished through the massive trade in animals, with India becoming the biggest exporter of leather in Asia and the biggest producer of milk in the world.[16] But under whose watch did India become such a renowned specialist in the mass exploitation of cows? Well, of course—because every good story needs irony—under that of the cow protectionists themselves, the Hindu right-wing Bharatiya Janata Party (BJP). And who but India's foremost animal activist and former *bahu* of the Indian National Congress Party is a star politician of the BJP?[17] Of course, Maneka Gandhi.

Gandhi's moral biography is as captivating and mercurial as she is. She was not yet sixteen when, at a cousin's party, a man approached her and asked if she would share her plate of mutton with him; she declined.[18] And so did Maneka Anand first meet Sanjay Gandhi, son of the prime minister, Indira Gandhi, and grandson of India's first prime minister, Jawaharlal Nehru—over a plate of lamb. Maneka, who was so apolitical that she did not know who Sanjay was, would marry into one of the world's great political dynasties and, as it happened, into a family of animal and environment protectionists. Nehru had made it his personal mission as prime minister to pass the Prevention of Cruelty against Animals (PCA) Act in 1960.[19] His daughter, Indira Gandhi, sponsored progressive environmental legislation and was known for her ambitious conservation initiative, Project Tiger.

Animal lovers perhaps, but the Nehru-Gandhis were meat eaters all, until one night at dinner when Maneka began pontificating about the treatment of animals. She was just putting a spoonful of meaty soup to her mouth when Sanjay said: "How can you go on about animal cruelty while eating meat? Stop eating meat or shut up." And just like that, she had an epiphany. So obvious to her was her hypocrisy that she dropped the spoon that very instant, the soup scalding her wrist. "See?" she said to me as she pulled up the sleeve of her kurta, "the scar is still there."[20] I will return to this point: the wound as trace, the scar as birthmark.[21]

That same year, the year she turned eighteen, she asked her husband for some property under an overpass in South Delhi, which he gave her as a birthday gift. In turn, she gave it to a friend, who started an animal shelter called Friendicoes. "So that was the beginning of your activism?" I asked. She laughed and replied: "What a stupid beginning! My husband was the boss of this city. My mother-in-law was the prime minister of India. And I asked for a shop under a flyover. This is one of my problems. And it was one of my husband's problems, too. Everybody talks about how wicked he was, but the truth is that he was just young. He had no idea what power he had. Neither of us did."[22]

People do talk about his wickedness. It is some sort of awful irony (once again) that he led a mass sterilization program of India's poor during his mother's autocratic emergency regime in 1975–77, anecdotally aided by Maneka Gandhi—who is responsible for instituting the increasingly popular Animal Birth Control program to sterilize stray dogs.[23] Since her husband's death in a plane crash in 1980, and her banishment from home and party at the hands of her mother-in-law shortly afterward, she has devoted herself to animals, founding India's largest animal rights organization, People for Animals.[24] She exploits her name for all it is worth. "I thank God every day," she told me once, "for making me a Gandhi." She works seven days a week, from morning to night, usually sitting behind a cluttered desk, wearing plain cotton *salwar kameez* (never silk or wool), thin from years of wear. She advocates on behalf of cows, pigs, dogs, cats, donkeys, and chickens by writing weekly newspaper columns; lobbying fellow members of parliament; and threatening over the phone to have people beaten, hanged upside down in their underwear, killed, maimed, and disappeared. Given her history, nobody takes these as idle threats. Putting her violence aside if possible—most of which consists of idle threats—Gandhi is tireless in her labors. The heavy bags under her eyes, the softening body, the more frequent battles with illness—all testify to the strains of a passion that will not let her go. "Why must you work so hard?" I asked her once while on a doctor-mandated walk. "Aren't you worried about the consequences, the enemies you make, the stress?"

It turns out I had asked the wrong question; she has nothing to do with it. She answered that she was "a machine that is designed to do this, exactly this, only this. It is a machine so sensitive," she continued, "that its skin literally prickles with another's pain. But there is no inside to the machine. There is just this skin." There is no inside—there is just this skin. What Gandhi pointed out to me was the limitation of my worldview, my assumption that she was a subject with volition, one who could stop and start at will. Perhaps she was once such a subject, but the day the soup scalded her skin she became something new: she became subject to the world, rather than insisting on being a subject in it. At the heart of this transformation lay a moment of radical humility, and her guiding principle: surrender. The activists she takes on as protégés are few, for they must be hardy sorts with thick skin as well as the kind that prickles, and they must share with Gandhi one thing: that "in the face of that which is bigger than you, stronger than you, you give yourself over to it, you surrender." The universe is such a thing (bigger, stronger) and what Gandhi pushed me to see is that the readiness to be transformed, even if by an unrelenting stream of stimuli (painful, god-awful) is not an act of extraordinary courage but the only thing that makes any sense. We are all bound to lose, standing up to the world. The only way to survive is to give ourselves over, to trust that we will be alternately battered and buoyed. And survive she must, to keep "sticking my fingers into all the holes in the dam." This sounds futile, but to her, and to the activists she trains, so is the notion of the rational actor, of someone who changes the world at will. And if everything is futile, including our very being, then what is so terrible about working in futility? And work she does.

THE PERPETUAL WITNESS

So I was surprised when she said to me one day, from behind her desk, wearing a tense, world-weary expression: "I only wish there were a slaughterhouse next door. To witness that violence, to hear those screams . . . I would *never* be able to rest."[25] As far as I could tell she never rested anyway, even without piercing screams to keep her pulse racing and her eyes open. She never rested, nor did the others: Abodh, the director of Welfare for Stray Dogs, whose personal cell phone serves as the default animal emergency line for all of Bombay and who has not had an uninterrupted night of sleep in fifteen years, and whose wife, however kind, is running out of patience; Abodh's fieldworker, Dipesh, who treats animals on the streets six days a week, voluntarily heals his own neighborhood animals on Sundays, and in his spare time—such as it is—works at another job to keep his ailing parents alive; Maya, who finally got engaged but had no time for love, and so lost it. All of them have witnessed something that allows them no respite; all, like Gandhi, having once been transformed are now forever compelled by something that, on the face of it, usurps their very (well-)being. I want to explore this thing called witnessing, specifically three things about it: first, the idea of witnessing as distinct from merely seeing; second, how witnessing requires a disciplined presence, or the witness's thereness; and third, the importance of movement in the witnessing of violence, both a movement toward the subject of intimacy and away from the self and its protective skin.

To witness, as Rogers and Gandhi each have used the term, means to see in a manner that is present, to root oneself when one might instead run or turn away. The same stubborn presence characterizes voyeurism of horror, but that differs from witnessing in two crucial ways. In witnessing and being present to pain as these activists describe it, they seek to place themselves in a situation in which they could—if brave enough—change the events that they are framed and marked by.[26] To witness is to be implicated and culpable in an event that is not inexorable. Furthermore, a voyeur heightens the affective experience of being alive in his or her own skin ("I have survived this moment and now I feel euphoric"), whereas in witnessing, that skin is shed, so that something in the person ceases to exist after the event is over. The fiction of the self is blown apart.

Or is it? Maybe the better question is: must it be?

I am suggesting an understanding of witnessing that blows the self apart, but witnessing can create truth as much as it can explode it, can concern the safely encased human self as much as the radically exfoliated one. Consider *witness* not as the thing one does but as the imperative. "Witness," says René Descartes, "the fact that the beasts have less reason than men . . . that they have no reason at all."[27] This is the other meaning of witness, witnessing as "we see that," witnessing as an appeal to evidence presumed to be commonly shared, witnessing—because of our privileged linking of ocularity to reason—that demands that each of us be in lockstep with the others who see. In witnessing, vision is not always singularly intimate; it is its opposite—common sense. That seems reason enough to be skeptical of the privileging of sight and of the politics of witnessing.

Jacques Derrida reminds us of another reason to be wary.[28] Witnessing, he says, is autobiographical, it is proof that I am, that we are. The animal is objectively staged for this purpose, it is seen but does not itself see, such as the animal in Descartes's discourse when he renders it an automaton, appealing to a man who witnesses an animal that does not see him in turn. This is the animal that exists as theoretical spectacle, an object for the human that says, "I am, because I see that." ("See that" here has two meanings: I see that thing, and I see that this is true.) Derrida calls the witnessed animal the "spectacle for a specular subject."[29] That specular subject becomes the subject he or she is in the act of seeing, but not through the act of being reflected back in the animal's gaze. This is the Levinasian animal, the one that does not have a face capable of compelling a relationship of ethical obligation.[30]

That is the Levinasian animal, but what kind of animal is Rogers's horse—the one with crows tearing the flesh off its back, and with bleeding sockets from which those crows have already pecked out its eyes? Does this animal have a face? Is this animal a theoretical spectacle, objectively staged for Rogers's story of "I am?" I don't know. That animal senses Rogers running toward it, and it turns to "face" Rogers. The animal, in other words, responds. Rogers is transformed, recognizing in herself an ethical responsibility at the moment of seeing the animal other. I have a hard time seeing her as only a specular subject. The specular subject becomes such through an act of differentiation owed to an ocular-centric logic of sameness and difference: "Because I see that ["see that" in both senses of seeing that thing and seeing reason], that is not me." The specular subject, furthermore, can only see himself reflected in his own gaze; the animal's gaze cannot reflect to him his soul.[31] Rogers is not that specular subject because she, I think, does see her soul reflected in the gaze of the animal: but that soul, like the sockets of the animal's eyes, is empty. The witnessing subject, in this case, is violently stripped away, revealed to be, and becoming, emptiness—the emptiness that, Agamben argues, is the nothing-space between human and animal, the space of ontological vulnerability.[32]

Yet we cannot take this nothingness too far. As Veena Das reminds us, the witness of violence is only a witness because she survives it—because she has witnessed, in fact, she has an obligation to live.[33] Recall Gandhi, who knows she must survive to keep working, and who knows that to survive she has no choice but to surrender. But she survives not as what she once was, before she became a perpetual witness. The scar she still wears from the night of the soup is indeed, as Sara Ahmed would suggest, a birthmark, a reminder of what she became: just skin.[34] To witness, then, might best be understood as a radical interpenetration of life and death: to maintain a disciplined presence to violence that opens up a death that then compels a new kind of responsible life in a previously unimaginable skin. In the case of animal activists, it is a skin also inhabited by the animal.

Carmelia Satija, a middle-aged Hindu animal rights activist in Delhi does not appear, on the face of it, to wear a skin unusual for a person of her social position. I first met her in the summer of 2010 while trying to track down an animal rights organization called Kindness to Animals and Respect for Environment (KARE). The address I had located through a website appeared erroneous. Instead of an NGO office or animal shelter, I found myself in front of Rio Grande, a small store with an armed guard in an upscale marketplace in South Delhi. It turned out that Satija was both the owner of the shop and the founding trustee of KARE, by then defunct. After learning from her sales clerk that I was there, she drove to her shop in a black SUV to meet me. We greeted each other, and she led me through the store to her second-floor office, where she offered me a seat across from her at her desk. She has an oval face, long black hair, and deep-set eyes. Her movements are elegant, with softly jangling jewelry and a clipped accent. Her perfume mixed with the jasmine incense wafting through her shop.

"So," she began, "does this really interest you, this activism of mine?" I answered that it did, and although she was unbelieving at first, she began to bring out reports, pamphlets, court filings, and photographs, all filed away behind store financial documents and inventories. (The basement of her house held much more material, filling entire shelving units.) "Thirty years of my life," she said, her face showing a mix of guilt and sadness. When I asked her to tell me about those years she began with images.[35]

The slaughterhouse footage she had in her possession, Satija said, was "more valuable to me than gold." She continued: "Those images reminded me of how horrible the world is, of the pain we cause. Even without watching the videos, just knowing that they were in the cabinet served a purpose. They would never let me stop." She then told me about her illicit visits to the Idgah slaughterhouse in New Delhi, whose horrors she filmed and later had shown on the state-owned broadcast service, Doordarshan (an effort by the government, no doubt, to whip up anti-Muslim sentiment under the guise of compassion). The Idgah slaughterhouse has the capacity to process 2,500 animals per day for meat, leather, and by-products, but instead it butchers upward of 13,000 animals daily, around 3,000 buffaloes and 10,000 goats.[36] The animals are brought in from miles away, thrown from the trucks into heaps by their limbs, most with their legs already broken, and some already crushed to death during the journey. Boys and men begin the process of hacking the animals into pieces and skinning them with rusty knives, the butchers barefoot and shin-deep in blood and shit. There are few sights more heartbreaking—or for those less sentimental than I, more ironic—than of sickly cows eating from the nearly one thousand pounds of cattle excrement, body parts, and clotted blood that the Idgah slaughterhouse dumps at a nearby landfill, a playground for kite-flying slum children, every day.

Telling me about her visits to Idgah, Satija continued: "It's not just the sights that you always remember. Worse even than the looks in the animals' eyes, worse than the screams, was the *stench* of death. It's not only the stench of blood and gore, it's the stench of *death*. Even now, I wake up in the middle of the night with that stench in my nostrils." The value for Satija of witnessing slaughter is that it forces her always to move, to stave off rest and the pretenses that enable it. The activism, then, compelled by witnessing (which, as I have suggested, is partly defined by a disciplined staying put in the face of horror) is also a kind of running—fervent movement away from the bounded self that only impotently remembers, and toward that which suffers on account of one's own life. This defining dynamic of witnessing as staying put in the face of death, only to then constantly move away from our own impotence and toward the other in a relation of intimacy that thins the human skin and thickens relationality, is one described by many of the people who have populated my narrative. Recall how Rogers runs toward the dying horse and keeps moving until her death thirty-five years later, homeless and almost penniless; Gandhi anticipates never resting while in the earshot of the nightmarish cacophony of death; the stench of death in Satija's nostrils tears her out of the tenuous refuge of sleep. These relationships among witnessing, animal activism, and the impossibility of respite also come into play in people's decisions not to involve themselves in the lives of animals. A woman in her early twenties explained to me why she did not volunteer at an animal shelter in Chennai, saying that she was "deathly afraid of caring too much." Is any other politics, I wonder, constrained by such a mortal fear of caring too much, of the heart bursting, the skin thinning, not being able to rest again? In other words, is any other politics so limited by the fear of intimacy, or so determined by the witnessed events that create it?

Satija's witnessing of the suffering of animals did more than force her to labor ceaselessly; that witnessing, I want to stress, constituted an intimate event in which her own social skin would be opened up, stripped away, and remade, thickening worldly relations. In her own words, such witnessing forced her—would force us all—to become the animal in pain. "To realize the suffering of animals," she said to me, "requires you to *become an animal that talks*. Because they cannot [talk], that becomes my responsibility." I want to think now, through the rubrics of humanism and its others, about what it means for Satija to "become an animal that talks."

BECOMING ANIMAL

Povinelli elaborates a history of the concept of intimacy in post-Enlightenment Western thought.[37] Intimacy here is the freely chosen bond between sovereign subjects, a foundational fiction of the autological society that sets itself apart from the genealogical one—in which people are incapable of intimacy because their bonds are already chosen for them in advance along such lines as tribe, caste, kin, and custom. Part of what interests me about this material on animals and witnessing in urban India is how it contributes to the project of destabilizing that fiction by showing how an act of intimacy—intimate because singular, because it exfoliates the social skin, and expands the boundaries of possible relationality—exceeds and even resists sovereignty. First, the animal subject is brought into its intimate relation with a human through its unfreedom. And second, by entering into intimacy with an animal in pain, the activist seeks not to be more free, but to render herself even more deeply subject to unequal relations of obligation and responsibility: in fact, to surrender.[38]

But the intimacy of human and animal, by showing that intimacy is other than a freely chosen bond between two sovereign (and thus presumably human) subjects, does not only explode the species divide. Intimacy also reintroduces and stabilizes that chasm. As Satija describes it, realizing the suffering of animals makes imperative a simultaneous sublimation and deployment of the self as a sovereign human subject to and for the needs of the unfree other. The activist simultaneously must become the animal (shedding her own skin in sublimation) and hyperembody herself as human by doing precisely that which defines what it is to be human: to speak or, here, to give voice to that unfree other that cannot speak, while the witness is safely encased in her human self. Satija exemplifies how voice itself emerges in the "zone between two deaths"—here, the death of the animal and the death of the woman whom the witness was in the moment before she witnessed.[39] But the voice that emerges in the zone between two deaths not only cries out against injustice; it also calls forth the very cleavage between human and animal that enables that injustice to thrive at all.

Or does it? Maybe the better question is: must it?

An obvious and eminently reasonable analysis of Satija's vision of becoming an animal is the one I just made: that despite its aim to break from violence, animal activism only reproduces the war between species through its anthropocentric humanism.[40] But that is just one interpretation, and perhaps its fatal flaw is precisely its eminent reasonability—a kind of approach to the world that also finds its foundation and value in the "bloody and lethal" tradition of metaphysical humanism.[41] What if I suggested that my very assumption of anthropocentric humanism in Satija's desire to "become an animal that talks" may well be the problem here: that my assumption of humanism results from my being locked in a closed, binary logic of representation in which I know what human and animal are, and I know that they are either different or that they are the same. Instead of hearing in her claim, "I = it" or "it = me," why am I not hearing "I + it + b + z = something you have never thought before?"[42]

Perhaps it would be useful to linger on Satija's use of the word *becoming*. She did not say she wanted to be an animal, but that she wanted to become one. The difference between being and becoming is similar to that between witnessing and specular subjects—a difference that lies, to use Brian Massumi's words, between rendering the self molar or dissolving the self into supermolecularity. We are all capable of becoming other, Massumi tells us; all we have to do is want it.[43] We have to want to escape our bodily and social limitations, a desire that may be sparked by politics, by philosophy, or by witnessing. But that desire may also be conflicted: oscillating between the desire for molarity (which manifests in being something other—say, an animal that talks—and is administered through the logic of sameness and difference) and the desire for supermolecularity (which does not, strictly speaking, ever manifest: it is only becoming and hyperdifferentiation). I do not know the nature of Satija's desires, but I am willing to say that my immediate unwillingness to accept that she does become animal in a way that is disruptive rather than productive of anthropocentric humanism unjustly limits in advance the potential effects of her, my, and the animal's becoming.[44]

I never saw Satija in the field (never saw her becoming animal with my own eyes), and therefore cannot say "I see that" her becoming is true—so let me move for a moment to something I did witness. In the summer of 2013 I spent a week with an American family, the Abrams-Meyers, who had moved from Seattle to a rocky, hilly village outside Udaipur, in the northwest Indian state of Rajasthan. They were Jim, Erika, and Claire, and when I stepped out of the Udaipur train station and gave the name of the village I wanted to get to, the rickshaw driver said, "Erika *ka ghar*?" [Erika's house?]. Erika had told me that might happen, but the proof of their local celebrity still tickled me. The driver brought me to their gate, and the sound of the engine brought Claire to the door, followed closely by Erika, who was quite literally flapping with excitement.

They were all abnormally tall, these Americans. Jim is a sturdy man who wears Dickies pants, a thin gray T-shirt, and heavy work boots. He rides to their shelter every morning on a Royal Enfield motorcycle, and when I sat behind him I was transfixed by the deep creases in his sun-reddened neck. He was once a professor of literature. Claire, in her early twenties, dresses simply and wears a bandana to keep the hair off a face that is beautiful in its classic symmetry, her Roman nose dotted with a stud. She was twelve when they left

Seattle and has not been formally schooled since, which might in fact account for her extraordinary curiosity and wisdom about the world. Erika—well, Erika, I have to say, is a lot like Big Bird. And I can say that because I know she does not mind, for she has nothing against either birds or muppets and is quite aware that she is tall, wild, and gangly. Erika almost always wears saris, but while I was there the family was moving their animal shelter to a larger site, which involved actually carrying animals in their arms, one by one, from a van into large outdoor enclosures. So I usually saw her in random house pants and kurtas, sometimes with glasses on her head, sometimes with her head covered with a bandana that she otherwise wears around her neck. I think I will always remember the sight of her, slightly disheveled, slightly mad looking, but somehow calm, with everything revolving around her in a steady, necessary orbit. In my mind, she is carrying a bucket full of water even though it has been a very long and hot day, and the dogs trail behind her, and she is harried but full of love. And I can see why an activist named Jaivardan says Erika "is like a god" to him; another activist named Rohit calls her "the mother of animals"; and Timmie Kumar—who directs Jaipur's renowned shelter, Help in Suffering, and has a cult following herself—told me that she "fell to the ground and wept when [she] first saw Erika with the animals." I know that sounds overly dramatic, but somehow it is not when you see this woman rolling in the dirt with salivating, joyous, romping three-legged dogs. I wish I had fallen to the ground in tears myself.

One of the things about Erika, as with any witness, is her mix of movement and stillness. She walked me to the large animals section of the shelter, populated mostly by donkeys, goats, and cows, with a couple of paralyzed pigs. We came upon a large lump on the ground, covered by burlap, and then I saw the hooves and tail showing from under it. I moved around and saw the nearly closed eyelids, the body rising and falling with laborious breaths: it was a dying cow, her neck bent unnaturally. Because of Rajasthan's antislaughter law, Erika could not euthanize her. She had been dying for days. Erika had assumed that the previous day was going to be the cow's last, and she told me what they do at times like those. Erika calls the workers over, one by one or perhaps two at a time, and she asks them to stop whatever work they are doing and just be there with the animal. She got down on the ground, next to this burlap and flesh, and demonstrated to me: "Just be silent next to its dying body, stroking its head if they feel they can, cradling it, kissing it, or just sitting there, body to body, life to life, death to death, soul to soul. Say you're sorry that it's leaving this world, if you feel moved to say that, say you're sorry that it lived in a world like this, if that's what you want to say. Whatever you do, just be there." In these moments of being-with, she added, the social boundaries between humans, too, fall apart, when they are together, from their varying backgrounds of caste and race, all with their butts equally on the shit- and piss-strewn ground and their hands on the crusted body of an animal in pain, sometimes crying, sometimes stoic, sometimes calm, but all the time and all of them there, facing the boundary between life and death that will one day hunt us all down, regardless of the skin we wear.

THESE ARE BECOMINGS, ALL

I turned to Erika to answer a question that Satija had provoked: can we become animal, become other, in a way that is disruptive rather than productive of anthropocentric humanism? Or to put it differently: can we become something other than the safely encased human self? I have no doubt that I watched some of Erika die in that instant with the cow, that I witnessed her becoming-other through her surrender to becoming-death. I simply would not feel right reducing that moment to a reproduction of anthropocentrism, though surely someone could make that argument if they wanted to. But more important, I want to suggest that it does not matter what she became; she affected me, forever, just as she affects all those who enter her orbit. The entire point of becoming, in the Deleuzian sense, is not to go from one thing to another, but to be a phenomenon, an event, an act of bordering in which both original categories are revealed to be infinitely other than what they are. Becoming is pure effectuation, the effect of affectively redefining the places we started from: in this particular case, woman and animal. In another case it was man and rat. This is from Gilles Deleuze and Félix Guattari's *A Thousand Plateaus*:

> When Hofmannsthal contemplates the death throes of a rat, it is in him that the animal "bares his teeth at his monstrous fate." This is not a feeling of pity, as he makes clear; still less an identification. It is a composition of speeds and affects . . . it makes the rat become a thought, a feverish thought in the man, at the same time that the man becomes a rat gnashing its teeth in its death throes. The rat and the man are in no way the same thing . . . but are expressed . . . in an affectability that is no longer that of subjects. *Unnatural participation.*[45]

Becoming; unnatural participation; turning the self not into another kind of self, but only into a "question-machine."[46] Social movements, in this sense, are full of becomings: they are defined and made by them. The phrase *unnatural participation*, in particular—because of its echoes, I suppose, of sexual policing and sodomy laws, but also of the emergent and perverse—takes me from the animal to the queer, to a pivotal moment in the history of queer organizing in India. (This might seem quite separate, but the queer and the animal have many connections between them.)[47] In 1998, a film called *Fire*, about the love affair between two sisters-in-law in a middle-class New Delhi home, was released throughout India.[48] What followed were violent public clashes instigated by right-wing activists who claimed that the film was an abomination: there are no lesbians in India, they said. Lesbians responded with three simple words: "Indian and Lesbian."[49]

Is this so unlike Satija's claim that she becomes an animal? Was not "Indian and Lesbian" an act of becoming par excellence? Certainly when those words were first uttered, they were as improbable as a wealthy, middle-aged Hindu woman saying, "I am an animal." The very identity of India, after all, rested on its exclusion of queer, and the very identity of queer rested on its exclusion from citizenship,[50] mirroring the mutual exclusions of human subject and animal abject. "Indian and Lesbian," during the riotous weeks that followed that utterance, was indeed a becoming, an effectuation, a question-machine. And it affectively redefined dominant categories of social understanding, birthing inbred monstrosities where there was once, so we had thought, a gaping abyss between this and that. Lesbians became Indian as blacks had become men in another radical becoming in Memphis in 1968, where the sanitation workers' strike gave rise to a mass of signs that also marked a singular becoming, this time with four words instead of three: "I Am a Man."

These are becomings, all: a lesbian becoming Indian, a black man becoming Man, a woman becoming animal. But putting it this way, there are at least two differences between the first two cases and the last one. The first two begin with a movement from the particular (molecular) to the general (molar), while the last one begins with a movement from the general-particular (human, but still only woman) to the particular. The first two, in other words, are majoritarian, the last one minoritarian. This first difference can probably explain the second, which is that we find the first two becomings credible (for who, really, would not want to be more, to be a man?), while most of us do not find the last one believable (for who, really, would want to be less, to become an animal?).

What is it for me, or anyone else, to critically question Satija's becoming animal? I question, in part, the motivation and effects of Satija's "animal that talks," describing it as more humanism. I call on the signs from our initial conversation: her references to mythology to suggest that Hindus, perhaps more than others, are inclined to compassion; her use of the phrase *stench of death*, unleashing a chain of references in my own mind that takes me quickly to a history of caste violence (though it could just as well take me to Omaha, Nebraska, where they use the same phrase to speak of slaughter);[51] and her wealth and comfortable life, which might signal to me a remove from struggle. But what do I know? What do I know of her heart other than what she tells me of it (and she tells me that she becomes an animal because she has witnessed an animal in pain)? Nonetheless, I think, "Can it be?" An Indian lesbian can be an Indian because she already is; a black man can be a man because he already is; but Satija cannot be an animal because I know what an animal is, and an animal is not this bejeweled woman with a daughter at an Ivy League school. Throughout all of this, I know. But what if we were to surrender to the spirit of becoming?[52] To truly, carnally enact a critique of Cartesianism by allowing other facets of the sensorium to reign? What if we were to become Satija; see what she sees; experience what inspires her to shed her skin and become the animal in pain, the animal that writhes at night, a smell in her nostrils, a flash in his mind's eye, a scream neither past nor present but here, in her bed, calling from below? What if we were to make her, and what she sees, a feverish thought coursing through our flesh? Could we feel, then, that she is not becoming or failing to become a subject, but becoming an event, an operation on the categories of thought and action that we hold onto, demanding that we not be something new, but let go of what we tell ourselves that we and our interlocutors are, so that we can sometimes, like her when she tries, become?

It would be to be like Maneka Gandhi, to give ourselves over. It would be to be like Timmie Kumar, to come apart in the face of something extraordinary. It would be to be like Erika, to put arms around the body of a dying animal, ear to its flesh, and be filled with the pulse of its enormous, failing heart. It would be to feel more ourselves and yet be ever less certain, and more curious, about what that even means. And is that not the point of all our multispecies ethnographic explorations?[53] Is that not what it means to do anthropology—not of *anthropos* as we believe we know it, but of life?[54]

Toward the end of my first meeting with Satija, she began showing me images from a collection of photographs. As we came on one of a dog with a mangled leg covered in maggots, I noticed her wet eyes. It reminded me of something that Frida Kahlo once wrote: "They say there are two things that don't mean anything: a dog's limp, and a woman's tears." In her witnessing, in her intimacies, and in her becomings, Satija tries and fails and tries again to make those things matter after all.

NOTES

1. M. Gandhi, *Heads and Tails*.
2. Though Gandhi presents Rogers's narrative as a direct quote, she actually paraphrases Rogers (I present Rogers's original version). The passages Gandhi uses about sight and the eyes are still accurate.
3. Rogers, *Mad Dogs and an Englishwoman*, 42–43.
4. M. Gandhi, *Heads and Tails*, 5.
5. Povinelli, *The Empire of Love*, 179.
6. Derrida, *The Animal That Therefore I Am*, 82.
7. Agamben, *The Open*, 38.
8. Jacques Derrida (*The Animal That Therefore I Am*) and Miriam Ticktin ("Human Rights/Humanitarianism Beyond the Human") have revealed how animal rights politics rely on humanist values such as compassion, thereby reproducing the very distinctions between action and passivity and between the noble and the mute that underlie other colonial and neocolonial forms of exploitation. This is an important reading of human action on behalf of animals—one I largely agree with—but I hope to show alternative ones.
9. L. Gandhi, *Affective Communities*. That said, as Leela Gandhi shows in *Affective Communities*, animal activism in India is also inseparable from an affective history of radicalism. Among her central figures is Mohandas K. Gandhi, the Mahatma, whose vegetarianism was part of a broader fin-de-siècle anticolonialism that created deep affective bonds between humans and humans, specifically whites and Indians. Indeed, part of what I demonstrate in this chapter is the difficulty of parsing the liberal or conservative from the radical—which might come down to what we are and are not able (and willing) to see. The Mahatma is a good example of this ambivalence, since his vegetarianism was part of a radical anticolonial pacifism as well as a masculinist politics of purity, though not one reducible to caste (see Roy, *Alimentary Tracts*, 75–115).
10. Mayo, *Mother India*.
11. Pandey, "Rallying Round the Cow."
12. Yang, "Sacred Symbol and Sacred Space in Rural India."
13. Dave, *Queer Activism in India: A Story in the Anthropology of Ethics*.
14. Roy, *Alimentary Tracts*, 8.
15. The anthropological literature on animal politics in India has largely focused on its failures, violences, and hypocrisies. For example, Parvis Ghassem-Fachandi (*Pogrom in Gujarat*) demonstrates that the Hindu right's enforced pacifism toward the cow serves as the ground for its mortal violence against non-Hindus and lower castes (see also Chigateri, "'Glory to the Cow'"). I could not agree more. But that is not all there is to say

about the politics of humans and animals in India. By telling stories from the perspective of animal activists who identify with progressive rather than conservative causes (see L. Gandhi, *Affective Communities*), and from theoretical perspectives other than that of how power reproduces itself in predictable ways, I hope to show that there are and must be other ways we conceive of human-animal engagements in India—ways that are not predetermined or fully determined by Hindu nationalism.

16 Federation of Indian Animal Protection Organizations, *The State of Dairy Cattle in India*.
17 *Bahu* is Hindi for "daughter-in-law." Maneka Gandhi joined the BJP after being cast out of the Congress Party by Indira Gandhi, her mother-in-law. See K. Singh, *Truth, Love, and a Little Malice*.
18 This is the story she told me (Maneka Gandhi, interview with the author, June 11, 2011, New Delhi). For a slightly different version, see K. Singh, *Truth, Love, and a Little Malice*.
19 For more details, particularly on the role of Rukmini Devi in the PCA Act, see Dave, "Witness"; Krishna and Gandhi, "Rukmini Devi and Animal Welfare."
20 Maneka Gandhi, interview with the author, May 29, 2008, New Delhi.
21 Ahmed, *The Cultural Politics of Emotion*, 27.
22 Maneka Gandhi, interview with the author, May 29, 2008, New Delhi.
23 See Tarlo, *Unsettling Memories*.
24 See K. Singh, *Truth, Love, and a Little Malice*.
25 This sentiment is like one expressed by Paul McCartney, Michael Pollan, or Timothy Pachirat, the feeling that seeing glass-walled slaughterhouses would inevitably transform our treatment of animals through horror and repugnance. Pachirat in fact calls for a "politics of sight," in which activists work to render transparent the violences we systematically conceal, creating a kind of reverse panopticon (*Every Twelve Seconds*, 242–43). But Pachirat's work is not entirely relevant here for at least two reasons. First, the activists discussed in this chapter are not concerned with motivating others to act; they are concerned foremost with disallowing complacency in themselves. Second, violence against animals in India is not nearly as concealed as it is in the United States, and the apathy created by the violence's ubiquity is more of a problem than is the tendency to conceal it.
26 Das, *Life and Words: Violence and the Descent into the Ordinary*.
27 Quoted in Derrida, *The Animal That Therefore I Am*, 77.
28 Derrida, *The Animal That Therefore I Am*, 77.
29 Derrida, *The Animal That Therefore I Am*, 82.
30 See Levinas, "The Name of a Dog, or Natural Rights." See also Calarco, *Zoographies*, 55–78.
31 Derrida, *The Animal That Therefore I Am*, 82.
32 Agamben, *The Open*, 92.
33 Das, *Life and Words*.
34 Ahmed, *The Cultural Politics of Emotion*, 27.
35 Carmelia Satija, interview with the author, June 11, 2010, New Delhi.
36 *Maneka Gandhi v. Union Territory of Delhi and Others*, Civil Writ No. 2961, 1992.
37 Povinelli, *The Empire of Love*.
38 See Mahmood, *Politics of Piety*.

39   Das, *Life and Words: Violence and the Descent into the Ordinary*, 61–62.
40   See Derrida, *The Animal That Therefore I Am*; Ticktin, "Human Rights/Humanitarianism Beyond the Human."
41   Agamben, *The Open*, 38.
42   Or, as Gilles Deleuze and Félix Guattari put it, riffing off Virginia Woolf, "Five o'clock is this animal! This animal is this place! . . . That is how we need to feel" (*A Thousand Plateaus*, 263).
43   Massumi, *A User's Guide to Capitalism and Schizophrenia*, 94.
44   João Biehl and Peter Locke also, via Deleuze, argue for an anthropology that recognizes that what we see does not exhaust the potential of what might be, and might become ("Deleuze and the Anthropology of Becoming").
45   Deleuze and Guattari, *A Thousand Plateaus*, 258 (emphasis in the original). Hugo von Hofmannsthal was an Austrian writer who published in the early twentieth century. Also in relation to Hofmannsthal, Deleuze and Guattari discuss writers who, through their "unnatural participation" beyond the human, act as "sorcerers" and are able to throw the self (and an openhearted reader) into radical upheaval (*A Thousand Plateaus*, 240).
46   Deleuze and Guattari, *A Thousand Plateaus*, 259.
47   See Chen, *Animacies*; Halberstam, *The Queer Art of Failure*; Haraway, "A Cyborg Manifesto."
48   Mehta, *Fire*.
49   Dave, "Indian and Lesbian and What Came Next."
50   Bacchetta, "When the (Hindu) Nation Exiles Its Queers."
51   Pachirat, *Every Twelve Seconds*, 30.
52   In asking what it would mean to believe a phenomenon that challenges our regimes of rationality, and not merely to believe that this phenomenon is true for our interlocutors, I am interested in a long-standing debate about belief and ethnographic method, one that Paul Nadasdy ("The Gift in the Animal") addressed. He persuasively asks us to inhabit alternative ontologies, to believe—in his case from the First Nations in the Yukon—that the animal gives itself as a gift to its hunter. I follow Nadasdy to a point, but I diverge to ask what it would mean to inhabit only becomings that traverse lines of sameness and difference, self and other.
53   Kirksey and Helmreich, "The Emergence of Multispecies Ethnography," 546, 559.
54   Kohn, *How Forests Think*.

IV

6

I Was Cannibalized by an Artist

Adriana Varejão, or Art as Flux

LILIA M. SCHWARCZ

INTRODUCTION, OR A STRING OF FALSE COINCIDENCES

I met Adriana by chance. Some years ago, I was on my way to Rio de Janeiro, and as I boarded the plane, I noticed a young family: a beautiful mother, a father, and a happy daughter. I also noted that the mother kept staring at me. I thought no more of it, but a string of coincidences was only just beginning; as it happened, I ended up sitting right behind them.

That was when the woman turned around to face me and said, very directly: "My name is Adriana Varejão. I love your books and want you to write an article about my work." I recognized the contemporary artist immediately, but I found it strange that she would recognize me. So I responded: "I am afraid I am not who you think I am. I am just (and at most) an anthropologist interested in art, or a historian, but not an art historian or an art critic."

Her reply was immediate: "I read your book *The Spectacle of the Races*, and that's why I want you to write something about my art." I was at a bit of a loss and let the matter drop.

Some months later, I was invited by Isabel Diegues, an editor at the arts publishing house Cobogó, based in Rio de Janeiro, to contribute to a book about Varejão's art. I responded as I had to Varejão on the plane, and Isabel replied: "But she wants to 'teach you about her art.'" To make a long story short, I decided to go to Rio de Janeiro, where I began a series of "classes" with the artist. We met and discussed her work, I watched her working, she gave me open access to her archive, and most importantly, we became friends.

I loved the stories Adriana told me in these meetings, and especially her way of "translating" formal information. I was enthralled by the opportunity to follow her creative process and to experiment with a new dimension of my own work as an anthropologist. I was starting to realize that, at least in my case, the boundaries between the author of knowledge and the subject of knowledge were really not so clear at all. Before my eyes, everything was transformed to fit Adriana's world and work. A reference from a book, old pictures, documents, ceramics, a research project—anything could trigger a new piece, anything could be "translated" into art.

I was particularly interested in how Adriana creates false tiles in her work and transforms them into allegories—perhaps the best instruments for difficult communication between such diverse settings as China, Brazil, and Portugal. Tiles have historically been used as part of the lucrative business that united different parts of these three countries and, at the same time, as symbols of different cultures. That is why *parody* is the best term from which to begin understanding her work. The artist does not create a new tile: she creates art as a tile. Contemporary art thus becomes a false document, which bears signs of the passage of time. At the same time, intentional imperfections can reveal the work of the operation. A false tile is not actually false, because it becomes real in a new work (plates 2 and 3).

Adriana can cheat with art: she creates tiles in her paintings to make them real: real tiles. This is one of her means toward poiesis, her way of showing that in art, everything is a parody—a parody of the self. Different cultures have used tiles as a way of exchanging products and as symbols. Tiles have also acted as a privileged language, with cultural difference inscribed in formats, drawings, colors, and techniques. For Adriana, tiles were also a way to express the ambiguities of colonization, insisting that colonization created suffering and leisure at the same time. What emerges in this work is a complex and ambiguous process combining violence and pleasure, death and miscegenation.

Colonization, in Adriana's work, is addressed alongside cannibalization as a way to understand order and disorder, present and future, and exchange and violence. The concept of cannibalization is prevalent in both Adriana's art itself and the way she comments on it. Drawing on modernist references from the writings of Oswald de Andrade[1] and the French traveler Jean de Léry,[2] she transforms meanings into images and images into other images. More than a biological function, to Adriana cannibalization was a way of managing questions of transformation and an important way of creating networks of communication: of being other, being the enemy, or incorporating the enemy's strengths. The subject has been studied by scholars at different stages in intellectual life, and there is not room enough to discuss all their ideas here. Better to consider Montaigne's famous essay from 1580,[3] or the writings of Manuela Carneiro da Cunha and Eduardo Viveiros de Castro on this subject.[4] There is a substantial difference between the concepts of anthropophagy (symbolic consumption) and cannibalism (the physical consumption of human flesh), of which Adriana was very much aware. The former has a ritual meaning; the latter, a biological one. The crucial point is that Amerindians did not eat their enemies because they were hungry. Eating the strongest prisoner was a way of receiving that person's strong spirit and a means of exchanging symbols, men, and messages. Cannibalism is, in fact, a central theme in Adriana's art (plates 1, 4, and 5). In her work, one can easily locate quotations, images, and documents from various times, but in all cases and at the same time, what is visible is a parody: a duplication of a document, a mirror that can reproduce but also distort or duplicate.

Let me return, once more, to my relationship with the artist. My first sensation, after those initial "classes," was a kind of vertigo. Who was the expert and who was the native in this brand-new situation? It is not my intention to rehash postmodern analyses of the rebellion of our objects and how this has affected anthropology as a discipline.[5] My concern here is a different one: I was afraid that I would be cannibalized! Instead of simply studying Adriana, she had started studying me and "translating" my own work for her own purposes.

But I thought no more of this worry. After my first series of meetings and dialogues with Adriana, I wrote an essay titled "Varejar, ladrilhar: uma cartografia ladrilhada da obra da artista" [A tile world map of the artist's work].[6] Later on the book in which it was included turned out beautifully, and the group of essays in it, written by different authors, offered a panorama of Adriana's work. I found it strange, however, that my article was not accompanied by the images I had included in it, which showed pieces I had discussed in the text. Instead, the editor (and, I imagined, Adriana) had opted for images of an installation called *Testemunhas oculares, x, y, z* [Eyewitnesses, x, y, z], a work consisting of portraits of three different Adrianas—one African, another Chinese, and a third indigenous—with a tray set out before each painting, and a single glass eye placed on each tray (plates 6, 7, 8, 9, 10, and 11).

The eyes, if one looks carefully, are egg-shaped, made specially by the artist. They open to reveal scenes of cannibalism copied from the work of Léry—scenes that were seared into the sixteenth-century European imagination. In his accounts of Brazil, Léry immortalized scenes of horrific rituals, with native women very naturally chomping on legs, arms, and other body parts of slain enemies. Their dancing, cooking, and feasting represented a kind of hell on earth. But the women were quite white, looking almost European and somewhat reminiscent of the witches that likewise haunted the European imagination. So in this case, indigenous women—and perhaps witches—were portrayed together in this very odd ritual. In this work, Adriana started a conversation about colonization, difference, and the forms through which we approach it, and its colors. The artist's self-portraits in "Eyewitnesses, x, y, z" show her performing not only three different races, but also three different colors.

It is not my intention here to interpret this piece. What shocked me at the time was why she had selected that particular work, which I had not mentioned even once in my essay, to accompany my text. I did not bring the subject up until one day when she invited me to have lunch with her. She was in São Paulo, the city where I live, and wanted to talk to me. We agreed to write a book together, and I immediately started imagining a project, as we academics always do. It was to be a retelling of Brazilian history with Adriana's work as a kind of guide.

We met again, and no sooner had she started talking than I realized that she had another plan, a visual plan, and that it was much, much better than my own. She wanted to abolish the notion of time altogether and instead work with the idea of cartography. She also wanted to explore, with my help, her process of creating art. Rather than using images as products that merely reflect reality, it would be better to introduce a less conservative methodology that could deal with art itself as production. I had the opportunity to establish a dialogue not about Adriana's work, but with Adriana, her work, and her world. In other words, instead of using images as illustrations, the idea was to understand how works of art can interfere in reality, creating and destroying customs, values, and symbols.

Before she starts painting, Adriana consults historical references such as documents, books, photographs, and old plates and tiles. I realized that this was a chance to understand not just one work, but the process by which she acquires a language—a Varejão language.

I accepted the invitation on the spot, but before we got started, there was one question I just had to ask: "Adriana, everything is fine, but why the hell did you decide to illustrate my essay with that particular image in your previous book?" She answered me frankly: "Because I read that story in your book."

She explained that my book *The Spectacle of the Races* had shown her that nineteenth-century scientific racial theories saw the eyes as a means of measuring madness, criminality, and even geniality.[7] She had found that story "terrific," she said. I was disappointed, because I knew I had never written anything on that subject!

The information itself was ultimately correct, part of a series of phrenological models used during the nineteenth century, in Brazil and elsewhere. It was also part of a wide range of models, known as racial theories, that were very fashionable at the time. But I was certainly not the author of, or even a commentator on, that argument. In short, Adriana thought she had read something in my book that wasn't actually there. She cannibalized me and my work in the same way that she cannibalizes other sources, mixing all of them together: she reads, sees, studies, and develops her work by "translating" it all into art.

This translation reminded me of Marshal Sahlins's conclusions on a different theme: cultures always intertranslate.[8] In this sense, each event is reinterpreted according to very different significations, even if they are somehow determined by prevailing cultural standards. Through this process, however, events can end up reorganizing culture. The great challenge for historical anthropology is not merely to know how events are ordered by culture, but how, in that process, culture itself is ordered.

During my own process of learning, seeing, and reading with Adriana, I also remembered some of the postcolonial theorist Homi Bhabha's explanations about the relationship between India and the West, which suggest that in a clash between two cultures, the resulting hybrid is different from the sum of its parts.[9] As Bhabha points out, one has to "move beyond the narratives of originary and founding subjectivities in order to focus (now) on those moments or processes that are produced by the articulation of cultural differences."[10] These in-between areas are where subjectivization strategies (singular and collective) are drafted.[11] This relates to Edward Said's ideas in *Orientalism*: we are always translating and inventing new repertoires and languages—political languages.[12] European culture, as Said puts it, "gained in strength and identity by setting itself off against the Orient as a sort of surrogate and even underground self."[13] These forms of "translation" between cultures act as a strategy replicated by Adriana, who similarly feeds her creativity in the sphere of art. She works from the subjectivities that underpin our colonization and sociability and creates art in which cultural differences in Brazil are articulated, always in an overtly political way.

As an anthropologist, I could understand that I was taking part in a game of mirrors and projections: I was becoming the other that would be transformed into a new image. An intermediate space, an in-between. But in this case, there was no otherness. The anthropologist was part of an anthropophagic ritual that excludes but also includes. Nevertheless, with time, things were going to become more and more digestible: there were books and ideas to be eaten.

PARENTHESES: PICTURING THEORY

The more I worked alongside Adriana, the more I felt familiarity but also distance before that 360-degree work of art, a sensation akin to the experience of discovering a new document. Whether the distance is between a curious tourist and a new country, a seasoned historian and an ancient parchment, or an anthropologist and images she is working with, we assume that it can never be fully bridged. Perhaps at that stage the best thing would have been, as the critic Michael Baxandall puts it, to try to recover "the causes of a painting" or the "intention" behind its production and form.[14] In other words, I should have tried to read the artwork, armed with other sources against which to compare my interpretation: elements from Adriana's own pictorial tradition and the context to which it belongs. In so doing, I would have been writing about "a place that may well be distant" but is always situated.[15] In this sense, and given that I am a social scientist, the best option would have been to examine the contexts in which the artist moves.

Yet the task remained unclear. The question that arose was: how do we reconcile writing and art? After all, to describe something in words is, first and foremost, as Baxandall once again shows, a representation of what we think about a work or our representation of it. It is never a written recovery of the work as such.

Furthermore, as we were dealing with an artwork, it was important not to overlook the analysis of its formal aspects. We might recall Claude Lévi-Strauss's well-known contention that art is expression, a form of knowledge located on the border between science and myth.[16] In all of these domains, art operates through concrete signs as opposed to concepts—and a fortiori "by his craftsmanship" the artist "constructs a material object which is also the object of knowledge."[17]

The theme of art is ever present in Lévi-Strauss's work, from the similarities between music and myth, as set forth in *The Raw and the Cooked*,[18] and observations about indigenous art in *Tristes Tropiques*,[19] to books that deal more specifically with the art world, such as *The Way of the Masks*[20] and *Look, Listen, Read*.[21] In this sense, Lévi-Strauss helps us understand and value perspectives like that of Ernst Gombrich, for whom, in the analysis of art, "form precedes content."[22] In other words, there is no dealing with the specificities of these documents without acknowledging that a work of art owes more to other works than to its context. Posing a daunting challenge for social scientists, the issue becomes how not to neglect the particular language of art, whose repertoire is very often specific, and no doubt self-referential.

However, the more sociological aspects (like place of origin, biography, gender, and ethnicity) that also affect artistic objects in their processes of production, circulation, and reception occupy limited space in the analyses of Lévi-Strauss, more keenly attuned as he was to the stylistic forms and symbolic meanings of a given piece. It is as if, like myths, works of art were in dialogue with each other more than with their contexts. In this sense, they are form—material that stands apart, to some degree, from social morphology.

Clifford Geertz's anthropological approach to art is rather different. Interested in analyzing the relativism of aesthetic taste and the definitions attributed to art, Geertz is invested in the idea that knowledge, even in this field, is always "placed" in some ethnographical setting: "such placing, the giving to art objects a cultural significance, is always a local matter; what art is in classical China or classical Islam, what it is in the Pueblo southwest or highland New Guinea, is just not the same thing."[23] Ever concerned with ethnographic contexts, Geertz denies the existence of any universal principle for the definition or analysis of the theme. In his essay "Art as a Cultural System," he introduces a "semiotic science of art," in which the meanings of works, based on their formal or prosodic characteristics, would be incorporated into the data derived from "specific patterns of life."[24] In other words, it is the broader cultural context that lends the work its meaning—or, better put, a particular meaning.

From this perspective, a work of art is framed as a sort of symbolic mediator within social relations. In this sense, and even more so in Geertz's vision, our attention should be directed not to the formal aesthetic characteristics of works, but rather to the context of their production. In this case, what really matters is the "external conception of the phenomenon."[25] So for Geertz, anthropological interest in artistic manifestations is limited to exploring what he calls an essentially collective sensibility wholly located in social life. Art therefore represents the materialized expression of a way of living and feeling, bringing "a particular cast of mind out into the world of objects, where men can look at it."[26] In other words, through art, anthropology understands how we think in society, not how art itself thinks.

The problem is that to think of art as a mere reflection of social life is to posit art as an organized and, in a sense, depoliticized whole, as if it arose devoid of conflict, entirely unified and homogeneous. In other words, art would be understood as a kind of obvious and passive product of its context. In Geertz's own words, "one could as well argue that the rituals, or the myths, or the organization of family life, or the division of labor enact conceptions evolved in painting as that painting reflects the conceptions underlying social life."[27] In this way, we might say that Geertz gives up on understanding the reflexivity of the artistic universe because, as he writes, there is no need to consider these items in terms of their heuristic value as producers of customs, values, or even concepts.

Alfred Gell, on the other hand, defends a position diametrically opposed to Geertz's. For Gell, art does not necessarily reflect anything. Above all, it articulates a network of clustered intentionalities and negotiates intentions and ways of conceiving them among producers, receptors, and intermediaries. In Gell's conception, art plays a relevant role as a practical mediator in social life. His perspective offers another way of approaching this domain, one geared toward evaluating the negotiations and agency of the artistic object. As Gell explains, with a jab in Geertz's direction, he is more "preoccupied with the practical mediatory role of art objects in the social process, rather than with the interpretation of objects 'as if' they were texts."[28] Gell launches a veritable methodological program for an anthropology interested in and concerned with art. "In place of symbolic communication," he writes, "I place all the emphasis on *agency, intention, causation, result* and *transformation*. I view art as a system of action, intended to change the world rather than encode symbolic propositions about it."[29]

With this perspective in mind, Gell broadens the concept of the "art object," moving beyond, for example, the opposition between art and artefact. Gell demolishes the concept: "The nature of the art object is a function of the social-relational matrix in which it is inserted.... But in fact anything whatsoever could, conceivably, be an art object from the anthropological point of view, including living persons, because the anthropological theory of art (which we can roughly define as the 'social relations in the vicinity of objects mediating social agency') merges seamlessly with the social anthropology of persons and their bodies."[30]

However, if Gell articulates cosmologies of the cultural environment with social interactions mediated therein, Lévi-Strauss seems less concerned with the ethnographic background of artistic objects. This lack of concern makes it difficult to consider the agency of subjects within the fabric of social relations.

With these models in mind, my challenge is, first and foremost, to seek out a different equilibrium between formal aesthetic analyses and the social studies of art. On the one hand, as social scientists, it is important for us to understand a work in its context, so as to assess to what extent it responds to its time. Even works of art are not just unique, autonomous products of an independent artist. In this sense, it is important to situate the artist and the art in their context. On the other hand, we cannot overlook the internal dialogues that works of art have within themselves based on patterns of intention: recurring references to preceding or contemporary works, or even conversations with earlier works in the artist's own oeuvre. It is an ongoing and imbricated exercise in communication and reciprocal influence, befitting an object imbued with its own languages. To grasp the citations and visual references an artist evokes is the task of the anthropologist, as it is part of the discipline's remit to rally its native's voice and thereby, in some way, to reclaim it.

Such an approach is also a way of taking seriously Baxandall's methodological proposition for an "inferential criticism," which reveals the dual effort to articulate concepts and objects: to describe is to explain, and vice versa.[31] He maintains that "the concept deepens the perception of the object and the object deepens the reference of the word."[32] Thus, in the process of describing a work, we can see how the act of description evinces its constitutive references, and how the inverse operates as well.

I wish to return here to the concepts of parody and intertextuality. According to Bruno Latour, the ways in which the "cascade of images is discernible in the artistic domain shows the firm and intricate connection which each image has with all others that have been produced, the complex relationship of sequestration, allusion, destruction, distance, citation, parody and dispute."[33]

However, it is just as important to avoid overpowering artwork by historicizing it, plucking it from the divine realm as Prometheus did with fire, and relegating it entirely to the world of man.[34] In other words, we might as well avail ourselves of our habit of critically questioning sources so as to refrain from falling for a reading that rather romantically wraps the artist and his oeuvre in a magical, demiurgic light. As Lévi-Strauss wrote about artistic production and its delusions of singularity: "When he claims to be solitary, the artist lulls himself in a perhaps fruitful illusion, but the privilege he grants himself is not real. When he thinks he is expressing himself spontaneously, creating an original work, he is answering other past or present, actual or potential, creators. Whether one knows it or not, one never walks alone along the path of creativity."[35]

Between a more formalist approach (concerned with aesthetic dispositions, canons, and relationships between stylistic elements, harmonies, and pictorial compositions) and a more historicist view (primed first and foremost to investigate the intrinsic content of the work of art and its contextualization in the historical and social moment of its production), it is important to heed Baxandall's reminder to analyze art by establishing "relations between the object and its circumstances," thereby moving beyond mere dichotomy.[36] Form is always content, so any separation of these domains might better serve didactic functions—that is, to resolve disputes between rival fields of knowledge—than unveil phenomenologically distinct worlds.

A SECOND TIME: CANNIBALIZATION WITH COLOR

Adriana and I started to work together more seriously in 2010. We used to meet every month. During those occasions, Adriana would explain her different series of works to me. We discussed books, ideas, places, references, and even the text I was writing. I used to read some parts of the book aloud. Eventually, each series became a chapter: one was about colonization, another about the rereading of academic art, another about saunas, another about her big artistic plates (plates 12 and 13), and, finally, one about her works related to the Yanomami Indians (plates 16 and 17).[37]

What I want to focus on here is not a conclusion, but rather a new beginning. Some time ago, Adriana called and told me she was working on a new project that she was sure "I would love." Together, we discussed at length the importance of terms for describing skin colors in Brazil, and also the relevance of thinking about color as a social classification in Brazil. I mentioned that the country's official census has five colors—white, black, yellow, indigenous (described as red), and *pardo* (an untranslatable word that refers to a kind of brown)—and noted that these color terms show the difficulties and ambiguities we face. In Brazil, we avoid discussing origins or social pasts by describing the world through different colors. Yellow is Oriental, red is indigenous, black and white need no explanation, and pardo is a kind of et cetera, otherness, or none of the above—a joker in the classification pack. We also discussed the social uses of these terms, and how color is a social marker of difference in Brazil. Color is a doppelgänger of race, and it is always circumstantial. It can change depending on social situation, economic status, the day in question, and other contextualized perceptions.[38] The sociologist Oracy Nogueira called it the prejudice of mark, or physical and external appearance, a form of categorizing people by phenotype or skin color.[39] The opposite of the model of prejudice of origin, this model is more ambiguous as it allows for greater flexibility, negotiation, and social use. As Edward Telles's research in various Latin American countries has shown, "pigmentocracy" is a powerful category in the social process of creating hierarchies.[40] Although I cannot address other countries here, at least in Brazil, color is a language—a way of dealing with differences through a kind of naturalization of hierarchy.

These were the kinds of issues that Adriana wanted to discuss. In her previous works, she frequently introduced different tones of (fake) skins. We also talked about the Pesquisa Nacional em Domicílios (PNAD),[41] a national survey in which Brazilians were asked to define their own skin color and collectively came up with 136 different terms.[42]

1	Acastanhada	somewhat chestnut-colored	F	
2	Agalegada	somewhat Galician[43]	F	
3	Alva	snowy white	F	
4	Alva escura	dull snowy white	F	
5	Alvarenta* (not in the dictionary; possibly dialect)	snowy white	F	
6	Alvarinta*	snowy white	F	
7	Alva rosada	pinkish white	F	
8	Alvinha	snowy white	F	dimin
9	Amarela	yellow	F	
10	Amarelada	yellowish	F	
11	Amarela-queimada	burnt yellow	F	
12	Amarelosa	yellowy	F	
13	Amorenada	somewhat dark-skinned	F	
14	Avermelhada	reddish	F	
15	Azul	blue	·	
16	Azul-marinho	sea blue	·	

17	Baiano	from Bahia	M	
18	Bem branca	very white	F	
19	Bem clara	very pale	F	
20	Bem morena	very dark-skinned	F	
21	Branca	white	F	
22	Branca-avermelhada	white going on red	F	
23	Branca-melada	honey-colored white	F	
24	Branca-morena	white but dark-skinned	F	
25	Branca-pálida	pale white	F	
26	Branca-queimada	burnt white	F	
27	Branca-sardenta	freckled white	F	
28	Branca-suja	off-white	F	
29	Branquiça*	whitish	F	
30	Branquinha	very white	F	dimin
31	Bronze	bronze-colored	·	
32	Bronzeada	suntanned	F	
33	Bugrezinha-escura	dark-skinned Indian	F	dimin + derogatory
34	Burro-quando-foge	disappearing donkey (that is, nondescript)		humorous
35	Cabocla	copper-colored (refers to civilized Indians)	F	
36	Cabo-verde	from Cabo Verde	·	
37	Café	coffee-colored	·	
38	Café-com-leite	café au lait	·	
39	Canela	cinnamon	·	
40	Canelada	somewhat like cinnamon	F	
41	Cardão	color of the cardoon, or thistle (blue-violet)	·	
42	Castanha	chestnut	F	
43	Castanha-clara	light chestnut	F	
44	Castanha-escura	dark chestnut	F	
45	Chocolate	chocolate-colored	·	
46	Clara	light-colored, pale	F	
47	Clarinha	light-colored, pale	F	dimin
48	Cobre	copper-colored	·	
49	Corada	ruddy	F	
50	Cor-de-café	coffee-colored	·	
51	Cor-de-canela	cinnamon-colored	·	

52	Cor-de-cuia	gourd-colored	·	
53	Cor-de-leite	milk-colored (that is, milk white)	·	
54	Cor-de-ouro	gold-colored	·	
55	Cor-de-rosa	pink	·	
56	Cor-firme	steady-colored (firm color)	·	
57	Crioula	Creole	F	
58	Encerada	polished	F	
59	Enxofrada	pallid	F	
60	Esbranquecimento	whitening	·	
61	Escura	dark	F	
62	Escurinha	very dark	F	dimin
63	Fogoió	having fiery-colored hair	·	
64	Galega	Galician or Portuguese	F	
65	Galegada	somewhat like a Galician or Portuguese	F	
66	Jambo	light-skinned (the color of a type of apple)	·	
67	Laranja	orange	·	
68	Lilás	lilac	·	
69	Loira	blonde	F	
70	Loira-clara	light blonde	F	
71	Loura	blonde	F	
72	Lourinha	petite blonde	F	dimin
73	Malaia*	Malaysian woman	F	
74	Marinheira	sailor woman	F	
75	Marrom	brown	·	
76	Meio-amarela	half yellow	F	
77	Meio-branca	half white	F	
78	Meio-morena	half dark-skinned	F	
79	Meio-preta	half black	F	
80	Melada	honey-colored	F	
81	Mestiça	half-caste (mestiza)	F	
82	Miscigenação	miscegenetic	·	
83	Mista	mixed	F	
84	Morena	dark-skinned, brunette	F	
85	Morena-bem chegada	very nearly morena	F	
86	Morena-bronzeada	sunburnt morena	F	
87	Morena-canelada	somewhat cinnamon-colored morena	F	

88	Morena-castanha	chestnut-colored morena	F	
89	Morena-clara	light-skinned morena	F	
90	Morena-cor-de-canela	cinnamon-colored morena	F	
91	Morena-jambo	light-skinned morena	F	
92	Morenada	somewhat morena	F	
93	Morena-escura	dark morena	F	
94	Morena-fechada	dark morena	F	
95	Morenão	dark-complexioned man	M	aug
96	Morena-parda	dark morena	F	
97	Morena-roxa	purplish morena	F	
98	Morena-ruiva	red-headed morena	F	
99	Morena-trigueira	swarthy, dusky morena	F	
100	Moreninha	petite morena	F	dimin
101	Mulata	mulatto girl	F	
102	Mulatinha	little mulatto girl	F	dimin
103	Negra	negress	F	
104	Negrota	young negress	F	
105	Pálida	pale	F	
106	Paraíba	from Paraíba	·	
107	Parda	brown	F	
108	Parda-clara	light brown	F	
109	Parda-morena	brown morena	F	
110	Parda-preta	black-brown	F	
111	Polaca	Polish woman	F	
112	Pouco-clara	not very light	F	
113	Pouco-morena	not very dark-complexioned	F	
114	Pretinha	black, either young or small	F	
115	Puxa-para-branco	heading toward white	F	
116	Quase-negra	almost negro	F	
117	Queimada	sunburnt	F	
118	Queimada-de-praia	beach bronzed	F	
119	Queimada-de-sol	sunburnt	F	
120	Regular	regular, normal	·	
121	Retinta	deep-dyed, very dark	F	
122	Rosa	rose-colored	F	
123	Rosada	rosy	F	
124	Rosa-queimada	sunburnt rosy	F	
125	Roxa	purple	F	

126	**Ruiva**	redhead	F
127	**Russo**	Russian	M
128	**Sapecada**	singed	F
129	**Sarará**	blonde negro	·
130	**Saraúba*** (possibly dialect)	untranslatable	·
131	**Tostada**	toasted	F
132	**Trigo**	wheaty	·
133	**Trigueira**	brunette	F
134	**Turva**	murky	F
135	**Verde**	green	·
136	**Vermelha**	red	F

Although this list has been around for many years, there is some continuity in the terms. In Brazil, color terms can be rainbow-like (black, white, yellow, and red, but also green, purple, or even blue); change because of gender (augmentative for the men, diminutive for women); change because of the sun (or the lack thereof); be modified depending on the day; and, most importantly, change with social situation. In Brazil, we might say that a person does not have a race: he or she is a race—if only temporarily. That is why race can be a language and a becoming. There is a popular expression that says "things are becoming black," which means that a situation is getting worse. On the other hand, becoming white is always aspirational, and the above examples of "quite white," "almost white," and "heading toward white" show how powerful whiteness is as a symbol in Brazil. The importance of the color white is also revealed in terms "approaching" this color. This sense of process or change is not unique to whiteness. People describe themselves not as one stable color but, most often, through examples of changing situations:

Half dark-skinned
Half-black
Honey-colored
Half-caste (mestiza)
Miscegenetic
Mixed
Dark-skinned, brunette
Very nearly morena
Sunburnt morena
Somewhat cinnamon-colored morena
Chestnut-colored morena

Light-skinned morena
Cinnamon-colored morena
Light-skinned morena
Somewhat morena
Dark morena
Dark-complexioned man
Purplish morena
Red-headed morena
Swarthy, dusky morena
Petite morena
Mulatto girl
Little mulatto girl
Negress
Young negress
Pale
From Paraíba
Brown
Light brown
Brown morena
Black-brown
Polish woman
Not very light
Not very dark-complexioned
Black, either young or small
Heading toward white
Almost negro
Sunburnt
Beach bronzed
Regular, normal
Deep-dyed, very dark

These terms show a series of agencies and negotiations. One has an approximate color or a color for now in Brazil, and describing one's color is always an ambiguous and complicated process. This explains the prevalence of terms that describe not essential or final situations but partial, changing descriptors: "quite," "almost," "not very," "heading for," "somewhat," "half," and so on. This is not to say that there is no such a thing as a regular color. On the contrary, many terms try to describe the color itself: 77 half-white, 88 chestnut brown,

124 burnt pink, 16 sea blue, 38 café au lait, 25 pale white, 28 off-white, 52 gourd-colored, 115 heading toward white, 58 polished, and 18 really white. Even so, the very attempt to describe one's color denotes the effort to make sure of it.

The list also includes numerous variations on white: white, rosy white, honey-white, beige, burnt white, freckly white, off white, whitish, and snow white. White is not just a color in Brazil, it is a kind of social objective. While some important changes in race relations have taken place since 1970, with the growth of black activism in the country and the increase in social inclusion programs, the deeply rooted belief in whiteness as a sign of superiority remains. This is visible in the PNAD survey responses, many of which are variants on white.

A second possible category for analysis is the use of color qualifiers in conjunction with feminine diminutives or masculine augmentatives, such as 60 becoming whiter, 30 quite white, 100 little dark-skinned girl, 62 little dark girl, 102 little mulatto girl, and 95 large dark-skinned man. Gender is another powerful social marker of difference, and as Anne McClintock reminds us, nationalism is raced and gendered.[44] It is common for race and gender to intersect in descriptions of social hierarchy. In this case, the use of the diminutive evokes sexual connotations.

The list also includes terms such as miscegenetic, mixed, and getting whiter, revealing the popularity of these concepts in responding to official surveys. In fact, miscegenation is a widely used term in Brazil, strongly connected with the ideology of the Estado Novo,[45] in which the idea of a racism-free country where everyone lived in harmony was officially formulated for the first time. Since then, these terms have become hackneyed, denoting not so much real miscegenation as the wish for miscegenation and processes of whitening.

Other terms show how race is often understood as a concept of circumstance. Beach bronzed, sunburnt, and toasted are descriptions that evince the distinction between *ser* (to be as a main verb, or an essential trait) and *estar* (to be as an auxiliary verb, or in a state of). In Brazil, a person may be one color temporarily, not permanently. It depends on social hierarchy, symbolic geography, to whom you are married, or where you live. If your partner is whiter than you, you immediately become whiter by association. If you live in a better part of a slum, you may look more white than if you lived in the worst part. Social markers of region interact with and help describe one's position in a particular society.[46]

There are also some possibly ironic terms in the list, revealing a series of allusions underlying their tone of mockery: runaway donkey color (a common jocular reference for a nondescript color), having fiery-colored hair, and honey-colored. These terms show how difficult it is for a person to define his or her color accurately, and how ambiguous this sort of definition can be. It is sometimes better to make a joke of it.

But the list also includes very common colors, some of them expected and others less so: blue, yellow, white, coffee-colored, copper-colored, orange, lilac, pink, purple, green, and red—a real rainbow, or possibly an "Aquarela do Brasil" (Watercolor of Brazil), to recall the famous 1939 song by Ary Barroso. Even back then, the popular poet and musician captured the myth of a color-coded racial democracy. In the words of Barroso's song: "Brazil, my Brazilian Brazil / My mulatto, wily scoundrel / Gonna sing you in my verses / Oh Brazil, samba will play / As the rhythm makes you sway / . . . / Brazil so fertile and delightful / Where the honey-colored eyeful / Sneaks an indiscreet peek / Oh, the coconuts fall from this palm tree / Where I string up my hammock / On nights aglow with bright moonlight / Brazil, for me . . . / Ah! this Brazil dusky and serene/ It's my Brazilian Brazil / Land of samba and the tambourine."[47]

While I cannot comment here on all the colors and their combinations that appear in the survey responses, one conclusion is clear. If the definitions themselves are multifarious, they have in common a certain consistency in their detailed references to color as an external and physical aspect, but also as a socially defined feature. It is interesting to note that in this extensive list, only a few of the 136 terms refer to a place of origin, and few used the word *pardo*. While things have undoubtedly changed in Brazil after almost forty years, it remains clear that people use color as language: a social language that contains information about gender, region, ethnicity, and social hierarchy.

And what about Adriana? While we were writing our book together, she was also creating a brand-new series of works based on color. She called the items in the series *Tintas polvo* (Octopus ink). She had invoked the octopus in earlier works, the creature appearing on her plates and in her panoramas (plate 9).

There is no coincidence here; instead, there is process. The octopus releases melanin, the same substance that gives our skin and hair their color. "We do not know it, but we are surrounded by ink," Adriana says. But let me remind you of another particularity of this complex animal. The Portuguese word *polvo* (octopus) closely resembles *povo* (people). The octopus can change color, as can Adriana. And she does so not just in this recent project, but in her work in general—in which we find a kind of ongoing visual reflection on color, skin, painting, and parody. She proposes a discussion using color as language.

In *Tintas polvo*, Adriana created a box of thirty-three paints whose colors she "invented," starting a new conversation about the different tones of ink, paint, or skin (plates 14 and 15).

Fogoió (flame-haired)
Branca suja (off-white)
Morena bem chegada (bordering on morena)
Amarelosa (yellowy)
Branca melada (honey-white)
Parda morena (dark-skinned girl)
Bugrezinha escura (dark Indian)
Café com leite (café-au-lait)
Azul marinho (sea-blue)
Branquinha (snow white)
Agalegada (Galician-like)
Chocolate
Burro-quando-foge (runaway donkey)
Morena-jambo (fair morena)
Turva (turbid)
Queimada de praia (beach bronzed)
Escurinha (very dark)
Mulatinha (little mulatto girl)
Encerada (varnished)
Sapecada (scorched)
Puxa para branca (heading toward white)
Bahiano (Bahian)
Cabocla (copper-colored [refers to civilized Indians] girl)
Cabo verde (Cape Verde)
Cor de cuia (gourd)
Cor firme (colorfast)
Mertiça (mestiza)
Pálida (pale)
Polaca (Polish)
Parda clara (fair pardo)
Retinta (deep-dyed, very dark)
Pouco clara (not so fair)
Meio preta (half black)

The translation of the terms into English—required by an exhibition in New York City that took place in 2014—proved especially challenging. It was difficult to translate the tones of skin, or even to translate popular terms or jokes, which are often strictly related to their cultural and social context. It was also difficult to create actual inks from terms that are always unstable, ambiguous, and sometimes untranslatable.

I played a role in this process, and I find it impossible to describe. We'd be better off just thinking about it. There is a semantics and a poiesis at work here. To create ink or paint is an act of producing representations, parodies, and classifications. It is a tribute to the different possibilities of discourse, the multiplicity that is a kind of common foundation of depiction in art. Art, of course, is not a reflex or a product of its context; it produces its own meanings, customs, and representations. One might call this a kind of visual literary fiction. As Horace said, "as is painting, so is poetry" ("*ut pictura poesis*").[48] The Greeks called this activity *ekphrasis*, meaning the description of images in words.

In fact, when looking at artworks, the challenge is how to walk the tightrope between more formalist analyses (those that place greater emphasis on the aspects treated in the history of art, such as form, color, background, and perspective) and more historicist readings (those that strive to draw connections between works and their contexts). If we social scientists feel more at home with analyses of a sociological ilk, we cannot neglect the reflexivity that emerges as an internal consequence of this kind of work. Works of art are products of their time, and as they depend on the receptiveness of their culture, they are capable of producing the realities in which they are situated. In this sense, as W. J. T. Mitchell noted, perhaps the best we can do is resist drawing theories from images, but rather to "picture theories."[49]

BECOMING THE OTHER

It is becoming very difficult for social scientists to deal with images. As Baxandall says, our attitude toward visual art is, to say the least, melancholic. We cannot describe in words what does not present itself in pages and notes, and it is difficult not to transform images into illustrations. But this case was different. When I started my research, I thought I would just describe Adriana's work and her creative process. However, she simultaneously cannibalized both me and the ideas of other scholars and transformed them into something else: another story, a visual argument, and another kind of discourse.

The French philosopher Jean-Jacques Rousseau once defined *alterity* as not only a way of discovering the other, but also a relationship in which that discovery was a form of denial or suspicion of oneself.[50] Maurice Merleau-Ponty saw in anthropology "a way of thinking in which the object is another and demands a transformation on our part."[51] Even Lévi-Strauss tried to describe anthropology as a science of the other.[52] I sincerely thought I was simply trying to translate Adriana's art, trying to understand my object, as we anthropologists like to believe we do. But in this case, the opposite took place without my knowledge (at least at first). Adriana tried to give visual space to certain theses I had in mind or had written about. She had selected me as her informant, not the other way around. Adriana is not an unknown artist. On the contrary, she is one of the most well-known contemporary artists in Brazil, and even internationally. One could say that through her art, she brings an alternative, distinctly globalized world into view (plates 18 and 19).

Perhaps Adriana's stature raises a different challenge for anthropologists, as we are not very accustomed to dealing with this kind of native. In my case, the most difficult part was understanding the kind of anthropology I was encountering in my research, which challenged all kinds of conventions. There was no strict division between the writer and the object, the owner of knowledge and the native, or the one who has the conditions to produce science and the other who passively follows.

Today, this duality is a caricature of the anthropologist's work, and what was happening in my case was an extreme example. I was selected by, and did not select, my object; I became the work of others; and I did not just create a work based on my own native philosophies.[53]

Perhaps my challenge was to stabilize what I had learned in describing Adriana's creative process. This challenge could also be a way of dealing with an anthropology of becoming—becoming food, theory, native, or art—and how our relationships with our subjects transform, create, or suggest new forms of communication and perhaps understanding. Gilles Deleuze tells us that "to write is certainly not to impose a form of expression on the matter of lived experience."[54] Literature and other written forms of expression are most often incomplete. This produces a kind of vertigo, a sense of always being in between or among different forms of expression.

In this engagement with the incompleteness of literature and writing one becomes the other (the subject of knowledge is transformed into the object), but sometimes the opposite is also true: literature can be a delirium, but also a destiny. We try to write about what is missing, but in so doing we create new possibilities.

This can be read as an act of anthropophagy, in the sense that the Brazilian modernist Oswald de Andrade gave to the term in the 1930s: we eat, we regurgitate, and we create a new product—a kind of mixture of different origins.[55] Using *anthropophagy* as a powerful metaphor for the Brazilian process of cultural production, Andrade created a new way of seeing people. Nothing is really new: everything is or can be transformed.

Here, we reach a certain plateau. To become, in this sense, means to create something new: new alternatives of making. Maybe we are close to an anthropology that is open to what results from the relationship established between the ethnographer and the native, the observer and the observed. Following the flux of these narratives, giving place to the philosophies of our informants, becoming part of those theories—as participant observers, and not just taking part in participant observation, as Bronislaw Malinowski used to urge—maybe we are talking about an anthropology with and not about, an anthropology that works together with its subjects, as opposed to simply producing books or essays about those people. That is, an anthropology that respects others in the sense that we not only listen to and write about them, but we also learn from their theories.

Following Adriana's work and listening to her explanations about art, the world, projects of life, and depictions of Brazil, we might experience a similar process. She can be considered a kind of Brazilian visual interpreter and together we created a new literary visuality and a new visual fiction. In the end, our roles really were reversed. Adriana was the one who listened to me and, respecting what I explained about my values and what I really care about, created a new becoming: becoming art.[56]

Cannibalization is a reflexive process in which one simultaneously reproduces forms of depiction and representation and produces new ones. That is perhaps an indication of the true incommensurability of language and image. Writing about what we see is almost a fruitless exercise, but even if it is "in vain, it is still our way of doing things and producing meanings, new meanings, for the subjects we engage with."[57] In these terms, the relationship between Adriana and me really did get flipped, and it produced another kind of anthropology: an anthropology that can incorporate relations, emotions, and a process of mutual translation.

NOTES

1 Andrade, "Manifesto antropófago."
2 Léry, *História de uma viagem feita à terra do Brasil.*
3 Montaigne, *Pensadores.*

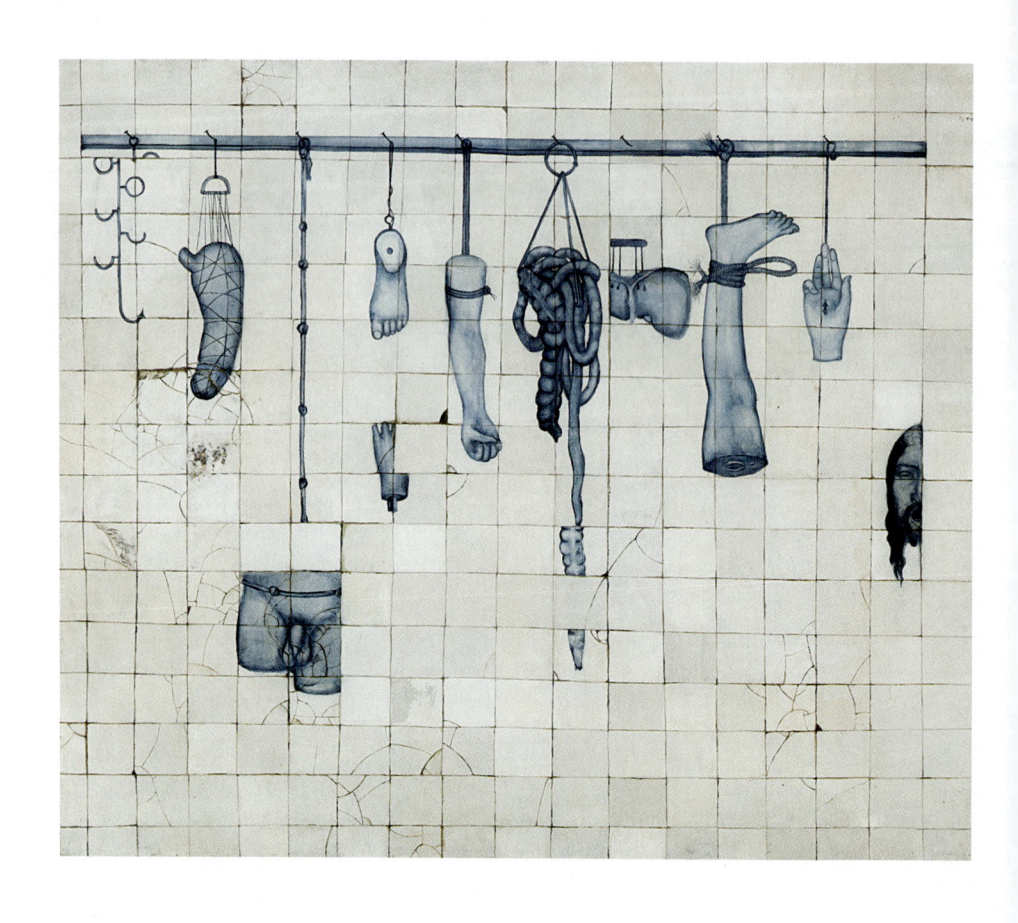

PLATE 1 (ABOVE)   Adriana Varejão, *Varal* [Rack], 1993

PLATE 2 (OPPOSITE, TOP)   Adriana Varejão, *Parede com incisões a la Fontana*, 2000

PLATE 3 (OPPOSITE, BOTTOM)   Adriana Varejão, *O sedutor*, 2004

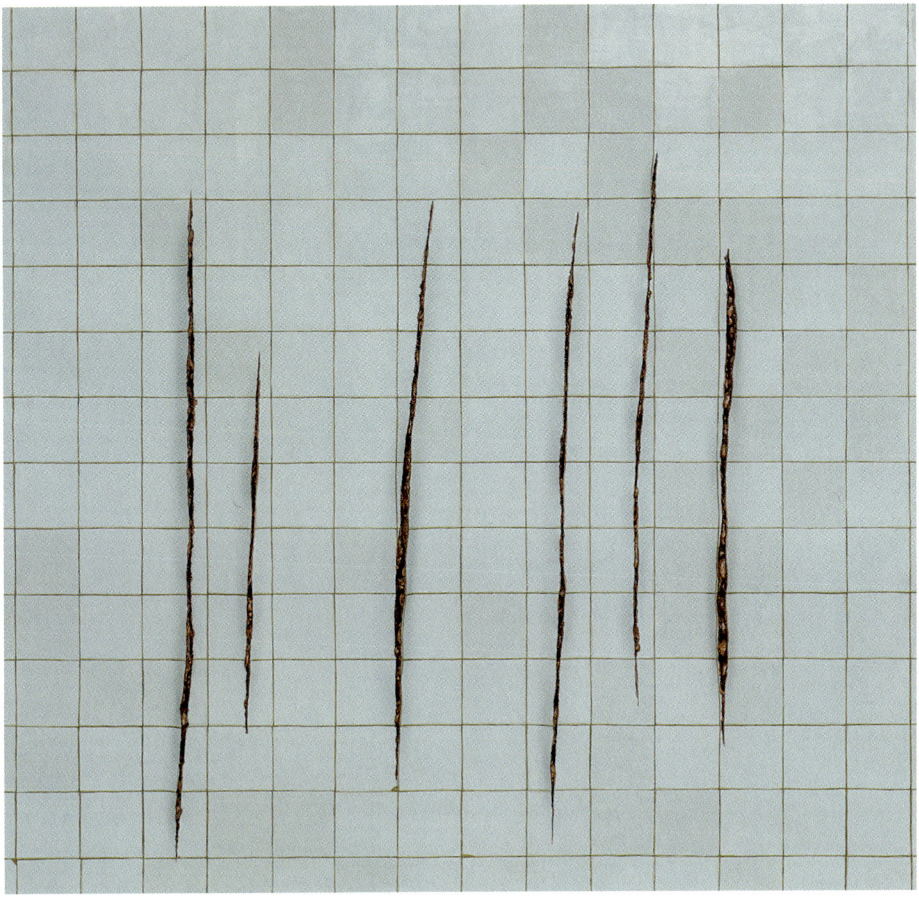

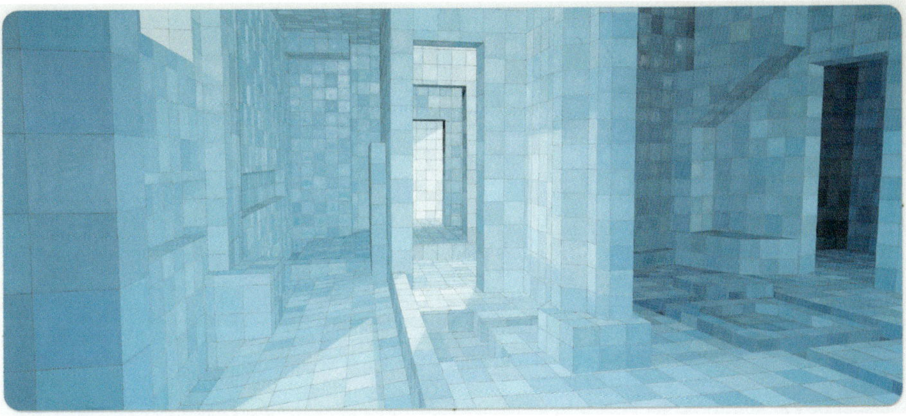

PLATE 4 Adriana Varejão, *Proposta para uma catequese—Parte I (díptico): Morte e esquartejamento*, 1993

PLATE 5 Adriana Varejão, *Proposta para uma catequese—Parte II (díptico): Aparição e relíquias*, 1993

PLATES 6–11 Adriana Varejão, details from *Testemunhas Oculares X, Y e Z*, 1997

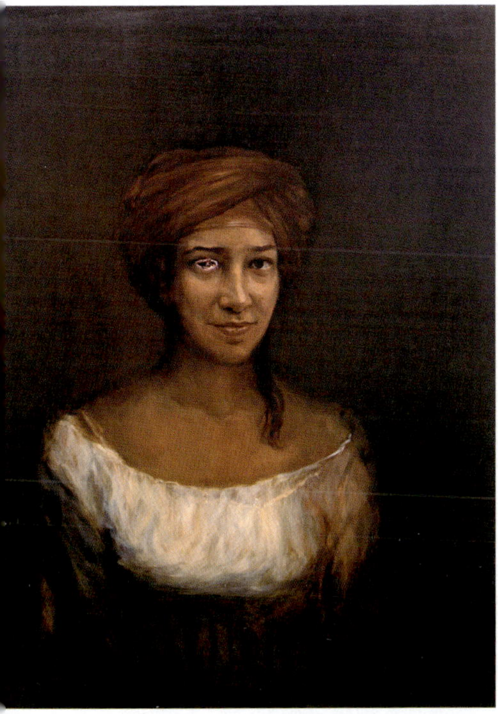
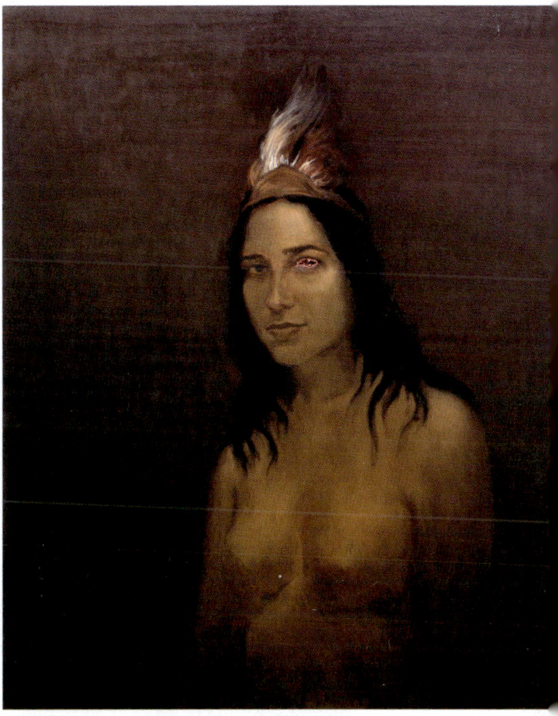
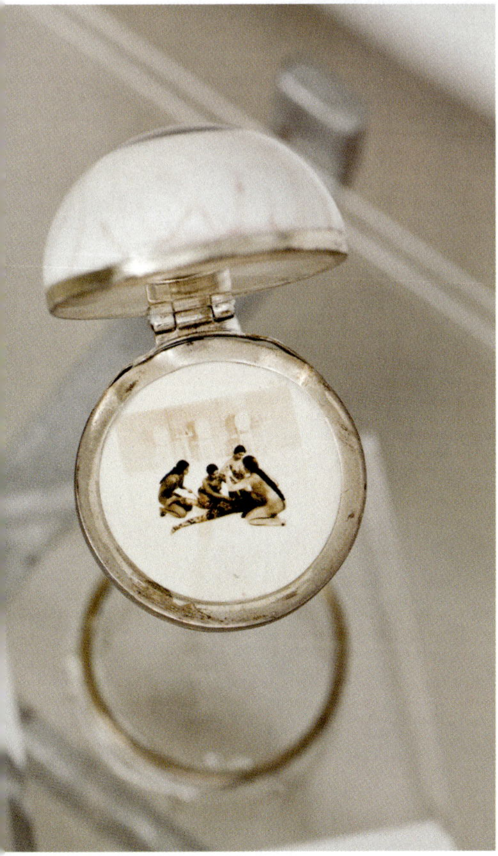
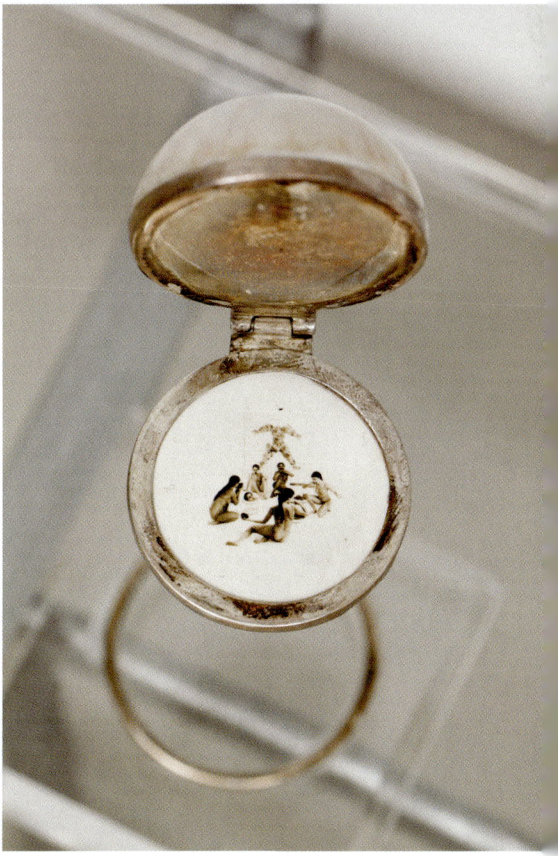

PLATE 12 Adriana Varejão, *Prato com mariscos*, 2011

PLATE 13 Adriana Varejão, *Mãe d'Água*, 2009

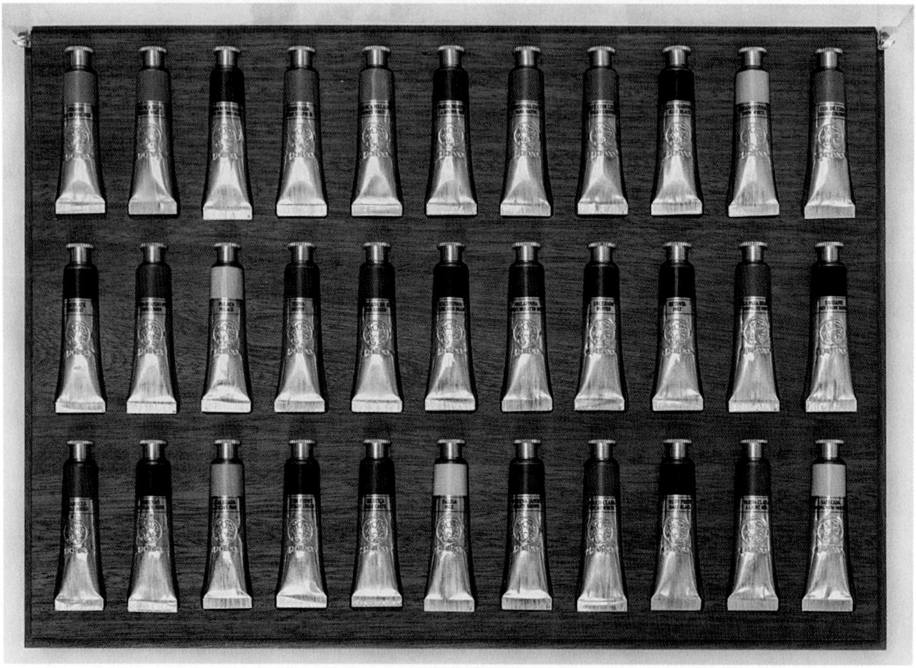

PLATE 14 (OPPOSITE) Adriana Varejão, *Tintas Polvo*, 2013

PLATE 15 (ABOVE) Adriana Varejão, *Polvo Portraits I (Seascape Series)*, 2014

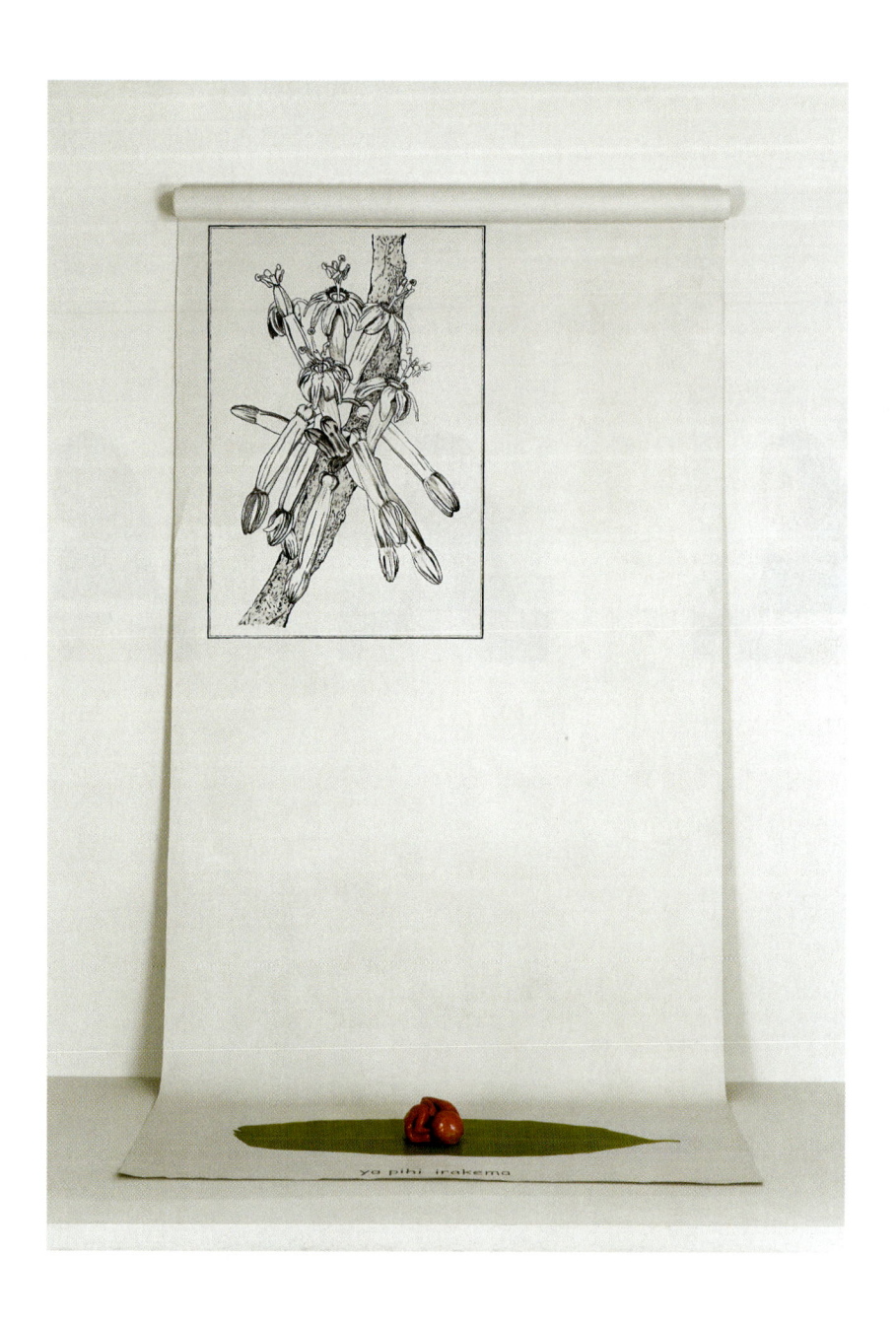

PLATE 16 (ABOVE) Adriana Varejão, *Em segredo*, 2003

PLATE 17 (OPPOSITE) Adriana Varejão, *Cadernos de viagem: Yãkoana*, 2003

Virola

Justicia pectoralis   Anadenanthera peregrina

PLATE 18 Adriana Varejão, *Éden*, 1992

PLATE 19 Adriana Varejão, *Mapa de Lopo Homem II*, 1992–2004

4   Carneiro da Cunha and Viveiros de Castro, "Vingança e temporalidade."
5   Clifford, *A experiência etnográfica*, and *The Predicament of Culture*; see also Rabinow, *Essays on the Anthropology of Reason*; Taussig, *Shamanism, Colonialism and the Wild Man*.
6   Schwarcz, "Varejar, ladrilhar."
7   Schwarcz, *The Spectacle of the Races*.
8   Sahlins, *Ilhas de história*.
9   Bhabha, *O Lugar da Cultura*.
10 Bhabha, *O Lugar da Cultura*, 26.
11 Bhabha, *O Lugar da Cultura*.
12 Said, *Orientalism*.
13 Said, *Orientalism*, 3.
14 Baxandall, *Patterns of Intention*, 37.
15 Baxandall, *Patterns of Intention*, 10. As Heliana Salgueiro shows in the introduction to that volume, it is hard to deal with the act of describing and visualizing. Distance, cultural difference, and a lack of synchrony are key concepts in this relationship to representation.
16 Lévi-Strauss, *The Savage Mind*.
17 Lévi-Strauss, *The Savage Mind*, 4.
18 Lévi-Strauss, *The Raw and the Cooked*.
19 Lévi-Strauss, *Tristes Tropiques*.
20 Lévi-Strauss, *The Way of the Masks*.
21 Lévi-Strauss, *Look, Listen, Read*. See also Menezes Neto, "Atravessando fronteiras," and "Boa para agir."
22 Gombrich, *Arte e ilusão*.
23 Geertz, "Art as a Cultural System," 1475–76.
24 Geertz, "Art as a Cultural System," 1481, 1475.
25 Geertz, "Art as a Cultural System," 1477.
26 Geertz, "Art as a Cultural System," 1478.
27 Geertz, "Art as a Cultural System," 1480.
28 Gell, *Art and Agency*, 6.
29 Gell, *Art and Agency*, 6 (emphasis in the original).
30 Gell, *Art and Agency*, 7.
31 Baxandall, *Patterns of Intention*, 69.
32 Baxandall, *Patterns of Intention*, 72.
33 Latour, *Jamais Fomos Modernos*, 141.
34 Menezes Neto, "Boa para agir."
35 Lévi-Strauss, *The Way of the Masks*, 148.
36 Baxandall, *Patterns of Intention*, 77.
37 Schwarcz and Varejão, *Pérola imperfeita*.
38 Valle Silva, "Aspectos demográficos dos grupos raciais."
39 Nogueira, *Tanto preto quanto branco*.
40 Telles, *Pigmentocracies*.
41 Fundação Instituto Brasileiro de Geografia e Estatística, "Pesquisa Nacional Por Amostra de Domicílios—1976."

42 In this list, *F* and *M* indicate feminine or masculine gender, respectively; *dimin* indicates diminutive form of the term, and *aug* indicates augmentative form.
43 Galician here implies historical origin in the Galician cultural/ethnolinguistic community of northwestern Spain.
44 McClintock, *Imperial Leather*.
45 Getúlio Vargas's dictatorship and populist government in Brazil (1937–45).
46 Moutinho, "Diferenças e desigualdades negociadas."
47 "Aquarela do Brasil."
48 *Ars Poetica*, 11, 361–65.
49 Mitchell, *Picture Theory*.
50 Rousseau, "Discourse on the Origins of Inequality."
51 Merleau-Ponty, "De Mauss a Claude Lévi-Strauss," 199–200.
52 Lévi-Strauss, *Antropologia estrutural*.
53 See Strathern, *O gênero da dádiva*; Viveiros de Castro, *A inconstância da alma selvagem*.
54 Deleuze, *Essays Critical and Clinical*, 1.
55 Andrade, "Manifesto antropófago."
56 The book that Adriana Varejão and I published in 2014 was a result of four years of dialogue and conversation (Schwarcz and Varejão, *Pérola imperfeita*).
57 Mitchell, *Picture Theory*, 63.

7

On Negative Becoming

LUCAS BESSIRE

AN ORIGIN STORY

"I do not know my own story," the young woman called Tié was whispering.

It was 2007, late on a cool night in a new village at the edge of an ancient forest that pulsed in the dark and exhaled a rolling wind. We were huddled around a double handful of embers in the wattle-and-daub shack of Tié's captors. The shack was theirs, but they were away and the others were asleep. Even so she sat in silence, and I didn't know why.

Her husband, Cutai, was by that time my hunting partner, the one who gave me his first find of the day and who received mine in turn. The pretext was laughable: I was only good at digging up turtles, but I'd like to think it opened out into other kinds of reciprocity, however topsy-turvy, later. I knew how quietly Cutai could move when necessary. One moment I was asleep, the next he was there murmuring to come with him because his wife wanted to tell me something. It was an odd request.

It was also a moment ripe with promise. Halfway through my dissertation fieldwork, I felt like I was getting nowhere. Moreover, I thought Cutai and Tié were exceptional. They were members of one of the world's last bands of voluntarily isolated nomads until 2004, when they fled the dwindling forests of northern Paraguay, haunted by memories of genocidal violence and the sounds of the bulldozers that never stopped. They settled near a group of their close relatives, who had been captured by missionaries and Ayoreo from an enemy group and had converted to evangelical Christianity.

When the 2004 band of holdouts came in, many imagined them to be "the last great hope for Ayoreo cultural revitalization."[1] Yet the aftermath of the 2004 contact unsettled this narrative. Up close, the 2004 group defied fantasies of redemption based on encountering an untouched primitive ideal. Like Ishi a century before, much of their life in the forest had been focused on the practical problems of concealment from the alien beings—trucks, cattle, and bulldozers—they thought were relentlessly pursuing them.[2]

They called the space of postcontact life Cojñone-Gari, or That Which Belongs to the Strangers. It was a New World in which nothing was certain. Everything had been recast in doubt and murk, especially the coordinates of humanity. From their relatives, Tié and the others learned that surviving in this world meant negating their past selves and transforming themselves into *Ichadie*, or New People. It was a fraught process, never complete. Of them all, Tié seemed most able to resist the transformations demanded of her. Or so I thought. She sometimes said she couldn't hear and often fell into deep silences, and I never knew what she meant to say, much less what she thought about anything.

On that night we sat passing a tin cup of *tereré* and breathing fragrant smoke and listening to the night wind rustle through leaves and branches and tarps and garbage. Tié began to speak in her throaty whisper, eyes averted, with long pauses after each phrase:

> I do not know where my story will go.
> I was born in the place called Aremia.
> I do not know what story to tell.
> I do not know what I will say.
> I do not know.
> I do not know my story.
> We looked for *doidie* roots.
> We found them near Cucarani.
> Little birds, in the afternoon.
> We painted our bodies.
> We were *sucio*, dirty, in the afternoon.
> We painted our bodies with ashes and down.
> Black and white.
> They were *sucio*, dirty.

Sucio.
They sang.
They told many stories.
They saw far away.
The old man was there, too.
He told stories.
I do not know what to say.
We ate honey.
We killed fish.
We were dirty.
I do not know my story.
I do not know what to say.
My thoughts and my memories are gone.
They will no longer come to me.
I do not know my own story.

We sat quietly for a long time. I can't forget her fractured story, even though it pains me to share and I still don't understand it. What was she trying so hard to convey, if not her own not-quite-ness, the way she was suspended between opposing objectifications of her humanity, none of which fit? How to make sense of the senseless delirium she seemed to communicate? What footings can such vertiginous perspectives suggest for a politically engaged anthropology of the contemporary? And how to resist the ways my recycled stories about these stories—despite my intentions otherwise—seem to amass, subtly and inexorably, a terrible affective weight of their own that threatens to drag them deeper and deeper into the dizzyingly mournful miasma of a death foretold?

ETHNOGRAPHIC DELIRIUM

In his short essay "Literature and Life," Gilles Deleuze evokes two poles of delirium: a "diseased" delirium of domination based on holding immanence accountable to the ideal types it imposes, and a "bastard" delirium that "ceaselessly stirs beneath dominations, resisting everything that crushes and imprisons."[3] It is this second form of delirium, he argues, that opens us up to the vital possibilities of becoming. For Deleuze, "to become is not to attain a form (identification, imitation, Mimesis) but to find the zone of proximity, indiscernibility or undifferentiation where one can no longer be distinguished" from the thing itself.[4] This apparent melding, however, is always interrupted by the constant slippage between category and content. Writing toward this slippage offers a technique for affirmative resistance when it fills in these gaps with fabulations of a missing people. Deleuze is quite specific about what kind of people are missing: "a minor people ... a bastard people, inferior, dominated, always in becoming, always incomplete."[5]

This is precisely the kind of Indigenous subject—bastardized, ex-, incomplete, and resolutely open-ended—that is all too often erased from and by much philosophically oriented anthropology no less than the ethnographic archives on which such formulations draw their claims of empirical weight.[6] In its refusal of the preemptive foreclosure of her humanity, the dizzying testimony of Tié unsettles this erasure. Instead, her unauthorized voice pushes against the limits of the common categories by which Indigenous life becomes intelligible and governed. Her palpable sense of dislocation reveals the generative power of negation and the paradoxical resilience of human life. More precisely, she calls attention to an unsettling art of living wherein immanence is collapsed into the terms of rupture in such a way as to make the affirmative power of desire or the leakiness of the social indistinguishable from a cascading chain of negations, at once deadly and vital. Common among Ayoreo and closely attuned to the global politics of Indigeneity, this delirious life project may be considered a mode of negative becoming.[7]

Such vital arts emerge from and reformulate the evolving conflict between the world-making projects of Ayoreo and the world-ordering projects of others. This life project arises from the efforts of people to live with and against several key contradictions in the politics of legitimate Ayoreo life[8]—a politics whereby cultural legitimacy is increasingly used to distinguish who is worthy of exceptional protection and who is allowed to die.[9] This collapse of cultural and biolegitimacy is causally related to the ways that the incoherence of the Indigenous category may, under certain conditions, reorganize the relationship between contingency and actualization for some of those to whom the Indigenous label partly sticks.[10]

Such global dynamics take particularly acute form among so-called ex-primitives: internally colonized Indigenous peoples struggling to survive on the margins of a dystopic New World, not least because their ties to legitimating cultural origins are now refused, impossible, tenuous, or suspect.[11] For these marginalized subjects, the diffuse collapse of culture and life may at times blur into the definitive operations of neocolonial governance, especially when it occurs against a schizoid backdrop of seemingly contradictory forms of violence aimed at people who refuse to stay within the authorized slots of Indigeneity. This is certainly true for Ayoreo people, who confront a dizzying conflation of bodily diminishment, voracious ecological destruction, the apocalyptic eschatology of millenarian faith, the exclusionary stigmas reserved for supposedly deculturated indigenes, the feverish pursuit of redemptive cosmologies, the caudillistic expenditures of advocacy nongovernmental organizations (NGOs), and the structural inequalities of neoliberal political economies.

Negative becoming does not merely instantiate these powerful forces of destruction—it also trips them up in their own contradictions. In such ways, this technique of negation illustrates a crucial point. It underlines how the sense-destroying axes of colonial dispossession engender not only well-documented coordinates of suffering but also novel vital experiments and unsettling kinds of immanence. The paradox, of course, is that such life projects often do not fit within or are imperceptible to many of the conventional analytic dichotomies used to understand emergence in Indigenous communities. This disconnect between analytic foreclosure and vital open-endedness is not coincidental. Rather, it is a crucial operation that calls attention to a wider system of expenditure and negation, a system to which Ayoreo sensibilities are more finely attuned than many analyses of it.[12] This begs the question: How might a more serious approximation to the creative and critical capacities of hypermarginalized Indigenous subjects help correct the mistakes of our past selves or negate the colonial genealogies of our own analytics and write more effectively against their systemic dispossession?

AFFIRMATIVE NEGATION

Aasi was one of the leaders of the forest band captured by armed missionaries and enemy Ayoreo in 1986. The story goes something like this: In late December the New Tribes Mission pilot spotted a column of smoke and later located a camp of forest Ayoreo. The following day, missionaries led a group of Christian Ayoreo to the camp. Led by Aasi, the forest people had seen the airplane and prepared defenses. The mission group approached the village at dawn, led by Aasi's brother—who had been captured in 1979. A fight broke out. Five Christians were killed and four badly wounded. The mission group retreated, and after much shouted discussion the forest people agreed to surrender. Four days later, the captives arrived at the mission on the back of a tractor-trailer. Afterward several of the New People starved themselves to death, and others died of "sadness." Aasi took the unprecedented step of renouncing his status as a *dacasute* warrior. Instead, he became widely known as an *ayaajingaque* peacemaker.

He was a slight man who rarely spoke but who radiated kindness and a calm strength. It was hard earned. He had found visions and killed jaguars alone with a spear and he had stood to defend his people in the face of death and he still carried the slug from a shotgun lodged against the base of his skull and he was the best tracker left alive although he could barely breathe in those days. He could find lost children or tell the sex and age of a tortoise from the slightest traces of its passage, whether over hard-packed earth or leafy detritus. When he sang the old songs with his gourd rattle, the other elders would gather and sit and listen until dawn to show their respect. He was a reluctant storyteller but masterful when the mood was upon him.

One of his funniest stories was about the time he made a mistake and fell from the top of a tall honey tree onto his face, breaking several ribs, bleeding internally, and losing consciousness. Eventually he crawled back to the camp, only to discover that everyone else had decided to move that day. He did not wish them to wait on his account, so he said nothing about his injuries. He told them to go ahead, and without a single word of complaint he picked up his heavy bag and followed as best as he could, stopping only to pass out from time to time before continuing his journey.

Aasi and I spent much time together in the twilight of his life around his hearth and under the fluorescent glare of hospital lights. I like to think that we were close, but like always that is a tricky game and I can never be sure. He told me that his life had changed in the mid-1990s. First, he contracted tuberculosis and began to suffer from the chronic wasting disease that later killed him. Next, he began to work on nearby ranches clearing the forest with an ax and hunting iguanas for their skins. Then, he became a Christian.

Few were so intimate with rupture. Contact, for Aasi and later the New People, meant entering a New World where Jesus was the ultimate arbiter of moral humanity. Aasi associated Cojñone-Gari with a set of causal relationships and orientations that were radically different from those he attributed to Erami, the forest world of the past. Life suited to this new world was created when God poured his spirit into a convert. This pouring erased the person's willpower, emotions, and memory and created a New Person who had a reconstituted kind of soul matter called the *ayipie*, and who was capable of surviving in the present. What was so striking about Aasi's take on this general project of rupture was that he explicitly related it to the originary differentiations of humans and nonhumans recounted in the *adode* myths now abandoned as satanic lies. These myths described the origins of moral humanity. They recounted an Original Time populated by the Ancestor Beings, an undifferentiated group of proto-humans, proto-animals, proto-plants, and proto-qualities. Each myth explained how these Ancestors were transformed into the nonhuman forms apparent in the world today. At the moment of transformation, each Ancestor Being gave two things to those who maintained a humanoid form. The first was a *puyaque* taboo, or a moral restriction on behavior and its associated punishment. The second was a prescriptive chant that could be used to relieve the illness or malaise caused by transgressing the restricted behavior through sympathetic magic.

The key point is that humanity emerges as a condensation of transformative processes in these retrospective descriptions of the complex of myths, taboos, and curing chants. The Original Time of the Ancestor Beings preceded the rise of human society. The Ancestors were not fully human. Rather, they were humanoids that were fundamentally amoral and unsocialized, lacking the means to reproduce a moral society. In fact, these Beings learned how to become moral humans—how to make fire, weave clothing, construct shelters, plant gardens, kill game, wage war, cure illness, and enlist metaphysical alliances—only through the embodied knowledge imparted by other Ancestor Beings as they transformed themselves. In other words, moral human life is defined as the capacity to harness and control the terms of transformation and rupture.[13] This notion is akin to an Ayoreo theory of becoming.

Confronted with the insoluble existential dilemmas of contact, many Ayoreo turned to this theory. Yet in a dizzying inversion, they argued that reclaiming the capacity of becoming in Cojñone-Gari meant negating the very coordinates of the moral in Erami: myths, curing chants, and ceremonies. The abandonment of tradition, in such a scheme, simply marked the most recent of several historical transformations of humanity. Citing and extending self-transformation through negation was a radical affirmation of Ayoreo capacities of becoming in the face of violent subjection. Continuity implied rupture and vice versa. Perhaps the peculiar agency drawn from the positive charge of rupture was why people like Aasi seemed to wear their self-negation so deeply and so lightly at once.

I could never share Aasi's ease with rupture. And I wish the story could end with his resilience, or that I could forget how these ideal trajectories of self-transformation would prove so illusory and crash so harshly against the insoluble contradictions of becoming an Indian in the Chaco. Even so, Aasi was one of the few who never lost his faith. Faced with the certainty of an undignified death hastened by appalling neglect in the local health care system, he was the one to comfort me. "I am not a child who cries with his fear of death," he told me. "If I cry, it appears as though I am a liar, as if I had no faith."

While this project of affirmative rupture may be carefully attuned to the upheavals of contact, the paradox is that within the peculiar double binds of internal colonialism it also made its Ayoreo proponents newly eligible for extermination. That is, Ayoreo subjects confronted a system in which two purportedly oppositional domains of dehumanization were conjoined and mutually sustaining: subjection due to their ostensive difference, and violent dispossession justified by the ostensive loss of legitimate difference, or culture death. Together, these operations animate an apparatus of consumption predicated on incoherence and the mutual interruption of contradictory schema of legitimate Indigenous life. Dysfunction is how it functions. This nonlinear apparatus, in turn, instantiates a wider political and moral economy aimed not so much at production as at senseless expenditures of life.

The colonizing force of nonsensical expenditures emerges from the embodied conjuncture of several projects focused on Ayoreo life: evangelical missionization, the culturalist protest against that evangelism, rampant ecological destruction, the hypervisibility of so-called isolated peoples, and the renewed conceptual investment in primitive cosmologies. Each can be considered a particular mode of delirium, and when they converge around expenditure, the delirium is intensified in politically instrumental ways.

The evangelical missionary project among Ayoreo, for instance, never claimed to be rational. Indeed, the entire mission order was predicated on a fundamental disorder: the irrational and excessive desire to hoard Indian souls. Ambiguity and efforts to eliminate doubt—efforts that in turn led to further ambiguities in need of domestication—were the primary technique and motor of the project. This principle, in which frustration blurred into faith and vice versa, emerged from the gap between missionary ideals of savagery, conversion, and salvation and the hard practicalities of managing unruly people. This delirious disorder linked various aspects of mission work. Missionaries saw themselves as ideally overwhelmed by the passion to collect Indian souls, or "brown gold," in lands dominated by Satan. Only by doing so could the Body of Christ's Bride be complete and the Rapture of the faithful occur.[14]

Yet dealing with the devil for Indian souls meant abandoning any clear distinctions between dark and light. The pursuit of souls meant that missionaries became complicit in local systems of slavery, epidemics, shamanism, and infanticide. The figure of savagery in need of contact was thus amplified not because the missions functioned smoothly but precisely because they did not.

The ever-increasing drive to hunt forest Indians was at least partly a response to the contradictions of running missions that resembled death camps. Repeated time and again, the Indian hunt can be considered the central ritual of the colonizing project. Its participants sought to track down, capture, enslave, and convert small groups of forest Indians in order to save and care for them by eradicating their difference. In doing so the Indian hunt created and amplified the figures of savagery to be hunted anew.

Culturalist critiques of missionary hunts also risked blurring into their opposite. The tragic outcome of the 1986 contact with Aasi and the others became the target of a vigorous international critique, which framed the Indian hunt as a form of ethnocide. This narrative of ethnocide became the foundational myth of Totobiegosode-Ayoreo humanity.[15] It is also an origin myth for the political anthropology of Indigeneity. The equation is simple: the death of culture is equivalent to the loss of the value of Indigenous life. "Genocide assassinates people in their bodies," Pierre Clastres wrote in his famous 1974 essay on the topic. "Ethnocide kills them in their minds."[16] For Clastres, "ethnocide is the systematic destruction of the ways of living and thinking of people different from those who lead this venture of destruction."[17] He finds this same "will to reduce difference and alterity" to be "at the very heart of the State's substance."[18] Moreover, he links ethnocide and the reduction of alterity to a modern drive for economic production: "Produce or die, this is the motto of the West.... Woe to the Indians caught in the path!"[19]

A special kind of woe was reserved for the Ayoreo. The Paraguayan ethnologist Ticio Escobar invoked Clastres's definition to summarize the aftermath of the 1986 contact with Totobiegosode-Ayoreo. In an evocative passage that helped galvanize the Indigenous rights movement in Alfredo Stroessner's Paraguay, he described the ethnocide of Ayoreo in the following terms:

> The most tragic effect of missionary ethnocide is that it breaks the spine of a people, it converts their members into caricatures of westerners and later, as it does not have any reasonable project to offer them, it pushes them irresponsibly to sell hides, to hand over their forests and symbols, and towards direct exploitation or it sends them to a marginal underworld of begging, prostitution, alcoholism and petty delinquency where they end as beings that have no place in their culture or the culture of others.... Once the community is dissolved, the pact that united it with nature according to its common designs is also dissolved; soon, the Indian finds himself in opposition to a universe with which he once identified himself and he sees his rela-

tions with his ecological environment adulterated; at the end, he himself is turned into a predatory destroyer. Collective tradition is also dissolved: the anathema launched against his ancient beliefs creates an artificial wall of forgetting that interferes with the transmitting metabolism of his culture: a phobic negation of the past and a schizophrenic fracture of time invents a pure present without ghosts or memories.[20]

What is difficult to understand is how recognizing Indians as the "shadows of men"[21] seems to require, almost despite itself, denying the strange agencies and vitalisms that surge from the former Savage's new role as consummate negator and destroyer, no less than they do from descriptions of that role. This denial arises from the reduction of the value of life to the limits of bounded traditional culture. By accepting this reduction, the model of ethnocide answers before it is posed the question of why any one of these shadowy ex-Indians would so eagerly invest in "opposition to a universe with which he once identified himself" and the "phobic negation of the past" or in a schizoid fracturing of time. It presumes these emerging vitalisms are not generative experimental forms finely adapted to wider colonial dynamics, but pathological disorders that are symptoms of contamination and death. In doing so, diagnosis and symptom are inverted. Ethnocide reappears not as pathology but as organizing principle and essential metanarrative. Yet it, too, is haunted by a delirious investment in the same dehumanizing logics as the Indian hunt. The unavoidable irony is that both this dismissive diagnosis and the feverish pursuit of the primitive not only sustain terrible violence but inadvertently birth a strange new subject: an interstitial, residual being caught between life and death, animated by profane desires and radiating decay yet somehow stubbornly still right there, refusing to assume a frozen pose, in your face, talking back, cracking wise, asking for a coin, trying to turn a trick in an outrageous outfit and with—could it be?—a raucous laugh.

One problem with this model lies in how it reproduces capitalist narratives of production. Yet the pursuit of capital in the Chaco is by no means rational. Cleared of most of its former Indigenous inhabitants, this once iconic wilderness is in the midst of a land rush. Because of the rising price of beef and the legal privileging of private property, land prices have skyrocketed. Many people with long-standing titles to large tracts of land, including most of the Mennonite ranchers in the area, have become multimillionaires. Much of this capital is reinvested in "improvements" and clearing more forest. The result is a shockingly fast transformation of an entire ecosystem, greater disparity in wealth, and one of the highest deforestation rates in the world. Many ranchers and government officials label this transformation as production, which is considered a moral value. In planetary terms, of course, this transition from a carbon-capturing and extremely biologically productive multistoried forest to a dystrophic grass monoculture used to feed beef cattle is senseless. Production blurs into its own economic and social opposites. It is not hard to share the common Ayoreo perception that the entire exercise is a wanton staging of destruction and a celebration of negative power, maximally expressed in the figure of the bulldozer: a massive howling machine of polished metal and inexorable treads that crushes all in its path, manned by rotating crews, never stopping.

It is no coincidence that the assault on the forest is accompanied by nostalgia for the wilderness and supposedly isolated primitives. The frustrated desires for pure difference are once again displaced onto the small bands of Ayoreo holdouts who, despite all odds, maintain a life of nomadic concealment in the shrinking forests. Like the New People before them, they have gained an international hypervisibility. They legally resemble elements of nature and are regularly celebrated as existing in harmony with nature.[22] While the hypermarginality of actual Ayoreo-speaking people is rendered politically invisible, a transnational moral economy is mobilized to preserve the haunting fantasy of a pristine Ayoreo life hidden in a besieged wilderness. The paradox, again, is that the terms by which this difference becomes appealing are the very terms that justify their abandonment to the fate that we think we already know, the sense of an inevitable end foreclosing their futures as surely as the bulldozers do.

The combined result is an incoherent colonial system predicated not on the rational accumulation of profits but on a series of violent, nonsensical expenditures that often converge around the consumption of Indigenous life. This resonates closely with Georges Bataille's startling insight that what he called "unproductive expenditures"—waste, destruction, sacrifice, and orgiastic consumption—were not merely dysfunctional but actually at the core of global political economies and their failed efforts to domesticate the excessive fecundity of natural and social life.[23] Bataille argues that the fetishization of positive production masks and sustains the operations of systemic negation, the true motor of capitalist civilization. The point for Bataille is that this negative expenditure, or *depensé*, paradoxically contains a latent affirmative force. That is, this kind of targeted destruction does not only destroy but also creates and sacralizes that which is negated. Only by intentionally amplifying this play of affirmation within negativity, he argues, could one have the slightest chance to reclaim in its midst a measure of "subversive sovereignty," the strange power that flows from inhabiting self-negation and embracing life beyond authorized utility.[24] From this perspective, the dynamics that meld the experiences of becoming Indian in the Chaco with ethnographic analyses of them—loss, abjection, insufficiency, and the breakdown of narrative itself—take on the shades of something more than lamentation. Instead, they voice an experimental resilience that continually reworks contingencies into becomings, violence into immanence.

BROKEN LINES OF FLIGHT

Aasi's nephew was a man I'll call Pejei. One evening, I noticed that he was missing from his customary place around the communal fire. Pejei didn't appear the next night or the night after that. It appeared that his entire household had left and that his shack was abandoned. No one was chopping wood or hauling water, and there was no fire inside. But someone was inside: I heard moans and mutters late at night. Then, suddenly, Pejei was back. His laugh was strained, his smile a little too quick, and he had nothing to say. The others were careful and gentle with him, making a point to share their food. When I asked him where he had been, an older woman interjected.

"His ayipie left him," she said. "But now he's okay again."

Pejei nodded and smiled. I learned that he had spent the last three days tied to a post with a coarse rope, thrashing and moaning and trying to run away to the forest. Pejei was one of several Totobiegosode who were susceptible to a form of madness called *urusoi*. A handsome man in his mid-fifties with the build of a weightlifter, he came from a long line of distinguished dacasute warriors and was said to resemble his father, Aasi's brother and the principal leader of the Totobiegosode whose band was hunted down and captured in December 1978.

By March 1979, Pejei's father had starved himself to death. The young Pejei was hired out to a local rancher, and when he returned several months later, he learned that most of his family had died in his absence. He then married a young woman who five years later gave birth to twins, traditionally considered taboo. Pejei's first bout of urusoi came when missionaries pressured the couple to keep both infants, despite the fact that Pejei saw a sign that indicated the death of his wife if they violated the prohibition. Back on the mission, they had little choice. True to Pejei's prophecy, his wife soon died. Since then, attacks of urusoi could strike him at any time. He had been told to take antipsychotic medication.

Urusoi could be caused by any profound fear. I was told that it was often triggered by frightening encounters with white men or things associated with them, such as the sudden appearance of a Cojñoi carrying a gun in the forest. The episode I witnessed with Pejei was attributed to an airplane that had unexpectedly passed overhead at dusk. The sound of this airplane and the air it pushed down, "its breath," touched Pejei, and the fright caused his ayipie to leave his body.

During my fieldwork, several people suffered from attacks of urusoi. One man kept ripping off his clothes, trying to grab his spear and moaning that he had to kill the Cojñone. Aasi's wife told me that it was the heat of a fever that made her want to cast off her clothes and run back to the forest. Yet urusoi itself was an unstable sign. Prior to contact, this affliction was attributed to transgressing the moral prohibitions of ritually powerful spirit beings, particularly Poji, or Iguana. In the past, a person struck with urusoi was thought to mimic and acquire the traits of Poji. Like an iguana, the afflicted ones would run to the forest, sleep in the daytime in a hole they dug underground, and eat raw food. They ran from their own people, lost their ability to speak, became afraid of fire, turned yellow, and jumped from one place to another at dizzying, impossible speed. Those afflicted by urusoi lost the defining core of their moral humanity. In the absence of the ayipie, they acted like nonhuman beings.

In the upheavals of contact, cases of urusoi proliferated. But those afflicted with urusoi in Cojñone-Gari experienced symptoms different from those experienced prior to contact. Postcontact victims of urusoi were not compromised by violating the taboos of a single spirit being, but by residues of their past selves embodied in their flesh. The other Totobiegosode explained that Pejei's sickness was caused not by his ayipie's vanishing or hovering in an indistinct state but by its returning to the past. If he ran out of medicine, his ayipie left his body and returned to the *cucha bajade,* or former practices now considered deeply offensive to God. Like Pejei, others afflicted by urusoi turned against the trappings of moral life in Cojñone-Gari. Like Pejei, they attempted to destroy all traces of Cojñone around them, particularly the symbols of contact. They tore their clothes, they broke their dishes, they refused to eat the foods of the whites, and they tried to run to the forest. They were usually restrained by being tied to a tree or a post. Ayoreo said that someone suffering from urusoi acted "like an animal," but the symptoms bore a striking resemblance to past forms of human life.

Ayoreo used the same word to describe the state of being drunk or high. During my fieldwork, huffing shoe glue or drinking grain alcohol were the chosen means of escape for a number of younger Ayoreo. To be sure, they had much to flee. Across the Chaco, Ayoreo were treated as subhuman matter out of place. This was particularly acute for the many who lived in unauthorized camps on the outskirts of towns and cities, where disease, poverty, rape, and murder were commonplace. The terrible irony is that Ayoreo projects of self-actualization through negation were most often legible to outsiders only as the loss of culture and a return to an essential savagery, a process that amplified the violent negativity such critiques ostensibly protested. In such disturbed conditions, urusoi was a radical technique for reworking the conditions of colonial subjection into a kind of negative vitality.

Ayoreo commonly say that those who indulge in intoxicants have a *vicio*, or a vice. The most extreme of the Ayoreo *viciosos* were those known as the *Puyedie*, or the Prohibited Ones.[25] They were a group of some two dozen Ayoreo who lived hidden in the tall grass of an abandoned lot behind the train station, where they supported themselves through sex work of the most marginal kinds. Puyedie were defined by two vices. The first was their addiction to smoking coca paste—an unrefined mash of coca leaves, sulphuric acid, and kerosene, gasoline, or benzol that was known in Ayoreo slang as *puyai*. Prior to contact, the word puyai referred to the set of moral prohibitions established through *adode* myths. Now it is applied to intoxicating drugs as well as to the domains of the past considered profane and immoral. The second vice of the puyedie was consuming dirt and bricks, which they pounded into dust and ate. In a series of remarkable interviews with the Bolivian anthropologist Irene Roca Ortiz, who directed the first Ayoreo public health project in 2012, some Puyedie said that any bricks would do, while others ate only the bricks used to line the bottom of open sewage ditches. The eating of bricks and dirt was not secondary to the coca smoking. Some said it was brick eating that led to the coca smoking, rather than vice versa. They said that some Puyedie eschewed any other kind of food and ate so many bricks that their skin turned yellow—like an iguana.

One Puye woman named Rosy told of passing out and waking up in strange places, snatches of incoherent conversation, bribing police with money or sex, and living a life defined by violent confrontations with Ayoreo and Cojñone alike.[26] She began sniffing gasoline in her early teens while living on an evangelical mission near the city, and she learned how to smoke coca paste from other Ayoreo. Rosy said that she knew her vices were dangerous: "The vices kill us." Many of her friends had already died from their vices—more than she could keep track of: "More than ten, more than twenty, I don't know." She herself was frequently sick these days, from what she didn't know: "When you are a viciosa, any illness will grab you, you know." Even so, she said she wouldn't give up her vices: "They are sweet to me." In her interviews with Roca Ortiz, Rosy emphasized that her deadly vices gave her life. She said that without her vices, she became more like an animal. She said she could not give them up: "You'd better tie me to a tree," she said, smiling, "or I won't stay." The same coarse rope is used to tie all those afflicted with urusoi or vice, to keep them from running off to an alterity at once inhuman and legitimating. And it is the same knot that always slips.

NEGATIVE BECOMING

How to account for such attitudes as something more than evidence of loss and disintegration? The voices recounted above provide some key clues. They imply that certain Ayoreo life projects emerge from those points at which two distinct labors of the negative collide: the incoherent negativity of internal colonialism manifested in oppositional schema for objectifying and governing legitimate Indigenous life, and an Ayoreo immanence premised on gaining mastery over this insoluble negativity by claiming, in distinct ways, the power of self-negation as a meaningful technique for reproducing moral life despite and through the terms of dehumanization. In other words, negative becoming as a vital technique flows from the delirium-inducing synergies between contradictory regimes of Ayoreo life. These include the fracturing of sympathetic magic and the frustrated promise of evangelical eschatology; the world-ending violence relentlessly stalking certain small Indigenous populations; the rampant ecological devastation of the Gran Chaco; the feverish pursuit of primitive cosmologies and their redemptive potentials by tradition-seeking anthropologists; the moral aspirations and economies of humanitarian NGOs focused on preserving culturalized life; the tenuous coordinates of causality for dispossessed peoples and the lightning-quick oscillations from reason to nonsense and back again that these engender; the irrepressible desires to assert humanity despite or through cataclysmic threats and in doing so to reclaim authority over the conditions of its possibility even if this means self-sacrifice; and the power of ethnography to conjure up and unleash spirit negatives in its efforts to effect a further transcendence of self and world. Ayoreo projects of negative becoming embrace and intensify the delirium of colonial subjection.

Among the most powerful of such contradictions is a conceptual operation and current trend in some anthropological theory that first measures the value of Indigenous life in terms of its continuity with an artificially limited set of cosmological positions glossed as nonmodern ontological exteriorities, then crafts the social orders of a future demanded by forecasted crises upon the disavowed exclusions of this ideal, and finally imposes the terms of this future back onto the present as a normative schema for a political anthropology aimed at solidarity with contemporary Indigenous peoples and their struggles. Such an operation, of course, cannot account for the projects of negative becoming. This lack of accounting, as Michael Taussig argues, is intrinsic to colonial violence and the "epistemic murk" on which it depends.[27] The persecution of difference under colonial regimes does not eradicate alterity but amplifies it through fetishized images of wildness in need of domestication. This amplification, in turn, draws force from and is predicated on what poses as its countermeasure, "the hermeneutic violence that creates feeble fictions in the guise of realism, objectivity and the like, flattening contradiction and systematizing chaos."[28]

Such contradictions, as Bataille reminds us, may be immanent not to language games but to an entire planetary economy wherein conventional framings of Indigenous struggles pose as metanarratives for masking what is actually a struggle over the means, methods, and modes of expenditure. If the capacity to control the terms of expenditure is inseparable from sovereignties of various kinds, the issue is not only how to limit expenditure but also how to better understand its uneven distribution.

What kind of ethnography is capable of writing towards such openings rather than their preemptive foreclosure? As outlined in this volume, the anthropology of becoming suggests several starting points.[29] In the first place, an analytical shift from being to becoming requires a theory of the Indigenous subject that goes beyond cultural determinism. Instead, ethnographers are challenged to attend to the critical capacities and creative agencies so forcefully retained by historically dispossessed people despite and through the nonsensical and constantly displaced footings of dehumanization. Doing so means presuming that the affirmative force of such emerging sensibilities lies not in their noninteriorizable qualities but in the experimental resilience they reflect and provoke under conditions of extreme marginality. This, in turn, challenges the sense of inevitability implied by many analytic tools and allows Indigenous subjects to reappear not as ideal types known in advance but as always unfinished, incomplete, and open-ended.

In such ways, the ethnography of becoming reclaims anthropological insights from their philosophical uses (including the primitivist genealogies of Deleuze and Guattari's original conceptualizations).[30] In doing so, it raises new questions and possible orientations for the political anthropology of indigeneity. Political critique can no longer be restricted to the defense of cultural continuity or the logics of cosmological alterity; indeed, restricting the search for revisionist potential to the ahistorical contents of primitive ontologies or a society against the state is no solution at all, but part of an updated mode of domination justified in the name of impending crisis. The anthropology of becoming interrupts this mode by refusing to take categories for granted, by staying close to contents to unsettle forms, and by finding actionable critique in the unruliness of that peculiar spark that unsettles, ignites, and always escapes, but not before illuminating the shape of a new humanistic politics and ethnography yet to come.

NOTES

1. Bartolome, *El Encuentro de la Gente y los Insensatos*, 308.
2. For more on Ishi, the member of the Yahi tribe who was caught in northern California in 1911 and later celebrated as "the last wild Indian in North America," see, for example, Kroeber, *Ishi in Two Worlds*.
3. Deleuze, "Literature and Life," 229.
4. Deleuze, "Literature and Life," 225.
5. Deleuze, "Literature and Life," 228.
6. See, for instance, Hage, "Critical Anthropological Thought and the Radical Political Imaginary Today"; Viveiros de Castro, "Introduction," and "Perspectival Anthropology and the Method of Controlled Equivocation."
7. Space constraints prevent a full discussion of these points here. For an elaboration of the arguments suggested in this chapter, see Bessire, *Behold the Black Caiman*.
8. For insightful analyses of the global politics of life in question, see especially Fassin, "Another Politics of Life Is Possible," and *Humanitarian Reason*.
9. Much has been written, of course, on the governmental force of the culture concept, especially within multiculturalism. See especially Hale, "Neoliberal Multiculturalism"; Jean Jackson, "Culture, Genuine and Spurious"; Povinelli, *The Cunning of Recognition*.
10. For a further development of these points, see Bessire, "Apocalyptic Futures," "The Politics of Isolation," and "The Rise of Indigenous Hypermarginality."
11. This notion of the ex-primitive is an expanded version of that developed so eloquently by Clifford Geertz in "Life among the Anthros."
12. My discussion of negativity is indebted to Gaston Gordillo's gripping analyses of "rubble" for criollo settlers in the Argentine Chaco (*En el Gran Chaco* and *Landscapes of Devils*). Gordillo reveals how the peculiar generative force of negativity resides in the ways people live alongside and appropriate the material detritus of state and corporate violence (*Debt*, 188–90). Such practices, Gordillo shows, go beyond any simplistic positivity, as they unsettle the totalizing force of negation itself.

13 For a related description of creation myths and cosmological tenets among the Kayapó, see Turner, "The Crisis of Late Structuralism."
14 See Johnston, *The Story of the New Tribes Mission*.
15 See Perasso, *Cronicas de Cacerias Humanas*.
16 Clastres, *Archeology of Violence*, 103.
17 Clastres, *Archeology of Violence*, 103.
18 Clastres, *Archeology of Violence*, 108.
19 Clastres, *Archeology of Violence*, 113.
20 T. Escobar, *Misión*, 37.
21 T. Escobar, *Misión*, 37.
22 See, for instance, Glauser, "Su presencia protege el corazón del Chaco Seco."
23 Bataille, *The Accursed Share*, vol. 3, and *The Unfinished System of Nonknowledge*.
24 Bataille, *The Accursed Share*, 3:198, 230–31.
25 This discussion is indebted to materials collected and shared by Irene Roca Ortiz. See also Roca Ortiz, *Pigasipiedie iji yoquijoningai*.
26 Irene Roca Ortiz, personal communication with the author, November 14, 2012.
27 Taussig, *Shamanism, Colonialism and the Wild Man*, xiii.
28 Taussig, *Shamanism, Colonialism and the Wild Man*, 132.
29 This use of becoming is borrowed from Biehl and Locke, "Deleuze and the Anthropology of Becoming," and inspired by discussions in Biehl, "CATKINE" and *Vita*.
30 Deleuze and Guattari, *Anti-Oedipus*, and *A Thousand Plateaus: Capitalism and Schizophrenia*. See also Biehl, "Ethnography in the Way of Theory." It is a noteworthy irony that the philosophical concept of becoming was initially inspired in part by a problematic ethnographic archive and latent primitivism, inherited from Antonin Artaud and Clastres. On Clastres's *Society against the State* and the repurposing of both within the project of ontological anthropology by Viveiros de Castro in "Introduction," see Deleuze and Guattari, *A Thousand Plateaus*.

V

8

Time Machines

The Matter of the Missing in Cyprus

ELIZABETH A. DAVIS

At the lab one afternoon in February—a few days after it had snowed in Nicosia for the first time in fifteen years, and all the scientists had left their tables and run outside in their white lab coats to play on the tarmac—M. and S. were working together on a case, S. dealing with the body and M. with the artifacts found with it in the grave. M. held up a watch for us to inspect. It was still in good shape, somewhat small for a man's watch, with a simple, round face and a cloth strap. M. pointed out that the watch had stopped when the date read "16." This body had come from a mass grave dating, it was thought, to August 16, 1974, immediately after the second Turkish invasion of Cyprus. M. and S. stopped for a moment and looked at the watch. S. explained to me that it might have been broken at the same moment when the man was killed. *We see lots of watches,* she said. *Usually, if they're not broken, you have to assume that they just kept working, keeping time long after the person was killed, which is weird—like a heart beating in a dead body. But then you see one like this, and you know it had the same fate as the person. It's like a time machine—it takes you right there.*

———

At this acute yet inchoate moment of polarizing conflict at the complex frontiers of global war, those frontiers may seem ever expansive—not only across geopolitical terrain but also across time. If the recent and ongoing conflicts in Iraq and Afghanistan, Darfur and Colombia, Gaza and Kurdistan, and Egypt and Syria are apprehended as the overdetermined effects of multiple vectors of empire, those vectors recur almost infinitely into the past, into many compound histories of violence, while their effects extend likewise into the future: into a "permanent war economy," as Ed Sard called it at the close of World War II;[1] a "permanent war," in the Reagan-era view of Sidney Lens;[2] or a "perpetual war for perpetual peace," in the words of Gore Vidal, just after 9/11.[3] The complementary threats of terrorism and security seem to petrify our political horizons as they define and legitimate state power along with domestic and transnational insurgencies. Like development, democratization, and debt, they appear as parts of the global unfolding of a systemic logic of sovereignty and capital, generating predictable forms and unyielding constraints for human life.

Yet in critical inquiries into war—past, present, or future—such closed visions of the political landscape are often animated by the search for contestatory and subversive, if not liberatory, spaces in the shadow of this apparent world machine. So it is imperative to ask by what criteria we may identify silence, reduction, conspiracy, and foreclosure in wartime—and also, on the contrary, how we might discern meaning, legitimacy, creativity, and possibilities of transformation. How do we distinguish the open and malleable aspects of war from those that are inevitably and intractably determined? Or, to borrow Eve Kosofsky Sedgwick's framing, how do we let paranoid hermeneutics interact with reparative ones in our "ecology of knowing"?[4]

I ask this question with a particular scene of perpetual war in mind. Since 2007, I have been visiting and working in Cyprus, a country still divided by the so-called Green Line, a de facto cease-fire line dating to 1958. It was designated as a United Nations (UN) cease-fire line following devastating episodes of civil and paramilitary violence in 1963, and it became the permanent partition line after the war of 1974. For the period between 1963 (when the first large-scale incidents of violence took place after Cyprus declared independence from Great Britain in 1960) and 1974 (when the cease-fire line definitively separated the island's populations), the government in the north reports 1,800 Turkish Cypriots killed and 502 missing, while the government in the south reports 3,000 Greek Cypriots killed, with 1,493 missing. During the same period, almost 215,000 Cypriots were displaced, or about a third of the Greek-Cypriot population and half the Turkish-Cypriot population.⁵ Although a political settlement for reunification has persisted as the dominant issue in Cyprus since 1974, the Green Line remains in place today.

The matter of this chapter arises from the forensic scene in which Cypriots reckon with war through the artifacts of death: the bones and belongings of those who went missing during the conflicts of the 1960s and 1970s. These artifacts objectify knowledge about the violence of the past that remains ever present in the ongoing division of people and places, in the Green Line and all its symbolic and material referents in Cypriots' everyday lives. But the forensic process of objectification does not exhaust their activity; the bones and belongings of the missing, fossils apparently "frozen" in the past, have come to be dynamic operators in complex time. Jane Bennett, parsing Deleuze, describes "an operator" as "that which, by virtue of its particular location in an assemblage and the fortuity of being in the right place at the right time, makes the difference, makes things happen, becomes the decisive force catalyzing an event."⁶ As operators in this sense, the artifacts of the missing tell many kinds of time in the performative rhythms of science and ritual; they materialize the temporalities of death, waiting, discovery, analysis, sanctification, and reburial.

The time machine that S. showed me that afternoon at the lab "takes you right there"—*there* being a *time*, the moment of a death. The literality of the watch's representation of time made it an ideal time machine, but in its capacity to materialize and stop time, it was no different from many other objects of forensic work. Layla Renshaw, writing of exhumations of the civil war dead in Spain, notes the "powerful material and aesthetic properties and affordances of the dead and their associated objects ... [which] actively shape the responses and representations that can be made by the living."⁷ The key to this insight lies in the "active" shaping of those representations by artifacts of the dead. I see this activity in the ways that bones tell time. They record the rhythms, patterns, and accidents of a person's life in traces left by eating habits, smoking habits, repetitive movements, diseases, injuries, and environmental elements. They also continue to tell time after death, aging at a different pace once buried in the ground. In this material and temporal capacity to tell time, bones are perhaps more like mechanical timepieces than they are like other organic matter of the body, such as the flesh—which quickly decomposes and disappears after death.⁸

These time machines, as I will call them, seemed to me during my fieldwork in Cyprus to generate what William Connolly, riffing on the final scene of *Barton Fink*, describes as "moment[s] of time without movement, engaging different zones of temporality"—moments that "arrest multiple sites and speeds of mobility that impinge on one another when in motion."[9] As I understand Connolly, it is the interference among these sites and speeds ("temporal force-fields") that actuates the experience of stopping ("time without movement"), but a focus is required (an image, object, or "multisensory memory") around which the past and present may coalesce in that moment.[10] What Sedgwick seeks as reparative hermeneutics can be found, I think, in Connolly's project to "amplify the experience of becoming" by harnessing such "protean moments"—dilated beyond the "punctual time" of decision and action—to new reflections on "ethics, politics, economics, and spirituality," and thus to develop an apprehension and appreciation of the uncertainty and essential openness of the world.[11]

I find this vision of a "world of becoming"[12] to be a vitalizing complement to the paranoid hermeneutics in which the violent history of Cyprus seems so deeply entrenched. Following Sedgwick's suggestion that paranoia is a chosen disposition to knowledge rather than a privileged path to truth, and that it may thus coexist and fruitfully interact with other dispositions to knowledge, I aim to develop a different orientation to these artifacts that are so often held to symbolize a Cyprus "frozen in time." In what follows, I explore how forensic objects in Cyprus refract and reorganize time, and how they thus summon and configure relationships between the past and the present, and the dead and the living. I examine the intimate and complex work scientists do to "see" a missing person in his or her bones—a work of reconstruction, simulation, imagination, conjuration, and humanization—and consider what this knowledge does to them in turn.

This chapter draws on the fieldwork I conducted in 2011–12 with the Committee on Missing Persons (CMP) in Cyprus. The CMP is a Greek-Cypriot/Turkish-Cypriot agency established in 1981 under UN auspices. Its mission is to determine the location and identity of the bodies of over 2,000 people, both combatants and civilians, who went missing during the violence of the 1960s and 1970s. The CMP has three political representatives: a Greek-Cypriot member and a Turkish-Cypriot member, appointed by their respective governments at the level of Minister, and another known as the "Third Member," selected by the International Committee of the Red Cross and appointed by the UN. Under the members' direction, since 2004, teams of Greek-Cypriot and Turkish-Cypriot archaeologists, physical anthropologists, and geneticists have been conducting investigations: exhuming remains on both sides of the

Green Line, analyzing them, and confirming their identity with DNA testing. Once a missing person's identity is confirmed, the remains are returned to the person's relatives—who also receive, if they wish, psychological counseling and financial support for burial.

For decades after the division in 1974, state authorities in the north and the south blocked the CMP's investigations, concealing information about the deaths of the missing and the location of their bodies, and either encouraging relatives to put the past behind them (in the north) or cynically nurturing the hope among relatives that their loved ones might still be alive (in the south). Exhumations of mass graves in Cyprus were conducted occasionally in the late 1990s and early 2000s by international nongovernmental organizations such as Physicians for Human Rights,[13] and by consulting agencies like the for-profit British Inforce Foundation and the nonprofit Argentine Forensic Anthropology Team. Even though the CMP had been established in 1981, it did not begin its own systematic investigations until 2004, when the recovery of the missing was "de-linked" from the prospect of a political settlement and newly framed as a "purely humanitarian issue"[14]—the outcome of efforts by officials in the Ministry of Foreign Affairs in the Republic of Cyprus, under pressure from the European Union (EU) and lobby groups formed by relatives of the missing.[15] Since then, of the 2,001 people counted officially as missing, 1,209 have been exhumed and 750 have been identified: 566 Greek Cypriots and 184 Turkish Cypriots.[16]

Although the CMP does not emphasize this point, its purview is limited to victims of inter-communal violence—that is, Greek Cypriots killed by Turkish Cypriots or Turkish military personnel, and Turkish Cypriots killed by Greek Cypriots or Greek military personnel. Many victims of violence cannot be counted in these communal terms. For example, it is well known that many Greek Cypriots, mostly leftists and other supporters of President Makarios at the time of the attempted coup in July 1974, were killed in that period by Greek-Cypriot members of EOKA-B,[17] a right-wing paramilitary organization, or by Greek officers and soldiers. Similarly, I have heard many accounts of the deliberate but secret bombing of Turkish-Cypriot homes and mosques by members of the TMT,[18] a Turkish-Cypriot paramilitary organization, or by the Turkish Army, which passed this violence off as Greek or Greek-Cypriot in order to stoke fear and hostility between the two communities and raise support among Turkish Cypriots for partition (*taksım*). At least two international agencies—the In-Force Foundation and Physicians for Human Rights—have investigated cases of Cypriots killed or hidden by members of "their own" communities, and a few archaeologists who now work at the CMP participated in those investigations, but the investigations themselves are organizationally unconnected to the CMP. Intra-communal violence in Cyprus, which has left unclaimed bodies throughout the island, is thus secreted within the mission of the CMP; forensic knowledge of these deaths is not legible to the politics of peace and reconciliation.

Despite the history of secrecy surrounding the fate of the missing, the CMP has received a great deal of media coverage in Cyprus in recent years, and the forensic teams have been featured in a number of television broadcasts and documentary films.[19] Images of scientists working with bones have become as commonplace as those of grief-stricken relatives in representations of Cyprus's violent history. This imagery originates and circulates in a very different way from the forensic photographs produced in the process of investigation and stored in the CMP's confidential archives. These very public photographs and films of scientists at work participate in a genre of representation that is well established outside Cyprus—in places like Argentina, Bosnia-Herzegovina, Chile, Guatemala, and Spain, where, as in Cyprus, forensic investigations of the missing and disappeared have become public forums for "witnessing" and "memory recovery."[20] Along with the forensic training and the infrastructure of investigation contributed to Cyprus by international agencies is this genre of publicity, which Francisco Ferrándiz and Alejandro Baer, documenting recent exhumations of leftists killed in the Spanish civil war, describe as a "global pool of images of repression, loss, terror and violence."[21] This genre features images of mourning women—the Mothers of the Plaza de Mayo in Argentina, for example, mirroring the Mothers of the Missing in Cyprus—as well as images of forensic teams working with bones in a scenario of grim science that Gregory Whitehead calls the "forensic theatre."[22]

Given the political sensitivity of the CMP's work, its visibility surprised me when I first began working with the forensic teams. But I have come to see this visibility as a defining feature of the CMP—a constitutive element in the synergetic dynamic of secrecy and publicity entailed by its mandate to conduct politically neutral investigations, detached from any prospect of justice for murder, rape, and other crimes of war. According to its terms of reference laid down in 1981, "the committee will not attempt to attribute responsibility for the deaths of any missing persons or make findings as to the cause of such deaths."[23] This mandate is grounded in an ideology of closure, a coercive expectation that confirming the deaths of the missing and returning their remains to their families will suffice to heal the wounds of the past and clear a path toward reunification. The bones and belongings of the missing, excavated painstakingly from mass graves and laid out on tables for analysis, identified and photographed, and catalogued and archived before their reburial, are scripted in the narrative of closure promoted by the CMP as the brute facts of death to be ascertained—and thus as substitutes for other truths that cannot be disclosed to the public. But the experience of time that these artifacts summon for the scientists who work with them, and for the relatives of the missing who ultimately claim them, may open up a different course. In focusing on these objects, I mean to show how they both stop and dilate time, summoning the dead into relationships with the living as they reckon with suddenly indeterminate histories and uncertain futures.

SECRETING EVIDENCE

Despite the CMP's stance of political neutrality and its interdiction on attributing responsibility for the deaths it investigates, the forensic scientists I knew made informal findings every day about the causes and circumstances of the deaths of the missing. F., an osteologist who had been working at the CMP for several years, told me that their lab reports were designed to prevent conclusions from being drawn about the cause or manner of death; the forms elicited information in discrete, quantitative chunks, rather than in what she called "narrative" form. F. had been trained to think in narrative terms, she said, assembling pieces of evidence that would lead to the conclusion that the event of death had transpired in a certain way. *A narrative like that needs a lot of description*, she told me. The CMP lab reports had boxes for recording measurements of each bone according to several different metrics, to determine the person's age, sex, injuries, and pathologies, but there were no spaces in which to write descriptions of the bones. Moreover, the forms required a kind of differential diagnosis; the scientists were asked to note any traumas or pathologies that might be related to the death, supplying evidence for multiple possible causes without drawing any conclusion. When I asked F. who would read these reports, she said: *No one! They just sit in the archive*. But she added that she thought the CMP was afraid that families might request the reports years down the line, so they wanted to limit the information recorded on the forms.

And so the production of forensic evidence yielded its own secrets, in turn. These secrets were not only a matter of what was concealed in the CMP's confidential archives. They were also a matter of what was quite literally destroyed in the process of investigation. When human remains are exhumed, the graves are destroyed. I have learned from archaeologists that such destruction is part and parcel of discovery, and that what is destroyed depends on what investigators are seeking. As the team leader at one excavation site told me, *The first thing I learned about excavations is that they destroy culture. Once you understand that, you understand that the question is how to learn as much as you can from a site while doing the least damage.* According to CMP protocols, material evidence recovered in an excavation would be removed from the site each day; brought to the lab; and washed, dried, catalogued, and stored in the climate-controlled annex until it was time for analysis—which could be a matter of weeks, months, or years. When the analysis was complete, any bones and fragments that could be identified conclusively were returned to the relatives of the victim, along with any associated artifacts. Artifacts that could not be associated with a specific person were retained by the CMP in storage. Any potentially dangerous materials, like munitions, were turned over to the UN to be destroyed by a bomb squad. Thus, according to procedure, most of the material evidence recovered by the CMP was reburied; some was stored anonymously; and some was destroyed.

In my work with the CMP, I saw nothing to indicate that the excavations conducted by its forensic teams were any more damaging to evidence than any others, but archaeologists did question the appropriateness of their excavations in a more general sense. For example, when I joined a team working at a large excavation site on a mountainside in the north, I heard a long debate over lunch between A., who worked part time curating exhibits at the Archaeological Museum in Nicosia, and G., who said he was altogether "against" excavation and exhibits. A. had started the conversation by announcing her plan that evening to see a new exhibition at the Archaeological Museum, just opened in celebration of the upcoming Cypriot presidency of the EU. G. asked her: *What is this? You spend all day working on an excavation and then at night you go to the archaeology museum?* Surprised, A. asked him: *Don't you like archaeology? Aren't you an archaeologist?* He told her that he preferred archaeological parks, where sites were opened with all the artifacts left in situ and glassed over so that visitors could see the site intact. He complained that the science of archaeology had not progressed much in a hundred years, that excavation techniques were still "very primitive" and did terrible damage to the history embedded in the ground. A. agreed that archaeological techniques were in some ways "too crude for proper excavations," but she contended that was exactly why they needed to continue their work—to improve their methods and keep learning about their civilization and their history. G. said:

History doesn't belong to us; it belongs to future generations. We should be preserving it for them. We could do that with satellite photography and three-dimensional photography—we don't need to excavate right now. People in the future will have better tools; they'll know what to do. A. asked him how they would know when that moment had arrived: *How long should we wait? Anyway, there are ways to excavate and preserve at the same time—you can excavate just a corner of a site, rather than the whole thing.* Gesturing across the massive site where they were working that day, G. pointed out: *If you only dig part of it, you don't get the whole picture; you just have little pieces, and little ideas that don't get at the whole. Look at how we do things—do you really think we're taking good care of these bones?*

S.'s criticism was ethical, not methodological. His team followed clear, established procedures as they had been trained to do. Archaeologists working in the field were acutely aware of the importance of following these procedures to ensure good evidence. They told me they were criticized "constantly" in the newspapers for doing sloppy work, not following proper procedures in their excavations, not storing bones safely, and in some cases, destroying evidence due to incompetence or political motivations. *People don't understand why investigations take so long*, P. told me: *We're attacked all the time, in the media—people say we're too young, we're lazy, we don't take the work seriously. They don't understand how hard it is.... On a lot of sites, we just don't have good information from witnesses, and we have to dig around for a long time before we find the grave. They don't understand how meticulous we have to be in order to recover entire bodies, rather than just a few fragments for identification, like they did in Bosnia. And then the analysis takes forever—we have so few people working in the lab, and we have to check and double-check everything to be sure we've got the right person. And then there's a huge backlog for DNA testing.* P. described the daily push by supervisors to go "faster, faster, faster" before the money ran out. When she first began working with the CMP, she told me, she had heard the project would continue for ten years or more—"as long as it took!" Now, however, the members were suggesting a much shorter horizon, of about three years. This reduction in the scope of the project had almost entirely to do with funding, P. said. The investigations were extremely expensive, and the CMP was wholly dependent on funding from the EU and UN, which were increasingly spare in their contributions. The lab manager told me that, given its short life span, the CMP would consider it an "excellent success" if 80 percent of the missing had been found by the time they shut down.

Under these pressures, one of the excavation supervisors was known to complain about the extensive documentation required of fieldworkers by "proper procedure." Recording everything in field notes and photos slowed down the excavations, and he could not see the point of collecting all those data when the important thing was to recover the bones and return them to the families as soon as possible. B., who had worked for several years in the field, objected to this. He told me that when it came to field photography, *more is better! The camera can see things you don't see. The whole process of excavating has to be recorded so that you can reconstruct it years later, if you need to.*

That prospect—reconstructing forensic investigations in the future—was, perhaps, the crux of the matter. At the time of my research, the CMP ensured the anonymity of witnesses and the confidentiality of forensic data in the present, but there was no guarantee for the future. Should a political settlement ever be achieved between the Republic of Cyprus and the Turkish Republic of Northern Cyprus, an essentially new state would emerge, with a new justice system. A truth-and-reconciliation process could be negotiated as part of this regime change—and with it, a new form and new role for the CMP, if it survived at all. Its confidential archives could be opened to the public, or at least to police and prosecutors. What the CMP treated as politically neutral deaths could become murders and assassinations. Field reports of excavations could become records of crime scenes; anthropological analyses could become autopsies. It was with that uncertain future of the state itself in mind that the CMP kept its secrets, even as it compiled a massive archive for future knowledge.

BECOMING HUMAN

The CMP had a proprietary relationship to the images of gravesites and bones generated by the forensic teams. The scientists oversaw an immense archive of forensic photographs containing thousands of images, but none of these images can be reprinted here. They are encrypted and stored in the CMP's database, and no one at the CMP has the right to reproduce or transmit them. Only scientists working on a case and relatives of the missing person in question would ever see these images. Even relatives were shown only a small selection of photographs: an image of the gravesite after the excavation was complete—but none of the excavation, when bones were still visible in the ground—and an image of the bones arranged in the form of a skeleton, as far as possible. One investigator told me that families could be "traumatized" if they were exposed to photographs of bones as they had been found in situ in mass graves, dispersed and disarticulated. Indeed, I had seen many photographs of skeletons in situ in the archives, and I had noted how different the bones looked after analysis, each one visible, clean, laid out on a white table in a rough approximation of body, if not quite to scale. The archaeological reports usually contained many photographs of a grave, unexcavated or in the process of excavation, showing bones looking uncannily like dead people, practically enfleshed: in the midst of action or in fallen positions, heads above feet, arms raised above heads or wrapped around others, bodies twisted to one side or the other, jaws open. Equally upsetting to relatives, however, according to this investigator, were photographs of bones being handled by strangers, even the scientists who worked with them so carefully. Before a viewing, the CMP psychologists, who counseled families during the course of an investigation, often showed relatives photographs of the bones arrayed on a lab table, to prepare them for what they would see in person. The photographs were intended as preparation for recognition.

One day at the lab, I followed Y., the forensic photographer, as he, not she hurried from table to table. She was taking multiple photographs of the bones and artifacts from a case, then uploading the best pictures into the database so the anthropologists working on the case could add captions and incorporate the images into their reports. Y. took individual photos of each item associated with the missing person as well as photos of the "whole body"—that is, as much of an entire skeleton as possible. He did the same with the artifacts, photographing each scrap of clothing separately and then placing the scraps into a meaningful array. He pointed out to me the case she was working on now, bodies from a family grave: a father, mother, grandmother, and two small children. He had created a folder in the database where she could put the photos of their bones and artifacts together—*like a family album, in a weird way*, he said.

That day, Y. got some help from K., an anthropologist, who had noticed that Y. was having trouble figuring out how the scraps of clothing fit together. K. knelt on the floor next to the white sheet where the fabric was laid out, and within half a minute had reconstructed almost an entire shirt, assembling scraps from the front and back, the breast pocket, the sleeves, the collar, the buttons. Y. whistled and praised her skills. K. replied that she liked working with the artifacts; it reminded her of housework and her family. *If you do enough laundry, you understand how clothes are put together*, she said, gesturing toward the old torn shirt on the floor. For whom was this old shirt repaired and summoned into the present? K., along with Y., me, and others in the lab who had gathered around for a moment, were the only audience for her deft handiwork. It was a fleeting moment; the shirt would be disassembled shortly afterward, the pieces placed in a plastic bag and set aside for a viewing with the relatives at some point in the future. Of the shots taken by Y., the best one would be uploaded to the digital case file, where, in all likelihood, no one would ever see it.

The care K. put into piecing the shirt together, which she likened to the care she put into doing her family's laundry, also mirrored the care she put into piecing skeletons together from bones and bone fragments, the analytic procedure that every anthropologist undertook when "working on a body." The scientific process of associating and ordering bones and bone fragments was oriented to the visual recognition of bodies. The anthropologists conducted their analysis "blind"—that is, without external references such as the case files of missing persons, which usually contained photographs of those persons from the time they went missing; descriptions given by relatives, noting habitual activities like smoking, or forms of labor that might have left traces of repetitive motion on their bones; and unique physical traits or medical conditions that might aid in identifying their remains. Working first without such antemortem data, anthropologists proceeded by areas of the body, locating all the pieces that belonged to each limb, the hands and feet, the pelvis, spine, skull (including teeth), and others, organizing them as far as possible in the form of a skeleton on a table. They ascertained whether the bones considered to be "associated" by the archaeologists who had bagged them at the excavation site did indeed belong to the same individual, and then they tried to associate any unassociated bones from the site with that or another individual. They measured each bone in several ways, using different metrics for different kinds of bones and bone features.[24] They provisionally determined the age, sex, stature, bone pathologies, and nutritional health of the individual, and they noted abnormalities like growths and discolorations, as well as indications of breaks and wounds.

Once this picture had been painted in the abstract, the anthropologist working on a body would consult the archaeological report from the excavation that had yielded the remains, as well as team members working on other bodies from the same gravesite, to associate the skeleton with a specific case file. D. told me that, after she finished an anthropological report, she would look at the antemortem data to see how close she had come to the information already known about the individual in question—his or her age, stature, medical conditions, habits, work. *That's the fun part!* she said, laughing. These were, after all, "just bones," in the context of an analysis that she likened to solving a mystery. In another sense, however, the bones were deeply and intimately known by the anthropologists who worked on them. Not only when and how the person had died, but also much about who he or she had been in life, were written on the bones.

We're surrounded by death, F. remarked, another day. She asked me if I found it strange to be in a room with all these bodies around. I told her it did not feel strange to me, but perhaps that was because I knew nothing about the people whose bodies these were; it might be harder if I understood more about who they had been before they died. *We don't know much about them, either,* F. told me. *The archaeologists usually know a lot more, since they sometimes have contact with witnesses at the excavation site. They know the reasons why the site is being excavated, the expected number of bodies, where they came from.* I said it seemed to me the anthropologists learned things about these victims that other people could not know, even their closest family members and friends. Even though the bodies were strangers, anthropologists knew all about their illnesses, injuries, and habits. *That's true,* F. said: *The bones become more human as we look at them.*

This becoming human of the bones in the hands of anthropologists evokes a series of rituals surrounding natural death in Cyprus: rituals of washing and dressing the corpse before the wake and funeral and, for Greek Cypriots, exhuming and inspecting the bones years later. In her ethnography of Inner Maniat women in Greece, Nadia Seremetakis describes this process as "adornment": "The preparation of the corpse before the burial and, later, the cleaning and ordering of the bones construct the dead as an effigy, as a 'doll.' . . . To remember and to adorn is to embody emotions."[25] In the mortuary rituals she examines, that adornment is performed by those who "shar[e] substance" with the dead—blood or, with fictive kin, tears.[26] In the lab, this adornment was performed by strangers, on behalf of kin who were not permitted to see or touch the bones during this process, but for whom they might, at a viewing, "become tangible emotive substitutes of the absent 'flesh,'" as Seremakis suggests.[27] The exhumation of bones would be their first visual encounter with the dead, unmediated by memories of a corpse or a burial—a disturbance that might inhibit their recognition of the bones as an "effigy" of the dead.

For anthropologists at the lab, the work of building a person from fragments was a scientific process of restoring and reconstructing, a simulation of the natural development of the human body. Yet as F. suggested, this was also a rehumanization of the dead, and as such a summoning of emotion and memory, or a semblance of memory. In this imaginary dimension of their work, the anthropologists were in a sense acting as proxies for the relatives of the dead, consigned to using guesswork rather than memory, but nevertheless conjuring a live person. The association of information from a file with an array of bones was an act of imagination, enlivening the bones with an image of the person. In this, the scientists—more than the relatives, ultimately—were the ones who could see a missing person in his or her bones.

Forensic work is thus perhaps not far from the work of divination captured by Seremetakis. Lamentation, dreaming, and exhumation make up the three scenes of women's work in what Seremetakis takes as the domain of death. These knowledge practices—composing the biography of a dead person in contrapuntal mourning songs, interpreting the "warnings" of death announced in dreams, and reading the condition of a person's soul in his exhumed bones—are dangerous, Seremetakis argues: polluting, violent, and threatening to the social order, especially the church. This secret divinatory knowledge—"a mode of knowing that looks beyond the immediate and the apparent to absence and the invisible"—grows from women's intimacy with death; it is an "instrument of cultural power" foreclosed in the public space of male power in Inner Mani (the space of law and property, of honor and murder) yet essential to the reproduction of Maniat society in its appropriation of alterity.[28] Seremetakis defines this powerful mode of knowing as a "fragment" of modernity, disconnected from other forms of women's work (agriculture, architecture, and hunting) by the domestication of women in the private space of the home and the depopulation of Maniat villages, yet reverberating with the valorization of labor, "helping," and kinship that they carry as a legacy.[29] Could the forensic work of Cypriot scientists at the CMP constitute some similar fragment of a divinatory tradition, from which they have been dislocated to the modern scene of science without fully knowing it? In this light, their insistence on the scientific value of their work and its bourgeois appeals—a decent salary, job security, social status—would only underscore their dislocation from ritual tradition.

I recall a visit to the lab by the third member of the CMP, who accompanied a foreign ambassador and guests on a tour of the facilities. He introduced the visitors to K., one of the team leaders, who gave them an overview of the forensic work undertaken at the lab and then a few details of the specific case her team was working on at the time. The visitors walked around the lab, looking at the bones and asking questions of the anthropologists at each table about the effects of soil conditions on the remains, the different colors perceptible on the surface of the bones, the different signs of injury. Later, when the visitors had reassembled by the front door, one of them asked the third member why so many of the anthropologists were women. He said he didn't know, but he guessed it might have to do with the "sensitivity" of their work and the fragility of the bones: *It takes a caring person.*

This imagination of careful women caring for bones was promoted on the CMP website. The scientists who appeared there in photographs of the lab were almost exclusively women. During the time I spent at the lab, two men worked there, on a team of twelve; another joined shortly before I left. Men were much better represented in CMP photographs of field excavations. A clear visualization of gender was at work in these representations: men along with women were shown doing the adventurous and dirty work of toiling in the fields, lifting buckets, wielding shovels and picks, operating machines, climbing hills, and descending into wells; while scenes of the lab, white and pristine, were populated by women in white lab coats, working alone, eyes cast down on the bones they handled dexterously yet tenderly. Their eyes and their hands were the forensic tools that mattered.

Such images of scientists performing this work contained a tension between scientization and sacralization, and between naturalization and humanization. The sober demeanor of the anthropologists, and their generational and temporal remove from the events of violence, did not fit the image of grief and mourning long established in the iconography of the missing. But it was precisely these forms of remove that qualified them as scientists and legitimated their proximity to the bones, an intimacy that might otherwise have been jarring or even wounding to relatives of the missing. That these strangers were women, already positioned for Cypriot audiences in a legacy of death work, perhaps tempered the pain of estrangement from the bones that mourners might experience on seeing them treated so clinically. Moreover, this death work was secluded in the protected if not private space of the lab, so far from the public space of state funerals for the missing that were dominated by the presence of clergy and politicians. In both scientizing and gendering forensic work in these ways, images of anthropologists working on bones depoliticized the knowledge of violence that the bones materialized. But these images do not convey a robust picture of their work; caring for the bones was much more than a representation. The intimate knowledge of the bones developed by scientists was, for some of them, a creative process, a labor of imagination, a work of empathy—a relationship between past and present, and between the dead and the living.

Up until the moment of provisional identification, the anthropologist who had worked so intimately and intricately with an individual's bones would not know his or her identity—nor, therefore, his or her "ethnic" identity. Yet having communicated with the archaeologists who had exhumed the remains and the investigators who had located the site, the anthropologist would likely know at least the general story of how the remains had ended up in that place, and therefore have a presumption of the victim's identity as either Greek Cypriot or Turkish Cypriot. Damir Arsenijević, writing in the aftermath of the genocide in Bosnia-Herzegovina, describes the moment at which remains are identified as the moment when "it" becomes "who"—"a moment of decision; a moment of naming."[30] His concern is to interrupt that moment, to recapture the bones of the dead from the multiculturalist politics of reconciliation that identify and consecrate bones in ethnic terms:

> The scientist, the bureaucrat and the priest assume the perspective of the perpetrator of the crime. For it is in the fantasy of the perpetrator that the executed person is the ethnic *other*.... But whose bone is the bone? Does it belong to the perpetrators who killed and buried the bodies? Does it belong to the family members of the missing persons? Does it belong to the diplomat in whose country peace in Bosnia was brokered? Does it belong to those, like me, who feel ashamed and wince every time the bone is touched? Yes and no. It belongs to all of us. It is a societal thing. It is thus precisely because the suffering and death which resulted from genocide are the effects of the politics of terror and, as such, are pre-eminently a public matter. The emancipated process of becoming a subject can only take place when the subject is freed from the shackles of a victim position or any other position that is merely focused on the interests of a particularist identity.[31]

Such identitarian interests weighed on scientists at the CMP, too, who were hired as representatives of either the Greek-Cypriot or the Turkish-Cypriot community in the postconflict game of balance and neutrality, and who were tasked with the identification of bones that were themselves communal representatives. In relation to the bones, scientists were positioned as either victim or perpetrator, sometimes forcibly and sometimes indeterminately. H. described to me the perversity of this positioning during a visit that some members of a Greek-Cypriot group had recently made to the lab. One of the visitors, a woman who was about his father's age—and thus had been a teenager in 1974—and who knew he was Turkish Cypriot, gestured across the whole room of bones laid out on tables and said to him: *Imagine, Turkey did all this!* H. told me he had felt that he could not say to her that there was not a single Greek-Cypriot bone in the whole room—that the bodies belonged to Turkish Cypriots killed by Greek Cypriots in 1964. He had kept quiet, but the experience had left him with a terrible feeling, as if the woman were accusing him of violence. *It's like we're being punished*, he said. *Turkish Cypriots have never denied what happened in 1974, but Greek Cypriots deny what happened before, to us.* He could not understand how someone of this woman's age could deny that there had been "trouble" in the early 1960s: *She was old enough to have lived through it!*

H. told me that story one morning just before Easter, when CMP employees would have a week-long holiday. (I learned that, in addition to two weeks off in August, all CMP employees had week-long holidays for both Easter and Bairam—in the name of balance. *We don't take any of the bad nationalist holidays on either side*, an archaeologist told me, laughing.) Some of the anthropologists—those who would not be celebrating Easter during the holiday—were exploring vacation itineraries online during their midmorning break. S. was looking into a trip to Izmir, and H., who had visited the city many times, asked if I had ever been. I had, and I told him my impression of its flatness, its shoddy and anonymous modernism, so unlike nearby cities such as Boursa—which made sense, I said, since the old city of Smyrna (now Izmir) had been burned to the ground in 1923 and rebuilt after the disastrous Greek campaign to reclaim Asia Minor from the Ottomans. T. chimed in: *Let me ask you: who burned Izmir?* I said, *That depends on who you ask!* This comment stirred a conversation among several of the anthropologists. H. and T. were of the opinion that it was the Greek soldiers who had set fire to villages in Anatolia and then Izmir as they fled from the Ottoman forces in defeat. R. said this made no sense to her, since at the time, the city was under Greek control and would have been retained by Greece if Prime Minister Eleftherios Venizelos had not made the mistake of trying to claim more land in Asia Minor. T. agreed that the whole Greek campaign in Anatolia had been a terrible mistake; what they disagreed about was who had destroyed Izmir. He told us he had heard that it was actually Armenian gangs who had burned down villages in Anatolia and killed the women and children left behind by their Turkish husbands who were serving in the army, and then moved on to Izmir.

I felt oddly stung by this comment, wanting to correct T.'s perspective on history, in which I heard ugly echoes of propaganda and conspiracy theory. I told him that I had studied the burning of Smyrna and had never come across a version in which Armenians were responsible; that, to my knowledge, the Armenian quarter of the city was the first to burn, and all the Armenians living there had died, so it was difficult to understand how Armenian gangs could have done it. But I had certainly come across accusations against both the Greek and Turkish armies. T. kept his patient demeanor as he continued to argue that the Turks had not burned Izmir. R. grew more visibly frustrated and upset, laughing uncomfortably: *Enough! No more talking about history!* She told T. that they both—she in Greece, he in northern Cyprus—had been given only one side of the story in school. *It's not our fault, it's how we're taught,* she said. *When you tell me what you've learned, I get upset, because I've learned the opposite!*

The conversation might have ended there, but S., who was still online, mentioned the headlines she was reading just then about the French law banning denial of the Armenian genocide, which had recently been struck down by the French supreme court. T. wondered why the court would come to that decision, unless it were to acknowledge that there had been no genocide. R. contended that the court's decision had been based on the constitutional protection of free speech: *You can't legislate what people are allowed to say, it's absurd to try and forbid people from saying things like this, even when they're obviously wrong.* H. pointed out that in Germany, it was illegal to deny the Holocaust. I suggested that was a different context, one where the prohibition was enforced in the same country where the genocide had taken place, so the same citizenry who had committed the genocide were now forbidden to deny it. Passing by at that moment, the lab manager, who had served in the Bosnian army during the war in the 1990s, told us that his country faced the same impasse: *When your population is made of the people who committed genocide and the people targeted for genocide, it's impossible to agree on whether a genocide has taken place—even if everyone knows it.* T. asked R. directly if she thought that a genocide against the Armenians had been carried out by Turkey. R. demurred, trailing off in a comment about different perspectives on history. As it turned out, though, T. was after a different point. He argued that it was soldiers in the Ottoman army, and not the Turkish, who had killed the Armenians: *The events took place in 1915, years before the Turkish Republic was founded. How can Turkey be blamed for this?* He reiterated that he thought Armenian gangs had been killing civilians and burning down villages throughout Anatolia at the time: *Of course the Ottoman army would try to kill them.* R. argued that taking up arms to fight the Ottoman soldiers was a natural reaction to oppression on the part of Armenian civilians; she drew a comparison with Chechens today, and the way the Russian army had branded them terrorists. T. acknowledged that Armenians had been targeted, and a million people could not have been killed by accident: *This happened on purpose. But my question is: can the Turkish government be blamed for it?*

If, for Arsenijević, "becoming a subject" is the path opening toward a "hopeful politics after genocide," this becoming requires not only the liberation of survivors from their ethnic identities as perpetrators or victims, but more than that, a rebuilding of relationships among the living and the dead: a reinvestment of bones in their relations with others, to bridge the gap between the remains of the dead and their names, their "full identity and history."[32] In the lab, it was bones from 1964, ethnically misnamed, that triggered the movement of these scientists from their workplace in 2012 to mass death in the burning of Smyrna in 1923 and onward, to the dying days of the Ottoman Empire and the Armenian genocide in 1915. These movements in time, across sites of ethnic memory crucial to these scientists' understanding of themselves as inheritors of either a Greek or a Turkish legacy of violence, were inflected by their work on the artifacts of death in Cyprus, and their unstated and utterly habitual understanding of the two-sidedness of conflict and loss demanded by that work. Their relationship to the bones of the Cypriot missing introduced a kind of indeterminacy into the legacies of violence that they had inherited and that they read back onto the bones. In their debate about those legacies—one of the few open arguments I witnessed during my time at the lab—they positioned themselves with deliberate distance, even if they could not sustain it; and in doing so, they participated, momentarily, in a reorganization of ethnic history.

CONCLUSION

For some Cypriots, forensic knowledge of the deaths of the missing inadequately stands in for knowledge of the causes and circumstances of those deaths, hindering the closure offered to relatives by the CMP and leaving their desire for truth and justice unsatisfied. But the matter of that knowledge—the bones and belongings of the missing—can open a different experience for the scientists who work with them so intricately and intimately: an experience of uncertainty and possibility in regard to the otherwise overdetermined history and future of conflict.

What significance do such experiences among forensic scientists have for Cypriot society and politics? Do their encounters with time machines bear on broader possibilities for recovery and reconciliation in the future? In her seminal work on classical law and politics, *The Divided City*, Nicole Loraux dwells on the question of reconciliation in the aftermath of a brutal war for Athens, probing the amnesty granted to the Thirty Tyrants by the democrats following their return from exile and their restoration of democracy in 403 BCE. Taking the sacred oath not to recall the war, on pain of death, was the procedure by which individuals became citizens after the war, and by which the city could once again be imagined "as a whole," devoid of division.[33] In Loraux's reading, the city as a political form is necessarily and essentially divided; it comes into being through division, which it must continually overcome by forgetting so as not to rekindle wrath and resentment in every democratic debate, since "recollection itself is a wound."[34] She warns that the "silence" that "surround[s]" *kratos*[35]—a term that, in Homeric sources, denotes "superiority and thus victory," or "to have the upper hand,"[36] but that, in modern Greek, simply means *the state*—marks the "repression" or "denial" of conflict, but not, in fact, its forgetting.[37] Indeed, she argues, the victorious democrats remembered all too acutely the violence, horror, and injustice of the war, and "it is precisely because they remembered the past that they forbade anyone to recall it."[38] But, she writes, "conflict cannot be forgotten without consequences . . . the prohibition of memory may affect the very definition of memory; and the will to memory may take refuge in recalling why memory limited its own existence."[39] In orations after the amnesty, she finds recurrent, insistent traces of this fixation on memory in the democrats' exhortations to all citizens of Athens to remain loyal to the amnesty, and in their ambivalent double-negations justifying it: "We were not unjust. . . ."[40]

The resemblances between Athens in 403 BCE and Cyprus in 2012—in the politico-theological underpinnings of the city-state, in the reckoning of citizens with civil war, and in their anxiety and ambivalence about their memory of war—are robust and easy to overstate. To identify contemporary Cyprus with the Athens of the amnesty would be to allegorize rather than analyze its political situation. I introduce Loraux's work here not to suggest such an easy comparison, but rather to extend her reflections on the dangers of forgetting conflict, even in the interest of peace. If amnesty in Athens wrought a distortion and hypertrophy of memory, fixing on the civil war as an event whose ever-present potential to recur required constant vigilance to avert, then what are the dangers of the closure to which the CMP is so committed? The work of healing the wounds of war by putting the dead to rest, rather than letting them lie, might appear to be a work of memory rather than forgetting; the public funerals of the missing after their remains are found and returned to families certainly emphasize this dimension of the CMP's mission. But in destroying or concealing evidence of violence in the name of political neutrality, the CMP does as much work to forget the conflict and to forgo justice.

An understanding of bones as things that tie the past to the future was implicit in the CMP's ideology of closure; digging up bones was widely promoted as "digging for a future"—the title of a documentary film commissioned by the CMP about its work.[41] This particular future is possible to imagine only when the past is conceived of in terms of loss, such that the future may be apprehended through healing—a future anterior contingent on forensic investigation. The temporality of political impasse in Cyprus is a historical temporality, punctuated by surges of hope for change ultimately reabsorbed into history as repetition, ever recurring to a closed set of past events in relation to which the future will have arrived (future anterior) when a political settlement is reached. Time machines made it possible to conceive of the future differently—not in the teleological terms of reconciliation but in terms of becoming something different in the present, which might also mean having been something else in the past. Thinking about the future in this way positions becoming as a supplement to secrecy—a closed hermeneutic, writing a script for infinitely unfolding future iterations of the "drama of revelation," in Michael Taussig's words.[42] I have focused on the temporality of forensic work here to show how this work was engrained in a history of violence concealed through secrecy, but also to show how the experience of time that forensic artifacts summoned for the scientists who worked with them, and for the relatives of the missing who ultimately claimed or disclaimed them, might open a different future.

In writing about the CMP, I have tried to avoid miming knowledge production as public exposure and thereby reproducing the ideology of secrecy. I have sought instead to capture the positivities of knowledge production at the CMP by documenting the contours and shadings between knowledge and its many obverse sides: what is known in relation to what is suspected; what is disclosed in relation to what is withheld; what is publicized in relation to what is kept confidential; what is concealed in relation to what is revealed; what is already known in relation what is new; what is evidence in relation to what is mere information; what is nonknowledge in relation to what is "deliberate deceit," in Taussig's formulation of public secrecy.[43] In the face of secrecy, ethnography has the assiduity and the durability to manifest such relational shadings—offering neither a fully paranoid nor a fully reparative interpretation, in Sedgwick's terms, but rather showing a complex oscillation between secrecy and becoming.

In this oscillation, there is room for both a critical analysis of the history of secrecy in Cyprus and the imagination of a future that diverges from the repetition of that history. In a different idiom, this might appear as an oscillation of myth and history, as Claude Lévi-Strauss presents them in *Myth and Meaning*: myth being "static," comprising combinations of a closed set of elements, in contrast to the "open system" of history.⁴⁴ As soon as he offers this distinction, however, Lévi-Strauss begins to unwrite it, showing the very same range of both variation and repetition among lineage accounts by native Canadians and historical accounts of French and North American wars. "I am not far from believing," he writes, "that, in our own societies, history has replaced mythology and fulfils the same function, that for societies without writing and without archives the aim of mythology is to ensure that as closely as possible—complete closeness is obviously impossible—the future will remain faithful to the present and to the past. For us, however, the future should always be different, and ever more different, from the present, some difference depending, of course, on our political preferences."⁴⁵

The vanishing distinction Lévi-Strauss finds here between myth and history turns on the "aim" of those undertaking to express them, either to reproduce the past with a little difference or to create "ever more" difference. He identifies that normative stance not as a cultural feature—since all of "us" are included in his "should"—but rather as a political disposition. Archives, in this imagination of history, operate like the time machines I have been writing about here: objects with the capacity to stop time, to stop its repetition and overdetermination, and to open experiences of uncertainty, possibility, and difference, even if only temporarily. Archives are also different from these other time machines, of course. The bones of the missing have distinctive, intrinsic, organic qualities that qualify them to tell time—and in telling time, they impinge in specific ways on the emotions and imaginations of the people who work with them. These artifacts can become human; they can become ethnic, and then unbecome it; they can become the effects of histories of conflict outside (yet still inside) Cyprus. Their activity is vitally political.

Arsenijević writes of the disturbance exerted by bones, imagining himself at the edge of a mass grave, wanting to "bear witness to anything resembling a human" and finding a "limit-experience" of the human in "the unpleasant corporeal remainder that, after genocide, stays with you, one which resists all the ideological mechanisms of quantification, identification, burial and sacralising—the excess of scattered bones, the dead-but-alive organic matter."⁴⁶ I hesitate to suggest that the resistances time machines bear to being successfully scripted in the CMP's drama of revelation and its ideology of closure are immanent in the matter itself—as Bennett, for example, argues for the "force" or "vitality intrinsic to materiality" exceeding complete semiotic capture.[47] In telling time, in killing time and filling time, the artifacts of the missing in Cyprus activate affects of hope, fear, and resentment and obligations toward the dead as well as the living, in the scientists who hold and behold them; but I do not presume that this dynamic capacity precedes or exceeds the meanings these people make of them. I therefore prefer to "vital materialism" the terminology of "projection" employed by Aslıhan Sanal, for one, to describe the relations between living persons and the dead.[48] The force operated by the artifacts of the missing lies in their capacity not to exceed but to slip between semiotic captures, to condense multiple temporalities and thus to accommodate discrepant meanings. They are in the right place at the right time to make things happen.

I think back, here, to the argument G. made against excavation, that spring afternoon on the mountainside—his assertion that *history doesn't belong to us; it belongs to future generations*, and his contention that the CMP should be preserving mass graves until proper excavations could be conducted. *People in the future will have better tools*, he said: *They'll know what to do*. And then A.'s response: *How long should we wait?* Perhaps among these technologies to come, these better tools to be wielded by future generations, might emerge new narrative tools as well—new ways of linking the present to the past, new ways of finding meaningful footholds in the flux of time. Perhaps we will know the time has come to use those tools when we discover that we already know what to do with them.

NOTES

1. Ed Sard, quoted in Walter J. Oakes, "Towards a Permanent War Economy?"
2. Sidney Lens, *Permanent War*.
3. Vidal Gore, *Permanent War for Permanent Peace*.
4. Sedgwick, *Touching Feeling*, 145.
5. Some 25,000 Turkish Cypriots moved into enclaves throughout Cyprus in 1963–64; approximately 45,000 Turkish Cypriots moved from the south to the north in 1974 while about 160,000 Greek Cypriots moved from the north to the south. See Demetriou and Gürel, "Human Rights, Civil Society and Conflict in Cyprus," who note that some of these figures are contested. Estimates provided by Nicos Trimikliniotis and Umut Bozkurt indicate that the population of Cyprus at the time of publication in 2012 was close to 1.1 million. Of that number, approximately 840,000 people lived in the Republic (about

200,000 of whom were non-Cypriot nationals, including undocumented migrants) and perhaps 300,000 people lived in the TRNC (including 120,000–230,000 migrants and settlers) ("Introduction," 3). The authors note that these numbers are approximate and contested. See also International Crisis Group, "Cyprus."

6   Bennett, *Vibrant Matter*, 9.
7   Renshaw, *Exhuming Loss*, 27.
8   On distinctions and affinities between bones and corpses, see Joost Fontein's discussion of the "agencies and affordances entangled in the affective presence and emotive materiality" of human remains vis-à-vis dead bodies in distinct historical moments of mass death in Zimbabwe ("Between Tortured Bodies and Resurfacing Bones," 436). He observes symbolic contrasts between the "dry bones" of the liberation war dead from anticolonial struggles in the 1890s and the 1950s–70s and the "fleshy, leaky bodies" of people killed in political contestations since the early 2000s (435 and 436)—but also their shared involvement in the "processes by which bones are formed from decaying bodies" in the "passage of time" from burial to decomposition, and in the transhistorical prophecy by liberation fighters in 1896–97 that "our bones will rise again" (432, 436, and 424).
9   Connolly, *Neuropolitics*, 2.
10 Connolly, *Neuropolitics*, 5, 2, and 4.
11 Connolly, *Neuropolitics*, 8, 5, and 10. João Biehl and Peter Locke take inspiration from Deleuze's thinking of becoming—that is, "those individual and collective struggles to come to terms with events and intolerable conditions and to shake loose, to whatever degree possible, from determinants and definitions" ("Deleuze and the Anthropology of Becoming," 317). In working through their own research experiences in situations of individual and social crisis, they urge an emphasis on "desire," "openness," and "flux" in "ethnographic efforts to illuminate the dynamism of the everyday and the literality and singularity of human becomings" (317 and 318).
12 Connolly, *A World of Becoming*.
13 According to an archaeologist I knew at the CMP, the Turkish-Cypriot side of the agency had insisted that the Greek-Cypriot side conduct investigations into Greek-Cypriot graves in the south before the CMP could proceed with investigations into Greek Cypriots' graves in the north. According to this archaeologist, Physicians for Human Rights still had a lab in Cyprus in 2012, but no one was working there.
14 For a detailed account of this breakthrough in the Republic's policy toward the problem of the missing, see Kovras, "De-Linkage Processes and Grassroots Movements in Transitional Justice."
15 Two organizations of relatives were formed in 1975: the Turkish-Cypriot Association of Martyrs' Families and War Veterans, and the Greek-Cypriot Organisation of Relatives of Undeclared Prisoners and Missing Persons. The only organization representing both Turkish-Cypriot and Greek-Cypriot families is the Bicommunal Initiative of Relatives of Missing Persons, Victims of Massacres and Other Victims of 1963–74 Events, which was founded in 2005.
16 These were the figures reported on the CMP website as of April 15, 2017, http://www.cmp-cyprus.org/content/facts-and-figures.

17 Εθνική Οργάνωση Κυπρίων Αγωνιστών/National Organization of Cypriot Fighters.
18 Türk Mukavemet Teşkilatı/Turkish Resistance Organization.
19 See, for example, Angastiniotis, *Voice of Blood*, and *Voice of Blood 2*; Evripidou and Nugent, *Birds of a Feather*; Committee on Missing Persons and Neocleous, *Digging for a Future*; Piault and Sant Cassia, *Dead or Presumed Missing?*; Tanpınar, *Kayıp Otobüs*; Tsiarta, *In This Waiting*; Zaim and Chrysanthou, *Parallel Trips*.
20 See Arsenijević, "Gendering the Bone," and "Mobilising Unbribable Life"; Crossland, "Buried Lives," and "Violent Spaces"; Ferrándiz, "The Return of Civil War Ghosts"; Ferrándiz and Baer, "Digital Memory"; Nelson, *Reckoning*; Renshaw, *Exhuming Loss*; Sanford, *Buried Secrets*.
21 Ferrándiz and Baer, "Digital Memory," 5.
22 Whitehead, "The Forensic Theatre." Ariel Dorfman points to the dependence of this theater on globalization: "We have grown strangely used to them over the last 25 years.... Mothers and daughters, wives and sisters, demanding to know the true fate of their men, demanding that they be returned to their families alive. A widespread, almost epidemic, image of tragedy and defiance.... Indeed, those marching women brandishing a black and white photo have become so natural to our eyes, so much a part of the mythical landscape of our time, that we tend to forget that there was a time, not very long ago, when photographs did not constitute an automatic ingredient of that sort of protest" ("The Missing and Photograph," 255–56).
23 See the CMP's "Terms of Reference," item 11, http://www.cmp-cyprus.org/content/terms-reference-and-mandate.
24 Among many sources they consulted were Brooks and Suchey, "Skeletal Age Determination Based on the Os Pubis," on the pubic symphysis; Işcan, Loth, and Wright, "Age Estimation from the Rib by Phase Analysis: White Females," and "Age Estimation from the Rib by Phase Analysis: White Males," on the sternal rib end; Lamendin, "A Simple Technique for Age Estimation in Adult Corpses"; Lovejoy et al., "Chronological Metamorphosis of the Auricular Surface of the Ilium," Osborne, Simmons, and Nawrocki, "Reconsidering the Auricular Surface as an Indicator of Age at Death," on the ilium and auricular surface; and Ubelaker, "Cranial Photographic Superimposition," on dentition. Since 2011, when the CMP purchased a license for ForDisc, the anthropologists have duplicated their measurements, recording all the information in their reports and then entering it again in the ForDisc database to calculate age estimates, which were then entered into the reports.
25 Seremetakis, *The Last Word*, 215–16.
26 Seremetakis, *The Last Word*, 216.
27 Seremetakis, *The Last Word*, 216.
28 Seremetakis, *The Last Word*, 200.
29 Seremetakis, *The Last Word*, 223. The association of women with death stands, for Seremetakis, as a "taxonomic linkage" that positions women as "iconic representatives of the dead in the world of the living" (*The Last Word*, 71 and 74). In writing about death in contemporary Athens, Neni Panourgiá perceives the relationships women sustain and build with the dead as artifacts of their labor—their caretaking of the dead before and

after burial—even though, as she notes, "women are not the only ones who tend the graves, nor are they the only ones who feel the pain of the loss" (*Fragments of Death, Fables of Identity*, 176).

30 Arsenijević, "Gendering the Bone," 194.
31 Arsenijević, "Gendering the Bone," 194–95.
32 Arsenijević, "Gendering the Bone," 194.
33 Loraux, *The Divided City*, 142, 48.
34 Loraux, *The Divided City*, 41.
35 Loraux, *The Divided City*, 57.
36 Loraux, *The Divided City*, 69.
37 Loraux, *The Divided City*, 68, 70.
38 Loraux, *The Divided City*, 263.
39 Loraux, *The Divided City*, 193, 263.
40 Loraux, *The Divided City*, 264.
41 Committee on Missing Persons and Neocleous, *Digging for a Future*.
42 Taussig, *Defacement*, 51.
43 Taussig, *Defacement*, 149. On the relationship between nonknowledge and public secrecy, see also Masco, *Theater of Operations*.
44 Lévi-Strauss, *Myth and Meaning*, 40.
45 Lévi-Strauss, *Myth and Meaning*, 43.
46 Arsenijević, "Mobilising Unbribable Life," 166.
47 Bennett, *Vibrant Matter*, 3. In like spirit, Yael Navaro-Yashin, exploring the relational "embroilment" and "codependence and co-determination" of the "inner and outer worlds" of humans (*The Make-Believe Space*, 24), develops a methodology of "sensing" to grasp the affects discharged by material environments in northern Cyprus—affects that are part of human experience but "excee[d] or g[o] further and beyond the human imagination" (18).
48 Sanal, *New Organs within Us*, 139.

9

Horizoning

The Work of Projection in Abrupt Climate Change

ADRIANA PETRYNA

The breath you just took contains about 400 parts of carbon dioxide (CO_2) per million molecules (ppm) of air. The safe level is considered to be 350 ppm. People living at the start of the Industrial Revolution would have inhaled about 278 ppm. Since then, levels of CO_2—the leading greenhouse gas driving changes in the climate—have doubled, and in a worst-case scenario that many experts believe is in fact the real scenario, will reach 1,450 ppm by 2150. In diverse contexts—medicine, agriculture, submarine engineering, and even beer making—experts control for overexposure to CO_2 that is deemed toxic. In hospital settings, excessive levels of CO_2, monitored through blood-gas exchange, are used to predict death. In factory farm settings, animal welfare advocates prefer CO_2 narcotic anesthetization to stunning as a more "humane" way of knocking cattle out before their slaughter. Amid the incendiary bombings of World War II, clouds of toxic gases, including CO and CO_2, killed untold numbers of people seeking refuge in air-raid shelters, tunnels, and cellars. Humans and animals have experienced unsafe CO_2 levels in multiple life and death settings. Exposure is not a distant threat or something happening in a faraway future; its harmful potential is being continually exploited or managed today.

Excessive atmospheric CO_2 is typically absorbed by the atmosphere, land, and ocean. But what kinds of oxygen-depleted worlds will we inhabit once

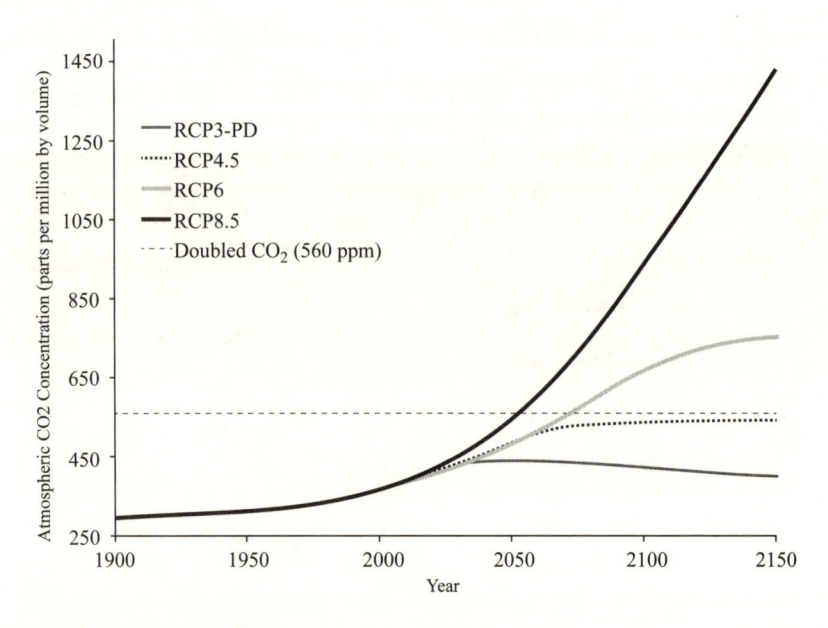

FIGURE 9.1 RCP Scenario Atmospheric CO_2 Concentrations

the Earth has lost its capacity to absorb this excess? Researchers are simply not sure where inordinate amounts of CO_2 will go, as the future availability of the Earth's carbon sinks is uncertain.[1] In fact, they note that nearly a third of all CO_2-offsetting reservoirs have already become fully saturated or have disappeared. This has occurred at a time when CO_2 levels have surpassed 400 ppm for the first time since "three to five million years ago—before modern humans existed."[2] How is it possible to even describe the dimensions of this loss of capacity?

There is no doubt that the world must immediately transition away from fossil fuels and toward energy efficiency, renewable energy sources, and sustainable agricultural practices. There is a burgeoning literature on resilience, and policy makers and government officials have adopted the term as a key buzzword. Yet it is at odds with the realities of cultural practice.[3] Figure 9.1 shows several scenarios for the trajectories over time of four greenhouse gas concentrations, adapted from the Fifth Assessment Report of the Intergovernmental Panel on Climate Change.

That lowest curve represents the luckiest (and increasingly unlikely) scenario, in which decreases in global greenhouse gas emissions will maintain global average temperatures below a target of a two-degree Celsius temperature rise (above preindustrial levels). That curve is really "where we need to be to be comfortable," but "culture and cultural practices create a certain reality ... that is nonetheless not going to get us into the [lowest curve] of the two-degree world in the future."[4]

In addition to the necessary work of dismantling a global political economy erected on fossil fuels, contemplating the physical dimensions of probable trajectories also inspires private terror and a string of associations. What is resilience, particularly in worlds that are conceivably nonadaptable? To pose this question is not to say that it is too late to fight climate change, but rather to open up a conversation about what it means when we look into the future and say we don't fully know. Such associations set the stage for reflection on what is, arguably, a need for a different curve—one that can grasp and project the urgent haste "in which evolution fails to furnish an immediate adaptive mechanism."[5] Yet in this space of haste, cognitive constraints can be significant; temporal horizons must be continuously recalibrated, incorporating the uncertainty of changing conditions while also giving weight to their existential challenges and moments of social reckoning over time. While studies on the so-called selfish agendas driving survival strategies in ant colonies and schools of fish are interesting, they employ a notion of the social that is reduced to self-regulating parts and mechanisms and that lacks such temporal horizoning. Also, this mechanistic approach to survival does little to shed light on the peculiar comforts of a socially organized denial and, hence, to reposition us in time on a more "comfortable" curve.[6]

Today's conditions beg for a sense of measure and cadence with respect to the kinds of changes that are at stake. The doubling of CO_2 beyond preindustrial levels is already causing significant disruptions. We know that the risks are here now and that they increase the longer we do not act. Occupational health specialists, deep-sea divers, and even submarine engineers have long known the incremental risks of atmospherically compromised settings. The U.S. Department of Labor, for example, considers 400 ppm the outdoor norm for CO_2 exposure and 800 ppm the indoor norm. According to a CO_2 monitor salesman I spoke with, 1,500 ppm "is when you start to see effects." In fact, the majority of his sales were to school districts because of concerns about the dangers of CO_2 on children's school performance: "We need to break up the CO_2 concentration in schools."[7] At 5,000 ppm, brewery workers experience narcosis and metabolic stress.

Asking if there is a limit to what humans can bear with respect to spiking atmospheric CO_2 seems commonsensical enough; yet it is also, somehow, a far-fetched thought experiment. This inconsistency suggests a paradox; while the risks of CO_2 are mostly considered in the context of global emissions leading to climate change, an everyday sense of palpable risk—calculated to a fault in some occupational domains—actually disappears.

Meanwhile, earth scientists who deal with an ultimate abstraction—the planet—are getting a better handle on CO_2 as an exposure event, and on what increases in CO_2 can mean for a variety of physical systems. Past a particular threshold, ocean acidification (caused by the overabundance of CO_2 in the seas) triggers widespread fish extinctions due to diminished coral reef ecosystems (which contain roughly 10 percent of the world's fisheries). Rising temperatures associated with increasing CO_2 mean that agricultural production in particular areas can be wiped out.[8]

As an anthropologist, I have been interested in the implications of this accelerated change and in the ability of humans (mostly experts and emergency service workers) to keep up with it. Today, there is a wide gap between "available information and how that information is being framed in the context of risk and uncertainty."[9] Stronger storms, more frequent fires, decreases in Arctic sea ice—many of these changes are not gradual, but are happening abruptly or within timescales that are much shorter than had been projected (within a few years or decades, not centuries). In a larger project from which this chapter draws, I look closely at how the realities of abrupt climate change are being reckoned with within basic science, applied technical fields, and social lifeworlds.

One of my empirical tasks is to trace the physics that transforms fires into megafires and storms into superstorms and accelerates species loss. Juxtaposing scientific uncertainty with the social fabric of emergency response, I reveal the stakes for the actors who bear the brunt of abrupt change but have been excluded from top-down governance models of collective action.

In this chapter, I ask who peoples abrupt change as its conceptualizers, navigators, and first responders, and I track how that change challenges our understanding of nature, time, and the future, as well as the notion of projection itself. Drawing on shifting understandings in environmental science—and of the environment itself—and the new heuristics and challenges they call forth, I explore the disconnects and ambiguities that characterize abrupt ecosystem dynamics for scientists and the rest of us in an "invisible present"[10] uncertainly projected into an unfamiliar and incompletely knowable future. Attuned to these uncertain projections, and how we manage and live with them, I argue for the importance of what I call horizoning work as a particular kind of intellectual labor that reconfigures possibilities for knowledge and action. Such work opens up a space for change in the face of apocalyptic thinking or denialism, reorganizing the moral and epistemological conditions of life on the brink of various thresholds or irreversible change, and invites new collectives in the collective action problem of abrupt change.

ABRUPT CHANGE NATURE

The year 2015 was the worst wildfire year on record in the United States. In California, about 3,400 wildfires were fought, a thousand more than the average number of the previous five years. Fire seasons are now lasting, on average, eighty-six days longer than over the last four decades. Between 1984 and 2006, a fifth of the southwest's forests were lost to wildfire and bark beetle outbreaks—both issues related to a warming climate.[11] Ecosystem modelers from different U.S. agencies see the fatal flaws of current tools meant to model these phenomena. These flaws pose problems not just for average citizens, but for on-the-ground emergency workers for whom the expected risks to life are falling outside the range of normal experience.

Bill Armstrong, one such worker, is a forest fuels specialist for the U.S. Forest Service and a veteran of an elite group of wildland firefighters. In an interview in July 2014, Armstrong described to me the many changes he has seen in the dynamics of fire.[12] He described the 1996 Dome Fire in northern New Mexico, the physics of which was unlike anything he had ever seen: "In the eighties, when I started, intense fires were anomalies. What we thought was a freak incident became a wake-up call that nobody woke up to. It was a plume-dominated fire—more like a firestorm, so much energy is released in such a small period of time. We just weren't expecting that kind of fire behavior."[13]

A plume-dominated fire is characterized by huge updrafts of burning embers and material that gets sucked high into clouds. Armstrong told me that "as material moves up through the clouds, it cools off, and when it cools off, the weight of the clouds can no longer sustain itself. Then the clouds collapse, and when they collapse, they throw shit everywhere."[14] In fact, they can do this many times.

Ten years later, the "freak incident" had become the norm. Armstrong was a first responder in the 2011 Las Conchas fire, which, like the Dome Fire, defied the behavioral assessments coming from the Forest Service's fire modelers in Missoula, Montana. Fires usually move with winds, but a plume-dominated fire like Los Conchas "burned with greatest intensities and greatest rates of spread against the wind. It actually managed to push its way up against the wind."[15] This meant that "with the power of the fire and what it was generating, with its own internal winds and its own weather system ... it was feeding itself."

Unlike previous fires, the Los Conchas fire burned aggressively: "It burned into areas where we thought there was absolutely nothing left to burn. It burned through the Cerro Grande wildfire scar [from 2000]. It burned through the old Dome Fire scar [from 1996]. We could not have predicted that kind of fire behavior."[16] In short, what Armstrong described to me is a potentially fatal mismatch between what modelers can model and what emergency workers face. In the absence of knowledge of novel or megafire dynamics, what accumulates is an intricate superstructure of surprise, consisting of overlaid events whose net physical interactions and intensities are unknown. According to Armstrong, a tipping point has been reached: "We should be treating these fires the same way we do hurricanes. *Get the hell out of the goddamn way.*"

CRITICAL THRESHOLDS

Critical thresholds of key planetary "life-support systems" have been crossed.[17] Abrupt shifts dominate planetary systems, reengineering ecosystems and the conditions for life. Tipping elements or bits of planet that could be switched under particular circumstances into "a qualitatively different state" require urgent attention.[18] A sequence of time-lapsed images from a film called *Chasing Ice* shows one photographer's trial-and-error (and then stunningly successful) attempts to create a multiyear record of a bit of planet that has been switched to a qualitatively different state.[19] The photographer James Balog set up twenty-eight cameras atop thirteen glaciers that snapped shots every half hour during daylight for several years. The time-lapse images revealed, in Balog's words, "the horror and miracle" of the rapidity of retreat of the world's glaciers (figures 9.2–9.4).[20] They captured what scientific literature on climate change calls abrupt change: shocks or sudden events that are either temporary, like a hurricane, or a shift in predictable long-term behaviors, like El Niño events or glacial cycles.[21]

Glaciers have probably never before moved the way the photographer showed they are now doing: an internal feedback mechanism called the albedo effect has taken over, and the glacier has passed some kind of critical threshold or tipping point. The category of abrupt change already entails cognitive losses and the relative lack of human ability to capture them, let alone predict where they go next. Viewed in fast forward, the photos from Balog's cameras capture an ecological field whose baselines are changing, crumpled up by some other complex of space-time and consumed by a "disordered chronological reality"

FIGURES 9.2, 9.3, AND 9.4 Stills from Jeff Orlowski's *Chasing Ice*, showing retreating ice at Columbia Glacier, Alaska

of an unfamiliar nature.[22] What strikes the senses is a blindsiding movement of a living and disappearing thing. What metrical concepts can grasp such crumpling of realities and render them sensible or visible?

I am interested in scientific scenarios, projections, diagrams, and graphs as material artifacts that render time sensible with respect to unknown thresholds or tipping points.[23] How do temporal horizons themselves become political, or how do they demarcate (or dissolve) a space of political action?

The concept of "stabilization wedges" from Princeton University scientists Steven Pacala and Robert Socolow provides a telling example of how environmental risk and possible futures can be visually presented and practically managed.[24] These wedges map a timetable of costs and consequences of inaction on mitigating carbon emissions, illustrating the divergent outcomes of business as usual versus more aggressive efforts to curb emissions over fifty years. For purposes of illustration, imagine a triangle whose base sits on an X-axis, roughly corresponding to a lowest emissions curve (discussed previously), and representing the most desirable or comfortable emissions scenario, in which a dangerous doubling of atmospheric CO_2 (as compared to pre-industrial levels) is avoided to ensure that global temperatures do not rise above a two-degree Celsius target. The upper trajectory (our triangle's hypotenuse) represents a predicted *total* amount of emissions (based on a "business-as-usual" scenario) that needs to be cut out to reach the temperature target. In the authors' formulation, multiple lines transect the interior of this triangle, making up "wedges" of stabilization. Each wedge represents a specific CO_2 reduction strategy (such as increased vehicle fuel efficiency, the use of wind and solar power, avoided deforestation, carbon sequestration, and so on) with which humanity could excise a chunk of CO_2 from its future and 'buy time' against an urgent threat.

As initially proposed (in 2004), concerted reduction strategies failed to get off the ground, and revisions of earlier projections (in 2011 and 2013) led to expanding the number of mitigation strategies (that is, wedges) to compensate for the unchecked increase in greenhouse gases in the intervening years. Inertia, intransigence, and the politics of old energy technology got so much in the way that more and more wedges are needed to achieve the same result. Today, studies estimate that it might require a staggering thirty-one wedges to drastically curb emissions over fifty years. A fifty-year engineered horizon was meant to act as a hyperpragmatic tool that would reorient the policies and ethos of modern energy consumption. What is concretized, instead, is a very climatologically costly, *delayed* trajectory in which the idea of living on borrowed time is no mere metaphor. Equally real are the uncertainties of what kind of time reckoning is required.

The stabilization wedge becomes a parable, of sorts, about a further unmooring from safety and danger. It begins to embody a situation not of returning to past CO_2 levels, but one of an ever-receding horizon of possible recoverability.

INVISIBLE PRESENT

Yet today there is something else making projections falter and time itself less linear and more abrupt—an "invisible present" whose potential for producing *jarring* or *unexpected* change is real. In 1983, the lake ecologist John Magnuson of the Center for Limnology at the University of Wisconsin and colleagues introduced the notion of the invisible present and started the conceptual work that would help capture the Earth as a tipping place.[25] The invisible present is a timescale of observable events, such as "acid deposition, . . . CO_2-induced climate warming, and deforestation," but it also captures processes "on multiple spatial and temporal scales to the generation of ecological pattern."[26] These processes are "hidden from view or understanding because they occur slowly or because effects lag years behind causes."[27]

According to Magnuson, the quality of experimental results is influenced by a choice of temporal frame. Samples taken from lake sediments representing longer timescales of "hundreds to thousands of years" provide only "a coarse history of past climatological events," and short-term ecological experiments, done without enough knowledge of the natural year-to-year variability of the system studied, make the interpretation of experimental results difficult.[28] To enhance interpretability, Magnuson identified the "invisible present" as a new kind of experimental medium—a meso-space of experimental time—that could capture the kinds of abrupt ecological change that Balog revealed through time-lapse photography.

Yet this experimental medium, too, was rife with problems of observation of and experimentation with "real" ecological change. As Magnuson wrote, "certain biological and physical processes simply take time, biological relics persist even after conditions change, movements across the landscape take time, the simultaneous occurrence of two or more necessary conditions for an event or process to occur can be rare, and a chain of events accumulates the lags between cause-and-effect events."[29]

Such were the indirect aspects of the invisible present, "the most elusive to uncover, yet the most interesting."[30] This is because phenomena that have gradually evolved can also be vulnerable to unforeseeable abrupt shifts, presenting a dimension of change that is *without* dimension. In short, Magnuson's "invisible present" captures an urgent kind of scientific nowhere. But it also requires a new kind of scientific person, someone who is both an experimentalist and a seer. Magnuson wrote, "It is the unusual person who observes changes that occur over decades, and even when observed, many of these changes are understood by no one."[31]

Yet he argued that the cultivation of science and publics in this present was crucial, as it is the "[time] scale within which our responsibilities for the planet earth are most evident." The invisible present thus poses critical moral and epistemological concerns: moral because it is a timescale in which ecosystems change "during our lifetimes and the lifetimes of our children and our grandchildren,"[32] and epistemological because it is about processes that we can only partly observe and can seriously misjudge, and "where a lack of temporal perspective can produce misleading conclusions."[33] Even so, we must choose to act, even with limited information. In other words, Magnuson's invisible present, an enigmatic experimental locus, also holds potential as a new kind of projective medium for reckoning with abrupt ecological change.

NONEQUILIBRIUM SPACES

Unraveling the dimensions of an invisible present and ecological change became key challenges for the American limnologist Stephen Carpenter, who joined Magnuson's Center of Limnology at the University of Wisconsin–Madison in 1990. Carpenter—whose research explores how lakes, which are not independently self-regulating ecosystems, are affected by a variety of activities in the landscape (including pollution from toxic agrochemicals)—won the Stockholm Water Prize in 2011. In July 2013, he told me about a shift in the 1970s that deeply affected his way of seeing ecological change and would begin to add dimension to a dimensionless invisible present: "One of the big break points in my thinking was realizing that the equilibrium models that dominated ecology for so many years were just simply wrong, and that everything that is really interesting occurs in relation to some sort of threshold transition in ecosystems." Those thresholds, Carpenter explained, could be occasioned by an internal (endogenous) "nonlinearity," a very large external shock, or the introduction of a new actor into an ecosystem, such as an invasive species or a new technology: "These are really the important events, and the dynamics around equilibria really are not."[34]

The dynamics around these not-so-important equilibria are linked to a once influential "balance of nature" theory in ecology. The theory suggests that ecosystems are in (or seek to be in) a stable equilibrium. When they are perturbed by pressures such as those linked to human exploitation, nutrient loading (pollution), and a rise in temperature, ecosystems tend to self-correct. They do so through negative feedback mechanisms that cancel out the perturbation, returning the ecosystem (or the Earth, for that matter) to a restored and balanced state. These activities are represented by a smooth and continuous curve in which forces are said to be canceling each other out to assume a predictable state.[35] Theories of nonequilibrium suggest a different trajectory. They also allow for self-correction through feedbacks, but the results are outcomes and alternative growth potentials calling for a different predictive skill. Researchers do not expect that a perturbed ecosystem will always return to a balanced state (nor do they see lack of balance as a sign of an ecosystem being on the verge of collapse), but study the dynamics around its thresholds or tipping points.

This nonequilibrium idea has several roots, among them the work of the mid-twentieth century French topologist and mathematician, René Thom, who developed a mathematical elaboration of what he called "structural stability."[36] In categorizing some of the ways living systems lose resilience, he noted that tipping points demarcate the boundaries between the structurally stable—those things that are knowable—and what lies beyond this knowability: all the things that scientists have yet to learn to satisfactorily account for why and how ecosystems do, or don't, bounce back from a perturbation, and how they might develop in the future.[37] Rather than focusing on evolutionary questions of why or how they evolve or how they adapt, Thom's "catastrophe theory" explores thresholds of what are called an ecosystem's "alternative stable states."[38]

Points F2 and F1 in figure 9.5 exhibit such thresholds. Note that there are not one but two equilibrium curves (theoretically, there can be many more) representing alternative stable states in ecosystems under pressure. Depending on that pressure, each equilibrium curve tips or breaks at some point. For example, F2 tips where there is too much pressure. It free-falls into an alternative stable state (F1) and will not return to a prior equilibrium. Why? The answer lies in the space of nonequilibrium, represented by the dotted line connecting the two points. The stretch from the outer and most unstable extreme (tipping point F1) of one stable state to that of another (tipping point F2) demarcates a space in which, for Carpenter, the most interesting ecological questions arise. In a nutshell, it shows a theoretical space linked to an abrupt change in nature, and how that change occurs.

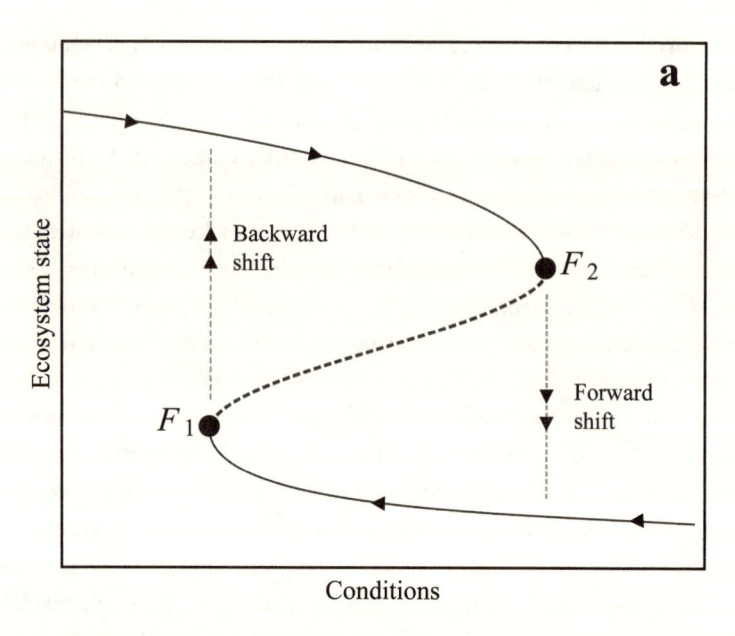

FIGURE 9.5 Regime shift curve. Adapted from Scheffer et al. 2001

If the balance of nature model relies on what the philosopher Manuel DeLanda calls "extensity," in which gradients are predictably defined and manage themselves within bounded entities, "far-from-equilibrium" states present an "intensity" of observation and experimentation.[39] Wind currents, hurricanes, thunderstorms, and cloud formations "inhabit our consciousness as meteorological phenomena, but we can't normally perceive the gradients in temperature, pressure, or speed that are responsible for their genesis." There is no "perfect cancellation of forces" here, but a change "based on some differential."[40] For DeLanda, what distinguishes intensity from extensity is the presence of what he calls "fuel." In zones of "higher intensity," DeLanda writes, "we can witness the birth of extensity."[41] Such zones rely on a host of system-stabilizing actors whose work is defined by incomplete information and restless uncertainty, and that always takes place on the edge of some potential and irreversible loss of remediating capacity or control of a system (a lake, an ecosystem, a world). I call these intensive actors horizon workers.

The whole-lake experiments on Lake Mendota in Wisconsin of Carpenter and his colleagues provided crucial tests of nonequilibrium dynamics under conditions of eutrophication (causing oxygen depletion, or hypoxia). It is caused by an external shock: in this case, an overabundance of chemical nutrients (runoff containing nitrogen and phosphorous from fertilizers) stimulates excessive plant growth, whose decomposition produces CO_2 and depletes oxygen. A stubborn environmental problem, it makes lakes appear turbid or become blanketed by thick accumulations of algae, a transformation inimical to food production and the survival of lake life. It would be all too easy to take a snapshot of a eutrophied lake and say "here is its new equilibrium state," and then proceed with a top-down removal of all the chemicals in the hopes of returning it to a prior, more "balanced," ecological state. The snapshot would be deceptive, and the lake would not bounce back. "In theory, eutrophication is reversible," says Carpenter, "but from the perspective of a human lifetime, once you push a lake over [a] threshold, eutrophication is a one-way trip."[42]

According to Carpenter, there will always be a disconnect between processes of observing a phenomenon of ecological change and thinking and acting coherently about that phenomenon. Observation does not always inform clear action. The real challenge is what to do about the disconnect. Carpenter states that making accurate assessments of the limits and uncertainties of ecological forecasting is a core challenge for ecologists: the "most important challenge of ecological forecasting is not the projections themselves. Many features of change are fundamentally unpredictable, so a big part of dealing with change is building resilience against the unpredictable and retaining the capacity to adapt when surprising things happen."[43] Carpenter collaborates with an interdisciplinary group of international scientists in quantifying threshold transitions or tipping points for different kinds of ecosystems under threat. Well-known in their respective fields (which include shallow lake ecology, deep lake ecology, coral reef ecology, earth systems, and others), these scientists are developing novel strategies for ecosystem management and are strongly committed to rapid policy change based on a science of critical transitions. What concerns these experts is not proving the existence of climate change, that is a settled case, but creating strategies for preserving existence in the face of undeniable threats.

Rather than focusing on specific tipping elements, I would like the reader to focus on the jarring nature of the "one-way trip" Carpenter mentions. We may have witnessed it. One day a lake seems perfectly normal. The next day it is brown or covered with a thick algae bloom or fish underbellies covering the lake as far as the eye can see. In this instance of ecological surprise, we can think of the lake as having crossed a threshold or tipping point. The relatively small scale of a lake has allowed researchers to see these threshold dynamics experimentally. Arguably, we are arriving at many such threshold moments on a larger scale; yet observations of these events and quasi-events often do not register with current models of scientific understanding and preparedness. There are inevitable disjunctures between the temporal and spatial modeling of climate change and moments when danger can no longer be actionably sensed: another kind of invisible present. In what follows, I explore the nature of projection in the context of ecosystem changes that are happening with surprising "speed." Attuned to the existential hazards at stake in a science of critical transitions, I argue for the importance of a distinct kind of intellectual and ethical labor, a horizoning work, amid physical worlds on edge.

PROJECTIONS

UNFREE ASSOCIATIONS

We can sample a myriad of abrupt shifts by opening the newspaper. When I did so one day recently, I found a story in the *New York Times* about emaciated sea lions that "washed ashore by the hundreds in California."[44] The mothers of these starved pups left them as they chased for fish that have been pushed out of their habitable zones by warming ocean temperatures. Images of pups with their ribs jutting out, now prey for dogs, show the effects of greenhouse gas emissions and associated warmer ocean temperatures. Their abandonment is a quiet fingerprint of how "ongoing greenhouse gas emissions can modify climate processes and induce shifts in ocean temperature, pH, oxygen concentration, and productivity, which in turn could alter biological and social systems."[45]

On another page in the same newspaper, I read that California has only one year's supply of water left due to the ongoing drought. The lack of surface water has spurred an unprecedented groundwater drilling boom, both legal and illicit. My mind jumps to friends living in the city of São Paulo, Brazil, where a massive drought means that the city reportedly has only a six-month supply of water left; and to Texas, where Cargill, a major multinational food-processing company, has not long ago shut down a major cattle slaughtering facility because of lack of water; and then to a recent scientific article that pinpointed the timing of a so-called climate departure, or the year when the projected mean climate of any given place moves beyond its "envelope," or "outside the bounds of historical variability under alternative greenhouse gas emissions scenarios." It shows when a "radically different" (and warmer) climate could begin for particular locations: 2048 for Los Angeles and Denver; 2047 for New York City, Philadelphia, and Washington; 2043 for Phoenix and Honolulu; 2029 for Lagos; and 2020 for Kuala Lumpur. At these dates, humans will be pushed "beyond historical analogues"—that is, familiar habitable zones.[46]

Such familiar zones suggest a climate envelope, or a range of suitable conditions for environmental adaptability. At the point at which various species are tipped into an "outside" existence, that is, unable to find the same range of suitable climatic conditions, their options are rapid adaptation (a culling process almost always involving high mortality), extinction, or migration to more suitable ecological niches. For humans, one cannot deny that such envelopes "may [also] shrink to nothing as conditions change—i.e., there may be no suitable conditions for a species in the future."[47] Mainstream media accounts bring images of biogeographical struggle into our daily routines, while also conveniently separating us from our own (humans, after all, can 'buy time'). An informed and acknowledging public is at a safe distance from a fringe ideology of climate change denialists. Yet the sociologist Kari Norgaard identifies a different kind of climate denier, beyond the extremist type.[48] Even with the public's adequate knowledge of climate change, she asks, why has action not been commensurate with the scale of the problem? Denialism, she argues, is not just a right-wing position, but is part and parcel of a deepening incommensurability between human and natural timescales and, I would add, of an inability to reconcile gradual changes with more recent rapid ones—that scientific nowhere in which projections are rapidly faltering. Arguably, we exist in a social "invisible present" that becomes a convenient abstraction in which many forms of denialism can be inserted. The question is how far some will attempt to go to "actively normalize climate change" before our envelope disappears.

THE WORK OF PROJECTION

Projections take us to interesting places, and often to places where we do not want to go. An interesting photographic coincidence occurred almost five decades ago that captured the Earth's many fates under different atmospheric conditions. Climate modelers perform "runs" into the future, based on certain parameters. Climate modeling was a nascent enterprise in the early 1970s, when ecological thinking transitioned in the way Carpenter described. In that decade, Syukuro "Suki" Manabe, a climatologist at the Geophysical Fluid Dynamics Laboratory in Princeton, NJ, pioneered the use of computers to simulate global climate change. When he pumped CO_2 concentrations of four to six times present-day concentrations into his computer model, he showed that such levels would take us into the Cretaceous period.

Manabe's more famous contemporary, the physicist James Hansen, produced yet another place with projection. In 1969, the not-yet-Bush-era whistleblower published a study on the atmospheric space of Venus, 97 percent of which is CO_2. Through a careful analysis of the composition of its surrounding molecules and dust, Hansen found that Venus may be the ancient relic of a planet that looked like Earth billions of years ago. Venus represents the conquest of a planet by a gas that is increasing on Earth at record pace. As an artifact of that runaway process, Hansen's Venus undermined the more hopeful image of the time, the iconic "blue marble" snapshot of Earth, taken in 1972 at a distance of 28,000 miles by moon-bound crew members of the Apollo 17 spacecraft.

Both modeling runs take us to very different places and, indeed, to various planetary limits, tipping points, and ends. If the blue marble captures the fantasy of a limitless biological regeneration of Earth, Venus is a picture of its disappearance, a kind of living extinction. Somewhere between these dueling images of deathless life and living extinction lies the troubling temporal imprecision of extinction events themselves. Answers to questions about extinction (what does extinction, near-extinction, or the hour of extinction look like?) are complicated, but they are critical to making the threat of climate change a more socially intuitive concept. How is extinction being understood, witnessed, and/or debated in the early 21st century?

Is the earth a wonderland, fertilized by runaway CO_2 levels, or a wasteland, suffocated to death by them? These choices are of course imaginary. Yet they speak to what the anthropologist Johannes Fabian called a lack of "coevalness," or an intersubjective sharing of the time and space of an other—in this case, the unknown or absent object of nature—and the need to regain proximity to ecological phenomena that are unstably configured, unfamiliar, or under stress.[49] Perhaps as a symptom of such a lack of shared time, an out-of-time thinking in which some keystone event becomes a popular image for the "end" of the world becomes common. I encountered this kind of thinking in my work on the nuclear disaster at Chernobyl.[50] The stark realities of the nuclear age and its biopolitics pushed many people, for better or worse, into an epochal kind of thinking that I consciously abandoned as I learned to examine how political practice and narrative forms of science shaped what was and was not knowable about the complexity of the disaster's biological outcomes. "They don't know how they survived" was a common refrain among physicians treating contaminated workers, who had absorbed six to eight times the textbook definition of a lethal dose of radiation. Such words point to an agonizing lack of knowledge about the actual physical states of those who survived, and where their survival ought to fit within larger schemes of knowledge. That is, they were at a loss to describe the dimensions of loss and of knowing how to project into the future: a dimensionless invisible present. Surprise, even bewilderment, among beings "born by accident" captures an aspect of what the philosopher Catherine Malabou calls "absolute existential improvisation" for a self that is literally "out of time."[51]

Today the epoch called the Anthropocene stands as a new geological era marking irreversible human activity on the Earth's ecosystems and, perhaps, an irretrievable self frozen in a time "whose future harbors nothing to come."[52] Arguably, the very name, Anthropocene, adds to this sense of deprivation: as it declares humans to be the central agents of massive damage, it puts the problem of climate change out of the bounds of human responsibility; human cognition is purportedly too limited to make sense of the causal potentials of our actions, now stretching across dimensions of geologic time and global space. As such, declarations of new eras run the risk of instilling fatalism in the face of rapid change and preclude capacities of calibrating the world with other forms of knowledge or from other zones of contact or influence. Norgaard's figure of the "common" climate change denier is salient here, overwhelmed by an invisible present and without an experimental and projective medium for forward movement. Abrupt change and tipping points—points that, if crossed, mean irreversible change—require a countertechnique, a continual capacity for recalibration, a horizoning work.

HORIZONING WORK

The word *horizon* derives from the ancient Greek ὁρίζω (horizō), meaning "I mark out a boundary," and from ὅρος (oros), meaning "boundary" or "landmark." Across time, people have used the concept of the horizon as a strategic point of reference in the navigation of varieties of physically incoherent worlds. Renaissance architects used horizon lines to properly orient objects in three-dimensional space. Early modern surveyors devised mercury-filled "artificial horizons" to create an image of a level surface against which the "inconstancy of the terrestrial horizon" could be judged.[53] Today, robotics engineers encode predictive horizons in remote machines, such as extraterrestrial rovers that can use them to make autonomous self-corrections in navigating craters on Mars. In meeting such course-plotting challenges, data from the past are useful, but only up to a point. And right when data are no longer useful and prediction capability derived from past or present information becomes misleading (or yields high computational cost or instability), a new predictive horizon is put into place.[54]

As these examples suggest, horizoning work is a specific kind of intellectual work undertaken in conditions in which the fate of entire systems is at stake. It involves the testing and assembly of empirical tools and appropriate "scaling rules"[55] for recognizing and "maintaining a safe distance from dangerous thresholds."[56] Such work requires demarcation or incrementing, using known parameters, but it is also a practice of continuous self-correction vis-à-vis changing baselines of safety and knowable risk. In the most extreme conditions, horizoning work entails a fine-tuned awareness of a system's exposure to jeopardy, without which navigators will inevitably be flying blind. Horizons of all sorts make complexity temporarily actionable within a particular human or technical frame. Horizon thinking makes good on faulty or fleeting information and allows movement forward or the prevention of a crash or disappearance of a whole system.[57] The fact that entire trajectories, machines, or worlds are at stake is precisely what makes horizons so real.

But what happens when horizons disappear? Restoring stability in systems on the verge of runaway change often starts with the construction of imaginary increments. Be it the navigation of treacherous seas or thinning ice, what escapes perception—a horizon line or a precarious patch of ice—is precisely what becomes an object of an acculturated thought experiment in "primitive" navigation. For example, aging mariners of the Canadian Bay of Fundy whom I interviewed in July 2013 were quite adept in mobilizing such thought experiments, before electronic direction finders, sonar depth sounders, and satellite navigation became available. They had crossed the highest tides in the world, and when they found themselves facing a thick fog, gale-force winds, or storms, they employed alternative scaling rules to determine their position and get themselves to their desired destination. In their dead reckoning, they constructed imaginary trajectories, deducing their position by employing their previously estimated location or fix—be it a view of some island meetinghouse, the smell of a certain forest, or patterns in tidal waters.

Such self-capacitation-in-seeing exercises, many of which were learned in childhood, started to generate an ordering of their own. These high-risk skippers moved along that trajectory on the basis of known or likely speeds over a specific time. As eighty-five-year-old Captain Burton Small, who holds the honor of being "the last fisherman in the Bay of Fundy to transport a load of herring to St. Johns using dead reckoning," told me, "chance is all we had." For Small, when horizons disappeared was when it became time to use dead reckoning. As dead reckoning suggests, sudden losses of visual imagery do not have to be "accompanied by impairments in performance on imagery tasks."[58] But how are these sudden losses themselves engineered?

ORIGINS OF EXTINCTION

In his essay "Air War and Literature," the German writer W. G. Sebald depicts the totality of destruction linked to the Allies' aerial carpet bombing of German cities in World War II. About the bombings, which left "31.1 cubic meters of rubble for every person in Cologne and 42.8 cubic meters of rubble for every inhabitant of Dresden," he notes that German writers "would not or could not describe the destruction of the German cities as millions experienced it."[59] He indicts the German literary establishment for breaking the correlation between experience and event, contributing to the privatization of the memory of this singular destruction, which left "bodies unrecognizable." Of the obliteration of Hamburg, Sebald wrote, "At one twenty A.M., a firestorm of an intensity that no one would ever before have thought possible arose.... At its height, the storm lifted gables and roofs from buildings, flung rafters and ... billboards through the air, tore trees from the ground and drove human beings before it like living torches."[60] The description gets much worse. But it is enough to say that Sebald's story of a great glossing over is also a story of an invisible present, a foreclosure of learning, and a refusal of horizoning work.

In my ethnography of the social and political aftermath of Chernobyl, I encountered this refusal of learning from one catastrophe to address the next, one that made "how they survived" ever more salient. These words indicate at least two distinct (yet linked) temporal dimensions—one linked to the lives of individual citizens, up close and relatively short term; the other linked to longer timescales and other events of similar magnitude (for example, in the case of Chernobyl, the nuclear disaster at Fukushima, or events comparable in terms of the magnitude of the public's refusal to address them). Such events, examined within a broader stretch of historical time, provide examples of failure, resourcefulness, and recovery (or not). Ideally, along this broader temporal stretch, one would hope to find lessons learned and opportunities taken for scientific knowledge to evolve a social science of survival. This social science would work, however tentatively, toward recovery and the creation of a safe distance, as it were, from inherent technological or anthropogenic risk. It would craft a learning curve that could stretch from one disaster to another. It would also engage the public in debates about what information is available or missing but required to produce a more adequate response the next time. It is about improving templates of data collection about what happened and using these data to predict and better respond to imminent threats. But in some important respects, as the emphatic words of the wildland firefighter ("get the hell out of the goddamn way") suggest, we are past this point of learning and engaging with collective realities that are well beyond the confines of recoverability and normal experience—a real tipping point.

Back in the Chernobyl's "dead zone," an area thirty kilometers in diameter surrounding the disaster site, it is ironic that we have better knowledge about recovering ecosystems—in that zone a herd of rare Przewalski's horses now runs wild, the decrease of certain birds' brain sizes has been observed, and information about the variability of species' response to radiation has been gleaned—than we do about how people and human conditions on the ground can recover. This absence of robust knowledge of Chernobyl's human toxicology is part of an invisible present.[61]

Ever since that catastrophe in Ukraine, scores of researchers have come to the zone to explore how the world's worst accidental release of radiation affected flora and fauna. Abandoned and stripped of human activities, the zone has become a site of heated debate about the long-term effects of exposure to radioactive chemicals. The terms of the debate are familiar: Is the zone an ecological wonderland or a technological wasteland? Some claim it is the former, given its lack of people and anecdotal sightings of large mammals there, such as wild boar, moose, and roe deer. No matter how contaminated the zone is, the accident at Chernobyl reconfirmed the fitness of animals in various ecological settings. Others that say the zone is a dangerous postindustrial wasteland, and that the fanfare over anecdotal sightings obscures the real chaos a few notches down in the animal kingdom, where the long-term presence of radiation acts as a kind of bio-ecological solvent in which certain bird species' reproductive rates have declined, the recruitment of potential mates is compromised, and some species have completely disappeared.[62]

There is an analogous debate going on with respect to climate change and about what might be considered competing horizons of expected ends. Conservatives promote the myth of infinite adaptability and have long defended CO_2 as enriching plants and leading to a richer and more verdant world. Even Svante Arrhenius, the Swedish Nobel prize–winning physicist who calculated the greenhouse effect in 1896, thought that the doubling of atmospheric CO_2 and related warming was "an attractive prospect." And given his projection of when such warming would take place (in 3,000 years), he lamented the fact that humanity had to wait so long to enjoy such prospects. Indeed, such projections butt up against real biological and geochemical limits in the amount of carbon the earth's oceans and forests can absorb—at a certain point these crucial carbon sinks may no longer be able to absorb all of the CO_2 that humans, machines, and the earth expire.

In a space of imperfect knowledge and inexorable threat, such origins of extinction require a radically new set of parameters for seeing and reckoning with nature's critical transitions and related potential risks. They usher in a new kind of intellectual effort, a horizoning work, involving the construction of appropriate scaling rules and cultivating "equipment" for modeling, managing, and facing a complex future that is right at hand.[63] This chapter has been about lines, curves, exposure events, points of no return, and recoverable and irreversible trajectories—scientific imagery suggesting that there is no safe distance from dangerous thresholds, only questions about the dimensions of loss and what comes next.

Lines depicting runaway CO_2 levels capture urgency as much as they do a sense of the unknown; they contain a form-blind myopia. Projected thresholds and tipping points have a seductive precision, but they also index an absence of expert knowledge about alternative states once certain thresholds are crossed. Post-threshold states, as suggested by the wildland firefighter's words and debates about the Chernobyl zone, suggest a loss of capacity for knowing the dimensions of loss and imaging form successions. Points-of-no-return occasion discourses on the origins of extinction as much as on the human art of horizoning work.

Horizons create a conceptual interiority, generating a space of decision making out of a line of inevitability, as well as new projective possibilities. They are age-old instruments, helping create effective perceptual ranges in invisible presents. As horizon workers (including ecologists, seafarers, and social scientists) learn to grasp the kinetics of real and observable situations in these presents, they enact a kind of labor in which the life of an entire system (a ship, an ecosystem, or a world) is at stake. Their dead reckoning allows for a constant reentry into a potential catastrophic present and a way to perform the difficult but necessary task of making the future less remote.

The reality of unconstrained abrupt change, with it mixes of human and natural causes, takes the issue of the unexpected—and what we do with it morally and scientifically—to a new level. Highlighting the mismatch between what modelers can now model and what others face, this chapter has moved the debate on collective action in response to abrupt climate change (which has largely focused on the failures of international diplomacy) to the realities of collective imagination on the ground. It has also troubled economistic cost-benefit reasoning about when and how to intervene, suggesting that there are hidden costs to a failure to act now, as well real limits to emergency response.

The centrality of horizoning work cannot be underestimated in ecological research and everyday life. The incongruities between what can be known about abrupt changes in nature tell of the level at which horizoning work becomes ever more central to political thought and practice. Never complete, horizoning work creates new projective possibilities in an "invisible present" and, in what is unfolding, a sustaining space for coordinating human action amid physical worlds on edge.

NOTES

1. Canadell et al., "Contributions to Accelerating Atmospheric CO_2 Growth from Economic Activity, Carbon Intensity, and Efficiency of Natural Sinks."
2. Shukman, "Carbon Dioxide Passes Symbolic Mark."
3. Norgaard, "Living in Denial," https://www.youtube.com/watch?v=f51N4-tBvVc.
4. Norgaard, "Living in Denial," https://www.youtube.com/watch?v=f51N4-tBvVc.
5. Thom, "Itinerary for a Science of the Detail," 389. As the mathematician René Thom noted, "man lives on projections" and must be able to use his "imaginary" faculties "on an unknown or absent object: nature" ("Itinerary for a Science of the Detail," 17).
6. Norgaard, *Living in Denial*.
7. CO_2 monitor salesman, telephone interview with the author, January 23, 2014.
8. National Research Council, "Abrupt Impacts of Climate Change."
9. Kunreuther et al., "Risk Management and Climate Change," 447.
10. Magnuson, Bowser, and Beckel, "The Invisible Present."
11. Williams et al., "Forest Responses to Increasing Aridity and Warmth in the Southwestern United States."

12 Armstrong is an advocate of controlled fires and a critic of the U.S. Forest Service's hundred-year-long policy of fire suppression, though he does admit a climate component to changing fire patterns.
13 Bill Armstrong, interview with the author, July 2014.
14 Bill Armstrong, interview with the author.
15 Bill Armstrong, interview with the author.
16 Bill Armstrong, interview with the author.
17 Rockström et al., "A Safe Operating Space for Humanity."
18 Lenton, "Environmental Tipping Points," 1.
19 Orlowski, *Chasing Ice*.
20 Quoted from *Chasing Ice*. The ice retreated further from 2001 to 2010 than it had in the previous hundred years.
21 Lenton, "Environmental Tipping Points."
22 On these other complexes, see Deleuze, *Francis Bacon*, xix. On "disordered chronological reality," see Cronon, "A Place for Stories," 1349.
23 Petryna, "What Is a Horizon?"
24 Pacala and Socolow, "Stabilization Wedges."
25 Magnuson, Bowser, and Beckel, "The Invisible Present," *L & S Magazine*.
26 First quote from Magnuson, "Long-Term Ecological Research and the Invisible Present," 495. Second quote from National Research Council, *The Bering Sea Ecosystem*, 13.
27 National Research Council, *The Bering Sea Ecosystem*, 13.
28 Magnuson, "Long-Term Ecological Research and the Invisible Present," 497.
29 Magnuson, "The Invisible Present," in *Ecological Time Series*, ed. Thomas M. Powell and John H. Steele, 454 (New York: Springer Science and Business Media, 1995).
30 Magnuson, Bowser, and Beckel, "The Invisible Present," *L & S Magazine*, 5.
31 Magnuson, "Long-Term Ecological Research and the Invisible Present," 495. Now an emeritus professor at the University of Wisconsin, Magnuson was one of the founders of the National Science Foundation–funded Long-Term Ecological Research Program. This program has been running since 1980, originally involving eleven sites representing a variety of ecosystems. Its goal is to draw together new expertise for conceptualizing relationships between scientific observation and the causes and effects of ecological change.
32 Magnuson, "Long-Term Ecological Research and the Invisible Present," 495.
33 Swanson and Sparks, "Long-Term Ecological Research and the Invisible Place," 502.
34 Stephen Carpenter, interview with the author, July 2013, via Skype.
35 The idea of a self-regulating and equilibrium-seeking ecosystem or Earth is reflected in the Gaia hypothesis.
36 Thom, *Structural Stability and Morphogenesis*.
37 Petryna and Mitchell, "On the Nature of Catastrophic Forms."
38 See, for example, Scheffer et al., "Catastrophic Shifts in Ecosystems."
39 DeLanda, "Space," 130.
40 DeLanda, *Deleuze*, 116.
41 DeLanda, "Space," 82.

42 Stephen Carpenter, quoted in Zagorski, "Profile of Stephen R. Carpenter," 9999. These configurations are separated by thresholds, "so, with enough pressure, you can move an ecosystem across a threshold, into a different configuration" (Stephen Carpenter, Skype interview with the author, July 2013).
43 Stephen Carpenter, quoted in Zagorski, "Profile of Stephen R. Carpenter," 10000.
44 Healy, "Starving Sea Lions," A12.
45 Mora et al., "Biotic and Human Vulnerability to Projected Changes in Ocean Biogeochemistry over the 21st Century."
46 See Mora et al., "The Projected Timing of Climate Departure for Recent Variability," 183.
47 *Britannica Guide to Climate Change* (2008), http://www.britannica.com/topic/climate-envelope.
48 See Norgaard, "Living in Denial."
49 Fabian, *Time and the Other*.
50 Petryna, *Life Exposed*.
51 Malabou, *The Ontology of the Accident*, 2.
52 Malabou, *The Ontology of the Accident*, 2.
53 M. Thomas, *The Artificial Horizon*.
54 Parunak, Belding, and Brueckner, "Prediction Horizons in Agent Models."
55 Griffen and Drake, "Scaling Rules for the Final Decline to Extinction."
56 Rockström et al., "A Safe Operating Space for Humanity," quoted in Hughes et al., "Living Dangerously on Borrowed Time during Slow, Unrecognized Regime Shifts," 6.
57 Verma, Langford, and Simmons, "Non-Parametric Fault Identification for Space Rovers."
58 Zeman et al., "Loss of Imagery Phenomenology with Intact Visuo-Spatial Task Performance," 145.
59 Sebald, *On the Natural History of Destruction*, 4 and 78.
60 Sebald, *On the Natural History of Destruction*, 27.
61 Williams and Baverstock, "Chernobyl and the Future."
62 See Petryna, "The Origins of Extinction."
63 Rabinow, *Anthropos Today*.

VI

10

Meantime

PETER LOCKE

In summer 2010, two years after my fieldwork in Sarajevo, I found myself in rural Sierra Leone with a group of undergraduates, studying and supporting the community health projects conducted by a small medical nongovernmental organization.[1] While my postdoctoral trajectory took me from one postconflict world reshaped by global humanitarianism to another—radically different in history, culture, and politics, to be sure—this was not in pursuit of a universalizing humanitarian anthropology that might suspend reflexive critique in the service of salvific narratives or a fetishization of suffering.[2] Scholarly suspicion of the kinds of solidarities and sympathies that often develop in fieldwork, especially among the world's most vulnerable people, is important to sustaining the rigor of our methods and analysis; yet such suspicion can too easily reinforce the questionable assumption that integrating greater empathy and moral commitment into our projects somehow invalidates the knowledge that we produce. The alternatives—to not engage, to mask our sympathies and politics, and to embrace a dispassionate critical distance or assess from an "armchair" position—are surely at least as problematic.

Over the course of three summers, my engagement in Sierra Leone helped me see my work in Bosnia-Herzegovina in new comparative light, juxtaposing the intersections of global humanitarianism, global health rhetorics and practices, and ordinary struggles to sustain life in these two disparate contexts. Above all, it illuminated the unevenness of global health's globalization: the ways in which reigning logics of aid and humanitarianism continue to map different sets of challenges onto different regions and populations.[3] Interventions operating under the label of *global health* in regions like West Africa largely seem to work according to what Peter Redfield has called a "minimal biopolitics"—preserving the basic biological conditions of life, and little more, for the majority of humanity that global capitalism treats as disposable or as market opportunities.[4] In contrast, international engagements in the former Yugoslavia have consistently stressed issues of democratic, multiethnic governance; reconciliation; and market reforms in a way that has neglected, and often diminished, the sort of "workable infrastructures" for a "livable life"— including health services—that most of my Sarajevan interlocutors told me they lacked and longed for.[5]

Recent events have drawn new attention to the consequences of these modes of global governance and care: in West Africa, in the unfolding of the Ebola epidemic and the deep deficits in public health infrastructure it threw into relief;[6] and in the Balkans, in bouts of political protests directed at the neoliberal order instituted in the wake of Yugoslavia's disintegration. In Bosnia-Herzegovina, a series of initially violent, but later peaceful and well-organized, protests against corrupt nationalist politicians began in February 2014 in the northeastern industrial hub of Tuzla, a community long held up as an exemplar of proletarian solidarity and skepticism toward ethnicized politics. Workers turned out to protest their sudden loss of jobs and benefits as privatization stripped five companies of their assets and led them to fold. These protests quickly spread throughout the country, spurring cautiously excited talk of a Bosnian Spring or Bosnian Occupy Movement.[7] Government offices, including the presidential headquarters in Sarajevo, were set ablaze, and there was some violent response from police forces in the upheaval's early days. Soon, though, the protests were consolidated into a set of remarkable, if relatively short-lived, experiments in direct democracy. Young activists, including the literary scholar Damir Arsenijević, at that time on the faculty of Tuzla's university, led the formation of open plenums, drawing in hundreds of fed-up citizens from across ethnic and demographic groups (including war veterans, the unemployed, students, retired people, and underpaid health workers and teachers) to formulate, vote on, and issue demands to municipal, regional, and national government bodies.[8]

The plenums succeeded in compelling the resignation of several cantonal administrators, and canton assemblies acceded to some plenum demands, which ranged from returning industries to public control and reforming health and pension policies to reducing the inflated salaries of government officials. One widely circulated image showed protesters holding up a spray-painted banner that read, "Neither Serb, Croat, nor Bosniak. Human beings first!" Slavoj Žižek, writing in the *Guardian*, insisted that "what brought the protesters together is a radical demand for justice.... The people of Bosnia have finally understood who their true enemy is: not other ethnic groups, but their own leaders who pretend to protect them from others. It is as if the old and much-abused Titoist motto of the 'brotherhood and unity' of Yugoslav nations acquired new actuality."[9]

The journalist Senad Hadžifejzović conducted a fascinating television interview with Arsenijević and his colleague Šejla Šehabović about the plenums.[10] Hadžifejzović seemed consistently bewildered by the sudden eruption and pace of events, as if they had come out of nowhere, pressing his interviewees to account for this emergent social movement. "It wasn't sudden," Arsenijević insisted. "You keep saying 'suddenly.' For twenty years politicians looked at the people with contempt. It's just the blindness of people who didn't see what was happening.... For over twenty years people have been complaining, we can't do this, we can't do that. Now people see that they can, and what a victory! In seven days we have saved one million marks [in government salaries]. That is a possibility achieved. A plenum is a protest for the creation of possibilities." He paused and looked directly into the camera for emphasis, as if trying to speak past Hadžifejzović to the entire country: "Now in Bosnia-Herzegovina, we're speaking about what is possible, not what is impossible." And later, he offered another powerful soundbite: "Bosnia today is a plenum."

The anthropologist Stef Jansen spent time with the protesters and plenums each day during this period. Like Arsenijević, he could easily perceive the roots of what was unfolding, but he also seemed to share the journalist's awe at such a dramatic turn of events. In an interview published online, he said:

> The rage existed, the protests and the strikes have always existed. Every month over the last few years you could see protests in Sarajevo, tent cities in front of the parliaments, farmers, workers.... But they were always standalone protests.... This time, protesters joined forces. In other words, it wasn't that the workers from one company wanted one thing, the pensioners another, the farmers another still. *It was a wondrous moment, and I don't know where that moment came from.* I was surprised by that moment when all those people realized that they have the same problem, that they

MEANTIME | 271

could publicly speak about it and that they could put it on the political agenda.[11]

The common thread of wonder that seems to weave through the reactions of the philosopher (Žižek), the journalist (Hadžifejzović), and the anthropologist (Jansen) resonates with the political theorist Jane Bennett's reflections on "enchantment"—deep, transfiguring, hard-to-anticipate modes of attachment to or investment in others and in the world—as a necessary and neglected precondition for "the *enactment* of ethical aspirations, which requires bodily movements in space, mobilizations of heat and energy, a series of choreographed gestures, a distinctive assemblage of affective propulsions."[12] The 2014 protests were perhaps all the more "wondrous" for longtime observers of postwar Bosnia-Herzegovina, who have noted that embittered disenchantment with politics—and certainly with airy aspirations like reconciliation—has been deep and widespread at least since the 1995 Dayton Accords. What are we to make of such striking reenchantments of politics, the countersolidarities they build, and their inevitable transience?

Indeed, the protests and plenums seem to have fizzled out after a matter of months, without leading to a radical revision of the Dayton constitutional structure and a new postethnic era of Bosnian politics, as some had dared to hope. The movement was overshadowed in part by catastrophic floods that struck the region later that spring—though, interestingly, this challenge, too, seemed to trigger unanticipated forms of intercommunity cooperation that disrupted any sense of Bosnia's population as being locked into the same ethnic animosities that characterize its politics. "The networks that had emerged with the uprising and the plenums have now transformed into a sort of humanitarian aid organisation," Arsenijević commented. "The plenums created the conditions for this kind of solidarity."[13] Moreover, as the Sarajevan-born writer Igor Štiks has argued in proposing the emergence of a post-Yugoslav "New Left," even after losing steam the protests have triggered "a series of movements struggling for 'social justice.' For the first time in Bosnia after the war, social issues such as inequalities and unemployment, as well as privatizations and corruption, overshadowed ethnic politics."[14]

On a similar note, Žižek, anticipating that the movement might fade, emphasized that "even if the protests gradually lose their power, they will remain a brief spark of hope, something like the enemy soldiers fraternizing across the trenches in the first world war. Authentic emancipatory events always involve ignoring of such particular identities."[15] Something, in other words, continues to resonate even when movements fade—the concrete fact of unanticipated public assembly that, as Judith Butler puts it, "delivers a bodily demand for a more livable set of economic, social and political conditions no longer afflicted by induced forms of precarity."[16]

For his part, Gilles Deleuze insisted emphatically on distinguishing processes of becoming revolutionary from the becoming of the revolution, and on the impossibility of assessing the former by the latter: "all revolutions fail," he quipped impatiently in the Abécédaire interviews—"everyone knows that."[17] Reflecting on the legacies of May 1968—"a becoming revolutionary without a revolutionary future"—Deleuze argued that "even if revolutions fail, go badly, that still never stopped people or prevented people from becoming revolutionary."[18] Such becomings, for Deleuze, are prompted not by aspirations to achieve abstract human rights or ideal types of government, but by "situations in which the only outcome for man [sic] is to become revolutionary"—situations in which, in other words, the preconditions for a livable life have become so far out of reach for so many that taking to the streets is less a result of any one group's or leader's intention than an organic inevitability.[19]

Butler's recent reflections on contemporary social movements, from the Arab Spring to Occupy Wall Street and Black Lives Matter, are illuminating. For Butler, such movements are, at their root, a reaction to the widespread conditions of precarity generated by decades of neoliberal politics and economics that have systematically undermined public infrastructures and services—the very preconditions of the rugged self-reliance and "responsibilization" that neoliberal ideology demands. "What does it mean to act together," she asks, "when the conditions for acting together are devastated or falling away?"[20] The transience of new modes of public assembly, for Butler, is an element of their critical function, a way in which they draw attention to the absence of "workable infrastructures" for democratic politics and "mutual dependency" in the world that neoliberalism has wrought.[21] "The bodies assembled," Butler argues, "'say' we are not disposable, even if they stand silently."[22]

I hesitate to directly connect the marginal solidarities and becomings I observed in my 2007–8 research with Wings of Hope to those on display throughout Bosnia-Herzegovina during the spring of 2014. Nevertheless, it is difficult not to interpret the protests and the grievances and aspirations they channeled as evidence that an anthropology attuned to becomings might be an especially helpful approach to better understanding the determinants, destinies, and possibilities of such social movements and upheavals (however fleeting they might be) and to exploring the complex relationships between becoming at individual, familial, and collective scales.

How, indeed, are small and marginal becomings and potentials related to such seemingly out of the blue, effervescent moments of radical political engagement and social transformation? Jansen expressed wonder at how splintered victim and protest groups—farmers, veterans, workers, retired people, and students—could so suddenly move from competitive atomization to a powerful and even world-altering solidarity. An anthropology of becoming might explore and illuminate what triggers the shift from the creative, if agonizing, arts of living practiced under heavy structural constraints and anomie to politics, to minor solidarities actualized as social movements. As Deleuze suggested, "the concrete problem" is not so much what ultimately becomes of those revolutions that manage to seize power—"whoever thought a revolution would go well? Who?"—but *"how* and *why...* people become revolutionary."[23] Thus, we might need to look for what triggers the movement from protecting the "I" and its identities, resources, and privileges to recognizing precarity as a shared experience of the failure of political and economic institutions that crosses ethnic, regional, and national divisions.

Meanwhile, brief return visits to Sarajevo in 2010, 2015, and 2016 have highlighted for me both the vital and deadening potentials of what Jansen has productively analyzed as the "yearnings in the meantime" (for a "normal" country and "normal" life) that were crystallized in the 2014 protests and that seem to characterize so much of Sarajevan sociality.[24] The material appearance of the city has continued to be rapidly transformed, with the most visible scars of the war gradually smoothed over, and the last of the iconic burned-out husks of old government buildings and shopping malls demolished and rebuilt as gleaming new tributes to the postwar reign of ethnonationalist oligarchs and a recent influx of investment from the Middle East. The enormous new American embassy, a fortress-like complex the size of two football fields that had been under construction throughout my fieldwork, has finally been completed. Hostels are proliferating to accommodate the increasing numbers of young North American and Australian backpackers passing through on their way to sunny adventures on neighboring Croatia's Adriatic coast.

Judging by appearances, one could almost imagine that things might be beginning to look up for many Sarajevans. But checking in with some of my old friends made it clear that behind the façades, people were still seething over the dysfunctional, byzantine, and ethnically divided government structures left behind by the Dayton Accords and still struggling to make ends meet and acquire basic necessities amid high unemployment and income inequality. Such grievances seemed particularly acute during my visit in the summer of 2015, a year that saw somber reflection and a renewal of collective grief on the occasion of the twentieth anniversary of the genocide of 8,000 Muslim men and boys at Srebrenica. At the same time, thousands of refugees from conflicts in the Middle East were moving through Serbia in their grueling struggle to reach hoped-for sanctuary in Western Europe, reminding many throughout the former Yugoslavia of their own arduous experiences of displacement, exile, and return, and their sense that little justice had been achieved to make up for what they had lost along the way.

My erstwhile research assistant, Mirza, was a man about my age who had lived through the siege of Sarajevo as a child; studied literature in college; and, during my fieldwork, helped me with interviews and translations while dreaming of getting a job as a cook or a cleaner on a Caribbean cruise ship. When I found him in 2010, just two years later, he had deteriorated considerably, becoming buried in alcohol and gambling addictions and deeply bitter about his future chances. He had given up on Bosnia, he said. But he had also given up on getting out. In subsequent years we lost touch, but I connected with him again in the summer of 2016. Still drinking, still gambling, he had stumbled into a strangely sustainable holding pattern—keeping his addictions enough in check to manage his ennui and resignation about life in Bosnia, without losing support from his family or letting his life collapse altogether. He seemed relaxed and content, and he contrasted his situation to that of civilians enduring Syria's civil war, saying, "Things could always be much worse."

My visits to Wings of Hope in the summers of 2015 and 2016 have been encouraging. Milan, Maja's young cousin who faced so many difficulties growing up in postwar Bosnia-Herzegovina, is now in his mid-twenties and flourishing. Though he was failing his math classes at the time of my fieldwork, after years of support from Maja, Milan has completed his studies in mining engineering, and he is now the manager of a Prijedor-based NGO that supports people living with disabilities. Maja herself is like a new person: frustrated and angry throughout my fieldwork in 2007–8, in the meantime she has attained significant personal and professional success, as well as a certain measure of peace and resigned humor vis-à-vis the often absurd sociopolitical realities that she faces daily. Having achieved independence for Wings of Hope from the founding organizations in Western Europe, Maja seems less stressed and relieved to be able to run things her way, without having to defend the value of her local knowledge. "We do use 'Western' knowledge, but adapted to the Bosnian reality," she told me in August 2016, describing how Wings of Hope's deliberately "multisystemic" approach to psychosocial support folds in multiple therapeutic modalities, biomedical health care, social work, and legal aid. Maja herself—despite her old distrust of psychologists—is now training in Gestalt therapy.

International organizations, Maja said, now reach out to her for "partnership" rather than trying to dictate and police how donor money must be spent. Accumulating successful programs that have drawn steadier funding, the organization has expanded its range of staff and specialists, engaging lawyers, pedagogues, social workers, counselors, and health care workers in providing holistic support to beneficiaries. She and her colleagues have relocated Wings of Hope to a big house farther from the city center with sweeping views of the Miljacka River valley and plenty of yard space for the children and teenagers she and her colleagues counsel and tutor. Word has spread throughout the city—and beyond—that Wings of Hope is a reliable and effective source of support. An invaluable mentor for me over a decade, Maja now also teaches the new cohorts of students I bring to join me in the field each summer.

Maja's response to my question about what might account for Wings of Hope's increasing success was simple: "because we are actually taking care of people." There is a wisdom in this—a commitment to caring for others in their day-to-day struggles, their arts of living amid constraint and frustration—that can inform and inspire our own commitment to people-centered approaches in anthropology, enriching everything from our mentoring of new generations to the effects of our scholarship in the world.

NOTES

1. Locke, "Anthropology and Medical Humanitarianism in the Age of Global Health Education."
2. Robbins, "Beyond the Suffering Subject."
3. Locke, "Global Health and Its Margins."
4. Redfield, *Life in Crisis*, 20. See also Abramowitz and Panter-Brick, *Medical Humanitarianism*; Biehl and Petryna, *When People Come First*; Livingston, *Improvising Medicine*; Nguyen, *The Republic of Therapy*; Ticktin and Feldman, *In the Name of Humanity*.
5. Butler, *Notes Toward a Performative Theory of Assembly*, 18 and 22.
6. See Farmer, "Who Lives and Who Dies"; Frankfurter, "The Danger in Losing Sight of Ebola Victims' Humanity."

Laura Jardim, the doctor who was overseeing Catarina's treatment, was positive that she could not have died from complications from Machado-Joseph Disease and requested an autopsy. The autopsy revealed that Catarina died as a result of intestinal bleeding.

The wear and tear of Vita, the silent work of killing, I still think.

When I made it back to southern Brazil in 2005, I wanted to get a headstone for Catarina's grave, and I decided to visit Vera and Marino, the adoptive parents of her youngest daughter, Ana. The couple had helped to organize Catarina's burial in Novo Hamburgo's public cemetery. The family, as Oscar had told me, "at least took the dead body home." Ana was helping at the family's restaurant when I arrived. At thirteen years of age, she had a face and gaze that were indeed extensions of Catarina's.

Vera did most of the talking. She lambasted every single member of Catarina's family, saying how "fake" they had all behaved during the funeral. Only Nilson, Catarina's ex-husband, had shown "respect," by offering to help defray some of the funeral's costs.

It was striking how Catarina's story continued to shift in the years following her death. In people's recollections, she was no longer seen as "the mad woman." Both Vera and the relatives I saw later that week now spoke of Catarina as having "suffered a lot."

As true as this was, such renderings left unaddressed the everyday practices that had compounded her intractability—most obviously, the cold detachment that accompanied care conceived solely as pharmaceutical intervention rather than as a relational practice too. Indeed, the plot of a life story is never securely in the possession of its subject. It is part of the ongoing moral work of those who live on.

One morning in August 2005, Vera and I drove to the cemetery. I used to visit this place as a child with Vó Minda, my maternal grandmother. We would make hour-long walks uphill to wash the white pebbles adorning her son's grave and to leave flowers from our backyard. Nowadays the cemetery occupies the whole hill, overlooking a city that has also changed beyond recognition. The cemetery has now become a site of pillage. Anything on the graves that might have had some monetary value, from the metallic letters spelling out the names of the deceased to religious icons, had been looted. So much for the value of memory, I told Vera. She shrugged, not knowing how to respond. I was not sure what I intended either, beyond giving voice to mourning.

The story of a life is always also the story of a death. And it is up to us to project the story into the future, helping shape its afterlife. Catarina had

FIGURE 11.1 Catarina's tombstone, Novo Hamburgo, 2011

been buried in a crypt together with her mother's remains. I made sure that the crypt was fully paid for, so that in the future their remains would not be thrown into the mass grave at the edge of the cemetery. And Vera was going to oversee the making of a marble headstone with Catarina's name engraved on it, along with a photo taken by my longtime collaborator and friend Torben Eskerod: a beautiful image of Catarina smiling that no one could take away.

TELL MY STORY

That winter I also returned to Vita.

Inside the infirmary, things had only gotten worse. The bedridden were not even brought into the sun's meager warmth. I asked for Iraci, Catarina's good friend. I found him crouched in bed. He said he was so happy to see me and began to cry silently. So did I. Yes, Catarina had died "all of a sudden," as had

India, the young woman Iraci called wife and had so dearly looked after. He then asked this simple and piercing question, which still haunts me: "Did you bring the tape recorder?"

I had not. Now it was his time to tell the story.

Iraci—much like Catarina—called on the ethnographer to help give shape to his own life story. In the recent lecture "Tell My Story," the literary scholar Stephen Greenblatt follows his "compulsive fascination with the power and pleasure of stories" to interrogate their stakes and possibilities.[1] Through a discussion of the Judeo-Christian origin myth, he explores our need for life stories: while Genesis glosses the lives of Adam and Eve in a few words and gives just sparing details, denoting only the barest trajectory of the fall and what came after, Greenblatt sees in the Apocrypha a response to our deep need for a story. If Genesis imagined the origin of life, the apocryphal texts imagine the origin of the story of *a* life: "Genesis tells us what it would have been like to be human, but not have human life stories." The Apocrypha, he tells us, "grope to supply these details."

Also drawing on Shakespeare's *King Lear* and attentive to the relationships between body, history, storytelling, and death, Greenblatt is interested in human longevity beyond reproductive life—"least relevant to the biological processes of life history." "This consciousness," he states, "has no claim on the attention of evolutionary biologists. It is, like the nonreproductive bodies of the very old, a kind of meaningless leftover." He goes on: "But for Shakespeare, and for literature, the leftover is the thing itself."

It is precisely here that the human story resides, as does the impulse that propels the Apocryphal texts to ask not only if Adam and Eve lived, but how. Where for biology, it is an "epiphenomenon" (at best, a ruse; at worst, an irrelevance), in literature, Greenblatt asserts, "life story is the platform for human experience." Beyond productive and reproductive life, he tells us, what matters most to Shakespeare is "what lies just ahead"—the rage, grief, madness, and fantasies of a redemption that will never come—the very stuff of stories.

How, then, does this stuff of our stories continue, drawing our subjects and ourselves into an ethnographic open system?

"YOU WILL REMEMBER MY CASE"

In November 2014, I received an e-mail message from someone I did not immediately recall: Andrea de Lima.

The subject line read: "Mr. João Guilherme [which is how I am addressed in Brazil]—MJD [which stands for Machado-Joseph Disease]—family case—Vita [where I met Catarina]." There was much more at work in that composite subject than I could immediately apprehend.

"Good morning, Mr. João Guilherme, she wrote, in a youthful, neighborly and respectful manner. "It is a great pleasure to be sending you this email."

The message seemed affectively important to her. "I got your contact information from Mr. Magnus at Vita, here in the state of Rio Grande do Sul, Brazil," she informed me. She had gone out of her way and into Vita, searching to establish contact with the anthropologist whom Catarina had known.

"My name is Andrea," she continued.

By then I knew who was writing. In *Vita*, I had named her Ana.[2]

A puzzling statement followed: "I'm looking for you for the following . . . you will remember my case."

How could I not? I felt deeply implicated. The character had acquired a Shakespearean ghostly tone, like in Hamlet: "Remember me."

Yet this was not just a call for personal recognition. The memory she invoked was that of her "case"—a broader story she was a part of. Andrea was looking for the ethnographer of Vita. She trusted that he knew of her particular situation and that she was not just an anonymous floating sample of something occurring in the world: "I am the daughter of Catarina Inês Gomes who spent years living in Vita with Machado-Joseph Disease and you accompanied her case."

My work with Catarina had unleashed something into the world, something that surfaced all these years later in Andrea. While Catarina had sought to detach herself from the logics that produced her abandonment, her daughter was, in a sense, trying to attach herself to something—to enter into the entanglements that brought kin, biology, and anthropologist together. Now it was Andrea who was trying to reassemble the dismembered family.

In her email, she wrote: "I was adopted by Vera. So my last name was changed. My siblings stayed with the blood family."

Catarina once told me that she had never signed the adoption papers. Indeed, given her supposed madness and recurrent psychiatric hospitalizations, she never got her day in court to contest her husband's decision to sign away custody of Andrea.

OPENING

Twice in this initial message, Andrea invoked the genre of the case: her own and her mother's. As the literary theorist Lauren Berlant notes, cases—legal, medical, or psychological—are defined by judgment. Linking the singular to the general, they express "a relation of expertise to a desire for shared knowledge."[3] But is the case only or always about judgment? And how does anthropological work—and the systems it engenders over time and space—enter into proximity with such cases?

Andrea knew that those who had seen her mother as unproductive, unfit, and mad had closed Catarina's life off. Yet by exploring how Catarina became a case—of psychosis, expert knowledge, and abandonment—anthropological work had made room for thinking reality and human figures otherwise. Ethnography brings crossroads (places where other choices might be made, other paths taken) out of the dustbin of history or the shadow of encased norms and deterministic analytics—the "leftovers," in Greenblatt's sense, that make up a life. Through ethnography, there is a refusal of encasing and its confines, including the values, systems, experts, and institutions through which the case is constituted. Andrea was curious about how her mother managed to survive in Vita and what her writing meant to her.

According to Berlant, cases can also trouble norms and create openings: "The case reveals itself not fundamentally as a form, but as an event that takes shape."[4] By breaking the case open, ethnography creates a spacetime separate from the event, which is the very spacetime that Andrea entered. In this way, a case "raises questions of precedent and futurity, of canons of contextualization, of narrative elucidation," writes Berlant, and "a personal or collective sensorium shifts."[5]

While cases can be—and indeed often are—domains of normative power and expert judgment, they are also a means of moving into the unknown. They offer not so much judgment as an invitation, entry point, or adjacency, or the becoming of a life story, which is an open system that the ethnographer in this case has become a part of. Ethnography thus makes the case "an opening within realism, suggesting where it might travel."[6]

In her e-mail Andrea told me, "I want the genetic test so that I can know whether I am negative or positive" for Machado-Joseph Disease.

Part of a dismembered family, Andrea knows that she also belongs to a biological system that exercises its own kind of agency. The knowledge she seeks is life-altering. If she tests positive, she will be diseased, so to speak, and left without a known treatment. I did not know how to take what I was reading or how to respond to her search, and I was thrown back to the core tension of my fieldwork with Catarina: how to sustain a sense of hope, as mortality hovers beneath the surface.

ONWARD

"I am very grateful that you attended to my mother and also to Adriano. For I know that some years ago, you helped him."

Andrea was right. A couple of years earlier, I had returned to southern Brazil to work on a visual documentary of the now-ubiquitous practice of litigation against the state for access to treatment. Torben had joined me in the field, and at that time we met with Laura Jardim, the doctor who had seen Catarina before her death, to discuss the plight of patients who are filing lawsuits for access to new and high-cost genetic therapies. At the end of the meeting, Laura mentioned that Catarina's son, Adriano, had recently visited her clinic and received the same diagnosis of Machado-Joseph Disease as his mother had had. He had been invited to enroll in the first clinical trial for a treatment that the genetics team hoped would slow the progression of the disease.

Fieldwork sets often surprising and unforeseeable processes in motion, changing something in the life course of all involved. My work with Catarina made me a part of what I have come to think of as an ethnographic open system. Between fieldwork's past and future, I was linked to both Catarina and her offspring. In contrast to the subjects of statistical studies and the figures of philosophy or social theory, our ethnographic subjects have a future, and we become a part of it in unexpected ways. Their stories become a part of the stories we tell, and we, too, become a part of their life stories.

I found Adriano, his wife, and their two children living in the poorest outskirts of the city of Novo Hamburgo, not far from where I grew up. The meeting with Adriano and his family taught me much about the dark underside of Brazil's ailing public health-care system. Unable to continue his work in the local steel factory, Adriano was getting by on a disability stipend that he had to reapply for every three months. His son had severe learning disabilities. After a year of trying, the family was still waiting for an appointment with a neurologist. His daughter was tiny, apparently undernourished; she had an umbilical hernia, and they were also having trouble making the appointment for her operation.

Living in the brutal stasis of poverty, Adriano and his wife seemed resigned to waiting. Their situation reveals the broad reality of public health among Brazil's poor: unless they learn to make themselves visible, demand fulfillment of their rights, and make the system care, they are left to live with their conditions and eventually die on their own.

Despite their difficult circumstances, there was something of Brazilian consumer society in Adriano's remote shack. The children sat on a sofa playing video games. Adriano dreamed of building a house with a yard for the kids to play in, he said, and he had managed to acquire an old Volkswagen Beetle—even though he did not have a driver's license. These possessions and desires helped him maintain a sense of worldliness and worthiness, I thought, as he now fought to escape Catarina's destiny—Vita.

"Onward," he said.

RETURN TO VITA

Together with Torben, I returned to Vita once more in August 2011.

"Welcome back," said Magnus, the soft-spoken senior citizen who had been in charge of Vita's daily operations for more than a decade. "Make yourself at home."

Vita has changed along with Brazil. It is now as much a makeshift institution of care as it is a zone of social abandonment. There is a nursing wing for the elderly and disabled, separate from the infirmary where I first met Catarina, and a social worker on staff is responsible for triage. Only people with retirement pensions or disability benefits and a certain level of well-being are accepted.

I interrupted Magnus to ask if two men seated in wheelchairs next to each other were Vaquinha (literally, "little cow") and Caminhãozinho (literally, "little truck"), the names I had come to know them by over the years. They were severely mentally impaired, and no one knew anything about their lives before Vita. I had actually written something about the pedagogical role the abandoned person/animal/object played for inmates who, by informally adopting men like Vaquinha and Caminhãozinho, were trying to rehabilitate and regenerate themselves as citizens.

In a striking turn of events and in line with Brazil's new rule of law, the abandoned had formally become citizens, I learned. During an audit by the Public Ministry, officials had demanded that the legal situation of everyone living at Vita be regularized. Vaquinha is now João Paulo Nestore Soares, and Caminhãozinho is Samuel Lopes. They had names and dates of birth invented for them and were issued social security and identity cards. With these cards in hand, João Paulo and Samuel were now entitled to disability benefits, which are channeled to the institution. Yes, formal channels of social inclusion are taking root even in places like Vita, but of course citizenship and care remain a money-making matter.

We found a bedridden man in a small room with an empty chair and a television. Caregivers refer to him as "uma antiguidade"—"an antique" or "a person of those earlier times"—because he has survived in Vita since its beginnings in the mid-1980s. Motionless, he was purged of specificity, a sort of human mineral with no human touch or voice to awaken flight, a person connected to nothing and no one. I know that no emotion or image within me can represent this life story, which, like most, will remain unknown.

A resident named Vilma beckoned us. She was unable to walk on her own. Three months earlier, Vilma had been left by her husband at Vita with a few clothes, a record of psychiatric prescriptions, and the prospect of a disability pension to be collected by Vita. Vita's administrators were adamant that, by and large, people who were left at Vita required full-time care and thus prevented another family member from working. Simply put, in today's economy, a family unburdened of day-to-day caregiving responsibilities can generate much more money.

It was uncanny how much Vilma's story mirrored Catarina's. As I listened to her, I was thrown back to the beginnings of Vita (both the place and the book), to knots of intractability, a reality that kills, and the desire to bring this reality to justice and tell it all.

But how?

HOW LITERAL THE VIRTUAL FIGURE IS

A few days later, we were back.

"I think that's Lili," I told Torben. "She was Catarina's roommate; you photographed her in 2001."

With a shaved head and aged beyond her years, yes, it was Lili, seated on a bench next to a man with a large build.

"Hi, Lili."

"Hi."

"Do you remember me?"

"I cannot remember you, sir."

"We talked many times, when Catarina was alive. I did not wear glasses then," I said, and I took my glasses off.

"Ah . . . yes, now I recall, *the times of Catarina.*"

"This is Torben, a friend of mine. He also photographed you. You told us about your family."

"Was it you who took me to the bank to get that money?"

"No," I said. Most likely it had been a Vita administrator taking her to collect her pension.

Lili then introduced us to Pedro: "I am married to this guy now. It is good to have someone, and they don't let us sleep together . . ."

Lili added that she had been "ill . . . of the nerves . . . I don't recall things . . . I had not recalled you."

"Do you take medication?"

"Yes. I am talking the red pill, the blue one, and the little white one, every day."

Torben asked to photograph the couple.

"But I have no money to pay for it," Lili said, to Pedro's laughter.

During the photo shoot, Lili asked me: "Are you married?"

"Yes. My wife's name is Adriana. And we have a son called Andre."

"I also have a son. There he is." She pointed to a volunteer who was helping an elderly man to his wheelchair.

I tried to shift the conversation to what I thought was real and asked: "Do you miss your son?"

"Now he is living nearby and he often comes to visit. My daughter-in-law also comes and brings me sweets."

I recalled that Lili had always spoken about going to church and quoted passages from the Bible. I asked her whether there were still worship services in Vita.

"No, they don't let us go to church now. . . . I used to go to the Assembly of God and to the God Is Love Church. I went to both."

"But you pray . . ."

"Yes, I pray. I think of God, but I never saw God."

I was puzzled. Lili meant it literally: "I only saw the Son of God on a crucifix. It was in a pamphlet they gave me at the hospital."

With a little trust restored between us, Lili spoke of everyday life in Vita: "I don't even know how long I have been here. Sometimes life here is good, sometimes it is bad." She lamented the cruel treatment inflicted by volunteers, with the exception of her "son."

She was referring to Jorge, the infirmary's head caregiver, who joined us. He had not overheard our conversation and revealed how literal the virtual figure is for the abandoned: "I am the one who is always joking with her. I tell her that I am her son."

And so, through and beyond the times of Catarina, the writing of Vita continues, amid cruelly optimistic yet sustaining attachments. People keep claiming the social roles and connections that have been denied to them, attaching themselves to the potentiality of words to create ties, allowing at least a minimal sense of personhood and human value.

UNTHOUGHT

"Please confirm that you received this message," Andrea pleaded in her e-mail to me. "You are very important in my history and in my family. I hope you will remember me or my family that you became a part of."

Besides family, biology, history and work ("I'm sending this e-mail from work," she said in a postscript), Andrea was also part of an ethnographic open system constituted by the circuits of fieldwork and the work of time.

"Thank you," Andrea concluded the message.

We began a conversation over e-mail and Skype. Andrea had finished high school, and when she turned eighteen, she said, it was time to leave the home of her adoptive parents: "Vera and Marino gave me a home and education, and I always had everything I needed. I cannot complain. But it was never an affectionate relationship."

Andrea was working as a computing and customer service assistant at a transportation company in Novo Hamburgo, and for the past three years, she had been living with her boyfriend, Anderson, and his working-class family. "Not a single day goes by that I don't miss my mother," she told me.

She only recalled having seen Catarina once. Her adoptive parents took her to Vita and "I did not know what to say. All that human misery. I regret so much not asking her any questions. I was afraid." She was ten at the time. Vera had told me that they had actually taken Andrea to Vita "for her to see what will happen to her if she does not start behaving."

Through the ethnographic complex, Andrea sought an identification with Catarina. She asked whether I could reach out to the same doctor who had tested and treated her mother and her brother, Adriano—which I did, although I was ambivalent about doing so. If it were me, I would not want to know if I had such a disease. I worried about what would happen to her current life, which seemed well-organized and stable, if she were found to have the genetic mutation for Machado-Joseph Disease. Yet Andrea was determined to know and went through a long process of evaluation and counseling. It was as if the lethal genetic knowledge would confirm that she was in fact the daughter of the mother who, encased in madness and abandonment, she never had.

A year later, in November 2015, Andrea e-mailed me again and asked if we could talk.

I thought she wanted to tell me the outcome of the genetic test. But that was not it. She had not yet been called to get the results. I knew from my geneticist colleagues that about half the people who get tested decide not to see their results, and I told her that this option was available to her.

"My sister and I found each other on Facebook," she told me.

That was the story Andrea wanted to tell. She was over the moon with happiness. The last time Andrea had seen her oldest sister, Adriana (who had been raised, together with Adriano, by a paternal grandmother), was at Catarina's funeral.

"I saw her message on a Sunday morning when I woke up," she told me. "Can you imagine? I cried a lot."

This is a snapshot of their digital encounter. The English translation of what they said is: "Hi Andrea, all good?" "I think I found the person I sought my entire life, the person I loved my entire life." "You are my little sister, right?"

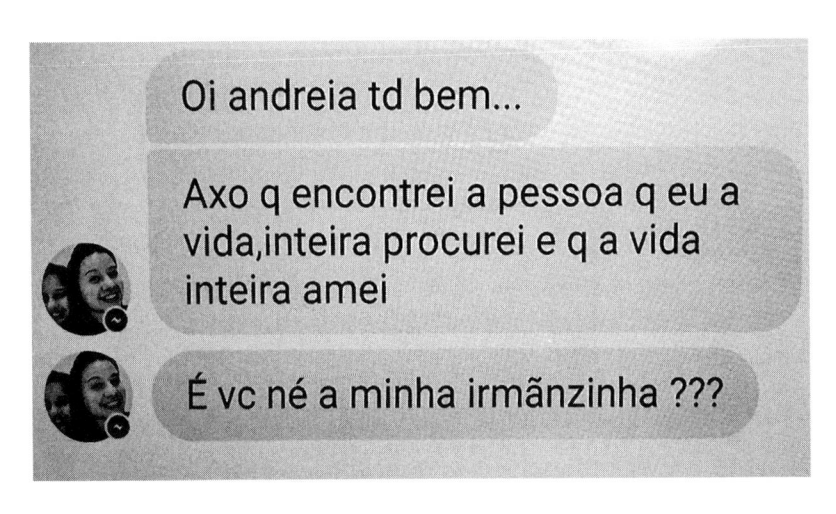

> Oi andreia td bem...
>
> Axo q encontrei a pessoa q eu a vida, inteira procurei e q a vida inteira amei
>
> É vc né a minha irmãnzinha ???

FIGURE 11.2 The sisters on Facebook, 2015

Adriana does not have Machado-Joseph Disease, Andrea told me. She has two children of her own and works as a supermarket cashier. "And what a coincidence," Andrea continued: "It was the Day of the Dead, and I had already bought flowers to take to my mother's grave."

The ethnographic memorial, an out-of-the-way effort to insist on the irreducible truth that a woman named Catarina Inês Gomes Moraes had once walked on the earth, was the site where the characters of the "tragedy generated in life" (in Catarina's own words) continued. In spite of all the time and prospects that people and institutions had taken from them, they continue to tell their family story, to live it a bit differently, and to graft each other anew: "It was there that we found each other, there in front of my mom's remains."

This is a photo Adriana took of Catarina's shrine, with the flowers she and her sister had brought. The sisters reached out to Adriano, who was now living by himself on disability benefits. With his disease progressing and conflict in the house, his wife left him for another man, taking the children with her. Adriano has found solace and support in the evangelical church he attends daily.

Catarina's scattered offspring were now forming the ties that she always imagined, and that had sustained her somehow: "to restart a home," she used to say. And now it was Andrea: "This is very important to me. What is happening is the brick that was lacking in my construction."

There was one more thing that Andrea wanted from the anthropologist who had "accompanied" Catarina's case: "Can you, please, tell me: what was my mom thinking in Vita?"

FIGURE 11.3 Andrea's photograph of the ethnographic memorial, 2015

FIGURE 11.4 Adriana, Adriano, and Andrea, 2016

I recalled Catarina's words: "In my thinking, people forgot me." But I didn't repeat her words, for Andrea was now living Catarina's hereafter. I told her I would love to meet the reassembling family and read parts of *Vita* and of Catarina's dictionary with them.

We met in January 2016 in Novo Hamburgo, the place of my own beginnings and departures.

It is such immanent negotiations (of people, social forms, time, worldliness, desire, storytelling and ethics)—in their impasses, stabilization, transience, excess, ruination, and creation—that animate the unfinishedness of ethnography and the critical work of human becomings.

NOTES

1 Greenblatt, "Tell My Story."
2 Biehl, *Vita*.
3 Berlant, "On the Case," 664.
4 Berlant, "On the Case," 670.
5 Berlant, "On the Case," 666.
6 Berlant, "On the Case," 669.

Afterword

Zen Exercises

Anthropological Discipline and Ethics

MICHAEL M. J. FISCHER

To catch the moment of becoming, emergence, phase transition, enlightenment, tipping point, switching point, Euclidean point, asymptote is a matter of approximation, finding parameters, modeling throughputs, a calculus of infinities, a receding mirage or fusion between cognition (it must be an illusion) and perception (but I can see, smell, taste, feel, or desire it), the unfinishedness of living, morphing through interactions, artificial life, algorithmic repetitions beyond the powers of understanding, materializations of seeming impossibilities. These are zen moments of enlightenment, zen exercises.

However, to approximate, triangulate, frame, or restage such moments are ethical exercises meant to keep things open to potentials, catch the metal fatigue before breakage occurs, anticipate and head off turbidity and hypoxia, shift uncontrolled anger into razor-sharp discipline, channel a mentor into a form of self-becoming other (more flexible and stronger), rebalance gut microbiome sensing, modulate a crowd's volatility with music or a speech, recognize when a fire's physics becomes plasma. These are pragmatic skills and apperceptions in which we can be trained; they are exercises for extreme environments (space, oceans), beyond anthropocentric hysteria, emotions for when we need to rely on risky dead reckonings.

What kind of biopolities and bioecologies will we live in, what role will violence play, what role will climate change play, what are the temporalities involved in all three of these basic anthropological, social-theoretical, humanistic questions (emergent forms of life)?[1] Does one answer them with grand theory, rapid model prototyping, and mathematical clarity or with microethnography, pragmatics, and building via imperfect understandings—or how do these inform and disturb each other (pebbles and labyrinths in the way of theory)?[2] What are the roles of writing, the tropes employed in writing, cultural genre forms, and writing's nondiscursive effectivities (changing the worlds we inhabit,[3] making, as João Biehl and Peter Locke say, the ethnography and theory "actionable" and, quoting Gilles Deleuze, making theory "multiple," a workman's "tool box")? Until and after death—always unfinished business, lives and afterlives—I want to keep the focus on people (the peopling of cultural technologies, "moral biographies of action and inaction" as Naisargi Dave puts it, people "becoming aggrieved" in Laurence Ralph's terms)[4]—people as biosensing membranes and biochemical channels; social hieroglyphs written across historical horizons; calligraphies or embodied inscriptions of experience (characters); poesis and lines of flight of desire, despair, and hope; inventor-explorers of life otherwise, generated from double binds, fostered in social pluralities; experimenters in devising new ethical plateaus for the time being, in the meantime.

This volume provides an exemplary series of case studies of, and among the best of intensive ethnographic writing about, such powerful affective anthropological zen exercises: living with ataxia, waiting years for politics to unfreeze, being forcibly converted to a new religious cosmology and enrolled in the margins of a strange society, feeling compelled to meditate on slaughterhouses cruelly run, having sons and neighbors shot without reason, being kidnapped and enduring coercive therapies in *anexos*. As in zen exercises, it is not the extremity of affect that is at issue but the overcoming, the recognition that more is going on in these partial accounts or situations; that biopolitical and bioecological subjectivities and agencies are at play that we can only partially understand; that we need, as Adriana Petryna suggests, human sciences of uncertainty rather than hubristic claims to analytic totalities.

I perform rereadings, repetitions with a difference, slippages, slightly different perspectives, threadings of other narratives, other horizons (1968, 2016, and 2036) and milieus, other pairings and juxtapositions, other questions or critiques in the service of care, and in the service, as Biehl and Locke say, of making our work "part of ethnographic open systems and . . . folded into lives, relationships, and [varied] swerves [tropes] across time and space."[5]

Seven elementary exercises follow: camaraderies and trajectories; swinging the pendulum (oscillation, contradiction, double binds); calligraphies; cannibalizing and indie-gestion; poisoned histories and dividing cities; horizoning and emergent forms of life; unfinished exercises and lifelines.

CAMARADERIES AND TRAJECTORIES

Biehl and Locke begin the volume with a musically rich quartet of pieces centered on, or spiraling outward from, the experiences of long-term, leaving-and-returning engagements with friends and acquaintances for life. Biehl and Locke, through the force of their writing, make us all accompaniers[6] on lifelines, lines of flight, and lines of stuckness (*avareh* in Persian, the word used by Iranian exiles for the feeling of being unable to move back or ahead in their lives). Only with such long engagements with people (what anthropologists call fieldwork in contrast to interviews, Google searches, and quick visits), Biehl and Locke observe, can one achieve antidotes to "the quick theoretical fix." Quick theoretical fixes miss what are often surprising developments.

The music—harmonies, dissonances, developments, and repeats—emerges over time: first encounters, meantimes, and hereafters. Thanks to different forms of camaraderie and accompaniment, doing what one can, Biehl has introduced Catarina to all readers of *Vita* as a world-revealing author, a life force against the entropy of her ataxia, a composer of poetic dictionaries with such startling social diagnoses and self-knowledge as "Desire is pharmaceutical. It is not good for the circus," "Documents, reality, tiresomeness, truth, saliva, voracious, consumer, saving, economics, Catarina, spirit, pills, marriage, cancer, Catholic church, separation of bodies, division of the state, the couple's children," and "Medical records, ready to go to heaven. Dollars, [Brazilian] *Real*, Brazil is bankrupted.... Things out of justice. Human body?" These refrains bear repetition.

Surprises and developments unfold over time: the ataxia is identified as Machado-Joseph Disease, a traceable epidemiology from founder populations beyond Brazil, allowing corrections of misdiagnosis and mismedication; a daughter reaches out through new media to an anthropologist a continent away; she reconstitutes a family with her siblings; and her brother is admitted to a new clinical trial with hopes for better treatment. Returning to the family and Vita (in 2005, 2006, 2011, and 2016), the anthropologist discovers new threads, new desires. "Did you bring the tape recorder?" asks Iraci, an elder in Vita, three years after Catarina died. "Should I take the test?" Ana/Andrea asks, including the anthropologist in her deliberations, posing an ethical dilemma for him, but making him part of further unfoldings of the crossing trajectories of lives and social struggles. These social struggles, importantly, include rights to medical care, now accessible through new institutional forms of judicialization supported by activist public prosecutors and judges against the "bankrupted" state, as Catarina astutely noted (despite, or perhaps because of, her position in a zone of abandonment, but with radio contact to the world). As she noted: "things out of justice" are significant for the "human body." Human bodies are always in question. Life is fragile.

The counterpoint for Locke is going and coming back to Bosnia-Herzegovina—the region, especially neighboring Serbia and Croatia, flooded now with other refugees (from Syria, Afghanistan, and parts of Africa), further adding to the aftermath of Yugoslavia's violent collapse, the unsolved forensics of bones and graves, and missing people—and being surprised to find in 2014 a hope-infused, coordinated protest movement, a Bosnian Spring. These were no longer isolated demonstrations but consolidated, if short-lived, experiments in direct democracy. The music here is not that these experiments fail—"all revolutions fail," Locke quotes Deleuze as saying—but that experience is created showing that new solidarities are possible (Deleuze's "one can become revolutionary without a revolutionary future").[7] One thinks here of the century-long repetitions in the revolution in Iran (variously narrated), and in particular the demonstrations of 2009 (crushed but never over)[8] and of Locke's note (quoting Biehl from another social context) that people in Bosnia-Herzegovina are nostalgic for, and waiting for, times of "a shared, against the odds 'will to live.'"

Music is but one of the arts of living on, and Locke urges us also to attend to language in a literary register, citing Deleuze on its distinction from language in a clinical register. He draws on Deleuze's line of thought that the unconscious is more about mobilization of desire than commemoration, as Sigmund Freud would have it, and that agency pulsates in language: people may be psychologically disturbed but do not simply become the diagnostic categories of quick theoretical fixes. Under the surface, a taxi driver notes, "something is not right," and people are "explosive" and "temperamental," "flying into a rage" at the slightest trigger. But more could be done with this harmonics/disharmonics and emic/etic diagnostics of clinical versus literary language and shifting cultural discourses of psychological accounting, as perhaps in the case of Iran[9] or Singapore.[10]

In this first set of zen exercises, becoming and new forms of life are apperceived and even tasted, if not institutionalized or stabilized. This is not to say that important institutional developments are not also happening in either Brazil or Bosnia-Herzegovina, and that leads to a second aporia and zen exercise in theory making.

SWINGING (ON) THE PENDULUM, SHIFTING THE PERIODICITIES

The pendulum swings back from times of social order to times of social disorder, back and forth, with different horizons calling up different resistances and different repressive forces. Inequalities become so gross that the privileged can neither see straight nor beyond their gated communities and personal automobiles. Or they distract and content themselves with attachments to experience-far, seemingly bright-line, moral causes elsewhere. Meanwhile the screams of the marginalized turn from immediate pain to reengaged assertions of "becoming aggrieved"; insistence on legal rights to medicine; the hard love of anexos' incarceration; charged oscillations between exposing and hiding poisonous histories; and sometimes disinfecting, but sometimes searing, sunlight. The pendulum is also the counterculture, do-it-yourself, punk resistance to always recuperating financialization, gentrification, and capital control. The *Jetztzeit*, to use Walter Benjamin's term,[11] of moments of revolt, euphoria, and solidarities (like those Locke describes in Sarajevo and Tuzla in 2014) result in afterlives and generational rejections or reappropriations, and occasionally there are shifts in collective common sense (like those Behrouzan describes in the discourses of Iranian psychology).[12]

The choice of words, the writing culture of today, intends intensities, electric shocks, and wake-up calls. The words are scalpels and sutures, experience-near tools that are not sensational but surgical. They intend to create affective-material effects in open wounds. They intend to pierce and lance to generate new skin, raw tenderness full of new nerve endings, and structures of feeling open to the biosensibilities of all that is touched and felt through the flesh's double-sided sensing, across membranes of self and other, interiority and recognition.

The affective-material shifts of life in the early decades of the twentieth-first century provide the matrix of becoming in today's world, the scaffolds of new metastable forms of socialities that no longer cannibalize themselves but seek symbiotic metamorphoses and kinships, softening old scars and deadening ends; and allowing exploratory health, growth, transformation, and even dead reckoning across unknowable tipping points and horizons. These are the found objects, the creativities of worlds in the here and now, the artistry that turns death back into regenerative biological, affective, and cognitive life and futures that can be invested in. In worlds of precarity, many of the old terms of politics have lost their purchase: Is the precariat the new proletariat? Is the optimism of "futures to invest in" what Lauren Berlant has called cruel optimism?[13]

These affective-material shifts or movements, insofar as we can perceive them, can also become new anthropological figures or templates for mindful reconstruction of our very cultural and philosophical fabrics, brought to life sometimes by graffiti and punk, transgressive defacements, and sometimes by the simple exhaustion of defensiveness, hatreds, and narrow causes that cannot grow beyond themselves or be self-sustaining, let alone allow mutualities of self and other.

Finding good examples, case studies, and cases worth study is a second form of zen exercise. Detachment from the world is not total indifference, but a meta-stable position from which critique and politics can emerge—a discipline of strength; breathing deeply, reoxygenating, and expelling the toxins; and finding ways to do so collectively, shifting the swing of the pendulum.

CALLIGRAPHIES

CHICAGO

Black lives matter. Names animate and call to life. Adam (meaning "human" in Hebrew), from *adamah* (meaning "earth" in Hebrew), is accorded the capacity to name.[14] "#Black lives matter" movements (and "taking the streets and community back," social reengagements yet again) grow urgent, picking up their histories again with contemporary hashtags, mobilizing over 680 urban demonstrations since the shooting deaths of Mrs. Lana's son Jo Jo in Eastwood (2013); Trayvon Martin (2013); Michael Brown, Tamir Rice, and Eric Garner (2014); and Alton Sterling and Philando Castile (2016). Unique individuals carry within themselves stratified and layered histories, middle passages, northward migrations, deindustrializations, blues, jazz, rap, hip hop, break dancing, footworkin', and shooting dice. They are social hieroglyphs and calligraphies composed of multiple lines: category lines ("radicals" in Chinese calligraphy); supple cartographic lines across multiple milieus; and lines of flight tracing desire and multiplicities of imagined worlds, utopias in the now, seen otherwise. Many Dannys wear many Cooks' boots, not taking them off since Cook was killed (as Laurence Ralph recounts). The cartographic radicals are not singular, exhaustive, or exclusive. There are other radicals: freemen artisans, sawmill merchants, Black Atlantic seamen,

Caribbean migrants, African students, intellectuals, physicians, educators, and policemen.

It is not the individual characters (from the Greek *kharassein*, meaning to engrave or scratch on the body) alone that draw attention, but also third spaces of interpretation, writings, and reports that awkwardly help try to suture reality. Marla hands police reports and therapy accounts to the ethnographer: she doesn't contest these reports but recognizes them as possible interpretable clues to what is going on in her mother's overwrought mind, her paranoia within reason (hardly irrational, if nonetheless mentally disturbed), and her need to warn neighbors and other community members about death, insisting that they protect their heads with hats and duct tape. Friedrich Nietzsche's hallucinatory figures (the rabble) were heads with atrophied bodies, dangling insatiable intestines and genitals.[15] Mrs. Lana's figures (friends and neighbors) are headless bodies with sounds emanating from their necks, collapsing all around her. She is mad with anger and apparitions, aggrieved, overwrought with concerns that her neighbors can recognize and respect. She is not outcast.

For all the stress on recognition and care for Mrs. Lana's mode of being aggrieved, Ralph narrates two more incidents, in which death at the hands of the police is the outcome of postpartum depression or bipolar disorder. In the latter case, family members called the police because the mentally ill woman became too much for them to handle—a situation not unlike Katkine's sedation and placement in a zone of abandonment.

In another work, Ralph gives us the hieroglyph of the large population of young men in wheelchairs, casualties of gang fights, but now serving, like Mrs. Lana, as elders working to damp down the internecine fighting.[16] Their community meetings are reminders of when gangs were community builders—another utopia, within memory, in these very same neighborhoods, self-organizing.

MEXICO CITY

The calligraphies in Mexico City, described by Angela Garcia, are body tattoos and amulets of "Nuestra Señora de la Santa Muerte (the Death Saint)"— "patron saint of prisoners, drug dealers and users, sex workers, victimized women, and Mexico's underclass," a "female personification of the grim reaper" who promises "deliverance from violence and a safe delivery to the afterlife." She is omnipresent, not only in Tepito—a poor neighborhood of tenement apartments and a sprawling market for pirated goods, where Magi works in her family's stall. Thousands of anexos, "informal, coercive residential treatment centers for addiction" across the city—part haven, part therapy, part safe house, part place of extreme rituals of corporal mortification and penance—are "set deep within other structures, like apartment buildings, commercial warehouses, churches, and even parking garages." Mexico has become a land of repeated reengagements of social protest movements (against the 1968 massacre of students, the Zapatista social justice movement, the War on Drugs in Mexico as both resistance and repression). These are all too easily enumerated, like logical demonstrations in numbers touted by grand philosophers and moralistic pundits—a tactic Garcia refuses to use, while still invoking empathetically obligatory personage-points-of-passage. Garcia brings us up close to Magi, Cabrito, and Rafa. Magi is kidnapped in open daylight, wrapped in a blanket, and taken to an anexo to keep her out of the way of the forces that abducted her cousin, too close for her parents' comfort, who presumably paid for her abduction and anexo stay. Cabrito relives and recounts over and over, in vivid present tense during the anexos' forced self-accounts, his failure to convince his grandmother to leave a war-torn Michoacan town—where he himself was caught and injured, but survived a spray of bullets. Rafa is a former small drug dealer who became addicted and spent long years in various anexos (paid for not just by his mother and ex-wife, but also by the drug organization he had worked for). He now runs an anexo, his wrists tattooed with black chains.

Calligraphy is zen par excellence: the perfect posture of holding the brush, bringing it down in decisive strokes with the whole body, concentrating the mind, becoming one, becoming many. Calligraphies of human lives, as noted above, are hieroglyphs of socialities, combinations of category (radical) lines, supple cartographic lines moving and connecting across milieus (cultural genres, forms, modes of thought), and lines of flight (desire, imagination, freedom). Individual characters (she's a piece of work, a character) are engraved, scratched, and scarred in muscle memory, neurological reflexes, and microbiomic assemblages, as well as on the skin. Their interpretation unfolds in storytelling and third spaces, not in one or two consciousnesses alone. The lines of storytelling disrupt data banks and superficial enumerations; they slow things down; they probe into possible motivations and the unseen backstage preparations. They explore the present tense (Cabrito in the anexo relives and recounts in the present tense, making what happened vivid, reexperienced, embodied), emplot with picaresque pleasure, and ethically pass the collective sense of rightness from person to person, acknowledging that no one person is always wise. Calligraphy and hieroglyphics are the zen exercises of anthropological method.

CANNIBALIZING AND INDIE-GESTION

GRAN CHACO, PARAGUAY

There are calligraphic characters on the resource frontiers, too, as shown by Lucas Bessire: Tié with her fractured story ("I do not know my story. I do not know what to say."); her husband, Cutai (Bessire's "hunting partner, the one who gave me his first find of the day and who received mine in return"); Aasi, who renounced his status as a *dacasute* (approximately in English, a "warrior"), becoming instead an *aya-ajingaque* (glossed as a "peacemaker") who sang the old songs with his gourd rattle, and was a " masterful [storyteller] when the mood was upon him"; Aasi's nephew, Pejei, with his susceptibility to attacks of madness; and Rosy, whose vices keep her, she says, from becoming animal. These figures, Bessire suggests, using Deleuze's term, compose a minority, "a missing people," "always in becoming, always incomplete," and, says Bessire, "all too often erased from and by much philosophically oriented anthropology."

Bessire reads Deleuze and Félix Guattari (authors of *Anti-Oedipus* and *A Thousand Plateaus*) as philosophers of the bipolar delirium of the Gran Chaco, where the last of the un-Christianized Ayoreo are hunted, ingested, digested, and evacuated by archstate (*Urstaat*) paranoid Christian missionaries, semantically and materially unable to allow anything or any demonic souls to remain unincorporated.[17] The indigenes, living their indie lives of "societies of refusal" (refusal of work, overwork, the state, and capitalism) give the *Urstaat* indigestion.[18] The last of the unconscripted, their lives in the forest were "haunted by memories of genocidal violence and the sounds of the bulldozers that never stopped" and were consumed in the practicalities of hiding from the violent primitive accumulation of the missionaries and Christianized Ayoreo who hunted them. For philosophers, they are sometimes romantically seen, following Pierre Clastres's 1972 *Society against the State*,[19] as societies of "anticipation-warding off," as figures of utopian thought who are made to stand in for, following Marshall Sahlins's phrase in his essay using it as a contrast to wealthy but constantly scarcity calculating societies,[20] original "societies of affluence," gaily living their lives of immediate expenditure, feasting and investing in ritual.

The New Tribes missionaries and Mennonite ranchers fulfill Carl Schmittian *nomos* of the earth of the *Urstaat*, the archstate's principles of land taking, state forming, and laying down the law. The Ayoreo are told by their mythology that they have been through this before in their original times, when amoral humanoids and human beings differentiated themselves, and through a number of earlier cosmic apocalyptic collapses, transformations, and renewals. So, terrified, they become *ichadie* ("the New People") finding their way in the nomos of the *cojñone-gari* (the strangers). Their old myths and rites have been revalued as satanic. And their old ways have been drained of meaning by anthropologically illiterate monoculturalists with no understanding of, or time for, other life-affirming ritual processes.

This last group of Ayoreo came in from the forest in 2004, joining relatives who had been hunted and Christianized in 1986 or 1979. The hunt, Bessire notes, is "the central ritual" of these Christians and of their colonizing project. They hunt "to collect Indian souls, or 'brown gold,' in lands dominated by Satan," complete with the frisson of risky bargaining with the devil involving them in minor sins like slavery in pursuit of a larger good of saving souls (tough love). After being brought into civilization, some New People starve themselves to death, or die of 'sadness,' not unlike the suicides chronicled by the anthropologists Maria de Lourdes Beldi de Alcantara and Toni Benites (himself a Guarani) among the Guarani of Brazil.[21] Others suffer attacks of madness fueled by sniffing glue or consuming alcohol, coca paste, dirt, or bricks, their skin yellowing like that of the otherworldly iguana.

Bessire sees Ayoreo strategy as one of taking on the apocalyptic as a form of inverted, negative life and an arduous effort to reconstitute their soul matter to survive in an estranged world. The hallucinatory poesis and third space (of the New Tribes, of the Ayereo, and of Bessire) is powerful, disturbing, and ravaging.

I am more persuaded by Bessire's charge against erasure "from and by much philosophically oriented anthropology" than by the Hegelian emphasis on negation, however true to Deleuze and Guattari's reworkings of nineteenth-century Hegelian and Marxian language for a transformed mid-twentieth century European world. Guillaume Sibertin-Blanc (and others) note that Deleuze and Guattari's *Anti-Oedipus* originally appeared in 1968 along with the era-defining urban explosions ("1968") in the United States, France, and Mexico, and along with (the slightly later) abandonment of the gold standard in 1971, the apparent freedom of the one being recuperated in the processes of the latter.[22] *A Thousand Plateaus* appeared a decade later, originally in 1980,[23] at roughly the same time as the Iranian revolution, the second oil crisis, the nuclear accident at Three Mile Island (all in 1979), and further freeing of global financialization (the Big Bang agreement in 1983 and its implementation in 1986). The hallucinatory analogies of schizophrenia as coding the desire-producing machine of capitalism fits the Gran Chaco ranchers as well as they fit Europe: "political confrontations shift into an impolitical dimension of violence that nullifies the very possibility of conflict" (the Ayoreo stand no chance against bulldozers and airplanes); a world capitalism destroys all exteriority (the turning of the forest into cattle lands, with devastating effects on both local and global ecology); the nation-state form is systematized in Europe after World War I, with "the correlated invention of the status of *minority as a 'permanent institution'*" (Hannah Arendt 1951), an invention that generated so-called ethnic wars in the 1990s and 2000s and new primitive accumulation and peripheralization within Europe, as well as globally.[24]

SÃO PAULO

The desiring machines of contemporary art and anthropology are, if not hallucinatory (which they can be), at least recombinatory, cannibalistic, colonizing, anthropophagic, and often allegorical. What is it that makes "Eyewitnesses," an installation of three eyeballs on trays in front of three portraits of the artist (as indigene, Chinese, and African) more than a simple metaphor of artist-subject mutual appropriation or anthropophagy? The anthropologist Lilia Schwarcz reports that the artist Adriana Varejão appropriates her and her work (albeit "Adriana thought she had read something in my book that wasn't actually there"). Nonetheless, Adriana "cannibalized me and my work" in the same way she used other sources, and Schwarcz also uses Adriana.

The egg-shaped eyeballs open or unfold into scenes of cannibal feasting by indigenous Tupinamba women, although they are painted here as if white like witches were in sixteenth-century France. The scenes are taken from a journal kept by French Calvinist Jean de Léry, who lived among the Tupinamba in the sixteenth century, in a blurry refraction of the Ayoreo story. Driven from France Antartique, an island in Rio de Janeiro Bay, by French Huguenots in a dispute over eucharistic theology, de Léry and other Calvinists took refuge among the Tupinamba. Under the governance of Nicolas Durand, who was given the title Chevalier de Villegaignon (and was at times a protector of, and at times an antagonist to, Protestants), the island was a capitalist entrepôt meant to export brazilwood (used in construction and to produce red dye). De Villegaignon became frustrated by the fighting between Catholics and Protestants and between Huguenots and Calvinists, and he expelled the Calvinists. This play of theological and economic gazes, as Michel Foucault might say—or mirrorings, inversions, and anthropophagies—confounds simple questions of who colonizes whom. In a similar vein, Varejão's art also includes faux tiles signifying the trade in and revaluation of ceramics among China, Brazil, and Portugal. These are lines of multiple cartographic milieus, lines perhaps even of cultural miscegenation, producing the 136 skin tones that Brazilians list if asked to describe themselves. The backstory of Villegaignon, intriguing on all sides, seems to remain hidden from the eyewitnesses, although the island today is named for him. A knight of the Order of Malta, he is described by Stefan Zweig as volatile and indulging in fantastic moods.[25] Huguenots believed he was a Catholic, while Catholics believed he was a Huguenot: "Nobody knows which side he is serving, and he himself probably doesn't know much more than that he wants to do something big."[26] Still, he would challenge Jean Calvin to a debate over the eucharist and become an antagonist of both Calvinists and Huguenots.

After he returned to France, de Léry wrote a response to de Villegaignon's accusations against the Calvinists, and in his account of the Tupinambas' cannibalism, de Léry spoke of the parallel anthropophagy of the Catholics' eating of the body and blood of Christ. The religious battles raging in Europe over the eucharist, de Léry claimed, were less palatable than the Tupinambas' cannibalism. Similarly, if inversely, the Jesuit José de Anchieta, who lived with the Tupinamba for some forty years, found their cannibalism preferable to the heinous Calvinist denial of the literal eucharist.

What is the play of art doing in this instance?

NEW DELHI

Only the pain of the Ayoreo's dispossession, conversion, and marginalization can match the intensity claimed by such animal protection workers as Maneka Gandhi (and perhaps her helpers Abodh, Dipesh, and Maya), Carmelia Satija, and Crystal Rogers (and perhaps less clearly Timmie Kumar; Erika Abrams-Meyers; her husband, Jim; and their daughter, Claire—about all of whom we are told too little by Naisargi Dave to know). The intensity here is directed inward, taking the form of an obsessive unwillingness to allow complacency in themselves rather than necessarily mobilizing others (albeit that mobilization is an important by-product of their activities). It is discipline with recognition that the work may be futile or may make only a marginal difference for a few animals. It is a cultural genre of world renunciation and inner discipline that is familiar in an Indian context. In this context, wearing a worn plain cotton *salwar kameez* (tunic and trouser) makes perfect sense, just as Mahatma Gandhi's *khadi* (handspun) wrap did, but the inner devotion does not necessarily prevent the devotee from wearing jewels, driving an SUV, or having a daughter studying at an Ivy League university. Maneka Gandhi's self-narration stresses both the feeling of becoming a machine designed to work unrelentingly and provides a biographical account of "coming to see" (the object of animal projection, as well as the reasons to surrender the self entirely to the cause). She stresses the machine of self-discipline: "I only wish there were a slaughterhouse next door. To witness that violence, to hear those screams ... I would *never* be able to rest."

But Dave stresses also the multiplicity, not always aligned into a singular perspective, and even the contradictions and double binds of reasons, rationales, and functions that such life-forms as Gandhi's self-discipline can entail. First, there is Maneka Gandhi's "moral biography of action and inaction," as an estranged member by marriage of a family of meat-eating, animal-protecting politicians. While they put in place a series of animal protection measures (Jawaharlal Nehru's Prevention of Cruelty against Animals Act and Indira Gandhi's Project Tiger initiative), they are also associated with the violence of sterilization campaigns. Maneka herself joined the Bharatiya Janata Party (BJP), a Hindu fundamentalist movement that puts religious identity above reason. And she is not above threatening opponents with violence. Second, Dave notes the morally ambiguous affective history of liberalism. It is glibly able to substitute in the same symbolic position as needing protection a female child or Hindu woman, a horse or other animal, thereby bolstering the need for imperial forces (historically) or the state (today)—either way, the *Urstaat*—in order to claim that they are protecting the vulnerable. Why is it, Dave muses, that many of those claiming to advance animal protection are also public and ostentatious meat eaters (to counter the Hindus' exclusive focus on cows? to express solidarity with Muslims?). It is the liberalism of a country that exports more leather than any other one in Asia and that looks the other way as slaughterhouses operate over capacity and with cruelty toward both the animals and the human laborers. Third, she points out, politics makes strange bedfellows: Doordarshan, the state-owned broadcast service under BJP ideology, shows slaughterhouse footage, filmed secretly by animal protection activists, "an effort by the government, no doubt, to whip up anti-Muslim sentiment under the guise of compassion."

The law in Rajasthan prevents euthanizing a dying cow in the name of animal (especially cow) protection, but in the face of such suffering in dying, the American Erika Abrams-Meyers (now a resident of Udaipur) summons workers one at a time or in pairs to sit with the animal, touching it and allowing it to feel accompanied. It is perhaps the most profound example of trans-species intimacy in Dave's essay, surpassing the story of Crystal Rogers coming face to face in 1959 with a dying horse that, sensing Cyrstal, turns its head toward her and shows its eyeless sockets pecked by birds, a horrifying, almost Guernica-like, scene. It is, however, a secondhand story that Maneka Gandhi tells as one of her own two experiences of a call to duty and inner need; the other is of eating meat soup while "pontificating about the treatment of animals" until her husband, Sanjay, unkindly pointed out the hypocrisy and told her to shut up.

What is most impressive about Dave's essay is its ability to track these countervailing desires and passions, justifications and reasons, and strange political bedfellows, and her insistence that while she can agree with this or that, she needs to press on to alternative possible interpretations or other perspectives to remain with the openness of the "moral biographies of action and inaction" that are always, as this volume insists, "unfinished."

Of course, the unfinishedness of moral and ethical struggles is also a characteristic of moral genre forms such as the Mahabharata, Jain, or Islamic stories,[27] or, as noted above, Benjamin's observations about storytelling where moral positionings pass among the characters, not residing in any one of them.[28] The fact that Dave stresses the metaphor of skin as the membrane of biosensing and intimacy in the world is a salutary contemporary libidinal touch, following the experiments with such terminology by Maurice Merleau-Ponty,[29] Deleuze and Guattari,[30] and Jean-François Lyotard.[31] The fact that she stresses the importance of foreigners, such as Crystal Rogers, in the animal rights movement, again flags an ambiguous mobile sovereignty of global humanism (as Mariella Pandolfi has warned of global moralities and initiatives that can displace local initiatives, understandings, and imperatives),[32] often admirable in the personal histories of those who take up its causes yet also ambiguous in its alliances and local implications. Thus, except for Maneka Gandhi (a character and a calligraphy of great complications), Carmelia Satija, and Timmie Kumar, Dave dismisses home-grown animal protection efforts as often being exclusively for cows (though Jains have bird hospitals, as well as *gaushalas* [cow shelters] and *panjorapors* [animal hospitals], that also care for other animals).

Indeed, what I read in Dave's essay is less an ode to compassion than, firstly, an anthropological map of moral conflicts and disagreements and, secondly, a concern with what I have been calling calligraphies and hieroglyphs, using camaraderies and trajectories as probes into socialities, politics, and historical horizons.

These three or four milieus along with the two earlier ones—Chicago, Mexico City, Gran Chaco, Sao Paulo-Rio de Janeiro, and New Delhi—form a set of cartographic lines, meta-stable moralities in places with connections and affinities traceable across time and space. How do they become otherwise? That is another exemplary zen exercise.

POISONED HISTORIES, DIVIDED CITIES

> "No, please! Get out!" screamed Rahmi, "I don't know anything! Leave this house at once!" ... "Ma, Mr. Nick is not a historian," he said in a commanding tone. "He does not want you to tell him any history." This stopped Rahmi in her tracks, "Not a historian?" she whispered, "But you said he was a researcher. Then what . . . ?" Anthropologist, Ma," replied Syahrial, "not a historian." There was a long pause, and then Rahmi began to laugh ... [the] chuckle of relief ..."I am so sorry," she gasped, "please forgive me. I misunderstood. I thought you were a historian. I was so scared."
> — NICHOLAS LONG, *Being Malay in Indonesia*

CYPRUS, 2011–2012

Elizabeth Davis beautifully pairs the ancient Athenian sacred oath on pain of death and as a condition of citizenship to not recall the fifth-century BCE civil war with the terms of the Cyprus Committee on Missing Persons (CMP) that forensic scientists not reveal much information about the bones they identify from the Cypriot civil war (1963–64), which eventuated in a cease-fire in 1974 and a population transfer. Between 1963 and 1974 a third of the Greek Cypriot population and half the Turkish Cypriot population were displaced. In 1974 some 45,000 Turkish Cypriots moved north, and 160,000 Greek Cypriots moved south. Indeed, although the CMP was established under the auspices of the United Nations in 1981, systematic forensic work was stalled until 2004, when it was agreed that such work could proceed only if it was delinked from any future political settlement, and only such information as could be quantitatively put on standardized forms would be collected and stored, with no narratives that might give information on causes, circumstances, locations, modes of death, or likely perpetrators. Instead of such information, a simple visitation with the bones, minimal funeral ceremony, return of the bones, and counseling were offered to families upon receipt of the bones for burial.

The ancient Greeks, as so often, provide a mythic charter, and contemporary Greeks provide classic and living ritual procedures: after the civil war against the Tyrants, the Erinyes (or Furies, female chthonic deities of vengeance) were turned into Eumenides ("seeing [only] good [Greek *eu*]"), and were given custody of the poisonous history of the civil war, and they and the citizens were warned lest their contained rage be revealed and destroy the peace. As Davis invokes the study by Loraux, "as guardians of dangerous knowledge, the Eumenides were consigned to live with their own rage and resentment, always on the verge of wreaking vengeance and thus destroying the peace of the city."[33] Women in ritual mourning, similarly, are custodians of the poisonous knowledge of intimate affairs encoded in dreams, warned about in mourning songs, and divined in inspections of the bones. So too, in contemporary forensic work, the lab work—the handling and preparation of the bones—is largely women's work (particularly when shown in publicity pictures), while both women and men do the excavations. But such patterns are not limited to the Mediterranean cultural area; they have cartographic resonances in other milieus elsewhere in the aftermath of communal warfare, where histories remain contested. The technologies of forensic work have been shared from Spain and Argentina to Chile, Guatemala, Bosnia-Herzegovina, and now Cyprus, but the rules and dynamics of secrecy and partial revelation vary from Bali and the Riau Islands to Beirut and Europe, where often perpetrators and victims must continue to live together. Intracommunal killings in Cyprus have their forensic experts, too (including both Physicians for Human Rights and the In-Force Foundation), but lest communal warfare be stirred up anew, this is rigidly separated from the CMP's identification of the bones of intercommunal killings.

Indeed, Davis makes two key points in terms of this volume's theme. First, the goal is not so much reconciliation as becoming something different in the future, an openness to narrating the past and what is to come differently. And second, the basis of politics lies in conflict, a kind of ritual process of renewal, repeatedly enacted and then repressed through the vote that reasserts a collective will. Forgetting, not transparency, is the goal. Justice (naming, punishment) is less needed for the time being than the identification and return of bones for family burial.

URFA, TURKEY, 2011

Bridget Purcell focuses our attention on another form of historical layering and simplification. Urfa is claimed by the local people to be the birthplace of Abraham and the place where he broke the idols. The Balıklıgöl shrine—with its cave of Abraham (chipped at for relics by pilgrims) and pools with sacred carp—has been undergoing restoration since the 1990s. Shrines contain densities of cultural references, and Urfa's many prior names index some of these: Urhoi in Syriac, Urha in Armenian, Orrha in Greek, Edessa under the Selucids, Justinopolis in Byzantine times, Ruha in Arabic, and Riha in Kurdish. A caravan stop along the fertile crescent routes, on a tributary of the Euphrates, it was one of the earliest of Christianized cities (363 CE). It still has a mixed population of Turks, Arabs, and Kurds; it used to also have Jews, Yezidis, Syriacs, and Armenians. Now instead it hosts large numbers of Shi'ite Iranian pilgrims (who are neither Sunni nor Alawi, as are the Turks and Arabs of the region).

Shrines across the Middle East, South Asia, and the Muslim World have been subject to cleansing and gentrification. Most extreme is the outright destruction of shrines, monuments, and other places of worship (by Wahhabis in the Arabian peninsula, the Taliban in the Bamiyan Valley, the Islamic State in Palmyra; by Sunni and Shiite forces at each other's shrines in Iraq, the BJP of the Babri Masjid in India). More common historically is the building of a conquering religion's mosques or churches on top of, or within, those of the conquered: in Cordova, there is a mosque inside the cathedral; in Jerusalem, the Dome of the Rock is on the Jewish temple mount, and the Holy Sepulchre is claimed by various Christian factions; in Istanbul, the name of the Sofia Mosque, with its Shiite inscriptions, reveals its previous identity as a church; and across Afghanistan, Iran, the Middle East, and North Africa, mosques have been built where Zoroastrian temples or Buddhist or Greek and Roman shrines once were. Urban renewal and restoration more recently has cleansed important shrines of adjoining houses and shops, creating green belts that can be more easily policed or occasionally, as in Mecca, increasing the clutter and congestion with high-rise hotels. A fourth process, the focus of Purcell's work, is the exclusion of folk and heterodox practices in the name of *salafi* Islam (a form of literalist fundamentalism).

Urfa sits in the contested South East Anatolia Development Project, planned to eventually have twenty-two irrigation dams, nineteen hydroelectric power plants, and 1.8 million hectares of irrigated land, thus involving the mass relocation and urbanization of villagers. Urbanization, Purcell points out, brings a certain literacy, and literacy under current Islamic conditions tends to mean (though she does not name it) salafi Islam. Urfa also sits in the tense borderlands that contain Islamic State fighters, Kurdish militants, and Turkish soldiers, and the area is now overfilled with half a million Syrian refugees.

Purcell focuses our attention at the microlevel, on the stresses of cultural change felt acutely by two women from a Kurdish village as they visit the shrine. She delightfully analogizes their identity struggles to those of Alice in Wonderland, becoming bigger or smaller as their frames of reference either expand to encompass vernacular practices and traces of the historical locality, or contract to exclude folk Islam in favor of newly learned salafi refusals of sacred fish or saint's tombs. Zehra thus says she cannot explain Islamic ideas in her native Kurdish, as she has studied the Quran and Islamic texts only in Turkish. Turkish and Arabic literacy thus function both as modernization and as alienation. She is married to an imam who helps enforce the unacceptability of local practices. These microshifts in styles of religiosity are felt at times as embarrassing, constraining, or empowering, and they are reflections of broader changes Turkey has been undergoing under President Recep Erdoğan.

Cyprus and Urfa are zen exercises in the mysteries of poisonous histories and divided polities, where conflict must be contained. They form an oscillating pair of changing ritualization in the contemporary world, one in a constrained space of modern forensic science, the other in a transforming political economy (from village to industrial irrigated agrarianism). In the interestices of social change, religious practices cover over or contain, like Eumenides, as much as they also cause frictions and anxieties among dominating and subordinated forces.

Like zen exercises, adjustments take time, repetition, mindfulness, and discipline.

HORIZONING AND EMERGENT FORMS OF LIFE

Both today's brave new worlds (worlds of precarity, climate change, big data, and smart control systems) and today's (Lacanian) real that periodically breaks through the façade of daily life are coming iteratively into focus. They are populated with calligraphies and hieroglyphs, peopled technologies, experimental models, and cartographies of explorations of milieus not yet understood. On the positive side, one thinks of President Barack Obama's administration's identification and pursuit of technological "moonshots" such as the $1.5 billion initiative to explore the brain; the SunShot effort to make solar energy as cheap as coal by 2020; the support of public-private manned Mars missions; the support for machine-learning technologies; and the support for the project of the University of California, Los Angeles, to make Los Angeles a sustainable city by 2050.

"1968" was an important predecessor horizon, as today (2017) is a horizon for today's ability to foresee; and, say, notationally, 2036 ("36" in Hebrew is the double numerological "hai," or double life) is one of many horizons for the near and further future. In 1960, updated in 1968, we get the Fischer (Mercury) Ellipsoid, a new geodetic world datum,[34] following on the 1957–58 International Geophysical Year, a breakthrough collaboration across Cold War lines. In 1968, from the first manned Moon orbiter, Apollo 8, William Anders takes the color earthrise photo that becomes an icon of a new phase of planetary environmental concern; in 1969, Apollo 11 lands Neil Armstrong and Buzz Aldrin on the moon. The first models of general circulation of the atmospheric climate combining oceanic and atmospheric processes were developed in the late 1960s. The International Biological Program (1964–75), with prominent collecting of blood and other biological human samples in Brazil and New Guinea for genetic mapping (and discovery of prions from the deadly "laughing disease" kuru in New Guinea) were precursors to today's genomics revolutions.[35] And in oceanography, the International Ocean Discovery Program began with Project Mohole (1961) and the Deep Sea Drilling Project (1968–83) that continues today as the Integrated Ocean Drilling Program.

As Petryna beautifully lays out, today's uncertainties about the future emerge from such modeling efforts to gain a purchase on how the world is changing around us. The dates 1968, 2017, and 2036 are, of course, arbitrary, but as a series they register a certain speed of transformations: in pervasive technologies, migration patterns, types of conflict, and awareness of the fragility of forms of life. Perhaps most unnerving is the unconsciousness of various forms of the real that are not available, or only partially available, to ordinary perception and, even then, only if one knows how to interpret the clues—air pollution, for instance, is partially available to sight in smog and to the lungs in asthma; and browning gardens after petrochemical plant flaring is an indication of toxic soils and air. Stephen Meyer divides the changing biodiversity of the globe into three categories: so-called weedy species comfortable living with humans (cockroaches, coyotes, raccoons, and other plants and animals evolved or adapted to high disturbance areas); relic or boutique species that we allow to live in managed enclaves (such as grizzly bears and elephants) but will never again have stable ecological niches; and ghost species that seem to be around but have passed the point of ecological collapse.[36]

Petryna's examples are somewhat more hopeful, focused on efforts to model and respond in the meantime, the now and near future. We are, she says, already breathing air with 400 parts per million (ppm) of carbon dioxide (CO_2), above the safe level of 350 ppm, though there's a way to go for catastrophic effects. A salesman for monitors tells her that at 1,500 ppm, one begins to see the effects on the performance of schoolchildren; and 5,000 ppm for workers, who at that level experience narcosis and metabolic stress. Still, Petryna points out, "occupational specialists, deep-sea divers, submarine engineers, and even anesthesiologists have long known the incremental risks of atmospherically compromised settings." About a third of all CO_2-offsetting reservoirs are already saturated. What draws her attention, and should draw ours, are the efforts of firefighters like Bill Armstrong to understand the physics of new phenomena of plasma-like fires that are unlike the worst natural firestorms of the past (excluding the fire-bombing of cities in World War II), of time-lapse photographers like James Balog to capture the kinetics of rapidly melting glaciers, of lake ecologists like John Magnuson and Stephen Carpenter to show that lakes suffering hypoxia (oxygen depletion) due to fertilizer runoff and industrial chemical dumping do not return over time to earlier equilibria for supporting life merely when the sources of pollution are cut off. Instead they go through phase transitions to new states, perhaps modeled best by the mathematics of chaos theory.

These new realities include more nuclear irradiated environments (Hanford, Oregon; Chernobyl, Ukraine; southern Belarus; and parts of Fukushima, Japan) and toxic landscapes full of hormone disrupters (from shale oil and gas fracking). Too often in the past such realities have been denied, preventing the kind of learning that we now will depend on. Of particular interest to Petryna is the work of Steven Pacala and Robert Socolow in modeling the time we have left and the costs associated with putting off remediation. They provide schematic timetables of the costs and consequences of inaction. As time goes by, shifting ratios of costlier strategies (called in the field "wedge stabilization") will be required.

The effort and logic here, as Petryna explains, is one of modeling horizons and tipping points, after which different combinations of resources and remediations will be required. Horizons, such as self-coordinated, balance-seeking equilibria of the earth (also called Gaia models), are meta-stable objects, moving, receding, characterized by recursive modeling, and pushing current understandings beyond their limits, or seeing as one says colloquially, "over the horizon." Models of temporary plateaus of semistabilized biochemicophysical interactions may allow for presumptively time-sensitive, but psychosocially calming, ethical mobilization and time for politics, persuasion, and discovering new options in material sciences, nanotechnology, undersea living, off-planet colonies, and other unexplored milieus.

Horizons, Petryna says, constitute what Magnuson calls "meso-spaces of experimental time," and their modelers are new kinds of scientists, experimentalists, and even, she suggests what Magnuson calls, "seers." Horizons are zen objects and exercises of deep consequence. Discussing the distant future, she cites James Hansen, who "published a study on the atmospheric space of Venus, 97 percent of which is CO_2. Through a careful analysis of the composition of its surrounding molecules and dust, Hansen found that Venus may be "the ancient relic of a planet that looked like Earth billions of years ago." Thus, Venus could be one of the futures for the Earth. In the meantime, she cites Svante Arrhenius among those who would rather think about shorter timeframes, such as the scenario of global warming that would make the Arctic available for agriculture (as well as oil drilling). Horizons are not singular, and they involve choices and actions as well as multiple scenarios and modeling efforts, requiring us to bring our best scientific instruments and minds to bear on problems that at best have solutions in the future.

UNFINISHED EXERCISES AND LIFELINES

From pressures and anxieties on all sides, anthropological exercises incrementally trace and illuminate new category lines ("radicals" in Chinese calligraphy), cartographic lines across multiple milieus, and lines of flight tracing desire and multiplicities of imagined worlds, utopias in the now that are seen otherwise and made newly possible with a push here, a shove there. In this sense, anthropologists are like artists: repetitive motions of drawing put one into meditative zones, emerging again and again for an analytic and evaluative gaze; whole body rhythms (of sculpting, printmaking, or painting) move resistant stone, wood, and metal into new shapes. So, too, the anthropologist attempts to access and draw out the forces and turbulences within third spaces beyond dualistic antagonisms and simplistic causal linear arguments.[37] The anthropologist repairs and compares, always using more than two cases, more than two dimensions, and more than two axes of comparison and contrast—shifting, adjusting, creating redesigns, new configurations, and new insights from ethnographic details, emic categories, tropes, and genres.

When politics freezes into black and white and is locked in place, it is often helpful to have some artwork[38] or anthropological ethnography to break the frame, reshuffle the pieces, and remind us that there is more going on; there are more ways to look at things; and from a certain (zen) point of view, the human comedy is as absurd as it is beautiful and inspired. If one can get on into the right swing and find the right point of leverage, the pendulum can move just a bit; the punctum or flash of insight[39] can allow us to see the world otherwise, and how little pieces of it can be reworked in the here and now. The gift of anthropology is a way (Chinese *dao*, as in zen exercises) of getting to know people in situ rather than in a planning document or a statistical table. It is a way of generating other planning documents, other statistical tables. Getting to know people in situ can change the tone, the structure of feeling, and the understanding. In all the discussions about climate warming, capitalism's not having an outside, and the like, a consensus seems to be emerging that all we can really do is try to live on—*su-vive*, to use a Derridian term.[40] That means we must try to get the ethnographic sensorium, as Biehl and Locke put it in the introduction, to function as a way finder. Pebbles and labyrinths of human interactions (and subjectivities that are raucous terrae incognitae, raucous because the unconscious and subjectivities are often zones of conflict and turmoil) cannot be swept out of the way, but they can be pieced together into new theories (ways of seeing), open to new relations (camaraderies and trajectories), mobilizing cartographies for social reengagements, and deploying tool boxes of varied swerves or tropes across time and space. In that work, the essays in this volume are exemplary: they are intensive points of beginning and so also unfinished, engaging equally unfinished lives and social forms of life.

NOTES

1. See the essays in M. M. J. Fischer, *Emergent Forms of Life and the Anthropological Voice*.
2. See M. M. J. Fischer, *Anthropological Futures*, 235–37 and 246.
3. The resonance is with the eleventh thesis from Karl Marx's "Theses on Feuerbach": "The philosophers have only interpreted the world, in various ways; the point is to change it" (13). In addition, the sentence is meant to resonate with concerns with writing and other media of anthropological intervention, from James Clifford and George Marcus's *Writing Culture* on. See especially M. M. J. Fischer, "The Peopling of Technologies" and "Time, Camera and the Digital Pen."
4. See also M. M. J. Fischer, "The Peopling of Technologies."
5. See K. Fortun, "Ethnography in/of/as Open Systems."
6. I adopt the term *accompaniers* from the work of Paul Farmer and Partners in Health, who use it to advocate for active participation in helping patients maintain commitment through serious side effects of medication.
7. Deleuze and Parnet, *Gilles Deleuze from A to Z*.
8. M. M. J. Fischer, *Anthropological Futures*, and "Repetitions in the Revolution."

9   Behrouzan, *Prozak Diaries*.
10 M. M. J. Fischer, "Ethnography for Aging Societies."
11 Benjamin, "Theses on the Philosophy of History."
12 Behrouzan, *Prozak Diaries*.
13 Berlant, *Cruel Optimism*.
14 Genesis 2:19–20. In the Quran, Adam is made from "sounding clay" (Sureh 15).
15 Nietzsche, *Thus Spoke Zarathustra*. The tropes and hallucinatory imagery are interesting here, deployed differently across communities that need constructive political agency and activation. Nietzsche's powerful imagery, intended to rouse people from habits and to make them be active in shaping their lives, in the section "Of Redemption" in *Thus Spoke Zarathustra*, was taken up by many other writers, including the Iranian modernist Sadegh Hedayat, when he describes the cowed "rabble—all identical, their faces expressing greed or money and sex, constructed 'only of a mouth and a wad of guts hanging from it'" (*The Blind Owl*, 73). In Nietzsche, Zarathustra sees "an ear as big as a man! . . . [U]nder the ear there moved . . . a thin stalk—the stalk, however, was a man! By the use of a magnifying glass one could even discern a little envious face . . . a turgid little soul was dangling from the stalk. The people told me, however, that the great ear . . . was a genius. But I have never believed the people when they talked about great men— and I held to my belief that it was an inverse cripple, who had too little of everything and too much of one thing" (*Thus Spoke Zarathustra*, 160).
16 Ralph, *Renegade Dreams*.
17 *Urstaat* is a term from Carl Schmitt that Deleuze and Guattari use to think about the power and apparatuses underlying all forms of the state.
18 *Societies of refusal* is a term from Pierre Clastres, *Chronicle of the Guayaki Indians*, who wrote of the Amazonian Indians not as predecessors to sedentarization and the state, but as those who are marginalized by the state and who actively refuse to be incorporated by it.
19 Clastres, *Society against the State*.
20 Sahlins, "Notes on the Original Affluent Society."
21 See Beldi de Alcantara, *Jouvens indigenas e lugares de pentencimentos*; Lyons, "A Brazilian Tribe's Suicide Epidemic."
22 Sibertin-Blanc, *State and Politics*. See also Deleuze and Guattari, *Anti-Oedipus*.
23 Deleuze and Guattari, *A Thousand Plateaus*.
24 Sibertin-Blanc, *State and Politics*, 14–15.
25 Zweig, *Brazil*.
26 Zweig, *Brazil*, 43.
27 M. M. J. Fischer, "Urban Mahabharata."
28 Benjamin, *Illuminations*.
29 Merleau-Ponty, *The Visible and the Invisible*.
30 Deleuze and Guattari, *Anti-Oedipus*, and *A Thousand Plateaus*.
31 Lyotard, *Libidinal Economy*.
32 See Fassin and Pandolfi, *Contemporary States of Emergency*; Pandolfi, "Contract of Mutual (In)difference."

33 Loraux, *The Divided City*.
34 See I. Fischer, *Geodesy? What's That?*
35 See Anderson, *The Collectors of Lost Souls*; M. M. J. Fischer, "In the Science Zone," and "In the Science Zone II."
36 Meyer, *The End of the Wild*, 7–14.
37 On third spaces, see M. M. J. Fischer, *Emergent Forms of Life and the Anthropological Voice*.
38 I have been working on a series of essays with artists about their artworks, reading their art anthropologically and as cultural critique. Older pieces were done with the Polish filmmaker Maria Zmarz-Koczanowicz (M. M. J. Fischer, "Filming Poland"), and the American printmaker Eric Avery (M. M. J. Fischer, "With a Hammer, a Gouge and a Wood Block"). As yet unpublished pieces are with the Iranian-American painter Parviz Yashar, the Indonesian artist Entang Wiharso, and the Singaporean videographer and photographer Charles Lim. Their work informs these paragraphs.
39 The poetics here resonate with Walter Benjamin's "aufblitzen" and "illumination" (*Illuminations*) and with Roland Barthes's "punctum" (*Camera Lucida*): the accident or detail in a photograph that jars one into an appreciation that is different from the staging or intention of the photographer.
40 *Su-viv* means not just to survive (bare life) but culturally to "live on." It also refers to the spectral "after life" or "super life," the "self contestatory attestation [that] keeps the community alive, i.e., open to something other and more than itself," "messianicity beyond any messianism" (Derrida, "Faith and Knowledge," 87).

Acknowledgments

"The blank page won't let me dream," the Brazilian poet João Cabral de Melo Neto writes: "It incites me to clear and exact poetry.... Not the form found, like a seashell, lost ... not the form obtained by a lucky or divine throw ... but the form attained like the end of a skein, which the spider of careful attention unrolls; like the furthest point of that fragile thread, inevitably snapped by the weights of huge hands. Mineral, the paper used for poetry, the poetry it is possible not to write."[1]

Thank you to all who have helped make this book possible.

Unfinished grew out of essay drafts and discussions generated at a workshop held at Princeton University in March 2014 on the anthropology of becoming. The workshop, in turn, was sparked by our 2010 article "Deleuze and the Anthropology of Becoming" and the fruitful exchanges it inspired with colleagues and students in subsequent years, including panels at the annual meetings of the American Anthropological Association in 2010 and 2014. In the workshop, we returned to that article and our ongoing field engagements to continue to explore productive tensions between ethnography and critical theory, and over the intervening years we exchanged drafts of essays with workshop participants and brought others into the conversation. The powerful work of the artist Adriana Varejão has been an inspiration to all of us, and we are honored to be able to include her art in the book. Many people have heard or read bits and pieces of the book's essays throughout the years, and we thank them for their generous and insightful rejoinders.

Special thanks are due to Naomi Zucker, a treasure beyond compare, whose brilliant thinking, sharp editing, and unwavering support have been absolutely essential at every stage of this project. We wish her a wondrous anthropological journey as she continues her doctoral studies at the University of Pennsylvania.

Our academic institutions have been indispensable sources of support and stimulation, both material and intellectual, and we thank the faculty, staff, and students of the departments and programs we are part of: at Princeton

University, the Department of Anthropology, the Global Health Program, the Center for Health and Wellbeing, the Program in Latin American Studies, and the Woodrow Wilson School of Public and International Affairs; and at Northwestern University, the Program in Global Health Studies, the Department of Anthropology, and the Buffett Institute for Global Studies. At Princeton, special thanks are due to the Committee on Research in the Humanities and Social Sciences for publication subvention. We also wish to thank Jessica Cooper, Sebastián Ramirez, and De'Sean Weber for their indispensable editorial assistance. Thanks also to the participants in the Princeton seminars Anthropology of Becoming (2014), Peopling Critical Theory (2014), and Keywords in Anthropology Today (2016) for their critical insights.

At Duke University Press, we have been most fortunate to be able to count on Ken Wissoker's luminous thinking and visionary editorial guidance at every step and turn. We are grateful to Duke's editorial staff, particularly Susan Albury, Matt Tauch, Chris Robinson, and Maryam Arain, for taking the best possible care of this project. We also wish to wholeheartedly thank the book's two anonymous reviewers for their close and generous reading, extraordinarily insightful feedback, and creative suggestions, which we have integrated to the best of our ability into the final manuscript.

The essay "The Anthropology of Becoming" is an extensively revised and updated version of our article "Deleuze and the Anthropology of Becoming," published in *Current Anthropology* 51 (3) (2010): 317–51 (with comments and a reply). Naisargi N. Dave's essay "Witness" is a revised version of her article "Witness: Humans, Animals, and the Politics of Becoming," published in *Cultural Anthropology* 29 (3) (2014): 433–56. Lilia M. Schwarcz's essay "I Was Cannibalized by an Artist" draws from her collaboration with Adriana Varejão for the book *Pérola imperfeita: A história e as histórias na obra de Adriana Varejão* (Cobogó, 2014). We are grateful to the wondrous Francis Alÿs for the film still from his creative video project *Reel/Unreel* that graces the cover of *Unfinished*. The estate of Alice Neel and the David Zwirner Gallery generously allowed us to include the arresting painting *James Hunter Black Draftee* in the book's opening pages.

Our biggest debt is to our families and our interlocutors in the field who continue to shape us and to the books we love reading. Thank you!

NOTE

1 Cabral de Melo Neto, *Education by Stone*, 27.

Bibliography

Abramowitz, Sharon. *Searching for Normal in the Wake of the Liberian War*. Philadelphia: University of Pennsylvania Press, 2014.

Abramowitz, Sharon, and Catherine Panter-Brick, eds. *Medical Humanitarianism: Ethnographies of Practice*. Philadelphia: University of Pennsylvania Press, 2015.

Abu-Lughod, Lila. *Dramas of Nationhood: The Politics of Television in Egypt*. Chicago: University of Chicago Press, 2005.

———. *Writing Women's Worlds: Bedouin Stories*. Berkeley: University of California Press, 1993.

Adams, Vincanne. "Evidence-Based Global Public Health: Subjects, Profits, Erasures." In *When People Come First: Critical Studies in Global Health*, edited by João Biehl and Adriana Petryna, 54–90. Princeton, NJ: Princeton University Press, 2013.

———, ed. *Metrics: What Counts in Global Health*. Durham, NC: Duke University Press, 2016.

Agamben, Giorgio. *Homo Sacer: Sovereign Power and Bare Life*. Translated by Daniel Heller-Roazen. Redwood City, CA: Stanford University Press, 1998.

———. *The Open: Man and Animal*. Translated by Kevin Attell. Redwood City, CA: Stanford University Press, 2004.

Agier, Michel. *On the Margins of the World: The Refugee Experience Today*. Cambridge: Polity, 2008.

Ahmed, Sara. *The Cultural Politics of Emotion*. New York: Routledge, 2004.

Alexander, Michelle. *The New Jim Crow: Mass Incarceration in the Age of Colorblindness*. New York: New Press, 2010.

Allison, Anne. *Precarious Japan*. Durham, NC: Duke University Press, 2013.

Amos, Jonathan. "Carbon Dioxide Passes Symbolic Mark." BBC News, May 10, 2013. Accessed April 16, 2017. http://www.bbc.com/news/science-environment-22486153.

Anderson, Warwick. *The Collectors of Lost Souls: Turning Kuru Scientists into Whitemen*. Baltimore: Johns Hopkins University Press, 2008.

Andrade, Oswald de. "Manifesto antropófago." *Revista de antropofagia* 1 (1928): 3–7.

Andreoli, S. B., N. Almeida-Filho, D. Martin, M. D. Mateus, and J. de J. Mari. "Is Psychiatric Reform a Strategy for Reducing the Mental Health Budget? The Case of Brazil." *Revista Brasileira de Psiquiatria* 29, no. 1 (2007): 43–46.

Angastiniotis, Tony, dir. *Voice of Blood*. 2004. DVD. https://www.youtube.com/watch?v=gwEF9H4PChk.

———, dir. *Voice of Blood 2—Searching for Selden*. 2005. DVD. https://www.youtube.com/watch?v=lVHfXd8ZEFg.

Appadurai, Arjun. "Mediants, Materiality, Normativity." *Public Culture* 27, no. 2 (2015): 221–37.

"Aquarela do Brasil." *Wikipedia, The Free Encyclopedia*, April 13, 2017. Accessed April 15, 2017. https://en.wikipedia.org/w/index.php?title=Aquarela_do_Brasil&oldid=775158473.

Arsenijević, Damir. "Gendering the Bone: The Politics of Memory in Bosnia and Herzegovina." *Journal for Cultural Research* 15, no. 2 (2011): 193–205.

———. "Mobilising Unbribable Life: The Politics of Contemporary Poetry in Bosnia and Herzegovina." In *Towards a New Literary Humanism*, edited by Andy Mousley, 166–80. London: Palgrave Macmillan, 2011.

———, ed. *Unbribable Bosnia-Herzegovina: The Struggle for the Commons*. Baden-Baden, Germany: Nomos Verlagenschaft, 2014.

Arsenijević, Damir, and Šejla Šehabović. Untitled interview by Senad Hadžifejzović, February 23, 2014. Accessed March 11, 2016. https://www.youtube.com/watch?v=rYb7-ojCmnA.

Asad, Talal. *Formations of the Secular: Christianity, Islam, Modernity*. Redwood City, CA: Stanford University Press, 2003.

———. *Genealogies of Religion: Discipline and Reasons of Power in Christianity and Islam*. Baltimore: Johns Hopkins University Press, 1993.

Astorga, Luis. *El siglo de las drogas*. Mexico City: Plaza and Janes, 2005.

Bacchetta, Paola. "When the (Hindu) Nation Exiles Its Queers." *Social Text* 61 (1999): 141–66.

Bachelard, Gaston. *The Poetics of Space*. Translated by Maria Jolas. Boston: Beacon, 1994.

Bainbridge, James. *Turkey*. 11th ed. New York: Lonely Planet, 2009.

Bambara, Toni Cade. *The Salt Eaters*. New York: Random House, 1980.

Barad, Karen. *Meeting the Universe Halfway: Quantum Physics and the Entanglement of Matter and Meaning*. Durham, NC: Duke University Press, 2007.

Barthes, Roland. *Camera Lucida: Reflections on Photography*. Translated by Richard Howard. London: Hill and Wang, 1981.

Bartolome, Miguel. *El Encuentro de la Gente y los Insensatos: La sedentarizacion de los cazadores ayoreo en el Chaco Paraguayo*. Asunción, Paraguay: CEADUC, 2000.

Bataille, Georges. *The Accursed Share*. Vol. 1. Translated by Robert Hurley. New York: Zone Books, 1989.

———. *The Accursed Share*. Vol. 3. Translated by Robert Hurley. New York: Zone, 1993.

———. *The Unfinished System of Nonknowledge*. Translated by Michelle Kendall and Stuart Kendall. Minneapolis: University of Minnesota Press, 2004.

Bateson, Gregory. *Naven*. Redwood City, CA: Stanford University Press, 1958.

———. *Steps to an Ecology of Mind: Selected Essays in Anthropology, Psychiatry, Evolution, and Epistemology*. Chicago: University of Chicago Press, 2000.

Baum, Kelly, Andrea Bayer, and Sheena Wagstaff. *Unfinished: Thought Left Visible*. New York: Metropolitan Museum of Art, 2016.

Baverstock, Keith, and Dillwyn Williams. "The Chernobyl Accident 20 Years On: An Assessment of the Health Consequences and the International Response." *Environmental Health Perspectives* 114, no. 9 (2006): 1312–17.

Baxandall, Michael. *Padrões de intenção: A explicação histórica dos quadros*. Translated by V. M. Pereira. São Paulo: Companhia das Letras, 2006.

———. *Patterns of Intention: On the Historical Explanations of Pictures*. New Haven, CT: Yale University Press, 1985.

Becker, Marjorie. *Setting the Virgin on Fire: Lázaro Cárdenas, Michoacán Peasants and the Redemption of the Mexican State*. Berkeley: University of California Press, 1996.

Behar, Ruth. *Translated Woman: Crossing the Border with Esperanza's Story*. Boston: Beacon, 1993.

———. *The Vulnerable Observer: Anthropology That Breaks Your Heart*. Boston: Beacon, 1996.

Behrouzan, Orkideh. *Prozak Diaries: Psychiatry and Generational Memory in Iran*. Redwood City, CA: Stanford University Press, 2016.

Beldi de Alcantara, Maria de Lourdes. *Jovens indígenas e lugares de pentencimentos: Analyse dos jovens indígenas da Reserva de Dourados, MS [Mato Grosso do Sul]*. São Paulo: University of São Paulo, Institute of Psychology, 2007.

Benedict, Ruth. *Patterns of Culture*. New York: Mariner, 2006.

Benjamin, Walter. *Illuminations*. Edited and with an introduction by Hannah Arendt. Translated by Harry Zohn. New York: Harcourt, Brace and World, 1968.

Bennett, Jane. *The Enchantment of Modern Life: Attachments, Crossings, and Ethics*. Princeton, NJ: Princeton University Press, 2001.

———. *Vibrant Matter: A Political Ecology of Things*. Durham, NC: Duke University Press, 2010.

Berlant, Lauren. *Cruel Optimism*. Durham, NC: Duke University Press, 2011.

———. "On the Case." *Critical Inquiry* 33, no. 4 (2007): 663–72.

———. "Slow Death (Sovereignty, Obesity, Lateral Agency)." *Critical Inquiry* 33, no. 4 (2007): 754–80.

Bessire, Lucas. "Apocalyptic Futures: The Violent Transformation of Moral Human Life among Ayoreo-Speaking People of the Gran Chaco." *American Ethnologist* 38, no. 4 (2011): 743–57.

———. *Behold the Black Caiman: A Chronicle of Ayoreo Life*. Chicago: University of Chicago Press, 2014.

———. "The Politics of Isolation: Refused Relation as an Emerging Regime of Indigenous Biolegitimacy." *Comparative Studies in Society and History* 54, no. 3 (2012): 1–32.

———. "The Rise of Indigenous Hypermarginality: Culture as a Neoliberal Politics of Life." *Current Anthropology* 55, no. 3 (2014): 276–95.

Bessire, Lucas, and David Bond. "Ontological Anthropology and the Deferral of Critique." *American Ethnologist* 41, no. 3 (2014): 440–56.

Bhabha, Homi. *The Location of Culture*. New York: Routledge, 1994.

———. *O local da cultura*. Translated by Myriam Ávila, Eliana Lourenço de Lima Reis, and Gláucia Renate Eliana Gonçalves. 2nd ed. Belo Horizonte, Brazil: Editora UFMG, 1998.

Biehl, João. "CATKINE . . . Asylum, Laboratory, Pharmacy, Pharmacist, I and the Cure: Pharmaceutical Subjectivity in the Global South." In *Pharmaceutical Self: The Global Shaping of Experience in an Age of Psychopharmacology*, edited by Janis Jenkins, 67–96. Santa Fe, NM: School of Advanced Research Press, 2011.

———. "Ethnography in the Way of Theory." *Cultural Anthropology* 28, no. 4 (2013): 573–97.
———. "The Judicialization of Biopolitics: Claiming the Right to Pharmaceuticals in Brazilian Courts." *American Ethnologist* 40, no. 3 (2013): 419–36.
———. "Patient-Citizen-Consumers: The Judicialization of Health and the Metamorphosis of Biopolitics." *Revista Lua Nova* 98 (2016): 77–105.
———. "The Postneoliberal Fabulation of Power: On Statecraft, Precarious Infrastructures, and Public Mobilization in Brazil." *American Ethnologist* 43, no. 3 (2016): 437–50.
———. *Vita: Life in a Zone of Social Abandonment*. Berkeley: University of California Press, 2005.
———. *Will to Live: AIDS Therapies and the Politics of Survival*. Princeton, NJ: Princeton University Press, 2007.
Biehl, João, Byron Good, and Arthur Kleinman. "Introduction: Rethinking Subjectivity." In *Subjectivity: Ethnographic Investigations*, edited by João Biehl, Byron Good, and Arthur Kleinman, 1–24. Berkeley: University of California Press, 2007.
———, eds. *Subjectivity: Ethnographic Investigations*. Berkeley: University of California Press, 2007.
Biehl, João, and Peter Locke. "Deleuze and the Anthropology of Becoming." *Current Anthropology* 51, no. 3 (2010): 317–51.
Biehl, João, and Amy Moran-Thomas. "Symptom: Technologies, Social Ills, Subjectivities." *Annual Review of Anthropology* 38, no. 1 (2009): 267–88.
Biehl, João, and Adriana Petryna, eds. *When People Come First: Critical Studies in Global Health*. Princeton, NJ: Princeton University Press, 2013.
Biehl, João, and Naomi Zucker. "The Masked Anthropologist." *HAU* 5, no. 2 (2015): 367–74.
Bloch, Ernst. *The Principle of Hope*. 3 vols. Translated by Neville Plaice, Stephen Plaice, and Paul Knight. Cambridge, MA: MIT Press, 1986.
———. *The Spirit of Utopia*. Translated by Anthony Nasser. Redwood City, CA: Stanford University Press, 2000.
———. *Traces*. Translated by Anthony Nasser. Redwood City, CA: Stanford University Press, 2006.
Boaz, Franz. *Race, Language and Culture*. New York: Macmillan, 1940.
Boon, James A. *Other Tribes, Other Scribes: Symbolic Anthropology in the Comparative Study of Cultures, Histories, Religions, and Texts*. Cambridge: Cambridge University Press, 1982.
Borneman, John. "Reconciliation after Ethnic Cleansing: Listening, Retribution, Affiliation." *Public Culture* 14, no. 2 (2002): 281–304.
Borneman, John, and Joseph Masco. "Anthropology and the Security State." *American Anthropologist* 117, no. 4 (2015): 781–85.
Bosnae, Amila. "Bosnia Floods: 'This Is Going to Stay with Us for the Next 20–30 Years.'" Bosnia-Herzegovina Protest Files, May 24, 2014. Accessed February 25, 2017. https://bhprotestfiles.wordpress.com/2014/05/24/bosnia-floods-this-is-going-to-stay-with-us-for-the-next-20-30-years/.
———. "Stef Jansen: 'The Plenum Is a Roar of Enraged People.'" Bosnia-Herzegovina Protest Files, February 27, 2014. Accessed March 15, 2017. https://bhprotestfiles.wordpress.com/2014/02/27/stef-jansen-the-plenum-is-a-roar-of-enraged-people/.

Bougarel, Xavier, Elissa Helms, and Ger Duijzings, eds. *The New Bosnian Mosaic: Identities, Memories, and Moral Claims in a Post-War Society*. Burlington, VT: Ashgate, 2007.

Boundas, Constantin V., ed. *Gilles Deleuze: The Intensive Reduction*. London: Continuum, 1991.

Bourgois, Philippe. *In Search of Respect: Selling Crack in El Barrio*. Cambridge: Cambridge University Press, 1995.

Bourgois, Philippe and Jeff Schonberg. *Righteous Dopefiend*. Berkeley: University of California Press, 2009.

Bozdoğan, Sibel. *Modernism and Nation Building: Turkish Architectural Culture in the Early Republic*. Seattle: University of Washington Press, 2001.

Bozdoğan, Sibel, and Reşat Kasaba. *Rethinking Modernity and National Identity in Turkey*. Seattle: University of Washington Press, 1997.

Briggs, Charles, and Clara Mantini-Briggs. *Tell Me Why My Children Died: Rabies, Indigenous Knowledge, and Communicative Justice*. Durham, NC: Duke University Press, 2016.

Brooks, Alison S., and Judy M. Suchey. "Skeletal Age Determination Based on the Os Pubis: A Comparison of the Acsádi-Nemeskéri and Suchey-Brooks Methods." *Human Evolution* 5, no. 3 (1990): 227–38.

Brown, Peter. *The Cult of the Saints: Its Rise and Function in Latin Christianity*. Chicago: University of Chicago Press, 1981.

Brown, Wendy. *Undoing the Demos: Neoliberalism's Stealth Revolution*. New York: Zone, 2015.

Burić, Fedja. "Becoming Mixed: Mixed Marriages of Bosnia-Herzegovina during the Life and Death of Yugoslavia." PhD diss., University of Illinois at Urbana-Champaign, 2012.

———. "Dwelling on the Ruins of Socialist Yugoslavia: Being Bosnian by Remembering Tito." In *Post-Communist Nostalgia*, edited by Maria Todorova and Zsuzsa Gille, 227–43. New York: Berghahn, 2010.

Butler, Judith. *Excitable Speech: A Politics of the Performative*. New York: Routledge, 1997.

———. *Frames of War: When Is Life Grievable?* London: Verso, 2009.

———. *Notes Toward a Performative Theory of Assembly*. Cambridge, MA: Harvard University Press, 2015.

———. *Precarious Life: The Powers of Mourning and Violence*. London: Verso, 2004.

Cabral de Melo Neto, João. *Education by Stone: Selected Poems*. Translated by Richard Zenith. New York: Archipelago, 2005.

Cadena, Marisol de la. *Earth Beings: Ecologies of Practice across Andean Worlds*. Durham, NC: Duke University Press, 2015.

Calarco, Matthew. *Zoographies: The Question of the Animal from Heidegger to Derrida*. New York: Columbia University Press, 2008.

Canadell, J. G., C. Le Quere, M. R. Raupach, C. B. Field, E. T. Buitenhuis, P. Ciais, T. J. Conway, N. P. Gillett, R. A. Houghton, and G. Marland. "Contributions to Accelerating Atmospheric CO_2 Growth from Economic Activity, Carbon Intensity, and Efficiency of Natural Sinks." *Proceedings of the National Academy of Sciences* 104, no. 47 (2007): 18,866–70.

Canguilhem, Georges. "The Decline of the Idea of Progress." *Economy and Society* 27, nos. 2–3 (1998): 313–29.

Cardoso, Fernando Henrique. "Notas Sobre a Reforma do Estado." *Novos Estudos do CEBRAP* 50 (1998): 1–12.

Carneiro da Cunha, Manuela, and Eduardo Viveiros de Castro. "Vingança e temporalidade: Os tupinambás." In *Cultura com aspas*, edited by Manuela Carneiro da Cunha. São Paulo: Cosac and Naify, 2009.

Carroll, Lewis. *Alice's Adventures in Wonderland*. Buffalo, NY: Broadview, 2011.

Cartwright, Nancy, and Jeremy Hardie. *Evidence-Based Policy: A Practical Guide to Doing It Better*. Oxford: Oxford University Press, 2012.

Caruth, Cathy. *Unclaimed Experience: Trauma, Narrative, and History*. Baltimore: Johns Hopkins University Press, 1996.

Chandler, David. *Bosnia: Faking Democracy after Dayton*. London: Pluto, 2000.

Chen, Mel Y. *Animacies: Biopolitics, Racial Mattering, Queer Affect*. Durham, NC: Duke University Press, 2012.

Chigateri, Shraddha. "'Glory to the Cow': Cultural Difference and Social Justice in the Food Hierarchy in India." *South Asia* 31, no. 1 (2008): 10–35.

Cixous, Hélène. *Reading with Clarice Lispector*. Minneapolis: University of Minnesota Press, 1990.

Clastres, Pierre. *Archeology of Violence*. Translated by Jeanine Herman. Los Angeles: Semiotext(e), 2010.

———. *Chronicle of the Guayaki Indians*. Translated by Paul Auster. New York: Zone, 1998.

———. *Society against the State: Essays in Political Anthropology*. Translated by Robert Hurley. New York: Zone, 1989.

Clifford, James. *A experiência etnográfica: Antropologia e literatura no século XX*. Translated by José Reginaldo Santos Gonçalves. Rio de Janeiro: Editora UFRJ, 2008.

———. *The Predicament of Culture: Twentieth-Century Ethnography, Literature and Art*. Cambridge, MA: Harvard University Press, 1998.

Clifford, James, and George E. Marcus, eds. 1986. *Writing Culture: The Poetics and Politics of Ethnography*. Berkeley: University of California Press, 1986.

Coleman, Gabriella. *Hacker, Hoaxer, Whistleblower, Spy: The Many Faces of Anonymous*. London: Verso, 2014.

Collier, Stephen J., and Aihwa Ong. "Global Assemblages, Anthropological Problems." In *Global Assemblages: Technology, Politics, and Ethics as Anthropological Problems*, edited by Aihwa Ong and Stephen J. Collier, 3–21. Malden, MA: Blackwell, 2005.

Comaroff, Jean, and John Comaroff. *Ethnography and the Historical Imagination*. Boulder, CO: Westview Press, 1992.

———. *Theory from the South: Or, How Euro-America Is Evolving Toward Africa*. New York: Routledge, 2012.

Connolly, William E. *Facing the Planetary: Entangled Humanism and the Politics of Swarming*. Durham, NC: Duke University Press, 2017.

———. *Neuropolitics: Thinking, Culture, Speed*. Minneapolis: University of Minnesota Press, 2002.

———. *A World of Becoming*. Durham, NC: Duke University Press, 2012.

Coole, Diana, and Samantha Frost, eds. *New Materialisms: Ontology, Agency, and Politics*. Durham, NC: Duke University Press, 2010.

Cronon, William. 1992. "A Place for Stories: Nature, History, and Narrative." *Journal of American History* 78, no. 4 (1992): 1347–76.

Crossland, Zoe. "Buried Lives: Forensic Archaeology and the Disappeared in Argentina." *Archaeological Dialogues* 7, no. 2 (2000): 146–59.

———. "Violent Spaces: Conflict over the Reappearance of Argentina's Disappeared." In *Matériel Culture: The Archaeology of Twentieth-Century Conflict*, edited by John Schofield, William Gray Johnson, and Colleen M. Beck, 115–31. London: Routledge, 2002.

Das, Veena. *Affliction: Health, Disease, Poverty*. New York: Fordham University Press, 2015.

———. *Life and Words: Violence and the Descent into the Ordinary*. Berkeley: University of California Press, 2006.

Das, Veena, Michael Jackson, Arthur Kleinman, and Bhrigupati Singh, eds. *The Ground Between: Anthropologists Engage Philosophy*. Durham, NC: Duke University Press, 2014.

Das, Veena, Arthur Kleinman, Margaret Lock, Mamphela Ramphele, and Pamela Reynolds, eds. *Remaking a World: Violence, Social Suffering, and Recovery*. Berkeley: University of California Press, 2001.

Dave, Naisargi N. "Indian and Lesbian and What Came Next: Affect, Commensuration, and Queer Emergences." *American Ethnologist* 38, no. 4 (2011): 650–65.

———. *Queer Activism in India: A Story in the Anthropology of Ethics*. Durham, NC: Duke University Press, 2012.

———. "Witness: Humans, Animals, and the Politics of Becoming." *Cultural Anthropology* 29, no. 3 (2014): 433–56.

Davis, Elizabeth Anne. *Bad Souls: Madness and Responsibility in Modern Greece*. Durham, NC: Duke University Press, 2012.

Deane-Drummond, C., and A. Fuentes. "Human Being and Becoming: Situating Theological Anthropology in Interspecies Relationships in an Evolutionary Context." *Philosophy, Theology and the Sciences* 1, no. 3 (2014): 251–75.

Deaton, Angus. *The Great Escape: Health, Wealth, and the Origins of Inequality*. Princeton, NJ: Princeton University Press, 2015.

———. "Instruments of Development: Randomization in the Tropics, and the Search for the Elusive Keys to Economic Development." Cambridge, MA: National Bureau of Economic Research, January 2009. Working Paper No. 14690. Accessed February 12, 2017. http://www.nber.org/papers/w14690.

Deeb, Lara. *An Enchanted Modern: Gender and Public Piety in Shi'i Lebanon*. Princeton, NJ: Princeton University Press, 2006.

DeLanda, Manuel. *Deleuze: History and Science*. New York: Atropos, 2010.

———. "Space: Extensive and Intensive, Actual and Virtual." In *Deleuze and Space*, edited by I. Buchanan and G. Lambert, 80–88. Edinburgh: Edinburgh University Press, 2005.

De León, Jason. *The Land of Open Graves: Living and Dying on the Migrant Trail*. Berkeley: University of California Press, 2015.

Deleuze, Gilles. *Bergsonism*. Translated by Hugh Tomlinson and Barbara Habberjam. New edition. New York: Zone, 1990.

———. *Desert Islands and Other Texts, 1953-1974*. Translated by David Lapoujade. Los Angeles: Semiotext(e), 2004.

———. *Empiricism and Subjectivity: An Essay on Hume's Theory of Human Nature*. Translated by Constantine V. Boundas. New York: Columbia University Press, 2001.

———. *Essays Critical and Clinical*. Translated by Daniel W. Smith and Michael A. Greco. Minneapolis: University of Minnesota Press, 1997.

———. *Francis Bacon: The Logic of Sensation*. Translated by Daniel W. Smith. Minneapolis: University of Minnesota Press, 2005.

———. "Having an Idea in Cinema: On the Cinema of Straub-Huillet." In *Deleuze and Guattari: New Mappings in Politics, Philosophy and Culture*, edited by Eleanor Kaufman and Kevin Jon Heller, 14–19. Minneapolis: Minnesota University Press, 1998.

———. "Lettre à un critique sévère." In *Pourparles 1972–1990*, 11–23. Paris: Editions de Minuit, 1990.

———. "Literature and Life." Translated by Daniel W. Smith and Michael A. Greco. *Critical Inquiry* 23, no. 2 (1997): 225–30.

———. *The Logic of Sense*. Translated by Mark Lester with Charles Stivale. New York: Columbia University Press, 1990.

———. *Negotiations, 1972–1990*. Translated by Martin Joughin. New York: Columbia University Press, 1995.

———. *Nietzsche and Philosophy*. Translated by Hugh Tomlinson. New York: Columbia University Press, 1983.

———. *Pure Immanence: Essays on a Life*. Translated by Anne Boyman. New York: Zone, 2001.

———. *Spinoza: Practical Philosophy*. Translated by Robert Hurley. San Francisco: City Lights, 2001.

———. *Two Regimes of Madness: Text and Interviews, 1975–1995*. Translated by David Lapoujade. New York: Semiotext(e), 2007.

Deleuze, Gilles, and Félix Guattari. *Anti-Oedipus*. Translated by Robert Hurley, Mark Seem, and Helen R. Lane. Minneapolis: University of Minnesota Press, 1983.

———. *Kafka: Towards a Minor Literature*. Translated by Dana Polan. Minneapolis: University of Minnesota Press, 1986.

———. *A Thousand Plateaus: Capitalism and Schizophrenia*. Translated by Brian Massumi. Minneapolis: University of Minnesota Press, 1987.

Deleuze, Gilles, and Claire Parnet. *Dialogues II*. Translated by Hugh Tomlinson and Barbara Hammerjam. New York: Columbia University Press, 2007.

———. *Gilles Deleuze from A to Z*. Los Angeles: Semiotext(e), 2011. DVD.

Demetriou, Olga, and Ayla Gürel. "Human Rights, Civil Society and Conflict in Cyprus: Exploring the Relationships. Case Study Report WP3." Rome: SHUR: Human Rights in Conflicts: The Role of Civil Society, 2008. Accessed April 15, 2017. https://www.prio.org/utility/DownloadFile.ashx?id=532&type=publicationfile.

Derrida, Jacques. *The Animal That Therefore I Am*. Translated by David Wills. New York: Fordham University Press, 2008.

———. "Faith and Knowledge: Two Sources of 'Religion' at the Limits of Reason Alone." In Jacques Derrida, *Acts of Religion*. Edited and with an introduction by Gil Anidjar, 40–101. New York: Routledge, 2002.

Descola, Philippe. *Beyond Nature and Culture*. Translated by Janet Lloyd. Chicago: University of Chicago Press, 2013.

Desjarlais, Robert. *Subject to Death: Life and Loss in a Buddhist World*. Chicago: University of Chicago Press, 2016.

Didion, Joan. *The Year of Magical Thinking*. New York: Knopf, 2006.

Donais, Timothy. *The Political Economy of Peacebuilding in Post-Dayton Bosnia*. New York: Routledge, 2005.

Dorfman, Ariel. "The Missing and the Photograph: The Uses and Misuses of Globalization." In *Spontaneous Shrines and the Public Memorialization of Death*, edited by Jack Santino, 255–60. New York: Palgrave Macmillan, 2006.

Dumit, Joseph. *Drugs for Life: How Pharmaceutical Companies Define Our Health*. Durham, NC: Duke University Press, 2012.

———. *Picturing Personhood: Brain Scans and Biomedical Identity*. Princeton, NJ: Princeton University Press, 2004.

Eager, Charlotte. "The War Is Over but Sarajevans Cannot Find the Peace They Seek." *Daily Telegraph*, September 6, 2003.

Easterly, William. *The Tyranny of Experts: Economists, Dictators, and the Forgotten Rights of the Poor*. New York: Basic Books, 2015.

Edkins, Jenny. *Trauma and the Memory of Politics*. Cambridge: Cambridge University Press, 2004.

Elias, Jamal. *Aisha's Cushion: Religious Art, Perception, and Practice in Islam*. Cambridge, MA: Harvard University Press, 2012.

Erickson, Patricia, and Steven Erickson. *Crime, Punishment, and Mental Illness: Law and the Behavioral Sciences in Conflict*. New Brunswick, NJ: Rutgers University Press, 2008.

Escobar, Arturo. *Encountering Development: The Making and Unmaking of the Third World*. Princeton, NJ: Princeton University Press, 2011.

Escobar, Ticio. *Misión: Etnocidio*. Asunción, Paraguay: Editora Liticolor, 1988.

Evripidou, Stefanos, and Stephen Nugent, dirs. *Birds of a Feather*. 2012. Accessed April 15, 2017. https://www.youtube.com/watch?v=1MRPMJgSmqE.

Fabian, Johannes. *Time and the Other: How Anthropology Makes Its Object*. New York: Columbia University Press, 2002.

Fanon, Frantz. 1963. *The Wretched of the Earth: A Negro Psychoanalyst's Study of the Problems of Racism and Colonialism in the World Today*. Translated by Richard Philcox. New York: Grove, 1963.

Farmer, Paul. "Challenging Orthodoxies: The Road Ahead for Health and Human Rights." *Health and Human Rights* 10, no. 1 (2008): 5–19.

———. *Infections and Inequalities: The Modern Plagues*. Berkeley: University of California Press, 2001.

———. *Pathologies of Power: Health, Human Rights, and the New War on the Poor*. Berkeley: University of California Press, 2003.

———. "Who Lives and Who Dies." *London Review of Books* 37, no. 3 (February 5, 2015): 17–20.

Farrar, Jeremy, and Peter Piot. 2014. "The Ebola Emergency: Immediate Action, Ongoing Strategy." *New England Journal of Medicine* 371 (2014): 1545–46. http://www.nejm.org/doi/full/10.1056/nejme1411471#t=article.

Fassin, Didier. "Another Politics of Life Is Possible." *Theory, Culture and Society* 26, no. 5 (2009): 44–60.

———. *Enforcing Order: An Ethnography of Urban Policing*. Cambridge: Polity, 2013.

———. *Humanitarian Reason: A Moral History of the Present*. Translated by Rachel Gomme. Berkeley: University of California Press, 2012.

———. "Humanitarianism as a Politics of Life." Translated by Rachel Gomme. *Public Culture* 19, no. 3 (2007): 499–520.

———. *L'ombre du monde: Une anthropologie de la condition carcérale*. Paris: Seuil, 2015.

———. *When Bodies Remember: Experiences and Politics of AIDS in South Africa*. Translated by Amy Jacobs and Gabrielle Varro. Berkeley: University of California Press, 2007.

Fassin, Didier, and Mariella Pandolfi, eds. *Contemporary States of Emergency: The Politics of Military and Humanitarian Intervention*. New York: Zone, 2010.

Fassin, Didier, and Richard Rechtman. *The Empire of Trauma: An Inquiry into the Condition of Victimhood*. Translated by Rachel Gomme. Princeton, NJ: Princeton University Press, 2009.

Federation of Indian Animal Protection Organizations. *The State of Dairy Cattle in India*. New Delhi: Federation of Indian Animal Protection Organizations, 2011.

Felski, Rita. *The Limits of Critique*. Chicago: University of Chicago Press, 2015.

Fennell, Catherine. *Last Project Standing: Civics and Sympathy in Post-Welfare Chicago*. Minneapolis: University of Minnesota Press, 2015.

Ferguson, James. *The Anti-Politics Machine: Development, Depoliticization, and Bureaucratic Power in Lesotho*. Minneapolis: University of Minnesota Press, 1994.

———. *Give a Man a Fish: Reflections on the New Politics of Distribution*. Durham, NC: Duke University Press, 2015.

———. *Global Shadows: Africa in the Neoliberal World Order*. Durham, NC: Duke University Press, 2006.

Fernando, Mayanthi. *The Republic Unsettled: Muslim French and the Contradictions of Secularism*. Durham, NC: Duke University Press, 2014.

Ferrándiz, Francisco. "The Return of Civil War Ghosts: The Ethnography of Exhumations in Contemporary Spain." *Anthropology Today* 22, no. 3 (2006): 7–12.

Ferrándiz, Francisco, and Alejandro Baer. "Digital Memory: The Visual Recording of Mass Grave Exhumations in Contemporary Spain." *Forum Qualitative Sozialforschung* 9, no. 3 (2008). Accessed April 15, 2017. http://www.qualitative-research.net/index.php/fqs/article/view/1152.

Fink, Bruce. *Fundamentals of Psychoanalytic Technique: A Lacanian Approach for Practitioners*. New York: W. W. Norton, 2007.

Fischer, Edward. *The Good Life: Aspiration, Dignity, and the Anthropology of Wellbeing*. Redwood City, CA: Stanford University Press, 2014.

Fischer, Irene Kaminka. *Geodesy? What's That? My Personal Involvement in the Age-Old Quest for the Size and Shape of the Earth with a Running Commentary on Life in a Government Research Office*. New York: iUniverse, 2005.

Fischer, Michael M. J. *Anthropological Futures*. Durham, NC: Duke University Press, 2009.

———. Comment on João Biehl and Peter Locke's article "Deleuze and the Anthropology of Becoming." *Current Anthropology* 51, no. 3 (2010): 337–38.
———. *Emergent Forms of Life and the Anthropological Voice*. Durham, NC: Duke University Press, 2003.
———. "Ethnography for Aging Societies: Dignity, Cultural Genres, and Singapore's Imagined Futures." *American Ethnologist* 42, no. 2 (2015): 207–29.
———. "Filming Poland: The Ethnographic (Documentary, Narrative) Films of Maria Zmarz-Koczanowicz." In *Cultural Producers in Perilous States*, edited by George Marcus, 91–150. Chicago: University of Chicago Press, 1997.
———. "In the Science Zone: The Yanomamo and the Fight for Representation." *Anthropology Today* 17, no. 4 (2001): 9–14.
———. "In the Science Zone II: The Fore, Papua New Guinea, and the Fight for Representation." *East Asian Science, Technology and Society* 5 (2011): 1–17.
———. "The Lightness of Existence and the Origami of 'French' Anthropology: Latour, Descola, Viveiros de Castro, Meillassoux, and Their So-Called Ontological Turn." HAU 4, no. 1 (2014): 331–55.
———. "The Peopling of Technologies." In *When People Come First: Critical Studies in Global Health*, edited by João Biehl and Adriana Petryna, 347–73. Princeton, NJ: Princeton University Press, 2013.
———. "Repetitions in the Revolution." In *Shi'ism, Resistance, Revolution*, edited by Martin Kramer, 117–32. Boulder, CO: Westview Press, 1987.
———. "The Rhythmic Beat of the Revolution in Iran." *Cultural Anthropology* 25, no. 3 (2010): 497–543.
———. "Time, Camera and the Digital Pen: Writing Culture Operating Systems 1.0–3.0." In *Writing Culture and the Life of Anthropology*, edited by Orin Starn, 72–104. Durham, NC: Duke University Press, 2015.
———. "To Live with What Would Otherwise Be Unendurable: Return(s) to Subjectivities." In *Subjectivity: Ethnographic Investigations*, edited by João Biehl, Byron Good, and Arthur Kleinman, 423–46. Berkeley: University of California Press, 2007.
———. "Urban Mahabharata: Health Care, Ordinary, Traditional, and Contemporary Ethics." *Medical Anthropology Theory* (2017).
———. "With a Hammer, a Gouge and a Wood Block: The Work of Art and Medicine in the Age of Social Re-Traumatization: The Texas Wood-Cut Art of Dr. Eric Avery." In *Para-Sites: A Casebook against Cynical Reason*, edited by George Marcus, 15–102. Chicago: University of Chicago Press, 2000.
Fontein, Joost. "Between Tortured Bodies and Resurfacing Bones: The Politics of the Dead in Zimbabwe." *Journal of Material Culture* 15, no. 4 (2010): 423–48.
Fortun, Kim. *Advocacy after Bhopal: Environmentalism, Disaster, New Global Orders*. Chicago: University of Chicago Press, 2001.
———. "Ethnography in/of/as Open Systems." *Reviews in Anthropology* 32 (2003): 171–90.
Fortun, Michael. *Promising Genomics: Iceland and deCODE Genetics in a World of Speculation*. Berkeley: University of California Press, 2008.

Foucault, Michel. "3 March 1982, First Hour." In *The Hermeneutics of the Subject: Lectures at the Collège de France, 1981–1982*. Translated by Graham Burchell, 331–54. New York: Palgrave Macmillan, 2005.

———. *Discipline and Punish: The Birth of the Prison*. Translated by Alan Sheridan. New York: Vintage, 1995.

———. *Ethics: Subjectivity and Truth*. Edited by Paul Rabinow. New York: New Press, 1997.

———. *The History of Sexuality*. Translated by Robert Hurley. New York: Vintage, 1990.

———. "Of Other Spaces: Utopias and Heterotopias." Translated by Jay Miskowiec. *Architecture/Mouvement/Continuité*, October 1984. Accessed April 15, 2017. http://web.mit.edu/allanmc/www/foucault1.pdf.

———. *Security, Territory, Population: Lectures at the Collège de France 1977–1978*. New York: Palgrave-Macmillan, 2007.

———. *The Use of Pleasure: The History of Sexuality*. Translated by Robert Hurley. Vol. 2. New York: Vintage, 1990.

Frank, Arthur. *The Wounded Storyteller: Body, Illness, and Ethics*. Chicago: University of Chicago Press, 1995.

Frankfurter, Raphael. "The Danger in Losing Sight of Ebola Victims' Humanity." *Atlantic*, August 22, 2014. Accessed April 15, 2017. https://www.theatlantic.com/health/archive/2014/08/the-danger-in-losing-sight-of-ebola-victims-humanity/378945/.

Freud, Sigmund. *Collected Papers*, edited by Ernest Jones, vol. 2. New York: Basic Books, 1959.

———. *Complete Psychological Works of Sigmund Freud, Volume 10: Two Case Histories (Little Hans and The Rat Man)*. New York: Vintage Books, 2001.

———. *Five Lectures on Psycho-Analysis*. Edited by James Strachey. New York: W. W. Norton, 1990.

———. "Mourning and Melancholia." In *The Standard Edition of the Complete Psychological Works of Sigmund Freud*, edited by James Strachey, 14:237–58. London: Hogarth Press, 1917.

Fukuyama, Francis. "The End of History?" *National Interest* (summer 1989): 3–18.

Fundação Instituto Brasileiro de Geografia e Estatística. "Pesquisa Nacional Por Amostra de Domicílios—1976." Vol. 1, no. 9: "Áreas metropolitanas: Rio de Janeiro e São Paulo." Rio de Janeiro: IBGE, 1979. Accessed February 18, 2017. http://biblioteca.ibge.gov.br/visualizacao/periodicos/59/pnad_1976_v1_t9_rj_sp.pdf.

Galton, Francis. "Visualised Numerals." *Nature* 21 (1880): 252–56.

Gandhi, Leela. *Affective Communities: Anticolonial Thought, Fin-de-Siècle Radicalism, and the Politics of Friendship*. Durham, NC: Duke University Press, 2006.

Gandhi, Maneka. *Heads and Tails*. Mapusa, India: Other India, 2000.

Garces, Chris, and Alexander Jones. "Mauss Redux: From Warfare's Human Toll to l'Homme Total." *Anthropological Quarterly* 82, no. 1 (2009): 279–309.

Garcia, Angela. *The Pastoral Clinic: Addiction and Dispossession along the Rio Grande*. Berkeley: University of California Press, 2010.

Geertz, Clifford. *After the Fact: Two Countries, Four Decades, One Anthropologist*. Cambridge, MA: Harvard University Press, 1995.

———. "Art as a Cultural System." MLN *Comparative Literature* 91, no. 6 (1976): 1473–99.
———. *Available Light: Anthropological Reflections on Philosophical Topics*. Princeton, NJ: Princeton University Press, 2000.
———. *The Interpretation of Cultures*. New York: Basic, 1973.
———. "Life among the Anthros." *New York Review of Books*, February 8, 2001. Accessed April 15, 2017. http://www.nybooks.com/articles/2001/02/08/life-among-anthros/.
———. *Local Knowledge: Further Essays in Interpretive Anthropology*. New York: Basic, 1983.
———. *Works and Lives: The Anthropologist as Author*. Redwood City, CA: Stanford University Press, 1988.
———. "The World in Pieces: Culture and Politics at the End of the Century." In Clifford Geertz, *Available Light: Anthropological Reflections on Philosophical Topics*, 218–63. Princeton, NJ: Princeton University Press, 2000.
Gell, Alfred. *Art and Agency: An Anthropological Theory*. Oxford: Clarendon Press of Oxford University Press, 1998.
Ghassem-Fachandi, Parvis. *Pogrom in Gujarat: Hindu Nationalism and Anti-Muslim Violence*. Princeton, NJ: Princeton University Press, 2012.
Gilbert, Andrew, Jessica Greenberg, Elissa Helms, and Stef Jansen. "Reconsidering Postsocialism from the Margins of Europe: Hope, Time and Normalcy in Post-Yugoslav Societies." *Anthropology News* 49, no. 8 (2008): 10–11.
Ginsburg, Faye. "Disability in the Digital Age." In *Digital Anthropology*, edited by Heather Horst and Daniel Miller, 101–26. London: Berg, 2012.
Ginsburg, Faye, and Rayna Rapp. "Disability Worlds." *Annual Review of Anthropology* 42 (2013): 53–68.
Glaude, Eddie. 2016. *Democracy in Black: How Race Still Enslaves the American Soul*. New York: Crown, 2016.
Glauser, Benno. "Su presencia protege el corazón del Chaco Seco. In *Pueblos indígenas en aislamiento voluntario y contacto inicial en la Amazonia y el Gran Chaco*, edited by A. Parellada, 220–34. Copenhagen: IWGIA, 2007.
Göle, Nilüfer. "Islam in Public: New Visibilities and New Imaginaries." *Public Culture* 14, no. 1 (2002): 173–90.
Gombrich, Ernst H. *Arte e Ilusão: Um estudo da psicologia da representação pictórica*. São Paulo: Martins Fontes, 1995.
Gonzalez, Solis. "Neoliberalismo y crimen organizado en Mexico: El surgimiento del Estado narco." *Frontera Norte* 25, no. 50 (2013): 7–34.
Good, Byron, Michael M. J. Fischer, Sarah Willen, and Mary-Jo DelVecchio Good, eds. *A Reader in Medical Anthropology: Theoretical Trajectory, Emergent Realities*. Malden, MA: Wiley-Blackwell, 2010.
Good, Byron, Mary-Jo DelVecchio Good, Sandra Teresa Hyde, and Sarah Pinto. 2008. "Postcolonial Disorders: Reflections on Subjectivity in the Contemporary World." In *Postcolonial Disorders*, ed. Mary-Jo DelVecchio Good, Sandra Teresa Hyde, Sarah Pinto, and Byron Good, 1–42. Berkeley: University of California Press.
Good, Mary-Jo DelVecchio, Sandra Hyde, Sarah Pinto, and Byron Good, eds. *Postcolonial Disorders*. Berkeley: University of California Press, 2008.

Gordillo, Gaston. *En el Gran Chaco: Antropologias e historias*. Buenos Aires: Prometeo, 2006.

———. *Landscapes of Devils: Tensions of Place and Memory in the Argentinean Chaco*. Durham, NC: Duke University Press, 2004.

———. *Rubble: The Afterlife of Destruction*. Durham, NC: Duke University Press, 2014.

Graeber, David. *Debt: The First 5,000 Years*. New York: Melville House, 2014.

———. *The Democracy Project: A History, A Crisis, A Movement*. New York: Spiegel and Grau, 2013.

———. "Occupy Wall Street Rediscovers the Radical Imagination." Hot Spots, *Cultural Anthropology* website, February 14, 2013. Accessed April 15, 2017. https://culanth.org/fieldsights/77-occupy-wall-street-rediscovers-the-radical-imagination.

Greenblatt, Stephen. "Tell My Story: The Human Compulsion to Narrate." Institute for Humanities Research, Denmark, March 18, 2014. Accessed April 15, 2017. https://www.youtube.com/watch?v=zvtgLkhij2s.

Greenhouse, Carol. *A Moment's Notice: Time Politics across Cultures*. Ithaca, NY: Cornell University Press, 1996.

———. *The Paradox of Relevance: Ethnography and Citizenship in the United States*. Philadelphia: University of Pennsylvania Press, 2011.

Griffen, B. D., and J. M. Drake. "Scaling Rules for the Final Decline to Extinction." *Proceedings of the Royal Society of London* 276, no. 1660 (2009): 1361–67.

Grosz, Elizabeth. *Architecture from the Outside: Essays on Virtual and Real Space*. Cambridge, MA: MIT Press, 2001.

Guidetti, Mattia. "The Byzantine Heritage in the Dār al-Islām: Churches and Mosques in al-Ruha between the Sixth and Twelfth Centuries." *Muqarnas* 26 (2009): 1–36.

Guscin, Mark. *The Image of Edessa*. Boston: Brill, 2009.

Gusterson, Hugh. *Nuclear Rites: A Weapons Laboratory at the End of the Cold War*. Berkeley: University of California Press, 1998.

Gutiérrez, Eduardo Guerrero. "Epidemias de violencia." *Nexos*, July 1, 2012. Accessed April 15, 2017. http://www.nexos.com.mx/?p=14884.

Hacking, Ian. "Making Up People." In *The Science Studies Reader*, edited by Mario Biagioli, 161–71. New York: Routledge, 1999.

Hage, Ghassan. "Critical Anthropological Thought and the Radical Political Imaginary Today." *Critique of Anthropology* 32, no. 3 (2012): 285–308.

Halberstam, Judith. *The Queer Art of Failure*. Durham, NC: Duke University Press, 2011.

Hale, Charles. "Neoliberal Multiculturalism." POLAR 28, no. 1 (2005): 10–19.

Hammoudi, Abdellah. *A Season in Mecca: Narrative of a Pilgrimage*. New York: Hill and Wang, 2006.

———. "Textualism and Anthropology: On the Ethnographic Encounter, or an Experience in the Hajj." In *Being There: The Fieldwork Encounter and the Making of Truth*, edited by John Borneman and Abdellah Hammoudi, 25–54. Berkeley: University of California Press, 2009.

Han, Clara. *Life in Debt: Times of Care and Violence in Neoliberal Chile*. Berkeley: University of California Press, 2012.

Haraway, Donna. "A Cyborg Manifesto: Science, Technology, and Socialist-Feminism in the Late Twentieth Century." In Donna Haraway, *Simians, Cyborgs, and Women: The Reinvention of Nature*, 149–82. New York: Routledge, 1991.
———. *Simians, Cyborgs, and Women: The Reinvention of Nature*. New York: Routledge, 1991.
———. *Staying with the Trouble: Making Kin in the Chthulucene*. Durham, NC: Duke University Press, 2016.
———. *When Species Meet*. Minneapolis: University of Minnesota Press, 2007.
Hart, Kimberley. *And Then We Work for God: Rural Sunni Islam in Western Turkey*. Redwood City, CA: Stanford University Press, 2013.
———. "The Orthodoxization of Ritual Practice in Western Anatolia." *American Ethnologist* 36, no. 4 (2009): 735–49.
Hayden, Robert. *Blueprints for a House Divided: The Constitutional Logic of the Yugoslav Conflicts*. Ann Arbor: University of Michigan Press, 2000.
———. "Moral Vision and Impaired Insight: The Imagining of Other People's Communities in Bosnia." *Current Anthropology* 48, no. 1 (2007): 105–31.
Haydn, Cori. *When Nature Goes Public: The Making and Unmaking of Bioprospecting in Mexico*. Princeton, NJ: Princeton University Press, 2003.
Healy, Jack. "Starving Sea Lions Washing Ashore by the Hundreds in California." *New York Times*, March 12, 2015, page A12.
Hedayat, Sadegh. *The Blind Owl*. Translated by D. P. Costello. London: John Calder, 1957.
Heinle, Kimberly, Cory Molzahn, and David A. Shirk. *Drug Violence in Mexico: Data and Analysis through 2014*. San Diego, CA: University of San Diego, 2015. Accessed February 18, 2017. https://justiceinmexico.org/wp-content/uploads/2015/04/2015-Drug-Violence-in-Mexico-final.pdf.
Helmreich, Stefan. *Alien Ocean: Anthropological Voices in Microbial Seas*. Berkeley: University of California Press, 2009.
Helms, Elissa. *Innocence and Victimhood: Gender, Nation, and Women's Activism in Postwar Bosnia-Herzegovina*. Madison: University of Wisconsin Press, 2013.
Herzfeld, Michael. *Cultural Intimacy: Social Poetics in the Nation-State*. New York: Routledge, 1997.
Hirschkind, Charles. *The Ethical Soundscape: Cassette Sermons and Islamic Counterpublics*. New York: Columbia University Press, 2009.
Hirschman, Albert O. *A Bias for Hope: Essays on Development and Latin America*. New Haven, CT: Yale University Press, 1971.
———. *Crossing Boundaries: Selected Writings*. New York: Zone, 1998.
———. *Exit, Voice and Loyalty: Responses to Decline in Firms, Organizations, and States*. Cambridge, MA: Harvard University Press, 1970.
Ho, Engseng. *The Graves of Tarim: Genealogy and Mobility across the Indian Ocean*. Berkeley: University of California Press, 2006.
Holling, Crawford S. "Resilience and Stability of Ecological Systems." *Annual Review of Ecology and Systematics* 4 (1973): 1–23.
Holmes, Seth. *Fresh Fruit, Broken Bodies: Migrant Farmworkers in the United States*. Berkeley: University of California Press, 2013.

Hromadžić, Azra. "Bathroom Mixing: Youth Negotiate Democratization in Post-Conflict Bosnia and Herzegovina." *Political and Legal Anthropology Review* 34, no. 2 (2011): 268–89.

———. "Once We Had a House; Invisible Citizens and Consociational Democracy in Postwar Mostar, Bosnia and Herzegovina." *Social Analysis* 56, no. 3 (2012): 30–48.

Hughes, Terry P., Cristina Linares, Vasilis Dakos, Ingrid A. van de Leemput, and Egbert H. van Nes. "Living Dangerously on Borrowed Time during Slow, Unrecognized Regime Shifts." *Trends in Ecology and Evolution* 28, no. 3 (2013): 149–55.

Ingold, Tim. *Being Alive: Essays on Movement, Knowledge, and Description*. New York: Routledge, 2011.

Ingold, Tim, and Gisli Palsson. *Biosocial Becomings: Integrating Social and Biological Anthropology*. Cambridge: Cambridge University Press, 2013.

Inhorn, Marcia. *Cosmopolitan Conceptions: IVF Sojourns in Global Dubai*. Durham, NC: Duke University Press, 2015.

Intergovernmental Panel on Climate Change. *Climate Change 2014: Synthesis Report*. Geneva: Intergovernmental Panel on Climate Change, 2014. Accessed February 23, 2017. http://ipcc.ch/report/ar5/.

International Crisis Group. "Cyprus: Bridging the Property Divide." 2010. Accessed February 21, 2017. http://www.observatori.org/paises/pais_69/documentos/210%20Cyprus%20-%20Bridging%20the%20Property%20Divide.pdf.

Isçan, M. Y., S. R. Loth, and R. K. Wright. "Age Estimation from the Rib by Phase Analysis: White Females." *Journal of Forensic Science* 30 (1985): 853–63.

———. "Age Estimation from the Rib by Phase Analysis: White Males." *Journal of Forensic Science* 29 (1984): 1094–104.

Jackson, Jean. "Culture, Genuine and Spurious: The Politics of Indianness in the Vaupes, Colombia." *American Ethnologist* 22, no. 1 (1995): 3–27.

Jackson, John L. *Harlemworld: Doing Race and Class in Contemporary Black America*. Chicago: University of Chicago Press, 2001.

———. *Real Black: Adventures in Racial Sincerity*. Chicago: University of Chicago Press, 2005.

Jackson, Michael. *In Sierra Leone*. Durham, NC: Duke University Press, 2004.

———. *Life within Limits: Well-Being in a World of Want*. Durham, NC: Duke University Press, 2011.

———. *Lifeworlds: Essays in Existential Anthropology*. Chicago: University of Chicago Press, 2012.

———. "Where Thought Belongs." *Anthropological Theory* 9, no. 3 (2009): 235–51.

Jain, S. Lochlann. *Malignant: How Cancer Becomes Us*. Berkeley: University of California Press, 2013.

James, Erica Caple. *Democratic Insecurities: Violence, Trauma, and Intervention in Haiti*. Berkeley: University of California Press, 2010.

Jansen, Stef. "On Not Moving Well Enough: Temporal Reasoning in Sarajevo Yearnings for 'Normal Lives.'" *Current Anthropology* 55, no. S9 (2014): S74–84.

———. "The Privatisation of Home and Hope: Return, Reforms and the Foreign Intervention in Bosnia-Herzegovina." *Dialectical Anthropology* 30 (2006): 177–99.

———. "Troubled Locations: Return, the Life Course, and Transformations of 'Home' in Bosnia-Herzegovina." *Focaal* 49 (2007): 15–30.

———. *Yearnings in the Meantime: "Normal Lives" and the State in a Sarajevo Apartment Complex*. New York: Berghahn, 2015.

Jardim, L. B., M. L. Pereira, I. Silveira, A. Ferro, J. Sequeiros, and R. Giugliani. 2001. "Machado-Joseph Disease in South Brazil: Clinical and Molecular Characterizations of Kindreds." *Acta Neurologica Scandinavica* 104 (2001): 224–31.

Jasanoff, Sheila. *The Fifth Branch: Science Advisors as Policymakers*. Cambridge, MA: Harvard University Press, 1998.

Jenkins, Janis H. *Extraordinary Conditions: Culture and Experience in Mental Illness*. Oakland: University of California Press, 2015.

Jenkins, Janis Hunter, and Robert John Barrett, eds. *Schizophrenia, Culture, and Subjectivity: The Edge of Experience*. New York: Cambridge University Press, 2003.

Johnston, Ken. *The Story of the New Tribes Mission: The First 40 Years*. Sanford, FL: New Tribes Mission Press, 1985.

Joseph, Gilbert, and David Nugent. *Everyday Forms of State Formation: Revolution and Negotiation of Rule in Modern Mexico*. Durham, NC: Duke University Press, 1994.

Karaboeva, Emiliya. "Death and Memory in the Context of the Contemporary Bulgarian Street Posted Obituary." In *Dying and Death in 18th–21st Century Europe*, edited by Marius Rotar and Adrina Teodorescu, 302–30. Newcastle upon Tyne, UK: Cambridge Scholars, 2011.

Kaufman, Sharon R. *Ordinary Medicine: Extraordinary Treatments, Longer Lives, and Where to Draw the Line*. Durham, NC: Duke University Press, 2015.

Keller, Catherine. *Face of the Deep: A Theology of Becoming*. New York: Routledge, 2003.

Kelley, Robin D. G. "Why We Won't Wait." *Counterpunch*. November 25, 2014.

Kelly, Anne, and Javier Lezaun. "Urban Mosquitoes, Situational Publics, and the Pursuit of Interspecies Separation in Dar es Salaam." *American Ethnologist* 41, no. 2 (2014): 368–83.

Kienzler, Hanna. "The Social Life of Psychiatric Practice: Trauma in Postwar Kosova." *Medical Anthropology* 31, no. 3 (2012): 266–82.

Kirmayer, Laurence J., Hanna Kienzler, Abdel Hamid Afana, and Duncan Pederson. "Trauma and Disasters in Social and Cultural Context." In *Principles of Social Psychiatry*, edited by Craig Morgan and Dinesh Bhugra, 155–78. 2nd ed. New York: John Wiley, 2010.

Kirskey, Eben. *Emergent Ecologies*. Durham, NC: Duke University Press, 2015.

Kirskey, Eben, and Stefan Helmreich. "The Emergence of Multispecies Ethnography." *Cultural Anthropology* 25, no. 4 (2010): 545–76.

Klein, Naomi. *This Changes Everything: Capitalism vs. the Climate*. New York: Simon and Schuster, 2014.

Kleinman, Arthur. "From Illness to Caregiving as Moral Experience." *New England Journal of Medicine* 368 (2013): 15.

———. *The Illness Narratives: Suffering, Healing, and the Human Condition*. New York: Basic, 1988.

———. *What Really Matters: Living a Moral Life Amidst Uncertainty and Danger*. New York: Oxford University Press, 2006.

Kleinman, Arthur, and Byron Good, eds. *Culture and Depression: Studies in the Anthropology and Cross-Cultural Psychiatry of Affect and Disorder*. Berkeley: University of California Press, 1985.

Kleinman, Arthur, and Iain Wilkinson. *A Passion for Society: How We Think about Human Suffering*. Berkeley: University of California Press, 2016.

Knight, Kelly. *addicted.pregnant.poor*. Durham, NC: Duke University Press, 2015.

Kohn, Eduardo. *How Forests Think: Toward an Anthropology beyond the Human*. Berkeley: University of California Press, 2013.

Kovras, Iosif. "De-Linkage Processes and Grassroots Movements in Transitional Justice." *Cooperation and Conflict* 47, no. 1 (2012): 88–105.

Krieger, Nancy. "Theories for Social Epidemiology in the 21st Century: An Ecosocial Perspective." *International Journal of Epidemiology* 30, no. 4 (2001): 668–77.

Krishna, Chinny, and Maneka Gandhi. "Rukmini Devi and Animal Welfare." In *Rukmini Devi Arundale, 1904–1986: A Visionary Architect of Indian Culture and Performing Arts*, edited by Avanthi Meduri, 67–84. Chennai, India: Motilal Banarsidass, 2005.

Kroeber, Theodora. *Ishi in Two Worlds: A Biography of the Last Wild Indian in North America*. Berkeley: University of California Press, 1961.

Kunreuther, Howard, Geoffrey Heal, Myles Allen, Ottmar Edenhofer, Christopher B. Field, and Gary Yohe. "Risk Management and Climate Change." *Nature Climate Change* 3 (2013): 447–50.

Kürkçüoğlu, Cihat. 2011. *Urfa: Fotoğraflarla Evvel Zaman İçinde* [Urfa: Once upon a time, through the eyes of photographs]. Ankara: Şanlıurfa Directorate of Culture and Social Affairs, 2011.

Kurtović, Larisa. "Who Sows Hunger, Reaps Rage: On Protest, Indignation, and Redistributive Justice in Post-Dayton Bosnia-Herzegovina." *Southeast European and Black Sea Studies* 15, no. 4 (2015): 639–59.

Lagerkvist, Bengt, Nermana Mehić-Basara, Dubravko Vaniček, and Vesna Puratić, eds. *The Mental Health Reform in Bosnia Herzegovina*. Sarajevo: SweBiH (Swedish Psychiatric, Social and Re-Habilitation Project for Bosnia-Herzegovina), 2003.

Lakoff, Andrew. *Pharmaceutical Reason: Knowledge and Value in Global Psychiatry*. Cambridge: Cambridge University Press, 2006.

Lakoff, Andrew, and Stephen J. Collier. *Biosecurity Interventions: Global Health and Security in Question*. New York: Columbia University Press, 2008.

Lakoff, Andrew, and Christopher Kelty, eds. "Ebola's Ecologies." Special issue, *Limn*, no. 5 (2015).

Lambek, Michael, Veena Das, Didier Fassin, and Webb Keane. *Four Lectures on Ethics: Anthropological Perspectives*. Chicago: HAU Books, 2015.

Lamendin, H., et al. "A Simple Technique for Age Estimation in Adult Corpses: The Two Criteria Dental Method." *Journal of Forensic Science* 37, no. 5 (1992): 1373–79.

Landecker, Hannah, and Aaron Panofsky. "From Social Structure to Gene Regulation and Back: A Critical Introduction to Environmental Epigenetics for Sociology. *Annual Review of Sociology* 39 (2012): 333–57.

Latour, Bruno. *Jamais Fomos Modernos*. Translated by Carlos Irineu da Costa. São Paulo: 34 Letras, 2008.

Latour, Bruno, and Steven Woolgar. *Laboratory Life: The Construction of Scientific Facts.* Princeton, NJ: Princeton University Press, 1986.

Laurell, Asa Cristina. "Three Decades of Neoliberalism in Mexico: The Destruction of Society." *International Journal of Health Services* 45, no. 2 (2015): 246–64.

Lens, Sidney. *Permanent War: The Militarization of America.* New York: Schocken Books, 1987.

Lenton, Timothy M. "Environmental Tipping Points." *Annual Review of Environment and Resources* 38 (2013): 1–29.

Léry, Jean de. *História de uma viagem feita à terra do Brasil.* São Paulo: Fundação Darcy Ribeiro, 2004.

Levinas, Emmanuel. "The Name of a Dog, or Natural Rights." In *Animal Philosophy: Essential Readings in Continental Thought*, edited by Peter Atterton and Matthew Calarco, 47–50. New York: Continuum, 2004.

Lévi-Strauss, Claude. *Look, Listen, Read.* New York: Basic, 1997.

———. *Myth and Meaning: Cracking the Code of Culture.* New York: Schocken, 1995.

———. *The Raw and the Cooked.* Translated by John Weightman and Doreen Weightman. Chicago: University of Chicago Press, 1983.

———. *The Savage Mind.* Chicago: University of Chicago Press, 1966.

———. *Structural Anthropology.* Translated by Claire Jacobson and Brooke Grundfest Schoepf. New York: Basic, 1963.

———. *Tristes Tropiques.* Translated by John and Doreen Weightman. New York: Penguin Books, 1964.

———. *The View from Afar.* Translated by Joachim Neugroschel and Phoebe Hoss. Chicago: University of Chicago Press, 1983.

———. *The Way of the Masks.* Translated by Sylvia Modelski. Seattle: University of Washington Press, 1979.

Lewis, Simon, and Mark Maslin. "Defining the Anthropocene." *Nature* 519 (2015): 171–80.

Li, Tania. *Land's End: Capitalist Relations on an Indigenous Frontier.* Durham, NC: Duke University Press, 2014.

Lindstrom, Nicole. "Yugonostalgia: Restorative and Reflective Nostalgia in Former Yugoslavia." *Eastern Central Europe* 32 (2005): 227–38.

Livingston, Julie. *Improvising Medicine: An African Oncology Ward in an Emerging Cancer Epidemic.* Durham, NC: Duke University Press, 2012.

Lock, Margaret. "Comprehending the Body in the Era of the Epigenome." *Current Anthropology* 56, no. 2 (2015): 151–77.

———. *Encounters with Aging: Mythologies of Menopause in Japan and North America.* Berkeley: University of California Press, 1993.

———. "The Epigenome and Nature/Nurture Reunification: A Challenge for Anthropology." *Medical Anthropology* 32, no. 4 (2013): 291–308.

———. "The Lure of the Epigenome." *Lancet* 381, no. 9881 (2013): 1896–97.

———. "Medicalization and the Naturalization of Social Control." In *Health and Illness in the World's Cultures*, vol. 1 of *Encyclopedia of Medical Anthropology*, edited by Carol R. Ember and Marvin Ember, 116–25. New York: Springer, 2003.

Lock, Margaret, and Nancy Scheper-Hughes. "The Mindful Body: A Prolegomenon to Future Work in Medical Anthropology." *Medical Anthropology Quarterly* 1, no. 1 (1987): 6–41.

Lock, Margaret, and Vinh-Kim Nguyen. "Local Biologies and Human Difference." In *An Anthropology of Biomedicine*, edited by Margaret Lock and Vinh-Kim Nguyen, 83–109. Malden, MA: Wiley Blackwell, 2010.

Locke, Peter. "Anthropology and Medical Humanitarianism in the Age of Global Health Education." In *Medical Humanitarianism: Ethnographies of Practice*, edited by Sharon Abramowitz and Catherine Panter-Brick, 193–208. Philadelphia: University of Pennsylvania Press, 2015.

———. "City of Survivors: Trauma, Grief, and Getting By in Post-War Sarajevo." PhD diss., Princeton University, 2009.

———. "'Everybody Loves Tito': Memory and Political Subjectivity in Post-War Sarajevo." Paper presented at the National Conference of the Midwest Political Science Association National Conference, Chicago, April 3–6, 2008.

———. "Global Health and Its Margins, from West Africa to Southeast Europe." Paper presented at the Annual Meeting of the American Anthropological Association, Denver, CO, November 21, 2015.

Lomnitz, Claudio. *Death and the Idea of Mexico*. New York: Zone, 2005.

Long, Nicholas. *Being Malay in Indonesia: Histories, Hope, and Citizenship in the Riau Archipelago*. Honolulu: University of Hawai'i Press, 2013.

Loraux, Nicole. *The Divided City: On Memory and Forgetting in Ancient Athens*. Translated by Corinne Pache with Jeff Fort. New York: Zone, 2002.

Lorraine, Tamsin. "Living a Time out of Joint." In *Between Deleuze and Derrida*, edited by Paul Patton and John Protevi, 30–45. New York: Continuum, 2003.

Lovejoy, C. Owen, Richard S. Meindl, Thomas R. Pryzbeck, and Robert P. Mensforth. "Chronological Metamorphosis of the Auricular Surface of the Ilium: A New Method for the Determination of Adult Skeletal Age at Death." *American Journal of Physical Anthropology* 68, no. 1 (1985): 15–28.

Lovell, Anne. "Addiction Markets: The Case of High-Dose Buprenorphine in France." In *Global Pharmaceuticals: Practices, Markets, Ethics*, edited by Adriana Petryna, Andrew Lakoff, and Arthur Kleinman, 136–70. Durham, NC: Duke University Press, 2006.

Lubkemann, Stephen C. *Culture in Chaos: An Anthropology of the Social Condition in War*. Chicago: University of Chicago Press, 2008.

Luhrmann, T. M. *Of Two Minds: The Growing Disorder in American Psychiatry*. New York: Knopf, 2000.

———. *When God Talks Back: Understanding the American Evangelical Relationship with God*. New York: Vintage, 2012.

Lutz, Catherine. *Homefront: A Military City and the American Twentieth Century*. Boston: Beacon, 2001.

Lutz, Catherine, and Jane Lou Collins. *Reading* National Geographic. Chicago: University of Chicago Press, 1993.

Lyons, Charles. "A Brazilian Tribe's Suicide Epidemic." *New York Times* (international edition), January 3, 2015.

Lyotard, Jean-François. *Libidinal Economy*. Translated by Iain Hamilton Grant. Bloomington: Indiana University Press, 1993.

Maček, Ivana. *Sarajevo under Siege: Anthropology in Wartime*. Philadelphia: University of Pennsylvania Press, 2009.

Magnuson, John J. "Long-Term Ecological Research and the Invisible Present." *BioScience* 40, no. 7 (1990): 495–501.

Magnuson, John J., C. J. Bowser, and A. L. Beckel. "The Invisible Present: Long-Term Ecological Research on Lakes." *L & S Magazine*, fall 1983, 3–6.

Mahmood, Saba. "Feminist Theory, Embodiment, and the Docile Agent: Some Reflections on the Egyptian Islamic Revival." *Cultural Anthropology* 16, no. 2 (2000): 202–36.

———. *Politics of Piety: The Islamic Revival and the Feminist Subject*. Princeton, NJ: Princeton University Press, 2005.

———. *Religious Difference in a Secular Age: A Minority Report*. Princeton, NJ: Princeton University Press, 2015.

Majstorović, Danijela, Zoran Vučkovac, and Anđela Pepić. "From Dayton to Brussels via Tuzla: Post-2014 Economic Restructuring as Europeanization Discourse/Practice in Bosnia and Herzegovina." *Southeast European and Black Sea Studies* 15, no. 4 (2015): 661–82.

Malabou, Catherine. *The Ontology of the Accident: An Essay on Destructive Plasticity*. Cambridge: Polity, 2012.

Malinowski, Bronislaw. *Argonauts of the Western Pacific*. Rev. ed. London: Routledge, 2014.

———. *Sex and Repression in Savage Society*. 2nd ed. New York: Routledge, 2015.

Malkki, Liisa. *The Need to Help: The Domestic Arts of International Humanitarianism*. Durham, NC: Duke University Press, 2015.

Malm, Andreas. "The Anthropocene Myth." *Jacobin Magazine*, 2015. Accessed April 16, 2017. https://www.jacobinmag.com/2015/03/anthropocene-capitalism-climate-change.

Marcus, George. "The End(s) of Ethnography: Social/Cultural Anthropology's Signature Form of Producing Knowledge in Transition." *Cultural Anthropology* 23, no. 1 (2008): 1–14.

Markowitz, Fran. *Sarajevo: A Bosnian Kaleidoscope*. Chicago: University of Illinois Press, 2010.

Markowitz, John C. "IPT and PTSD." *Depression and Anxiety* 27, no. 10 (2010): 879–81.

Martin, Emily. *Bipolar Expeditions: Mania and Depression in American Culture*. Princeton, NJ: Princeton University Press, 2008.

———. *The Woman in the Body: A Cultural Analysis of Reproduction*. Boston: Beacon, 1987.

Marx, Karl. "Theses on Feuerbach." In *Ludwig Feuerbach and the End of Classical German Philosophy*. Edited by Ludwig Feuerbach, 12–15. Moscow: Progress Publishers, 1969.

Masco, Joseph. *The Theater of Operations: National Security Affect from the Cold War to the War on Terror*. Durham, NC: Duke University Press, 2014.

Massumi, Brian. *Parables for the Virtual: Movement, Affect, Sensation*. Durham, NC: Duke University Press, 2002.

———. *A User's Guide to Capitalism and Schizophrenia: Deviations from Deleuze and Guattari*. Cambridge, MA: MIT Press, 1992.

Mattingly, Cheryl. *Moral Laboratories: Family Peril and the Struggle for a Good Life*. Berkeley: University of California Press, 2014.

Mauss, Marcel. "L'expression obligatoire des sentiments (rituels oraux funéraires australiens)." *Journal de Psychologie* 18 (1921). Accessed April 16, 2017. http://anthropomada.com/bibliotheque/MAUSS-Marcel-lexpression-obligatoire-des-sentiments.pdf.

———. "The Notion of Body Techniques." In *Sociology and Psychology: Essays*, translated by B. Brewster, 95–119. London: Routledge and Kegan Paul, 1979.

Mayo, Katherine. *Mother India: Selections from the Controversial 1927 Text*. Edited and with an introduction by Mrinalini Sinha. Ann Arbor: University of Michigan Press, 2000.

Mbembe, Achille. *On the Postcolony*. Berkeley: University of California Press, 2001.

McClintock, Anne. *Imperial Leather: Race, Gender, and Sexuality in the Colonial Contest*. New York: Routledge, 1995.

Mehta, Deepa, dir. *Fire*. New York City: Zeitgeist Films, 1996.

Menezes Neto, Hélio Santos. "Atravessando fronteiras: Uma releitura da Antropologia da Arte proposta por Alfred Gell a partir de um Ibiri de Mestre Didi." *Revista da Universidade Federal de Minas Gerais* 22, no. 1 (2015): 104–23.

———. "Boa para agir: Arte afro-brasileira e seus diálogos de fronteira entre Antropologia e Arte." *Jornadas de Antropologia John Monteiro 2015* (November 3, 2015). Campinas: Instituo de Filosofia e Ciências Humanas-Unicamp.

Merleau-Ponty, Maurice. "De Mauss a Claude Lévi-Strauss." *Os pensadores*. São Paulo: Abril Cultural, 1984.

———. "From Mauss to Claude Lévi-Strauss." *Signs*. Translated by Richard C. McCleary, 114–25. Evanston, IL: Northwestern University Press, 1964.

———. *The Visible and the Invisible*. Edited by Claude Lefort. Translated by Alphonso Lingis. Evanston, IL: Northwestern University Press, 1968.

Metzl, Jonathan. *The Protest Psychosis: How Schizophrenia Became a Black Disease*. Boston: Beacon, 2006.

Meyer, Stephen M. *The End of the Wild*. Cambridge, MA: MIT Press, 2006.

Mitchell, W. J. T. *Picture Theory: Essays on Verbal and Visual Representation*. Chicago: University of Chicago Press, 1995.

Mittermaier, Amira. "Dreams from Elsewhere: Muslim Subjectivities beyond the Trope of Self-Cultivation." *Journal of the Royal Anthropological Institute* 18, no. 2 (2012): 247–65.

Mol, Annemarie. *The Body Multiple: Ontology in Medical Practice*. Durham, NC: Duke University Press, 2002.

Montaigne, Michel de. *The Complete Essays*. Edited and translated by M. A. Screech. Reprint. New York: Penguin Books, 1993.

———. *Pensadores*. São Paulo: Abril Cultural, 1971.

Moore, B. *Social Origins of Dictatorship and Democracy: Lord and Peasant in the Making of the Modern World*. Boston: Beacon, 1966.

Mora, C., C. L. Wei, A. Rollo, T. Amaro, A. R. Baco, D. Billett, L. Bopp, et al. "Biotic and Human Vulnerability to Projected Changes in Ocean Biogeochemistry over the 21st Century." *PLoS Biology* 11, no. 10 (2013): e1001682.

Mora, C., A. G. Frazier, R. J. Longman, R.-S. Dacks, M. M. Walton, E. J. Tong, J. J. Sanchez, et al. "The Projected Timing of Climate Departure from Recent Variability." *Nature* 502 (2013): 183–87.

Morris, Rosalind, ed. *Can the Subaltern Speak? Reflections on the History of an Idea.* New York: Columbia University Press, 2010.

Morrison, Toni. *Sula.* New York: Knopf, 1974.

Moss, Richard, Mustafa Babiker, Sander Brinkman, Eduardo Calvo, Tim Carter, Jae Edmonds, Ismail Elgizouli, et al. *Towards New Scenarios for Analysis of Emissions, Climate Change, Impacts, and Response Strategies.* Geneva: Intergovernmental Panel on Climate Change, 2008. Accessed February 23, 2017. https://www.ipcc.ch/pdf/supporting-material/expert-meeting-ts-scenarios.pdf.

Moutinho, Laura. "Diferenças e desigualdades negociadas: Raça, sexualidade e gênero em produções acadêmicas recentes." *Cadernos Pagu* 42 (2009): 201–48.

Mujkić, Asim. "In Search of a Democratic Counter-Power in Bosnia-Herzegovina." *Southeast European and Black Sea Studies* 15, no. 4 (2015): 623–38.

Murakawa, Naomi. *The First Civil Right: How Liberals Built Prison America.* Oxford: Oxford University Press, 2014.

Nadasdy, Paul. "The Gift in the Animal: The Ontology of Hunting and Human-Animal Sociality." *American Ethnologist* 34, no. 1 (2007): 25–43.

Nading, Alex. *Mosquito Trails: Ecology, Health, and the Politics of Entanglement.* Durham, NC: Duke University Press, 2014.

National Research Council. "Abrupt Impacts of Climate Change: Anticipating Surprises." Washington, DC: National Academies Press, 2013. Accessed February 23, 2017. https://www.nap.edu/catalog/18373/abrupt-impacts-of-climate-change-anticipating-surprises.

———. *Committee on the Bering Sea Ecosystem, Polar Research Board.* Washington, DC: National Academies Press, 1996.

Navaro-Yashin, Yael. *The Make-Believe Space: Affective Geography in a Postwar Polity.* Durham, NC: Duke University Press, 2012.

Nelson, Diane M. *Reckoning: The Ends of War in Guatemala.* Durham, NC: Duke University Press, 2009.

———. *Who Counts? The Mathematics of Life and Death after Genocide.* Durham, NC: Duke University Press, 2015.

Neocleous, Elmos, dir. *Digging for a Future.* Nicosia, Cyprus: Mediabox, 2010. DVD.

Nettelfield, Lara, and Sarah Wagner. *Srebrenica in the Aftermath of Genocide.* Cambridge: Cambridge University Press, 2013.

Nguyen, Vinh-Kim. *The Republic of Therapy: Triage and Sovereignty in West Africa's Time of AIDS.* Durham, NC: Duke University Press, 2010.

Nietzsche, Friedrich. *Thus Spoke Zarathustra.* Translated by R. J. Hollingdale. Harmondsworth, UK: Penguin, 1961.

———. *Twilight of the Idols; Or, How to Philosophize with a Hammer.* Translated by Duncan Large. New York: Oxford University Press, 2009.

———. *The Use and Abuse of History.* Translated by Adrian Collins. New York: Macmillan, 1955.

———. *Will to Power.* Translated by R. Kevin Hill. New York: Penguin Classics, 2017.

Nixon, Rob. *Slow Violence and the Environmentalism of the Poor.* Cambridge, MA: Harvard University Press, 2013.

Nogueira, Oracy. *Tanto preto quanto branco: Estudos de relações raciais*. São Paulo: T. A. Queiroz, 1985.

Norgaard, Kari M. *Living in Denial: Climate Change, Emotions, and Everyday Life*. Cambridge, MA: MIT Press, 2011.

Norgaard, Kari M. "Living in Denial: Climate Change, Emotions and Everyday Life." Keynote lecture at Climate Change and Cinema, Earth 101, Reykjavik, Iceland, October 4, 2013.

Noys, Benjamin. *The Persistence of the Negative: A Critique of Contemporary Continental Thinking*. Edinburgh: Edinburgh University Press, 2010.

Nuccitelli, Dana. "A Glimpse at Our Possible Future Climate, Best to Worst Case Scenarios." *Skeptical Science*, February 13, 2013. Accessed February 28, 2017. http://www.skepticalscience.com/climate-best-to-worst-case-scenarios.html.

Oakes, Walter J. "Towards a Permanent War Economy?" *Politics* 1, no. 1 (1944): 11–17.

Oktem, Kerem. 2004. "Incorporating the Time and Space of the Ethnic 'Other': Nationalism and Space in Southeast Turkey in the Nineteenth and Twentieth Centuries." *Nations and Nationalisms* 10, no. 4 (2004): 559–78.

O'Neill, Kevin. *Secure the Soul: Christian Piety and Gang Prevention in Guatemala*. Berkeley: University of California Press, 2015.

Ong, Aihwa, and Stephen J. Collier, eds. *Global Assemblages: Technology, Politics, and Ethics as Anthropological Problems*. Malden, MA: Blackwell, 2005.

Orlowski, Jeff, dir. *Chasing Ice*. New York: New Video Group, 2013.

Ortner, Sherry. "Dark Anthropology and Its Others: Theory since the Eighties." *HAU* 6, no. 1 (2016): 47–73.

———. "Power and Projects: Reflections on Agency." In *Anthropology and Social Theory: Culture, Power, and the Acting Subject*, 129–53. Durham, NC: Duke University Press, 2006.

Osborne, Daniel L., Tal Simmons, and Stephen Nawrocki. "Reconsidering the Auricular Surface as an Indicator of Age at Death." *Journal of Forensic Sciences* 49, no. 5 (2004): 1–7.

Pacala, Steven, and Robert Socolow. "Stabilization Wedges: Solving the Climate Problem for the Next 50 Years with Current Technologies." *Science* 305, no. 5686 (2004): 968–72.

Pachirat, Timothy. *Every Twelve Seconds: Industrialized Slaughter and the Politics of Sight*. New Haven, CT: Yale University Press, 2011.

Pandey, Gyan. "Rallying Round the Cow: Sectarian Strife in the Bhojpuri Region, c. 1888–1917." In *Subaltern Studies*, edited by Ranajit Guha, 2:60–129. Oxford: Oxford University Press, 1983.

Pandian, Anand. *Reel World: An Anthropology of Creation*. Durham, NC: Duke University Press, 2015.

Pandolfi, Mariella. "Contract of Mutual (In)difference: Governance and the Humanitarian Apparatus in Contemporary Albania and Kosovo." *Indiana Journal of Global Legal Studies* 10, no. 1 (2003): 369–81.

Panourgiá, Neni. *Fragments of Death, Fables of Identity: An Athenian Anthropography*. Madison: University of Wisconsin Press, 1995.

Panter-Brick, Catherine. "Health, Risk, and Resilience: Interdisciplinary Concepts and Applications." *Annual Review of Anthropology* 43 (2014): 431–48.

Park, Alice. "Post Partum Depression and Miriam Carey: Stopping the Silent Scourge." *Time*, October 4, 2013. Accessed April 16, 2017. http://healthland.time.com/2013/10/04/post-partum-depression-and-miriam-carey-stopping-the-silent-scourge/.

Parunak, H. Van Dyke, T. C. Belding, and S. A. Brueckner. "Prediction Horizons in Agent Models." In *Engineering Environment-Mediated Multiagent Systems*, ed. D. Weyns, S. A. Brueckner, and Y. Demazeau. Lecture Notes in Computer Science, vol. 5049, 88–102. Berlin and Heidelberg, Germany: Springer, 2008. http://link.springer.com/chapter/10.1007%2F978-3-540-85029-8_7.

Pearson, Heath. "The Prickly Skin of White Supremacy: Race in the 'Real America.'" *Transforming Anthropology* 23, no. 1 (2015): 43–58.

Pearson, Michael, Lateef Mungin, and Deborah Feyerick. "Source: Mental Health Paperwork Found at Home of Miriam Carey after Capitol Chase." CNN *Politics*, October 4, 2013. Accessed April 16, 2017. http://www.cnn.com/2013/10/04/politics/u-s-capitol-shooting/.

Pederson, Morten Axel. *Not Quite Shamans: Spirit Worlds and Political Lives in Northern Mongolia*. Ithaca, NY: Cornell University Press, 2011.

Perasso, Jose. *Cronicas de cacerias humanas: La tragedia Ayorea*. Asunción, Paraguay: El Lector, 1987.

Petryna, Adriana. *Life Exposed: Biological Citizens after Chernobyl*. With a new introduction by the author. Princeton, NJ: Princeton University Press, 2013.

———. "The Origins of Extinction." *Limn*, no. 3 (2013): 50–53.

———. "What Is a Horizon? Navigating Thresholds in Climate Change Uncertainty." In *Modes of Uncertainty: Anthropological Cases*, edited by Paul Rabinow and Limor Samimian-Darash, 147–64. Chicago: University of Chicago Press, 2015.

———. *When Experiments Travel: Clinical Trials and the Global Search for Human Subjects*. Princeton, NJ: Princeton University Press, 2009.

Petryna, Adriana, Andrew Lakoff, and Arthur Kleinman, eds. *Global Pharmaceuticals: Markets, Practices, Ethics*. Durham, NC: Duke University Press, 2006.

Petryna, Adriana, and Paul Mitchell. "On the Nature of Catastrophic Forms." *BioSocieties* (2017). doi:10.1057/s41292-017-0038-3.

Pfeiffer, Mary Beth. 2007. *Crazy in America: The Hidden Tragedy of Our Criminalized Mentally Ill*. New York: Carroll and Graf, 2007.

Piault, Colette, and Paul Sant Cassia, dirs. *Dead or Presumed Missing?* Paris: Les Films du Quotidien, 2003. DVD.

Piketty, Thomas. *Capital in the Twenty-First Century*. Translated by Arthur Goldhammer. Cambridge, MA: Belknap Press of Harvard University Press, 2014.

Piot, Charles. *Nostalgia for the Future: West Africa after the Cold War*. Chicago: University of Chicago Press, 2010.

———. *Remotely Global: Village Modernity in West Africa*. Chicago: University of Chicago Press, 1999.

Poitras, Laura, dir. CITIZENFOUR. New York: Radius-TWC, 2014. DVD.

Pomeroy, John C., Joyce Sprafkin, and Kenneth D. Gadow. 1988. "Minor Physical Anomalies as a Biologic Marker for Behavior Disorders." *Journal of the American Academy of Child and Adolescent Psychiatry* 27, no. 4 (1988): 466–73.

Poniatowska, Elena. *La Noche de Tlatelolco: Testimonios de historia oral*. Mexico City: Ediciones Era, 1971.

Pope Francis. *Encyclical on Capitalism and Inequality: On Care for Our Common Home*. Edited by Sam Lavigne. London: Verso, 2015.

Povinelli, Elizabeth. *The Cunning of Recognition: Indigenous Alterities and the Making of Australian Multiculturalism*. Durham, NC: Duke University Press, 2002.

———. *Economies of Abandonment: Social Belonging and Endurance in Late Liberalism*. Durham, NC: Duke University Press, 2011.

———. *The Empire of Love: Toward a Theory of Intimacy, Genealogy, and Carnality*. Durham, NC: Duke University Press, 2006.

———. *Geontologies: A Requiem to Late Liberalism*. Durham, NC: Duke University Press, 2016.

———. "The Will to Be Otherwise/The Effort of Endurance." *South Atlantic Quarterly* 111, no. 3 (2012): 453–75.

Prentice, Rachel. *Bodies in Formation: An Ethnography of Anatomy and Surgery Education*. Durham, NC: Duke University Press, 2012.

Pupavac, Vanessa. "International Therapeutic Peace and Justice in Bosnia." *Social and Legal Studies* 13, no. 3 (2004): 377–401.

———. "Securing the Community? An Examination of International Psychosocial Intervention." In *International Intervention in the Balkans since 1995*, edited by Peter Siani-Davies, 158–71. New York: Routledge, 2003.

Purdy, Jedediah. *After Nature: A Politics for the Anthropocene*. Cambridge, MA: Harvard University Press, 2015.

Rabinow, Paul. *The Accompaniment: Assembling the Contemporary*. Chicago: University of Chicago Press, 2011.

———. *Anthropos Today: Reflections on Modern Equipment*. Princeton, NJ: Princeton University Press, 2003.

———. *Essays on the Anthropology of Reason*. Princeton, NJ: Princeton University Press, 1996.

———. *Making PCR: A Story of Biotechnology*. Chicago: University of Chicago Press, 1996.

———. *Marking Time: On the Anthropology of the Contemporary*. Princeton, NJ: Princeton University Press, 2008.

Rabinow, Paul, and Nikolas Rose. "Biopower Today." *Biosocieties* 1, no. 2 (2006): 195–217.

Raffles, Hugh. *Insectopedia*. New York: Pantheon, 2010.

Raikhel, Eugene, and William Garriott, eds. *Addiction Trajectories*. Durham, NC: Duke University Press, 2013.

Ralph, Laurence. *Renegade Dreams: Living through Injury in Gangland Chicago*. Chicago: University of Chicago Press, 2014.

Ramet, Sabrina P. *Balkan Babel: The Disintegration of Yugoslavia from the Death of Tito to the War for Kosovo*. 3rd ed. Boulder, CO: Westview, 1999.

Rancière, Jacques. *The Emancipated Spectator*. Translated by Gregory Elliott. Reprint edition. London: Verso, 2009.

———. *Moments Politiques: Interventions 1977–2009*. Translated by Mary Foster. New York: Seven Stories, 2014.

Rapp, Rayna. *Testing Women, Testing the Fetus: The Social Impact of Amniocentesis in America*. New York: Routledge, 2000.

Rasza, Maple. *Bastards of Utopia: Living Radical Politics after Socialism*. Bloomington: Indiana University Press, 2015.

Redfield, Peter. *Life in Crisis: The Ethical Journey of Doctors without Borders*. Berkeley: University of California Press, 2013.

Reguillo, Rossana. "The Narco-Machine and the Work of Violence: Notes Toward Its Decodification." *New York University: E-misférica* 8 no. 2 (2014). Accessed April 16, 2017. http://hemisphericinstitute.org/hemi/en/e-misferica-82/reguillo.

Renshaw, Layla. *Exhuming Loss: Memory, Materiality and Mass Graves of the Spanish Civil War*. Walnut Creek, CA: Left Coast, 2011.

Richard, Nelly. *The Insubordination of Signs: Political Change, Cultural Transformation, and Poetics of the Crisis*. Durham, NC: Duke University Press, 2004.

Rieff, Philip. *The Triumph of the Therapeutic: Uses of Faith after Freud*. With a new preface by the author. Chicago: University of Chicago Press, 1987.

Rimbaud, Arthur. *Complete Works*. Translated by Paul Schmidt. New York: Harper and Row, 1975.

Rios, Victor. *Punished: Policing the Lives of Black and Latino Boys*. New York: New York University Press, 2011.

Robbins, Joel. "Beyond the Suffering Subject: Toward an Anthropology of the Good." *Journal of the Royal Anthropological Institute* 19, no. 3 (2013): 447–62.

Roca Ortiz, Irene, ed. *Pigasipiedie iji yoquijoningai*. Santa Cruz de la Sierra, Bolivia: Apoyo al Campesino-indigena del Oriente Boliviano (APCOB), 2012.

Rockström, Johan, Will Steffen, Kevin Noone, Åsa Persson, F. Stuart Chapin III, Eric F. Lambin, Timothy M. Lenton, et al. "A Safe Operating Space for Humanity." *Nature* 461 (2009): 472–75.

Rogers, Crystal. *Mad Dogs and an Englishwoman: The Memoir of Crystal Rogers*. New Delhi: Penguin, 2000.

Roitman, Janet. *Anti-Crisis*. Durham, NC: Duke University Press, 2013.

Rorty, Richard. *Achieving Our Country: Leftist Thought in Twentieth-Century America*. Cambridge, MA: Harvard University Press, 1998.

Rouse, Carolyn. *Uncertain Suffering: Racial Health Care Disparities and Sickle Cell Disease*. Berkeley: University of California Press, 2009.

Rousseau, Jean-Jacques. *Discourse on the Origin of Inequality*. Translated by Donald A. Cress. Indianapolis: Hackett, 1992.

Roy, Parama. *Alimentary Tracts: Appetites, Aversions, and the Postcolonial*. Durham, NC: Duke University Press, 2010.

Sahlins, Marshall. *Ilhas de história*. Rio de Janeiro: Zahar, 1997.

———. *Islands of History*. Chicago: University of Chicago Press, 1987.

———. "Notes on the Original Affluent Society." In *Man the Hunter*, edited by Richard B. Lee and Irving DeVore, 85–89. New York: Aldine, 1968.

Said, Edward W. *Orientalism*. New York: Vintage, 1970.

Salgueiro, Heliana Angotti. Introduction to Michael Baxandall, *Padrões de intenção: A explicação histórica dos quadros*. Translated by Vera Maria Pereira, 9–24. São Paulo: Companhia das Letras, 2006.

Sanal, Aslihan. *New Organs within Us: Transplants and the Moral Economy*. Durham, NC: Duke University Press, 2011.

Sanford, Victoria. *Buried Secrets: Truth and Human Rights in Guatemala*. New York: Palgrave Macmillan, 2004.

Savić, Senka. "Diskursne osobine citulja." *Zbornik Matice Srpske za Filologiju i Lingvistiku* 41, no. 2 (1998): 141–52.

Schafer, Jessica. *Soldiers at Peace: Veterans and Society after the Civil War in Mozambique*. New York: Palgrave-Macmillan, 2007.

Scheffer, Marten, Steve Carpenter, Jonathan A. Foley, Carl Folke, and Brian Walker. "Catastrophic Shifts in Ecosystems." *Nature* 413 (2001): 591–96.

Scheper-Hughes, Nancy. *Death without Weeping: The Violence of Everyday Life in Brazil*. Berkeley: University of California Press, 1992.

———. "The Global Traffic in Organs." *Current Anthropology* 41, no. 2 (2000):191–224.

———. "Parts Unknown: Undercover Ethnography of the Organs-Trafficking Underworld." *Ethnography* 5, no. 1 (2004): 29–73.

Schielke, Samuli. "Being Good in Ramadan: Ambivalence, Fragmentation, and the Moral Self in the Lives of Young Egyptians." *Journal of the Royal Anthropological Institute* 15, no. 1 (2009): 24–40.

Schmitt, Carl. *The Nomos of the Earth in the International Law of the Jus Publicum Europeaeum*. Translated by G. L. Ulmen. New York: Telos, 2003.

Schultz, Dorothea. "(Re)Turning to Proper Muslim Practice: Islamic Moral Renewal and Women's Conflicting Assertions of Sunni Identity in Urban Mali." *Africa Today* 54, no. 4 (2008): 21–43.

Schwarcz, Lilia Moritz. *The Spectacle of the Races: Institutions, Scientists and Racial Theory in Brazil: 1870–1930*. New York: Farrar, Straus and Giroux, 1999.

———. "Varejar, ladrilhar: Uma cartografia ladrilhada da obra da artista." In Adriana Varejão, Silviano Santiago, Lilia Moritz Schwarcz, Karl Erik Schollhammer, Luis Camillo Osorio, Zalinda Cartaxo, *Entre Carnes e Mares*. Rio de Janeiro: Cobogó, 2012.

Schwarcz, Lilia Moritz, and Adriana Varejão. *Pérola imperfeita: A história e as histórias na obra de Adriana Varejão*. Rio de Janeiro: Cobogó, 2014.

Scott, Michael W. "To Be a Wonder: Anthropology, Cosmology, and Alterity." In *Framing Cosmologies: The Anthropology of Worlds*, edited by Allen Abramson and Marin Holbraad, 31–54. Manchester, UK: Manchester University Press, 2014.

Sebald, W. G. *On the Natural History of Destruction*. New York: Random House, 2004.

Sedgwick, Eve Kosofsky. *Touching Feeling: Affect, Pedagogy, Performativity*. Durham, NC: Duke University Press, 2003.

Segal, Judah B. *Edessa: The Blessed City*. Piscataway, NJ: Gorgias, 2001.

Segal, Lotte Buch. *No Place for Grief: Martyrs, Prisoners, and Mourning in Contemporary Palestine*. Philadelphia: University of Pennsylvania Press, 2016.
Seremetakis, C. Nadia. *The Last Word: Women, Death, and Divination in Inner Mani*. Chicago: University of Chicago Press, 1991.
Shakespeare, William. *Hamlet*. Edited by A. R. Braunmuller and Stephen Orgel. New York: Penguin Classics, 2016.
Shapiro, Nicholas. "Attuning to the Chemosphere: Domestic Formaldehyde, Bodily Reasoning, and the Chemical Sublime." *Cultural Anthropology* 30, no. 3 (2015): 368–93.
Sharp, Lesley. *The Transplant Imaginary: Mechanical Hearts, Animal Parts, and Moral Thinking in Highly Experimental Science*. Berkeley: University of California Press, 2013.
Sheikh, Fazal, and Eyal Weizman. *The Conflict Shoreline: Colonialism as Climate Change in the Negev Desert*. Göttingen, Germany: Steidl, 2015.
Sibertin-Blanc, Guillaume. *State and Politics: Deleuze and Guattari on Marx*. Translated by Amos Hodges. Los Angeles: Semiotext(e), 2016.
Silverstein, Brian. "Islamist Critique in Modern Turkey: Hermeneutics, Tradition, Genealogy." *Comparative Studies in Society and History* 47, no. 1 (2005): 134–60.
Simpson, Audra. *Mohawk Interruptus: Political Life across the Borders of Settler States*. Durham, NC: Duke University Press, 2014.
Singh, Bhrigupati. *Poverty and the Quest for Life: Spiritual and Material Striving in Rural India*. Chicago: University of Chicago Press, 2015.
Singh, Kushwant. 2003. *Truth, Love, and a Little Malice: An Autobiography*. New Delhi: Penguin, 2003.
Solomon, Christopher. "Emerging from the Shadow of War, Sarajevo Slowly Reclaims Its Lost Innocence." *New York Times*, February 5, 2006. Accessed April 16, 2017. http://www.nytimes.com/2006/02/05/travel/emerging-from-the-shadow-of-war-sarajevo-slowly-reclaims-its-lost.html.
Sorabji, Cornelia. "Bosnian Neighborhoods Revisited: Tolerance, Commitment, and Komšiluk in Sarajevo." In *On the Margins of Religion*, edited by Frances Pine and João de Pina-Cabral, 97–114. New York: Berghahn, 2008.
——— . "Managing Memories in Post-War Sarajevo: Individuals, Bad Memories, and New Wars. *Journal of the Royal Anthropological Institute* 12, no. 1 (2006): 1–18.
Spivak, Gayatri. "Can the Subaltern Speak?" In *Marxism and the Interpretation of Culture*, edited by Cary Nelson and Lawrence Grossberg, 271–313. Urbana: University of Illinois Press, 1988.
Stasch, Rupert. "The Poetics of Village Space When Villages Are New: Settlement Form as History Making in Papua, Indonesia." *American Ethnologist* 40, no. 3 (2013): 555–70.
Stevenson, Lisa. *Life Beside Itself: Imagining Care in the Canadian Arctic*. Berkeley: University of California Press, 2014.
Stewart, Kathleen. *Ordinary Affects*. Durham, NC: Duke University Press, 2007.
——— . "Precarity's Form." Paper presented at the Annual Meeting of the American Anthropological Association, November 25, 2011. Accessed April 5, 2017. https://supervalentthought.files.wordpress.com/2011/12/precarity-aaa-11.docx.

Štiks, Igor. "'New Left' in the Post-Yugoslav Space: Issues, Sites, and Forms." *Socialism and Democracy* 29, no. 3 (2015): 135–46.

Stoler, Ann L. *Along the Archival Grain: Epistemic Anxieties and Colonial Common Sense.* Princeton, NJ: Princeton University Press, 2009.

———. *Carnal Knowledge and Imperial Power: Race and the Intimate in Colonial Rule.* Berkeley: University of California Press, 2002.

———, ed. *Imperial Debris: On Ruins and Ruination.* Durham, NC: Duke University Press, 2013.

———. *Race and the Education of Desire: Foucault's History of Sexuality and the Colonial Order of Things.* Durham, NC: Duke University Press, 1995.

Strathern, Marilyn. "Negative Strategies." In *Localizing Strategies: Regional Traditions of Ethnographic Writing*, edited by Richard Fardon, 204–16. Edinburgh: Scottish Academic Press, 1990.

———. *O gênero da dádiva.* Campinas: Ed. da Unicamp, 2006.

Sullivan, Winnifred Fallers, Elizabeth Shakman Hurd, Saba Mahmood, and Peter G. Danchin, eds. *Politics of Religious Freedom.* Chicago: University of Chicago Press, 2015.

Summerfield, Derek. "A Critique of Seven Assumptions behind Psychological Trauma Programmes in War-Affected Areas." *Social Science and Medicine* 48, no. 10 (1999): 1449–62.

Swanson, Carl. "What Happened to 'James Hunter Black Draftee'? A Mystery at the Met Breuer." *Vulture: Devouring Culture*, March 8, 2016. Accessed June 24, 2017. http://www.vulture.com/2016/03/are-you-the-guy-in-this-famous-met-painting.html.

Swanson, Frederick J., and Richard E. Sparks. 1990. "Long-Term Ecological Research and the Invisible Place." *BioScience* 40, no. 7 (1990): 502–8.

Taibo, Paco Ignacio. *'68.* Translated by Donald Nicholson-Smith. New York: Seven Stories, 2004.

Tambar, Kabir. *The Reckoning of Pluralism: Political Belonging and the Demands of History in Turkey.* Redwood City, CA: Stanford University Press, 2014.

Tanpınar, Fevzi, dir. *Kayıp Otobüs.* 2007. DVD.

Tarlo, Emma. *Unsettling Memories: Narratives of Emergency in Delhi.* Berkeley: University of California Press, 2003.

Taussig, Michael. *Defacement: Public Secrecy and the Labor of the Negative.* Redwood City, CA: Stanford University Press, 1999.

———. *Mimesis and Alterity: A Particular History of the Senses.* New York: Routledge, 1993.

———. *Shamanism, Colonialism and the Wild Man.* Chicago: University of Chicago Press, 1987.

Taylor, Keeanga-Yamahtta. *From #BlackLivesMatter to Black Liberation.* Chicago: Haymarket, 2016.

Telles, Edward. *Pigmentocracies: Ethnicity, Race, and Color in Latin America.* Princeton, NJ: Princeton University Press, 2014.

Thom, René. "At the Boundaries of Man's Power: Play." *Substance* 8, no. 4 (1979): 11–19.

——— . "Itinerary for a Science of the Detail." *Criticism* 32, no. 3 (1990): 371–90.

——— . *Structural Stability and Morphogenesis: An Outline of a General Theory of Models*. Reading, MA: Benjamin, 1975.

Thomas, Deborah. *Exceptional Violence: Embodied Citizenship in Transnational Jamaica*. Durham, NC: Duke University Press, 2011.

——— . *Nationalism, Globalization, and the Politics of Culture in Jamaica*. Durham, NC: Duke University Press, 2004.

Thomas, Martyn. *The Artificial Horizon: Reading a Colonised Landscape*. Melbourne, Australia: Melbourne University Publishing, 2010.

Thompson, Peter, and Slavoj Žižek, eds. *The Privatization of Hope: Ernst Bloch and the Future of Utopia*. Durham, NC: Duke University Press, 2013.

Ticktin, Miriam. *Casualties of Care: Immigration and the Politics of Humanitarianism in France*. Berkeley: University of California Press, 2011.

——— . "Human Rights/Humanitarianism beyond the Human." Paper presented at the Annual Meeting of the American Anthropological Association, San Francisco, November 16, 2012.

Ticktin, Miriam, and Ilana Felman, eds. *In the Name of Humanity: The Government of Threat and Care*. Durham, NC: Duke University Press, 2010.

Trimikliniotis, Nicos, and Umut Bozkurt. "Introduction: Beyond a Divided Cyprus, a Society in a State of Transformation." In *Beyond a Divided Cyprus: A State and Society in Transformation*, edited by Nicos Trimikliniotis and Umut Bozkurt, 1–21. New York: Palgrave Macmillan, 2012.

Trouillot, Michel-Rolph. *Global Transformations: Anthropology and the Modern World*. New York: Palgrave Macmillan, 2004.

——— . *Silencing the Past: Power and the Production of History*. Boston: Beacon, 1997.

Tsiarta, Anna, dir. *In This Waiting*. Nicosia, Cyprus: Roads and Oranges Film Productions, 2011. DVD.

Tsing, Anna L. *Friction: An Ethnography of Global Connection*. Princeton, NJ: Princeton University Press, 2005.

——— . *The Mushroom at the End of the World: On the Possibility of Life in Capitalist Ruins*. Princeton, NJ: Princeton University Press, 2015.

Tuğal, Cihan. *Passive Revolution: Absorbing the Islamic Challenge to Capitalism*. Redwood City, CA: Stanford University Press, 2009.

——— . "The Urban Dynamism of Islamic Hegemony: Absorbing Squatter Creativity in Istanbul." *Comparative Studies of South Asia, Africa, and the Middle East* 29, no. 3 (2009): 423–37.

Turkle, Sherry. 2015. *Reclaiming Conversation: The Power of Talk in a Digital Age*. New York: Penguin, 2015.

Turner, Terence. "The Crisis of Late Structuralism: Perspectivism and Animism; Rethinking Culture, Nature, Spirit and Bodiliness." *Tipiti* 7, no. 1 (2009): 3–42.

Ubelaker, D. H. "Cranial Photographic Superimposition." In *Forensic Sciences*, edited by C. H. Wecht, 3–38. New York: Matthew Bender, 2002.

Uludağ, Sevgül. *Oysters with the Missing Pearls: Untold Stories about Missing Persons, Mass Graves and Memories from the Past of Cyprus*. Nicosia, Cyprus: IKME Sociopolitical Studies Institute, 2006.

Üngör, Uğur Ümit. *The Making of Modern Turkey: Nation and State in Eastern Anatolia, 1913–1950*. Oxford: Oxford University Press, 2011.

United Nations Development Program. *Social Inclusion in Bosnia and Herzegovina: National Human Development Report 2007*. Accessed April 16, 2017. http://hdr.undp.org/sites/default/files/bosnia_and_hercegovina_2007_en.pdf.

Valle Silva, Nelson do. "Aspectos demográficos dos grupos raciais." *Estudos Afro-Asiáticos* 23 (1992): 7–15.

———. "Black-White Income Differentials: Brazil, 1960." PhD diss., University of Michigan, 1980.

———. "Uma nota sobre raça social no Brasil." *Estudos Afro-Asiáticos* 26 (1994): 67–80.

Van Bruinessen, Martin. *Agha, Shaikh, and State: The Social and Political Structures of Kurdistan*. London: Zed, 1992.

Vargas, João. "Black Radical Becoming: The Politics of Identification in Permanent Transformation." *Critical Sociology* 32, nos. 2–3 (2006): 475–500.

Verma, Vandi, John Langford, and Reid Simmons. "Non-Parametric Fault Identification for Space Rovers." *International Symposium on Artificial Intelligence and Robotics in Space (iSAIRAS)*, June 2001. Accessed April 16, 2017. http://citeseerx.ist.psu.edu/viewdoc/download;jsessionid=591E373199815301CC651AEC2DC299F0?doi=10.1.1.21.3513&rep=rep1&type=pdf.

Vidal, Gore. *Perpetual War for Perpetual Peace: How We Got to Be So Hated*. New York: Thunder Mouth Press/Nation Books, 2002.

Viveiros de Castro, Eduardo. *A inconstância da alma selvagem*. São Paulo: Cosac and Naif, 2002.

———. "Cosmological Deixis and Amerindian Perspectivism." *Journal of the Royal Anthropological Institute* 4, no. 3 (1998): 469–88.

———. "Introduction: The Untimely, Again." In Pierre Clastres, *Archeology of Violence*, 9–52. Los Angeles: Semiotext(e), 2010.

———. *Métaphysiques cannibales*. Translated by Oiara Bonilla. Paris: Presses Universitaires de France, 2009.

———. "Perspectival Anthropology and the Method of Controlled Equivocation." *Tipiti* 2, no. 1 (2004): 3–22.

Volćić, Zala. "Yugo-Nostalgia: Cultural Memory and Media in the Former Yugoslavia." *Critical Studies in Media Communication* 24, no. 1 (2007): 21–38.

Wagner, Sarah. *To Know Where He Lies: DNA Technology and the Search for Srebrenica's Missing*. Berkeley: University of California Press, 2008.

Walley, Christine. *Exit Zero: Family and Class in Postindustrial Chicago*. Chicago: University of Chicago Press, 2013.

Walton, Jeremy. "Practices of Neo-Ottomanism: Making Space and Place Virtuous in Istanbul." In *Orienting Istanbul: Cultural Capital of Europe?*, edited by Deniz Göktürk, Levent Soysal, and Ipek Türeli, 88–103. Abingdon, UK: Taylor and Francis, 2010.

West, Paige. *From Modern Coffee Production to Imagined Primitive: The Social World of Coffee from Papua New Guinea*. Durham, NC: Duke University Press, 2012.

Whitehead, Gregory. "The Forensic Theatre: Memory Plays for the Post-Mortem Condition." *Performing Arts Journal* 12, nos. 2–3 (1990): 99–109.

Whyte, Susan Reynolds, ed. *Second Chances: Surviving AIDS in Uganda*. Durham, NC: Duke University Press, 2014.

Williams, A. Park, Craig D. Allen, Constance I. Millar, Thomas W. Swetnam, Joel Michaelsen, Christopher J. Still, and Steven W. Leavitt. "Forest Responses to Increasing Aridity and Warmth in the Southwestern United States." *Proceedings of the National Academy of Sciences* 107, no. 50 (2010): 21289–94.

Williams, Dillwyn, and Keith Baverstock. "Chernobyl and the Future: Too Soon for a Final Diagnosis." *Nature* 440 (2006): 993–94.

Winslow, Deborah. "Living Life Forward: Technology, Time, and Society in a Sri Lankan Potter Community." *Economic Anthropology* 3, no. 2 (2016): 216–27.

Winter, Jay, and Emmanuel Sivan, eds. *War and Remembrance in the Twentieth Century*. Cambridge: Cambridge University Press, 1999.

Wolf, Eric. *Europe and the People without History*. Berkeley: University of California Press, 1982.

World Health Organization. *Mental Health Atlas 2011*. Geneva: World Health Organization Department of Mental Health and Substance Abuse, 2011.

Yang, Anand. "Sacred Symbol and Sacred Space in Rural India: Community Mobilization in the 'Anti-Cow Killing' Riot of 1893." *Comparative Studies in Society and History* 22, no. 4 (1980): 576–96.

Young, Allan. *The Harmony of Illusions: Inventing Post-Traumatic Stress Disorder*. Princeton, NJ: Princeton University Press, 1995.

Zagorski, Nick. "Profile of Stephen R. Carpenter." *Proceedings of the National Academy of Sciences* 102, no. 29 (2005): 9999–10001.

Zaim, Derviş, and Panikos Chrysanthou, dirs. *Parallel Trips*. 2004. DVD.

Zamudio, Carlos. *Las redes del narcomenudeo*. Mexico City: CEAPAC Ediciones, 2012.

Zeman, Adam Z. J., Sergio Della Sala, Lorna A. Torrens, Viktoria-Eleni Gountouna, David J. McGonigle, and Robert H. Logie. "Loss of Imagery Phenomenology with Intact Visuo-Spatial Task Performance: A Case of 'Blind Imagination.'" *Neuropsychologia* 48 (2010): 145–55.

Žižek, Slavoj. "Anger in Bosnia, but This Time People Can Read Their Leaders' Ethnic Lies." *Guardian*, February 10, 2014.

Zweig, Stefan. *Brazil: Land of the Future*. New York: Viking, 1943.

Contributors

LUCAS BESSIRE is Associate Professor of Anthropology at the University of Oklahoma. He is the author of the award-winning book *Behold the Black Caiman: A Chronicle of Ayoreo Life* (2014), director of the films *Asking Ayahai: An Ayoreo Story* and *From Honey to Ashes*, and creator of the Ayoreo Video Project. He is currently working on a literary echnography of ground water and responsibility on the High Plains.

JOÃO BIEHL is Susan Dod Brown Professor of Anthropology and Woodrow Wilson School Faculty Associate at Princeton University. He is the codirector of Princeton's Global Health Program. Biehl is the author of the award-winning books *Vita: Life in a Zone of Social Abandonment* (2005, updated 2013) and *Will to Live: AIDS Therapies and the Politics of Survival* (2007). He coedited the books *When People Come First: Critical Studies in Global Health* (with Adriana Petryna, 2013) and *Subjectivity: Ethnographic Investigations* (with Byron Good and Arthur Kleinman, 2007). Biehl is also the coeditor of the book series Critical Global Health (with Vincanne Adams) at Duke University Press.

NAISARGI N. DAVE is Associate Professor of Anthropology at the University of Toronto. Her award-winning book, *Queer Activism in India: A Story in the Anthropology of Ethics* (Duke University Press, 2012) explores the relationship among queer politics, activism, and affect. Her second book, *The Social Skin: Humans and Animals in India*, engages critically with humanism and the privileging of reason to consider myriad facets of working with and for urban and working animals in India.

ELIZABETH A. DAVIS is Associate Professor of Anthropology at Princeton University, in association with the Program in Hellenic Studies. Her award-winning book, *Bad Souls: Madness and Responsibility in Modern Greece* (Duke University Press, 2012), explores humanitarian psychiatric reform in the borderland between Greece and Turkey. She is currently writing a new book addressing knowledge production about the violent conflicts of the 1960s–1970s in Cyprus, in the domains of forensic science, documentary film, and "conspiracy theory."

ANGELA GARCIA is Associate Professor of Anthropology at Stanford University. She is the author of the award-winning *The Pastoral Clinic: Addiction and Dispossession along the Rio Grande* (2010), an ethnographic study of intergenerational heroin use, historical loss, and the ethics of care in northern New Mexico. Garcia is currently engaged in ethnographic research on the intersection of criminal and therapeutic violence within coercive treatment centers for drug addiction in Mexico City.

PETER LOCKE is Assistant Professor of Instruction in Global Health Studies and Anthropology at Northwestern University. Locke has conducted fieldwork in Bosnia-Herzegovina, where he explored psychosocial support services for poor families living in postwar Sarajevo, and in Sierra Leone, where he studied medical humanitarian interventions in collaboration with a small community healthcare organization. He established and directs Northwestern's summer academic program on comparative public health and postconflict studies in the former Yugoslavia, based in Belgrade and Sarajevo. His work has appeared in the book *Medical Humanitarianism: Ethnographies of Practice* (2015) and in the journals *Current Anthropology* and *Intergraph: Journal of Dialogic Anthropology*.

MICHAEL M. J. FISCHER is Andrew W. Mellon Professor in the Humanities and Professor of Anthropology and Science and Technology Studies at MIT, and a lecturer in the Department of Global Health and Social Medicine at Harvard Medical School. His books include *Anthropological Futures* (2009), the award-winning *Emergent Forms of Life and the Anthropological Voice* (2003), *Anthropology as Cultural Critique* (with George E. Marcus, 1986, 1999), *Mute Dreams, Blind Owls, and Dispersed Knowledges* (2004), *Debating Muslims: Cultural Dialogues in Postmodernity and Tradition* (with Mehdi Abedi, 1990), and *Iran: From Religious Dispute to Revolution* (1999). He is the editor (with Byron Good, Sarah Willen, and Mary-Jo DelVecchio Good) of *A Medical Anthropology Reader: Theoretical Trajectories and Emergent Realities* (2010). Fischer is the coeditor of the book series Experimental Futures (with Joseph Dumit) at Duke University Press.

ADRIANA PETRYNA is the Edmund J. and Louise W. Kahn Term Professor in Anthropology at the University of Pennsylvania. She is the author of the award-winning books *Life Exposed: Biological Citizens after Chernobyl* (2002, updated 2013) and *When Experiments Travel: Clinical Trials and the Global Search for Human Subjects* (2009). She coedited *Global Pharmaceuticals: Ethics, Markets, Practices* (with Andrew Lakoff and Arthur Kleinman, Duke University Press, 2007) and *When People Come First: Critical Studies in Global Health* (with João Biehl, 2013).

BRIDGET PURCELL is Visiting Assistant Professor in the Department of Anthropology at Rutgers University. Her research interests include Islam, urban anthropology, and the ethical and experiential dimensions of state power. She is currently at work on her first book manuscript, titled "The City That Hides Itself: Turkish Geographies of the Otherwise," based on ethnographic research in a Turko-Syrian border city. Her work has appeared in the journal *City & Society*.

LAURENCE RALPH is Professor of African and African American Studies and Anthropology at Harvard University. He is the author of the award-winning book *Renegade Dreams: Living through Injury in Gangland Chicago* (2014), and he has published articles in *Anthropological Theory, Disability Studies Quarterly, Transition,* and *Identities: Global Studies in Culture and Power*. As an Andrew Carnegie Fellow, he is currently studying policing, gun violence, and public mobilization in Chicago.

LILIA M. SCHWARCZ is Professor of Anthropology at the University of São Paulo and a Visiting Professor at Princeton University. The author of numerous award-winning books in Portuguese, her books in English include *Spectacle of Races: Scientists, Institutions and Racial Theories in Brazil at the End of the XIXth Century* (1999) and *The Emperor's Beard: D. Pedro II, a Tropical King* (2004). Her recent books in Portuguese include *Brasil: Uma Biografia* (2015), *Pérola Imperfeita: A História e as Histórias de Adriana Varejão* (2014), *Histórias Mestiças* (2016) and *Lima Barreto: Triste visionário* (2017).

List of Illustrations

PLATE 0.1 Alice Neel (American, 1900–1984), *James Hunter Black Draftee*, 1965. Oil on canvas. 60 × 40 in. (152.4 × 101.6 cm). COMMA Foundation, Belgium. © The Estate of Alice Neel.

FIGURE 9.1 RCP Scenario Atmospheric CO_2 Concentrations, in Dana Nuccitelli, "A Glimpse at Our Possible Future Climate, Best to Worst Case Scenarios," *SkepticalScience*, February 13, 2013. Accessed February 23, 2017. http://skepticalscience.com/climate-best-to-worst-case-scenarios.html.

FIGURES 9.2, 9.3, AND 9.4 Stills from Jeff Orlowski's *Chasing Ice*, showing retreating ice at Columbia Glacier, Alaska.

FIGURE 9.5 Regime shift curve, from Marten Scheffer, Steve Carpenter, Jonathan A. Foley, et al., "Catastrophic Shifts in Ecosystems." *Nature* 413 (October 11, 2001): 591–96. doi: 10.1038/35098000.

FIGURE 11.1 Catarina's tombstone, Novo Hamburgo, 2011. Photo by Torben Eskerod.

FIGURE 11.2 The sisters on Facebook, 2015.

FIGURE 11.3 Andrea's photograph of the ethnographic memorial, 2015.

FIGURE 11.4 Adriana, Adriano, and Andrea, 2016. Photo by João Biehl.

PLATE 1 Adriana Varejão, *Varal* [Rack], 1993. Oil on canvas. Photo by Eduardo Ortega, Acervo Atelier Adriana Varejão.

PLATE 2 Adriana Varejão, *Parede com incisões à la Fontana* [Wall with incisions à la Fontana], 2000. Oil on canvas and polyurethane on aluminum and wood support. Photo by Eduardo Ortega, Acervo Atelier Adriana Varejão.

PLATE 3 Adriana Varejão, *O sedutor* [The seducer], 2004. Oil on canvas. Photo by Eduardo Ortega, Acervo Atelier Adriana Varejão.

PLATE 4 Adriana Varejão, *Proposta para uma catequese — Parte I (díptico): Morte e esquartejamento* [Proposal for a catechesis — Part I diptych: Death and dismemberment], 1993. Oil on canvas. Photo by Eduardo Ortega, Acervo Atelier Adriana Varejão.

PLATE 5 Adriana Varejão, *Proposta para uma catequese—Parte II (díptico): Aparição e relíquias* [Proposal for a catechesis—Part II diptych: Apparition and relics], 1993. Oil on canvas. Photo by Eduardo Ortega, Acervo Atelier Adriana Varejão.

PLATES 6–11 Adriana Varejão, details from *Testemunhas Oculares X, Y e Z* [Eyewitnesses x, y and z], 1997. Oil on canvas, porcelain, photography, silver, glass, and iron. Photo by Eduardo Ortega, Acervo Atelier Adriana Varejão.

PLATE 12 Adriana Varejão, *Prato com mariscos* [Plate with clams], 2011. Oil on fiberglass and resin. Photo by Vicente de Mello, Acervo Atelier Adriana Varejão.

PLATE 13 Adriana Varejão, *Mãe d'Água* [Water deity], 2009. Oil on fiberglass and resin. Photo by Jaime Acioli, Acervo Atelier Adriana Varejão.

PLATE 14 Adriana Varejão, *Tintas Polvo* [Octopus ink], 2013. Mixed media. Photo by Vicente de Mello, Acervo Atelier Adriana Varejão.

PLATE 15 Adriana Varejão, *Polvo Portraits I* [Seascape series], 2014. Oil on canvas. Photo by Jaime Acioli, Acervo Atelier Adriana Varejão.

PLATE 16 Adriana Varejão, *Em segredo* [Secretly], 2003. Oil on canvas and sculpture in resin. Photo by Vicente de Mello, Acervo Atelier Adriana Varejão.

PLATE 17 Adriana Varejão, *Cadernos de viagem: Yãkoana* [Travel log: Yãkoana], 2003. Oil on linen. Photo by Patrick Gries, Acervo Atelier Adriana Varejão.

PLATE 18 Adriana Varejão, *Éden* [Eden], 1992. Oil on wood. Photo by Vicente de Mello, Acervo Atelier Adriana Varejão.

PLATE 19 Adriana Varejão, *Mapa de Lopo Homem II* [Map of Lopo Homem II], 1992–2004. Oil on wood with suture thread. Photo by Jaime Acioli, Acervo Atelier Adriana Varejão.

Index

Page references followed by *f* indicate an illustrated figure or photograph.

Aasi (Ayoreo people), 201–2, 203
abandoned: Biehl on pedagogical role in rehabilitation by the, 285; Brazil's new rule of law making citizens out of, 285–86
abandonment: Brazil's institutionalized zones of, 52–53; Catarina's daughter Ana (Andrea de Lima) reconnecting after, 1, 279, 281–84; Catarina's narration on her story of, 1, 10, 17, 30, 41, 44–45, 46, 51–55, 58–65. *See also* family bonds
Abécédaire interviews (Deleuze), 273
Abodh (Welfare for Stray Dogs director) [India], 156
Abraham (Old Testament), 133
Abrams-Meyers, Claire, 162–63, 304
Abrams-Meyers, Erika, 162, 163–64, 166, 304, 305–6
Abrams-Meyers, Jim, 162, 304
accompaniers on lifelines, 295, 314n6
accountability and "response-ability," 28
Adam and Eve story, 281
addiction centers. See *anexos* residential centers (Mexico)
adornment of dead, 229
Adorno, Theodor, 12
Adriana (Catarina's daughter), 289*f*, 289–91
Adriano (Catarina's son), 284–85, 289–91, 295
affective-material shifts, 297–98
African Americans: #BlackLivesMatter as response to devalued black lives of, 22, 98–99, 273, 298; Butler's theory of grief to understand systematic dehumanization of, 12, 28, 95, 122; "I Am a Man" radical becoming in Memphis (1968), 165. *See also* Eastwood neighborhood (Chicago)

Agamben, Giorgio, 152, 158
Ahmed, Sara, 158
"Air War and Literature" (Sebald), 261
Akineton (biperiden), 1, 45
Alice in Wonderland (character), 135, 148
Altamir (Catarina's brother), 54, 61
Ana. *See* Lima, Andrea de (Catarina's daughter)
Anatolia (Turkey): dispute over Armenian genocide history of, 233–35; Smyrna (now Izmir) burning [1923] in, 233–34, 235
Anchieta, José de, 304
Anders, William, 311
Andrade, Oswald de, 174, 194
anexos residential centers (Mexico): Bar Heavens mass kidnapping (2013) and increased residents in, 123–24; coercive nature of addiction treatment at, 118; description of the widespread, 118–19; folding together violence and religion, 25, 121–22, 126; forced testimonies central to therapeutic programs of, 119, 121–22, 129n35; kidnappings engaged in by, 124–27; utopia suggested as potential reality by, 127; zen exercise on living with, 295, 299–300. *See also* Grupo Centro (Mexico City)
Animal Birth Control program (India), 155
animals: animal activism political engagement between humans and, 152–53; cow protection (*gauseva*) in India, 153–54; Derrida on human action on behalf of, 167n8; epigenetic field's understanding of evolution of, 14; Friendicoes animal shelter (India) for, 155; Idgah slaughterhouse (New Delhi) violence against, 159–60; the Levinasian, 157–58; multispecies ethnography on the human, material, and,

animals (continued)
    14–16; Nadasdy on gift of itself to hunter by, 169n52; witnessing as an intimate event followed by becoming an, 160–64; witnessing the violence against, 156–64. *See also* Indian animal activism
Anthropocene epoch, 13–14, 259
anthropology: bastardized indigenous subject often erased by philosophically oriented, 200; conditions leading to incompleteness of understanding in, 7–8; and critical theory, 11–13; Deleuze's exchanges between philosophy and, 7–10, 17, 47; humanism as the foundation of, 16–17; impact on becomings by concepts and theories of, 30–31; Marcus's assessment of intellectual health of, 48–49; as science of the Other, 193; subjectivities as *terrae incognitae* for inquiry of, 57
anthropology of becoming: on categories important to human experience, 43–44; commitment to ethnographic empiricism by, 7, 47–51; crafting stories from instances of, 29–33; ethnographic reclaiming it from philosophical uses, 212–13, 214n30; ethnographic sensorium of moments and stories of, 1–3; examining the Eastwood neighborhood experience as, 96, 109n7; experiences of time, space, and desire dimension of, 6; how anthropological concepts have impacted, 30–31; illuminating crossroads of assemblage, 79–80; informed by Deleuze's work, 7–10, 14, 42, 62, 148, 199, 213, 240n11; moving from judgment to constructive questions on, 32–33; plasticity dimension of, 3–6, 22–23; power of art invoking human potential by, 84; revelations from disseminating evidence with other disciplines, 81–84; the unknown dimension of, 6–7. *See also* becomings; zen exercises
anthropology of disability: Chicago's Eastwood neighborhood study, 29, 94–107, 109n5, 298–99; how digital technologies impact the, 24; humanitarian psychiatry and psychologization of postwar BiH study, 45–47, 65–81, 295–97; Mexican *anexos* residential treatment centers study, 25, 118–27, 129n35, 299–300. *See also* medicalization; psychiatric rationality; Vita (Brazil)
anthropology of Islam: individuals orienting themselves in shifting ritual landscape, 135–36; limited literature on shifting ritual landscape in, 134–35; Turkish "orthodoxization" of local religiosity, 137–38. *See also* Islam
anthropophagy (symbolic consumption), 175, 194
Anti-Oedipus (Deleuze and Guattari), 301, 302
Apollo 8 (1968), 311
Apollo 17 "blue marble" Earth photograph (1972), 258
Appadurai, Arjun, 16
Apocrypha, 281
"Aquarela do Brasil" (Watercolor of Brazil), 190
Arab Spring, 22, 273
archaeological excavations: becoming human through Cyprus's forensic, 220, 226–31; public criticism of CMP's, 225–26; revealing time machines of moment of a death, 219–20; understanding how they destroy culture, 224–25. *See also* history
Archaeological Museum (Nicosia, Cyprus), 224
Argentina: Argentine Forensic Anthropology Team of, 221; Mothers of the Plaza de Mayo in, 222
Armenian genocide: legal and historic dispute over the, 234–35; Smyrna (now Izmir) burning [1923], 233–34, 235
Armstrong, Bill, 247, 248, 312
Arrhenius, Svante, 263, 313
Arsenijević, Damir, 232, 235, 238–39, 270, 271, 272
art: as both object of knowledge and material object, 178–82; cannibalization and colonization in, 2, 174–75, 182–94, 303; cultural context lending meaning of, 179; customs, values, and symbols impacted by material objects and, 16; *ekphrasis* (images in words), 192; exploring multiple meanings of, 16, 174–78; learning from Adriana Varejão about, 16, 173–78; reconciling writing and, 178; social life and relations framing, 179–80; as system of action, 180. *See also* images
"Art as a Cultural System" (Geertz), 179
artistic objects: customs, values, and symbols impacting, 16; Gell on the nature of, 180–81; "inferential criticism" of, 181–82; as object of knowledge, 178–79
Asai (Ayoreo people), 3
assemblages: anthropology of becomings as illuminating crossroads of, 79–80; Bosnia-

Herzegovina as an, 79; as concretization of power, desire, of territoriality, 55–56; expressions of the collective, 80
Athens (403 BCE): comparing modern Cyprus reconciliation and amnesty of, 236–37, 307; Thirty Tyrants amnesty granted by, 236
ayipie (soul matter), 202
Ayoreo Cojñone-Gari aftermath: Aasi's story on living through the, 201–2, 203; drunkenness and substance abuse increase during, 210–11; evangelical missionary project and ethnocide after, 204–8; reclaiming capacity of becoming in, 201; of the 2004 contact with Ayoreo people, 197–98, 201–3; *urusoi* (madness) experience after the, 208–10
Ayoreo negative becoming: affirmative negation beginnings of, 201–3; anthropologic of becoming study of the, 3, 11; bastard delirium of colonial subjection and, 201–8, 211; dehumanization of, 211–13; examining the process of, 201–13; missionary ethnocide role in, 204–8, 302; reclaiming capacity through affirmative rupture with past, 203–4
Ayoreo people (Paraguay): Aasi of the, 201–2, 203; cannibalizing and indie-gestion zen exercise, 295, 301–3; conflict between outside world-ordering projects and those of the, 200–201; Cutai of the, 197; evangelical missionary project and ethnocide of, 204–8; examining process of negative becoming experienced by, 201–13; land rush over former habitation of the, 206–8, 301, 303; living in postcolonial and neocolonial violence, 26, 31; Original Time myths of the Ancestory Beings of, 202–3, 302; Pejei of the, 3, 208–9; recognizing them as "shadows of men," 206; rejection of former ways of life by postcontact, 17; Rosy of the, 210–11; susceptible to *urusoi* (madness), 208–9; Tié of the, 197, 198–99, 200; Totobiegosode-Ayoreo 1986 contact, 205–6; transforming themselves into *Ichadie* (New People), 198, 202, 302; the 2004 Cojñone-Gari (That Which Belongs to the Strangers) contact with, 197–98, 201–3; *viciosos* (Puyedie, or Prohibited Ones) with vices among, 210–11. *See also* indigenous populations; Paraguay
Ayotzinapa Normal School students' disappearance (Mexico, 2014), 111, 115, 127n1

Bachelard, Gaston, 54
Baer, Alejandro, 222
balance of nature theory: equilibria association with, 252–56; reliance on "extensity," 254
Balikligöl ritual center (Urfa, Turkey): Kadir Gecesi (Night of Power) celebrated in, 133, 140–41; poetic density of overlapping ritual space of, 138–41; politics of purification practiced in, 141–43, 149n28; restoration (late 1990s) of, 133–34, 137, 142–43; zen elementary exercise on becoming of, 308. *See also* Urfa ritual space
Balog, James, 248, 312
Bar Daisan, 140
Bar Heavens mass kidnapping (Mexico City, 2013), 123–24, 125, 126, 127
Barroso, Ary, 190
Barton Fink (Connolly), 220
bastard delirium: of Ayoreo's colonial subjection, 201–8, 211; Deleuze on becoming through experience of, 199–200; Tié as indigenous subject experiencing, 200
Bataille, Georges, 31, 207–8, 212
Bateson, Gregory, 13
Baxandall, Michael, 178, 181, 182, 192
Bay of Funday mariners (Canada), 260–61
becomings: bastard delirium as opening us up to, 199–200; of the colonized subject, 12–13; driven by unfinished processes of, 114–15; enlarging our sense of what is possible, 84; ethnographic work on dynamism of everyday, 43–44; geographies of, 55–57; "I Am a Man" radical becoming (Memphis, 1968), 165; informed by Deleuze's work, 7–10, 14, 42, 62, 148, 199, 213, 240n11; letting go of assumptions on human condition to study, 9–10; moving from judgment to constructive questions on, 32–33; negative, 201–13; self turned into a question-machine through, 17, 164; as style of noticing dynamics of power and flight in social world, 10; understanding the nuances of the struggles of, 17–18; zen exercises on catching moments of, 293, 295–314. *See also* anthropology of becoming; zen exercises
bedua (curse), 145–46
Behrouzan, Orkideh, 297
Being Malay in Indonesia (Long), 307
Beldi de Alcantara, Maria de, 302
Benites, Toni, 302

INDEX | 361

Benjamin, Walter, 12, 297, 306
Bennett, Jane, 16, 219, 239, 272
Berlant, Lauren, 20, 22, 283
Bessire, Lucas, 17, 31, 197, 301, 302
Beverly, Mrs. (Eastwood resident), 104, 106
Bhabha, Homi, 177
Biehl, João, 1, 21, 30, 41, 44, 51–55, 65, 83, 294, 314
Big Bang agreement (1983), 302
big data: challenge of understanding societal changes using, 26–28; Snowden's revelations on dark side of, 23–24
biological processes: epigenetic field's understanding of evolution and, 14; multispecies ethnography on human and animal, 14–16
biopower concept, 55
Biosocial Becomings (Ingold and Palsson), 14
biperiden (Akineton), 1, 45
Black Chicago. *See* Eastwood neighborhood (Chicago)
#BlackLivesMatter, 22, 98–99, 272, 298
Black Power era (Eastwood neighborhood), 96
Bloch, Ernst, 31, 111, 113–15, 117, 120, 126, 128n15
body. *See* human bodies
bones: CMP image of careful women caring for, 231, 308; Cyprus forensic investigations working with, 227–31; distinctions between corpses and, 240n8; photographs from Cyprus mass graves, 226–27. *See also* human bodies
Borneman, John, 47
Bosnia-Herzegovina (BiH): as an assemblage, 79; Bosnian Spring or Bosnian Occupy Movement (2014) eventual failure in, 22, 270–73, 296; comparing global health interventions in West Africa and, 269–76; confronting the effects of international neoliberalism on, 30; Dayton Accords (1995) ending the war in, 67, 272, 274; failure of postwar governance of, 66–67; international protectorate over, 67; NGOs providing psychosocial services in postwar, 66, 67–70; Srebrenica massacre and collective grief in, 2, 275; therapeutic governance and humanitarian psychiatry in, 45–47, 65–72; UN Development Program report on "huge dependency syndrome" of, 73–74; volatile economies and faltering infrastructures of, 41–42; wartime deaths and population displacements in, 67; when "it" becomes "who" in genocide of, 232; "Yugo-nostalgia"

by people in, 73, 74, 78. *See also* former Yugoslavia; Sarajevo (Bosnia-Herzegovina, BiH)
Bosnian Spring (or Bosnian Occupy Movement): hope and struggle for social justice legacy of, 22, 271–73, 296; open citizens' plenums formed out of the, 270–71, 272; Senad Hadžifejzović's television interview with leaders of, 271; Tuzla protests (2014) evolving into, 270, 297
Bosnian war, 3
Brazil: Adriana Varejão's skin color ink project in, 2, 182–92; anthropophagy (symbolic consumption) metaphor for cultural production in, 175, 194; Catarina's story on pharmaceuticalization of mental health care in, 45; drought in São Paulo, 256; new regime of public health in, 59–60; new rule of law formally making the abandoned into citizens, 285–86; Novo Hamburgo of, 278f, 278–80, 284–85, 291; Pesquisa Nacional em Domicílios (PNAD) survey on skin color in, 183–90; population living in poverty or indigent in, 52; skin color functioning as a language in, 183; volatile economies and faltering infrastructures of, 41–42; zones of abandonment institutionalized in, 52–53. *See also* Vita (Brazil)
British Inforce Foundation, 221
Brown, Michael, 98, 298
Brown, Wendy, 19–20
Butler, Judith, 12, 28, 95, 122, 273

Cabrito (Grupo Centro resident), 121–22, 129n35
California: diminishing water supply in, 256–57; wildfires (2015) in, 247
calligraphies: Chicago's Eastwood neighborhood, 298–99; in Mexico City, 299–300; zen exercise through, 295
Calvin, Jean, 304
Caminhãozinho (Samuel Lopes) [Vita resident], 285–86
cannibalization: becoming the Other through artistic, 192–93; comparing concepts of anthropophagy and, 175; "Eyewitnesses" (Varejão) example of, 303–4; prevalent in Varejão's art, 174–75, 182–94, 303–4; simultaneously reproducing forms of depiction and producing new ones, 194; Varejão's making ink for skin color project expression of, 2, 182–92; as way of managing questions of

transformation, 175; zen exercise through indie-gestion and, 295, 301–3
Capital in the Twenty-First Century (Piketty), 20
capitalism: Catarina's story and implications regarding, 45; "cruel optimism" of, 20–21; Deleuze's understanding of plasticity of power and techno-, 24, 26; driving land rush over former Ayoreo habitation (Paraguay), 206–8, 301, 303; ethnographic sensorium to demystify power and, 22–23; expansion of inequality through underregulated, 20; fantasy and attachment in contemporary, 20; ideologies and political choices propelling, 22; postwar Sarajevo's privatization mafia form of, 75; social reconfigurations of power, discipline, and profit of, 24–28. *See also* ideologies
carbon dioxide (CO_2): Arrhenius's greenhouse effect projections (1896) on, 263; Hansen's study on Venus levels of, 258, 313; health risks of, 245–46; Manabe's climate modeling of increased levels of, 257–58; rising levels of, 243–44, 244f; stabilization wedges for managing levels of, 250–51, 312; U.S. Department of Labor standards on, 245
Cargill (food-processing company), 256
Carlos, Luis (Vita resident), 62, 64
Carneiro da Cunha, Manuela, 175
Carpenter, Stephen, 252, 253, 254–55, 312
Carroll, Lewis, 135, 148
cartography, 7, 56–57, 176. *See also* geographies of becomings; place (territory)
cases (legal, medical, psychological): Berlant on the way that judgment defines, 283; how they trouble norms and create openings, 283
caste violence/cow protection (*gauseva*) association, 153–54
Castile, Philando, 298
Catarina/Catkine (Catarina Inês Gomes Moraes): connecting with Catarina's daughter Andrea, 1, 279, 281–84, 288–91; death and burial at Novo Hamburgo cemetery, 278–80, 280f; Deleuze's work used to understand struggles of, 45; early life and progressive illness of, 58–59; ethnographic memorial of, 280f, 290f, 290–91; on her detachment from accepted truth, 30; on her needs and desires, 54, 64, 295; on her "rheumatism," 61; her struggle for understanding and becoming, 44–45, 46, 57–58; her three children sharing and continuing her story, 290f, 290–91; her writings defining a subjectivity, 80–81; highlighting pharmaceuticalization of mental health care in Brazil, 45, 46, 51–55, 59–60, 63–64; on living with signification through her memories, 64; Machado-Joseph Disease diagnosis and legacy of, 59, 279, 281, 282, 283, 284–85, 288–89, 295–96; naming herself after Akineton (biperiden), 1, 45; recalling her abandonment at Vita, 1, 10, 17, 30, 44–45, 46, 51–55, 58–65; refusal to depict herself as a victim, 64; on society of bodies living at Vita, 52–53; violent response to learning her family would not visit, 83; visiting Lili, former roommate of, 286–88. *See also* missing people; *Vita* (Biehl); Vita (Brazil)
Catarina's dictionary: capturing the messiness of her world, 57–58; Catarina on the world created in, 44, 295; as ethnographic theory of the leftover subject, 62–65; as evidence of struggles to define subjectivity, 80–81; failure to take her back home, 83; implications of "separation of bodies" written in, 41, 53; new name and identity created in, 1, 45, 46, 57–58, 59, 60–61, 63. *See also* stories; writing
catastrophe theory, 253–54, 254f
cave of Abraham (Turkey), 138–39, 140, 144, 308
Center for Limnology (University of Wisconsin), 251, 252
Cerro Grande wildfire (2000), 248
change. *See* climate change; social transformations
Chasing Ice (film), 248–49, 249f
Chernobyl nuclear disaster, 258–59, 261, 262, 263, 312
Chicago. *See* Eastwood neighborhood (Chicago)
Christianity: adopted in early Urfa (Turkey), 139–40; "cult of the saints" in Eastern, 140; Greenblatt on Judeo-Christian origin myth and need for life stories, 281; missionary ethnocide of Ayoreo people, 204–8
City of Survivors (Locke), 41
Clastres, Pierre, 205, 301
Clifford, James, 48
climate change: available information on, 246; carbon dioxide (CO_2) levels and impact on, 243–46; changes in dynamics of wildfires,

climate change (continued)
247–48; crossed critical thresholds of planetary life-support systems and, 248–52; denialism of, 257, 261–62; El Niño, 248; exploring the implications of accelerated, 246–47; Fifth Assessment Report of the Intergovernmental Panel on Climate Change on, 244; horizoning work to counter tipping points of, 259–61, 263–64, 295, 310–13; "invisible present" potential for producing unexpected, 251–52, 256, 259, 261; modeling projections of, 257–59, 264; *New York Times* stories reporting on, 256–57; stabilization wedges concept to manage, 250–51, 312; tipping points of, 3, 5, 248–50, 253, 255, 258, 263, 311; trajectories over time of four greenhouse gas concentrations, 244f, 244–45. *See also* Earth; ecology; environment; global warming

climate modeling: Arrhenius's greenhouse effect projections (1896), 263; description and early history of, 257–58; keystone event image of the "end" thinking, 258–59; Manabe's carbon dioxide (CO_2) levels, 257–58; mismatch between reality and current capabilities of, 264

climate scientists: examining the intellectual labor and becomings of, 27, 29; horizoning work by, 259–64, 295, 310–13; quantitating threshold transitions of tipping points, 255, 263

climate tipping points: causing irreversible change, 3, 5, 250; climate modeling, 258, 311; horizoning work to counter, 259–64, 295, 310–13; quantitating threshold transitions of, 255, 263; Thom on structural stability and, 253; triggering albedo effect of glaciers, 248, 250

Clóis (Vita resident), 62, 64
Cobogó publishing house (Rio de Janeiro), 173
Cojñone-Gari aftermath. *See* Ayoreo Cojñone-Gari
Coleman, Gabriella, 24
Collier, Stephen, 55
colonization: combined with cannibalization prevalent in Varejão's art, 174–75; subjectivities underpinning our, 177–78; Varejão's art expressing the ambiguities of, 174, 303
colonized subject: Ayoreo people's bastard delirium as, 201–8, 211; Comaroffs' work on Tswana people as, 12; Fanon's political "I" deconstructing reality of, 12; missionary ethnocide of the, 204–8; negative becoming of Ayoreo as, 201–8, 211; notion of becoming applied to the, 12–13. *See also* indigenous populations

Comaroff, Jean, 12
Comaroff, John, 12
Connolly, William, 31, 219–20
control societies: Deleuze on shift toward, 23–24, 27; what Deleuze's failure to consider digital media tools and, 25
Cook (Eastwood resident), 101, 298
counterknowledge resistance, 24
cow protection (*gauseva*) [India], 153–54
critical theory: becoming notion and ethnographic peopling of, 11–14; Comaroffs' work on anthropology and, 12–13; focusing on people's plasticity and experiences, 11–12
Cruel Optimism (Berlant), 20
Crutzen, Paul, 13
cultures: Adriana Varejão's art created from subjectivities of, 177–78; anthropology on dichotomies of nature and, 14; epigenetics understanding of evolution conditioned by, 14; how archaeological excavations destroy, 224–25; impacting material objects and art, 16; inventing new repertoires to translate between, 177–78
Cutai (Ayoreo people), 197
Cyprus: declaring independence from Great Britain (1960), 218; EOKA-B paramilitary organization of, 221; forensic examination of the mass graves of, 217; Green Line (1958) cease-fire line in, 218–19, 221; Mothers of the Missing in, 222; potential for a truth-and-reconciliation process in, 226, 236–37; reparative "ecology of knowing" framing study of perpetual war in, 218; resemblances between Athens 403 BCE and 2012, 236–37, 307–8. *See also* Republic of Cyprus; Turkish Republic of Northern Cyprus
Cyprus Committee on Missing Persons (CMP), 220–39, 240n13, 307; accomplishments and number of missing identified by, 221; "digging for a future" promotion by, 237; ideology of closure and neutrality mandate of, 222–23; image of careful women caring for bones used by, 231, 308; learning history through moment of naming, 232–35; media coverage of the, 222, 237; mission to identify missing victims, 220;

origins and political representatives in the, 220, 240n13, 307; public criticism of excavations done by, 225–26; secreting forensic evidence of cause of death in work of, 223–26, 237–39; work limited to inter-communal violence, 221–22. *See also* witnessing

Cyprus forensic investigations: becoming human process through, 220, 226–31; CMP's secreting cause of death in their, 223–26, 237–39; CMP's work limited to inter-communal violence, 221–22; "forensic theatre" images of international work in, 222, 237, 241n22; functioning as time machine to moment of death, 217, 219–20, 226–31; image of careful women caring for bones during, 231; photographs of bones from mass graves, 226–27; public criticism of CMP's, 225–26; restoration of history and collective memory through, 220, 226–39; working with the bones and bodies during, 227–31

Cyprus inter-communal violence: Committee on Missing Persons (CMP) working to identify victims of, 220–30; events of the, 307; forensic examination of the mass graves as time machines to, 217, 219–20; Green Line (1958) cease-fire line of the, 218–219, 221; potential for a truth-and-reconciliation process ending, 226; between Turkish Cypriots and Greek Cypriots in, 218–19, 221–22

Cyprus time machines: death artifacts functioning as, 217, 219–20, 226–32; experience of becoming human through, 220, 226–31. *See also* temporalities

Daily Telegraph (Great Britain), 71
Danny (Eastwood resident), 101, 107
darkness: Bloch's view of securing a better future out of the, 31, 111, 113–15, 117, 120, 126, 127, 128n15; manifestations of Mexican, 115–16, 123–27. *See also* negativity
Das, Veena, 158
Dave, Naisargi N., 17, 29, 151, 294, 304, 305, 306
Davis, Elizabeth A., 16, 31, 217, 307, 308
Dayton Accords (1995), 67, 272, 274
death: association of women with, 241–42n29, 308; Catarina's burial and, 278–80, 280f; death artifacts creating time machines of moment of, 217, 219–20, 226–32; Greenblatt on connection between bodies, history, storytelling,

and, 281; Inner Maniat women adoration ritual over the dead, 229, 230; story of a life as also a story of, 279–80. *See also* grief; mourning; witnessing

death artifacts: association of women with death and, 241–42n29; becoming human through work with Cyprus, 220, 226–31; creating time machines of moment of a death, 217, 219–20, 226–32; distinctions between bones and corpses, 240n8; image of careful women caring for bones and, 231; Inner Maniat women adoration of the dead ritual, 229, 230; restoration of Cyprus history and collective memory through, 220, 226–39

Deep Sea Drilling Project (1968–83), 311

dehumanization: of black lives in Eastwood neighborhood, 96–99; #BlackLivesMatter as response to black, 22, 98–99, 273; Butler's theory of grief to understand systematic black lives, 12, 28, 95, 122; Eastwood's community-driven alternative framework of care response to, 108–9; impacting the Eastwood neighborhood residents, 96–99; negative becoming and self-negation as part of, 211–13. *See also* racism

DeLanda, Manuel, 254

Deleuze, Gilles: Abécédaire interviews of, 273; on benefits of moving from criticism and judgment, 32; on cartographic approach to defining subjects, 56–57; Catarina's capacity for living reflecting ideas by, 45; on diseased and bastard types of delirium, 199–200; distinction between clinical language and literature language by, 74; emphasizing potentials of desire, transformation of social fields, and unfinishedness, 43, 55; "ethical plateaus" of, 13; ethnography used to explore ideas of, 42–44; examining Sarajevo's social transformation through work by, 46–47; on exchanges between anthropology and philosophy on becoming, 7–10, 17, 47; formulation of the minority by Guattari and, 113; on Freud's philosophy of memory, 55–56, 296; his theory of individuation and formation of social fields, 8–9, 55; on how people become revolutionary, 273, 274; on invoking potentials of people, 84; on the multiple construction of subjects, 42; on nature of becoming, 8, 9, 10, 14, 42, 148, 199, 213, 240n11; on our lack of belief in the world, 18; on plasticity of power and

INDEX | 365

Deleuze, Gilles (continued)
  techno-capitalism, 24, 26; on shift to "control societies," 23–25, 27; on theory as multiple "tool box" for action, 32, 294; value of ethnographic microanalysis reaffirmed by ideas of, 81; what he might say about Sarajevo's subjectivity as a milieu, 74; on writing as process of becoming, 62; on writing for benefit of a "missing people," 45, 50, 63, 76, 200
Deleuze titles: *Anti-Oedipus* coauthored with Guattari, 301, 302; *Essays Critical and Clinical* by, 41; "Literature and Life," 199–200; "Many Politics," 8; *A Thousand Plateaus*, coauthored with Guattari, 111, 164, 301, 302; "What Children Say," 56
Delić, Alma (pseudonym), 71, 72–73, 74–75
delirium. *See* bastard delirium
democracy. *See* liberal democracy
Derrida, Jacques, 157, 167n8, 314, 316n40
Descartes, René, 157
desire: assemblage concretization of power and, 55–56, 79–80; becoming through experiences of time, space, and, 6; BiH as assemblage of places, peoples, hopes, grievances, and, 79; Catarina's story on her needs and, 54, 64, 295; Deleuze on potentials of transformation of social fields, unfinishedness, and, 43, 55; differentiating between hope and, 115
Diegues, Isabel, 173–74
digital technologies: Deleuze's control society concept and implications of, 25; societal changes due to the, 23–24. *See also* social media
Dipesh (Indian animal activist), 156
Dirty War, The. *See* Mexican drug war
disability. *See* anthropology of disability; mental illness
disciplinary society: evolving modes of control implications for global poverty, 26–27; reconfigurations of power, profit, and, 24–28; transition from sovereign to, 23, 25–26
Discipline and Punish (Foucault), 55
diversity backlash, 18–19
Divided City, The (Loraux), 236
Dome Fire (1996), 247, 248
Dome of the Rock, 309
domination, Fanon's political "I" struggling over, 12
Dresden bombings (World War II), 261

drug war. *See* Mexican drug war
Durand, Nicolas (Chevalier de Villegaignon), 303–4

Earth: Anthropocene epoch of, 259; Apollo 17 "blue marble" photograph of, 258; global warming of, 244f, 244–45, 257–58, 257–59. *See also* climate change; environment
Eastwood neighborhood (Chicago): community-driven alternative framework of care for Mrs. Lana by, 104–8; dehumanization of black lives impacting the, 96–99; demographics and poverty of, 96; "describe your neighborhood" interviews with residents of, 100–104; history of economic decline and homicide rates of, 97; the "lunch money" corner of the, 100–101, 106–7; medicalized interpretation of mental illness versus the, 94–96; once known as Sacred City, 96; providing alternative framework of care for Mrs. Lana, 104–8; as pseudonym for neighborhood fieldwork, 109n5; relationship between mourning and mental illness in, 94; stories of becomings in the inner-city of, 29; symbols of mourning seen in, 101. *See also* African Americans
Ebola epidemic (West Africa), 19, 270
ecology: balance of nature theory in, 252–53; horizoning work to restore stability in, 259–61, 263–64, 295, 310–13; Long-Term Ecological Research Program (NSF) on, 265n31; nonequilibrium spaces and dynamics in, 252–56. *See also* climate change
"ecology of knowing," 218
economic forces, entanglement of material objects with, 16
ecosystems: catastrophe theory on thresholds of, 253–54, 254f; DeLanda's balance of nature theory on ecology and, 252–54; horizoning work to restore stability in, 259–61, 263–64, 295, 310–13; Lake Mendota experiments (Wisconsin), 254–55
ekphrasis (images in words), 192
El Niño, 248
encobijado (murdered body) [Mexican drug war image], 126
environment: Arrhenius's greenhouse effect projections (1896) on the, 263; balance of nature theory in ecology, 252–53; Chernobyl nuclear

disaster to the, 258–59, 261, 262, 263; crossed critical thresholds of planetary life-support systems of the, 248–52; denialism of damage to the, 261–62, 275; Fukushima nuclear disaster to the, 261; global warming of the, 244f, 244–45, 247–48; Hansen's study of Venus, 258, 313; horizoning work to restore stability in, 259–61, 263–64, 295, 310–13; increase of nuclear irradiated, 312; "invisible present" potential for unexpected changes to, 251–52, 256, 259, 261; modeling projections on the, 257–59, 264; *New York Times* stories reporting on changes to the, 256–57; nonequilibrium spaces and dynamics, 252–56; stabilization wedges concept on risks and possible futures of, 250–51, 312. *See also* climate change; Earth

EOKA-B (Cyprus paramilitary organization), 221

epigenetic field: on becomings of people and ecosystems, 14; on a post-Darwinian understanding of evolution, 14

equilibrium dynamics: catastrophe theory on thresholds of ecosystem, 253–54, 254f; De-Landa's balance of nature theory on, 252–56; Lake Mendota whole-lake experiments on, 254–56

Erdoğan, Recep, 310

Escobar, Ticio, 205–6

Eskerod, Torben, 280, 285, 286, 287

Essays Critical and Clinical (Deleuze), 41

ethics: Bennett's "enchantment" investment in the world as precondition for, 272; challenges of ethical "response-ability," 28; "ethical plateaus," 13; Foucault on state power vs. individual, 137–38, 149n20

ethnocide: of Ayoreo people through missionary hunt, 204–8; Clastres on outcomes of, 205; Ticio Escobar on Totobiegosode-Ayoreo 1986 contact, 205–6

ethnographic empiricism: anthropology of becoming's commitment to, 7, 47–51; bastardized indigenous subject often erased by, 200; on dynamism of everyday becomings, 43–44; revelations about our world through, 17–18

ethnographic sensorium: of incomplete moments and stories of lifeworlds, 1–3; for maintaining space for political engagement, 22–23; plasticity of the, 3–6, 22–23; providing us a way back into worldliness, 17–18,

21–23; revealing transformative visions and potentials, 11

ethnography: anthropology of becoming's commitment to empirical, 7; capturing the implications and impact of theories on reality, 30–32; developing area of multispecies, 14–15; emerging from unfinished subjects and realities, 31–32, 60; exploring Deleuze's ideas in context of, 42–44; of Inner Maniat women of Greece, 229, 230; knowledge as "placed" in setting of, 179; power of art invoking human potential by, 84; to understand plasticity of social fields, 12; value of becomings analysis done through multiple disciplines and, 81–84; as way of staying connected to changing social processes, 10–11

Eumenides ("seeing good") [ancient Greece], 307–8

European Union: BiH international protectorate role of, 67; doubts about continued viability of the, 19; UK's 2016 Brexit vote to leave, 18

evolutionary epigenetics, 14

experiences: anthropological work on categories important to, 43–44; Butler's study of self-empowerment and role of, 12, 28, 95, 122; ethnographic peopling of critical theory through study of, 11–14; Zehra's story on her "small-scale" religious, 143–47, 148, 149n32, 310

"Eyewitnesses" (Varejão), 303–4

Fabian, Johannes, 258

family bonds: Andrea (Catarina's daughter) reclaiming her, 1, 279, 281–84, 288–91; Catarina/Catkine's story on mental health care remaking, 44–45, 46; Catarina's narration of her abandonment and cut, 51–55; how Brazil's new regime of public health has impacted, 59–60; psychologization of war aftermath in Sarajevo and remaking of, 46–47; Sarajevo's wartime destruction of, 65–66. *See also* abandonment

Fanon, Frantz, 12

Fassin, Didier, 82

femicide pandemic (Mexico), 126

Ferguson civil unrest (2014), 98

Ferrándiz, Francisco, 222

Fifth Assessment Report of the Intergovernmental Panel on Climate Change, 244

Fire (film) [India], 165

Fischer (Mercury) Ellipsoid (1968), 311
Fischer, Michael M. J., 11, 13, 57, 293
flight: becoming as style of noticing social world dynamics of, 10; Deleuze's writing on lines of, 7, 8–9, 55, 285
forensic investigation. *See* Cyprus forensic investigations
"forensic theatre" images, 222, 237, 241n22
former Yugoslavia: Dayton Accords (1995) ending the war in, 67, 272, 274; humanitarian psychiatry and psychologization of war's aftermath in, 45–47, 65–81; President Tito of, 73; prewar foreign debts and economy of, 73; "therapeutic governance" of international intervention in, 67–68; "Yugo-nostalgia" for the prewar, 73, 74. *See also* Bosnia-Herzegovina (BiH); Sarajevo (Bosnia-Herzegovina, BiH)
fossil fuels. *See* greenhouse gases
Foucault, Michel: *Discipline and Punish* by, 55; "heterotopic" space concept of, 138; *History of Sexuality* by, 55; on "philosophy in activity" detachment, 30; on power of state vs. individual ethics, 137–38, 149n20; on transition from sovereign to disciplinary societies, 23
Frank, Arthur, 95
French Calvinists, 303, 304
French Huguenots, 303, 304
Freud, Sigmund: on "allo-plastic" capacity of altering reality, 12; Deleuze on philosophy of memory and unconscious, 55–56, 296; Little Hans study by, 56; "mourning and melancholia" distinguished by, 94; oedipal theorizing by, 81
Friendicoes animal shelter (India), 155
Fukushima nuclear disaster, 261, 312

Gaia models, 312
Gandhi, Indira, 154, 155
Gandhi, Leela, 167n9
Gandhi, Maneka Anand, 151–52, 153, 154–57, 160, 166, 304–5, 306
Gandhi, Sanjay, 154–55, 306
Garcia, Angela, 5, 26, 31, 111, 299–300
Garner, Eric, 98
Geertz, Clifford, 18, 50, 179–80
Gell, Alfred, 180–81
Genesis (Old Testament), 281
genocide: Armenian, 233–35; Arsenijević on when "it" becomes "who" in, 232; becoming a subject path toward hopeful politics after, 235; Bosnia-Herzegovina (BiH) wartime population displacements and, 67; denial of Holocaust, 234; Srebrenica genocide anniversary (BiH), 2, 275. *See also* violence; war
geographies of becomings, 55–57. *See also* cartography; place (territory)
Geophysical Fluid Dynamics Laboratory (Princeton), 257
Ginsburg, Faye, 24
glaciers: *Chasing Ice* (film) on retreating, 248, 249f; tipping point triggering albedo effect of, 248, 250
global health interventions: comparing the BiH and West African experiences with, 269–76; Ebola epidemic and recent revelations of deficits in, 19, 270; operating at "minimal biopolitics" in West Africa, 270. *See also* humanitarian psychiatry (Sarajevo, BiH); medicalization
global warming: Arrhenius's greenhouse effect projections (1896) on the, 263; changes in dynamics of wildfires linked to, 247–48; denialism of, 257, 261–62; Fifth Assessment Report of the Intergovernmental Panel on Climate Change on, 244; horizoning work to slow down, 259–61, 263–64, 295, 310–13; modeling projections of, 257–59, 264; trajectories over time of four greenhouse gas concentrations and, 244f, 244–45. *See also* climate change
Gomrich, Ernst, 179
Graner, Eric, 298
Greece: Inner Maniat women adoration of the dead in, 229, 230; resemblances between Cyprus of 2012 and Athens 403 BCE, 236–37, 307–8; Smyrna (now Izmir) burning [1923] dispute over role, 233–34, 235
Greek Cypriots: CMP working to identify intercommunal conflict victims among, 220–31; conflict between Turkish Cypriots and, 218–19, 221–22, 239–40n5, 307; denial of inter-communal violence (1974) by, 233
Greenblatt, Stephen, 281, 283
greenhouse gases: Arrhenius's greenhouse effect projections (1896), 263; barriers to dismantling economy based on fossil fuels, 245; carbon dioxide (CO_2), 243–46, 250–51, 258, 263; *New York Times* stories on environment effects of, 256–57; stabilization

wedges concept on reductions of, 251–52, 312; trajectories over time of concentrations of four, 244f, 244–45
Green Line (Cyprus, 1958), 218, 219, 221
Gregory, Mr. (Eastwood resident), 106
grief: Butler's *Precarious Life* study reconceptualizing madness as, 12, 28, 95, 122; a communal framework of grief for both mourning, madness, and, 104–8; expressed by Jo Jo's peers in care for Mrs. Lana, 105; racial inequality of grievable and ungrievable lives, 122; Srebrenica massacre anniversary and expression of collective, 2, 275. *See also* death; mourning
Grupo Centro (Mexico City): as *anexo* to addiction treatment, 118; Cabrito's testimony given at, 121–22, 129n35; description of the, 117; individuals confined (*anexados*) and living at, 118; Magi's internment at, 124–27; Padrino Rafa founder of, 119–20, 124, 125, 300; the twelve *anexados* living in, 120–27. See also *anexos* residential centers (Mexico)
Guattari, Félix: *Anti-Oedipus* coauthored with Deleuze, 301, 302; on becoming turning the self into question-machine, 17, 164; concerned with the idea of becoming, 7, 42, 213; "ethical plateaus" concept of, 13; formulation of the minority by Deleuze and, 113; on interpreting symptoms, 74; *A Thousand Plateaus* by Deleuze and, 111, 164, 301, 302; writing with Deleuze on assemblages, 55, 80
Güneydoğu Anadolu Projesi (GAP) [Urfa, Turkey], 148n14

Hacking, Ian, 70
Hadžifejzović, Senad, 271, 272
Hamlet (Shakespeare), 282
Hammoudi, Abdellah, 47
Hansen, James, 258, 313
Haraway, Donna, 28
Help in Suffering shelter (India), 163
"heterotopic" space, 138
Hindu nationalism, cow protection (*gauseva*) association with, 153–54
Hirschman, Albert, 29, 48
history: Armenian genocide, 233–35; becoming as not being part of, 8, 10; as belonging to future generations, 225, 239; Cyprus CMP's forensic work to name missing and restore to, 220, 226–39; Cyprus CMP's secrecy and oscillation of myth and, 223–26, 237–39; dispute over Smyrna (now Izmir) burning [1923], 233–34, 235; epigenetics understanding of evolution conditioned by, 14; Greenblatt on connection between bodies, death, storytelling and, 281; Purcell on persistence of layered, 10; when "it" becomes "who" in genocide, 232. *See also* archaeological excavations
History of Sexuality (Foucault), 55
Holocaust denial, 234
hope: Bennett's reflections on "enchantment" investment in the world and, 272; Bloch on better future through, 31, 111, 114–15, 117, 120, 126, 128n15; Bosnian Spring (or Bosnian Occupy Movement) legacy of, 22, 271–73, 296; differentiating between desire and, 115; Mexico City demonstration (2014) as expression of, 116; negativity linked to positive trajectory of, 117; social movements creating both a demand for better future and, 271–73; violence as force for annihilation and also for, 127
Horace, 192
horizoning work: by Canadian Bay of Fundy mariners, 260–61; description and examples of, 259–60; Gaia models, 312; 1968 predecessor horizon, 310–11; Obama administration's pursuit of, 310; providing space of environmental decision making, 263–64; for restoring stability in changing systems, 260; World War II bombing of German cities as refusal of, 261; zen elementary exercise using, 295, 310–13
human bodies: Catarina's abandonment at Vita of her, 51–55, 58–59; Foucault's biopower concept on reterritorializing, 55; Greenblatt on connection between history, death, storytelling and, 281; Vita's society of abandoned, 52–53. *See also* bones
human condition: anthropological work on categories important to, 43–44; letting go of assumptions to study becoming, 9–10
human dignity ("I" struggle), 12
Humane Society International, 153
humanism: becomings of Indian animal rights activists in context of, 17; as foundation of anthropological thought, 16–17; historic roots of crisis over our world and, 19–20; witnessing to become animal or anthropocentric, 160–64

INDEX | 369

humanitarian psychiatry (Sarajevo, BiH): Deleuze's thoughts used to understand "missing people" of, 46–47; events leading to institutionalization of, 45–47, 65–68; language used for interpretation of symptoms, 74–75; legacy of the, 71–72; Locke's investigation into "missing people" in system of, 47, 65–72, 80–81; NGOs (nongovernmental organizations) role in providing, 66, 67–70; psychological language incorporated into local sense making, 68; UN's report on "huge dependency syndrome" of BiH reinforcing, 73–74; "The War Is Over but Sarajevans Cannot Find the Peace They Seek" (*Daily Telegraph* article) on, 71. *See also* global health interventions; mental health care; psychiatric rationality

Hurtić, Zlatko, 73

"I Am a Man" radical becoming (Memphis, 1968), 165

Ichadie (New People): Ayoreo people renaming themselves the, 198, 302; creating New Person by reconstituting *ayipie* (soul matter), 202

identity: Catarina/Catkine creating a more livable reality and, 1, 45, 46, 57–58, 60–65, 80–81, 83; missionary ethnocide fracturing collective, 205–6; naming the missing to restore history and, 232–35; reemergence of religion in public sphere of, 19

ideologies: CMP's neutrality mandate and closure, 222–23; ethnographic fieldwork revelations about, 17. *See also* capitalism; neoliberalism

Idgah slaughterhouse (New Delhi), 159–60

images: cannibalization and colonization of, 2, 174–75, 182–94; of careful women caring for bones by CMP, 231; *ekphrasis* (images in words), 193; of forensic photographs of bones from Cyprus mass graves, 226–27; "forensic theatre," 222, 237, 241n22; incommensurability of language and, 194; Mexican drug war *encobijado* (murdered body), 126; mourning women, 222, 241n22. *See also* art

inclusion: examining social orders and exclusion and, 27; growing backlash against progressive, 18–19

India: Animal Birth Control program in, 155; becomings of animal rights activists in, 17, 29; Bharatiya Janata Party (BJP) of, 154; cow protection (*gauseva*) association with caste violence and Hindu nationalism, 153–54; Friendicoes animal shelter in, 155; how affective history of liberalism is linked to animal activism in, 153–56, 167n9; Idgah slaughterhouse in New Delhi, 159–60; Indian and lesbian activism in, 165, 166; mass sterilization program of the poor (1975–77) in, 155; Prevention of Cruelty against Animals (PCA) Act of 1960, 154, 305; Project Tiger conservation initiative of, 154

Indian and lesbian activism, 165, 166

Indian animal activism: Animal Birth Control program, 155; anthropological literature on animal politics and, 167n15; Crystal Rogers on event triggering her, 2, 151–52, 153, 158, 160, 306; Help in Suffering shelter, 163; how affective history of liberalism linked to, 153–56, 167n9; influence of foreign NGOs on development of, 153; Kindness to Animals and Respect for Environment (KARE), 158–59; People for Animals organization, 155; perceived as having anti-Muslim sentiments, 153–54; political engagement between humans and animals through, 152–53; Project Tiger conservation initiative, 154; Welfare for Stray Dogs, 156; zen elementary exercise on, 295, 304–7. *See also* animals

Indian animal activists: Abrams-Meyers family, 162–64, 165, 166, 304, 305–6; Carmelia Satija's work as, 158–60, 164, 165–67, 304, 306; Crystal Rogers's work as an, 2, 151–52, 153, 157, 158, 160, 304, 306; Maneka Gandhi as well-known, 151–52, 153, 154–57, 160, 166, 304–5, 306; stories of becomings from, 29; their becoming in context of humanism, 17; Timmie Kumar, 163, 166, 304, 306; witnessing role of, 156–64

indigenous populations: contradictions in anthropological theory on, 211–13; missionary ethnocide of, 204–8; negative becoming among, 211–13; "societies of refusal" among, 310, 315n18; violence stalking small, 211. *See also* Ayoreo people (Paraguay); colonized subject

individuals: Deleuze's control societies making "dividuals" out of, 23; Deleuze's theory of individuation and formation of, 8–9, 55; examining how they orient themselves to multiplicity, 28–29; exploring social world through collaboration of individuals and unified voice, 51. *See also* lifeworlds; self; subjects

Industrial Revolution, 243

inequalities: Anthropocene geological era on global workings of, 13–14; Fanon's political "I" struggling over, 12; fueling the illegal drug trade in Mexico, 129n32; underregulated capitalism and expansion of, 20. *See also* poverty

In-Force Foundation, 221, 308

Ingold, Tim, 14

Inner Maniat women study (Greece), 229, 230

Integrated Ocean Driving Program, 311

International Biological Program (1964–75), 311

International Committee of the Red Cross, 220

International Geophysical Year (1957–58), 311

International Ocean Discovery Program, 311

Internet: Deleuze's control society concept and implications of, 25; societal changes due to the, 23–24. *See also* social media

intimacy: post-Enlightenment Western thought on, 160–61; of witnessing, 152, 160–64

"invisible present" concept, 251–52, 256, 259, 261

Iraci (Vita resident), 280–81, 295

Iranian revolution (1979), 302

ISIS (Islamic State of Iraq and Syria): destruction of ancient ritual sites by, 134; Urfa buffer zone between Kurdish and Turkish military and, 2, 138

Islam: *salafi*, 309; Sunni, 137, 141–43, 149n17. *See also* anthropology of Islam; Quran

Izmir (then Smyrna) burning [1923], 233–34, 235

Jansen, Stef, 271–72, 274

Jardim, Laura, 279, 284

Jetztzeit (moments of solidarities), 297

Jorge (Vita infirmary caregiver), 288

Joyce, James, 84

Judeo-Christian origin myth, 281

judgment: anthropology of becoming moving to constructive questions form, 32–33; Deleuze on benefits of moving from criticism and, 32; how legal, medical, psychological cases are defined by, 283

Justin (Eastwood resident), 93

Kadir Gecesi (Night of Power), 133, 140–41, 148n1

Kafka, Franz, 80, 84

Kahlo, Frida, 167

Karadžić, Radovan, 70

Kearns, Officer, 96, 97

Keller, Catherine, 113

kharassein (engrave or scratch body), 299

kidnappings. *See* Mexican kidnappings

Kindness to Animals and Respect for Environment (KARE) [India], 158–59

King Lear (Shakespeare), 281

King, Martin Luther, Jr., 97

Kirskey, Eben, 15

Kleinman, Arthur, 95

knowledge: anthropological use of sociology and politics of production of, 49–50; art as construction of material objects and object of, 178–82; complexity of secrecy and becoming in Cyprus CMP production of, 223–26, 237–39; Deleuze's writing on totalizing forms of power and, 7–9, 10; openness to the Others, 33; as "placed" in ethnographical setting, 179; subject transformed into the object through writing, 193. *See also* scientific knowledge

Kumar, Timmie (Indian animal activist), 163, 166, 304, 306

Kurdish militias, 2, 138, 148nn12,13

kutsal baliklar (sacred fish), 133

Lake Mendota experiments (Wisconsin), 254–55

Lana, Mrs. (Eastwood resident): arrested for duct tape incident, 102–3, 299; community-driven alternative framework of care for, 104–8; driven mad after witnessing the shooting death of her son, 93–94, 97, 101–2, 298; examining differing perspectives of mental illness and care of, 1, 10–11, 29, 93–94; her refusal to accept son's death codified as mental illness, 103; Marla on challenges of mother's madness, 103–4; neighbors invited to visit, 105–6; physician versus neighborhood perspective on madness of, 94–96, 101–2

language: Catarina's creation of a new identity through her dictionary's, 1, 45, 46, 57–58, 59, 60, 63; Deleuze's distinction between clinical and literary, 74; for expressing interpretation of symptoms in Sarajevo, 74–75; expressing "Yugo-nostalgia" (Sarajevo, BiH), 73, 74; humanitarian psychiatry incorporated into BiH, 68; incommensurability of image and, 194; translating and inventing new repertoires and, 177–78

Las Conchas fire (2011), 247–48
Latour, Bruno, 181
Lens, Sidney, 218
Léry, Jean de, 174, 303–4
lesbian activism (India), 165
Levinasian animal, 157–58
Lévi-Strauss, Claude, 75, 178–79, 181, 182, 193, 238
liberal democracy: Bosnian Spring's open citizens' plenums experiments in, 270–71, 272, 296; declining faith in politics of, 18–19; *homo oeconomicus's* lost capacity for, 21–22; impact of neoliberalism encroachment into social life and, 19–20; Indian animal activism's relationship to, 153–56, 167n9
lifelines (accompaniers on), 295, 314n6
lifeworlds: affective-material shifts in, 297–98; as always also a story of death, 279–80; collective becomings to understand many Sarajevan, 65–80; ethnographic sensorium of incomplete views onto, 1–3; ethnographic theory as emerging from unfinished subjects and, 31–32; psychologization of war aftermath in Sarajevo and remaking of, 46–47; writing for missing people and their, 45, 47, 50, 63, 65–72. *See also* individuals; stories; worlds/worldliness
Lili (Vita resident), 286–88
Lima, Andrea de (Catarina's daughter): connecting with sister on Facebook, 289; photograph with siblings, 290f; reconnecting after abandonment, 1, 279, 281–84, 288–91; requesting Machado-Joseph Disease test, 283–84, 288–89, 295–96; sharing mother's memorial and continuing story with siblings, 290f, 290–91
line of flight, 7, 8–9, 55, 295
literature: on animal politics in India, 167n15; becoming the Other through engagement with incompleteness of, 193; Deleuze's distinction between clinical language and language of, 74; Margaret Lock's review of medicalization, 87n95–88n95; on racism and poverty increasing risk for mental illness, 100. *See also* writing
"Literature and Life" (Deleuze), 199–200
Little Hans study (Freud), 56
Ljubović, Senadin, 65–66
Lock, Margaret, 14, 70, 87–88n95
Locke, Peter, 1, 30, 41, 45, 46, 51, 65–72, 269, 294, 296, 297, 314

Loga, Slobodan, 71, 73
Long, Nicholas, 307
Long-Term Ecological Research Program (NSF), 265n31
Look, Listen, Read (Lévi-Strauss), 179
Loraux, Nicole, 236, 308
Lorraine, Tamsin, 146
Lyotard, Jean-François, 306

Machado-Joseph Disease: Catarina's daughter Adriana testing negative for, 290; Catarina's daughter Andrea requesting a test for, 283–84, 288–89, 295–96; Catarina's diagnosis of, 28, 59, 279, 295; Catarina's son Adriano's diagnosis of, 284–85
Mad Dogs and an Englishwoman (Rogers), 151–52
madness. *See* mental illness
Magi (Grupo Centro resident), 124–27
Magnus, Mr. (Vita employee), 281, 285
Magnuson, John, 251–52, 259, 312, 313
Mahmood, Saba, 135
Maja. *See* Šrić, Marija (Maja) [Sarajevo resident]
Makarios, President (Cyprus), 221
Malabou, Catherine, 259
Malinowski, Bronislaw, 12, 50
Manabe, Syukuro "Suki," 257–58
"Many Politics" (Deleuze), 8
Marcus, George, 48–49
Marino (adoptive father of Catarina's child), 279, 288
Mario (Grupo Centro senior anexado), 124
Marla (Mrs. Lana's daughter): on challenges of her mother's madness, 103–4, 105; on death of brother triggering her mother's madness, 93, 94, 101–2; on her mother's arrest and Mental Health Court hearing, 102–4, 299; inviting the neighbors to begin communal care of her mother, 105–8
Martin, Trayvon, 98, 298
mass media: Bosnian Spring coverage on social media and, 271–73; Cyprus Committee on Missing Persons (CMP) coverage by social media, 222, 237; Deleuze's failure to consider control societies and tools of social media and, 25; dependence of forensic theatre on social media and, 222, 237, 241n22; U.S. presidential election (2016) role of social media and, 36n88

material objects: art as construction of object of knowledge and, 178–82; customs, values, and symbols impacted by art and, 16; multispecies ethnography on the human, animal, and, 14–16; social, political, and economic entanglement with, 16

Mauss, Marcel, 12

Maya (Indian animal activist), 156

Mayo, Katherine, 153

"May you go to the blue lake" (*bedua* curse), 145–46

meaning: cultural context in art, 179; Cyprus CMP's secrecy and oscillation of history and mythical, 223–26, 237–39; multiple nature of art's, 16, 174–78; of stasis as social death, 12

Médecins Sans Frontières, 71

media. *See* mass media; social media

medicalization: anthropological work to understand politics and ethics of, 46; Catarina's abandonment by family facilitated through, 1, 10, 17, 30, 41, 44–45, 46, 51–55, 58–65; Eastwood neighborhood interpretation of mental illness versus, 94–96, 101–2; Margaret Lock's review of literature on, 87–88n95; Mrs. Lana's refusal to accept son's death codified as mental illness, 103; of PTSD in postwar Sarajevan, 71, 73, 74, 78, 79. *See also* anthropology of disability; global health interventions; psychiatric rationality

medications: Brazilian public health regime and distribution of free, 59–60; Catarina's renaming of herself after Akineton (biperiden), 1, 45; Catarina's story on pharmaceuticalization of mental health, 44–45, 46, 51–55, 59–60, 63–64

melancholia vs. mourning (Freud), 94

memories: Athens (403 BCE) Thirty Tyrants amnesty distortion of, 236, 307–8; Catarina on living with signification through her, 64; Catarina's narration of her abandonment, 51–55; Cyprus forensic restoration of history and collective, 220, 226–39; Deleuze on Freud's philosophy of psychoanalysis through, 55–56, 296; Inner Maniat women's "adornment of the dead" ritual of, 229; missionary ethnocide fracturing collective, 205–6; of World War II Dresden bombings, 261; "Yugo-nostalgia" for prewar, 73, 74, 78

mental health care: Brazil's new regime of public health and, 59–60; Catarina's story on pharmaceuticalization of, 44–45, 46, 51–55, 59–60, 63–64; Eastwood's community-driven alternative framework of, 104–8; enabling hybrid ways of remaking lives, families, and social roles, 44–46. *See also* humanitarian psychiatry (Sarajevo, BiH); psychiatric rationality

mental illness: Ayoreo people's susceptability to *urusoi* (madness), 208–10; a communal framework of grief for both mourning, grief, and, 104–8; Eastwood neighborhood vs. medicalized interpretation of, 94–96; Freud's "mourning and melancholia" distinguished by, 94; Metzl's argument on political nature of treatments for, 99–100; Mrs. Lana's grief triggering her madness, 93–94, 97, 101–2, 298; physician vs. neighborhood perspective on Mrs. Lana's, 94–96, 101–2; PTSD (post-traumatic stress disorder), 71, 73, 74, 78, 79; relationship between mourning and, 94; shift in diagnosis of schizophrenia in the U.S., 99. *See also* anthropology of disability

Merleau-Ponty, Maurice, 193, 306

Metzl, Jonathan, 99, 100

Mexican drug war: *anexos* residential addiction treatment centers arising from, 25, 118–27, 129n32, 294, 295, 299–300; apocalyptic visions related to, 127n2; considering the brutal toll of the, 5; The Dirty War (*Guerra Sucia*) period of the, 128n23; *encobijado* (murdered body) image of the, 126; racial inequality of grievable and ungrievable lives evidenced in, 122; research on factors fueling the illegal drug trade, 129n32. *See also* substance abuse

Mexican kidnappings: Bar Heavens mass kidnapping (2013), 123–24, 125, 126, 127; the drug war's increased violence connection to, 123–24; engaged in by *anexos*, 124–27; of forty-three Ayotzinapa Normal School students (2014), 111, 115, 127n1

Mexico: Bloch on securing a better future out of darkness of, 31, 111, 113–15, 117, 120, 126, 127, 128n15; disappearance of Ayotzinapa Normal School students (2014) in, 111, 115, 127n1; ethnographic tracing of crises shaping present, 113; femicide pandemic declared in, 126; as land of repeated social protests

Mexico (continued)
movements, 300; manifestations of darkness in, 115–16, 123–27; "Nuestra Señora de la Santa Muerta (the Death Saint)" patron saint in, 123, 299–300; violence and religion folded together in *anexos* of, 25, 119–22, 126, 294

Mexico City (Mexico): Bar Heavens mass kidnapping (2013) in, 123–24, 125, 126, 127; demonstration protesting missing forty-three students in, 1–2, 11, 111–12, 116; Grupo Centro *anexo* for addiction treatment in, 117–27, 129n35, 300; increased violence and kidnappings in, 123–24; Taibo on 1968 massacre of student demonstrators in, 116–17

Milan (Sarajevo resident), 76–78, 275

Mirza (Sarajevo resident), 275

missing people: CMP working to identify bodies of the Cyprus war, 220–39; Deleuze on writing for benefits of a, 45, 50, 63, 76, 200; "forensic theatre" media coverage of, 222, 237, 241n22; restoring to history by naming the, 232–35; writing for Sarajevo's, 47, 65–72, 80–81. *See also* Catarina/Catkine (Catarina Inês Gomes Moraes)

missionary ethnocide: of Ayoreo people (Paraguay), 204–8, 302; Clastres on outcomes of, 205

Mitchell, W. J. T., 192

Moraes, Nilson (Catarina's husband), 58, 279

Mother India (Mayo), 153

Mothers of the Missing (Cyprus), 222

Mothers of the Plaza de Mayo (Argentina), 222

mourning: Black Chicago understanding of mental illness and, 94; a communal framework of care for both grief, madness, and, 104–8; Eastwood neighborhood vs. medicalized interpretation of, 94–96, 101–2; Freud's distinguishing between melancholia and, 94; images of women in, 222, 241n22; symbols visible in Eastwood neighborhood, 101. *See also* death; grief

Muhammad, Prophet, 133, 141, 142

multiplicity: Deleuze on construction of subjects, 42; examining how individuals orient themselves to, 28–29; of meanings of art, 16, 174–78; reworking classification schemas of race, 29–30

multispecies ethnography, 14–16

Mushroom at the End of the World, The (Tsing), 15–16

Myth and Meaning (Lévi-Strauss), 238

myths: Ayoreo people's Original Time myths of the Ancestor Beings, 202–3, 302; Cyprus CMP's secrecy and oscillation of history and, 223–26, 237–39; Judeo-Christian origin myth, 281. *See also* stories

naming: Catarina/Catkine creating a more livable reality through, 1, 45, 46, 57–58, 60–65, 80–81, 83; of Cyprus missing through CMP's forensic work, 220–39; restoring identity and history by, 232–35; when "it" becomes "who" in genocide through, 232

nation-states: transition to disciplinary societies from sovereignty of, 23, 25–26; Urstaat (state power) of, 301, 305, 315n17. *See also* political sphere

Nature (journal), 13

negative becoming: Ayoreo's affirmative negation beginnings of, 201–3; capitalist land rush and exploitation role in, 206–8, 301, 303; dehumanization of, 211–13; missionary ethnocide role in, 204–6

negativity: positive trajectory of hope linked to, 117; as revelatory practice replacing darkness, 113. *See also* darkness

Negri, Antonio, 18

Nehru, Jawaharlal, 154, 305

neoliberalism: humanitarian psychiatry and psychologization of postwar Sarajevo, 45–47, 65–81; impact of encroachment into social life, 19–20; Sarajevo's confrontation of the effects of international, 30; self-reliance and "responsibilization" demanded of, 273. *See also* ideologies

New York Times: diminishing California water supply story in, 256–57; emaciated sea lions story in, 256; travel writer of the, 72

NGOs (nongovernmental organizations): Argentine Forensic Anthropology Team, 221; India's People for Animals, 155; influence on animal activism in India by foreign, 153; In-Force Foundation, 221, 308; Kindness to Animals and Respect for Environment (KARE) [India], 158–59; legacy of therapeutic governance and humanitarian psychiatry in BiH, 70–72; Médecins Sans Frontières's psychosocial programs, 71; Physicians for Human Rights, 221, 240n13, 308; providing psychosocial services in postwar Sarajevo, 66, 67–70; Wings of Hope (Sarajevo, BiH), 66, 69, 76–77, 78–79, 273–76

Nietzsche, Friedrich, 8, 298, 314n15

Nimrod, King (Old Testament), 133, 140

Nogueira, Oracy, 183

nonequilibrium dynamics: balance of nature theory ecology on, 252–56; catastrophe theory on thresholds of ecosystem stability, 253–54, 254f; Lake Mendota whole-lake experiments on, 254–56

Norgaard, Kari, 257, 259

Novo Hamburo (Brazil), 278–80, 280f, 284–85, 291

Noy, Benjamin, 113

nuclear disasters: Chernobyl, 258–59, 261, 262, 263, 312; Fukushima, 261, 312; more nuclear irradiated environments due to, 312; Three Mile Island, 302

"Nuestra Señora de la Santa Muerta (the Death Saint)," 123, 299–300

Obama, Barack, 310

objects: artistic, 16, 178–79, 180–81; cartography, 7, 56–57, 176; material, 14–16; subject of knowledge transformed by writing into the, 193

Occupy Wall Street, 22, 273

Ong, Aihwa, 55

Orientalism (Said), 177

Orlowski, Jeff, 249

Ortiz, Irene, 210, 211

Oscar (Vita's chief caretaker), 278, 279

Other, the: *alterity* as suspicion of self and discovery of, 193; anthropology as a science of the, 193; artistic cannibalization for becoming the, 192–93; Fabian on lack of intersubjective sharing of time and space of, 258; "mimetic faculty" or capacity to become the, 12; openness to knowledge of the, 33; when "it" becomes "who" in genocide naming the, 232; writing that becomes the, 193

Ottoman Empire: dispute over Armenian genocide history of, 233–35; Smyrna (now Izmir) burning [1923] in, 233–34, 235

Özlem (Islamic theology student), 2, 134, 135

Pacala, Steven, 250, 312

Palsson, Gisli, 14

Pandolfi, Mariella, 67, 306

Paraguay: land rush over former Ayoreo habitation in, 206–8, 301, 303; New Tribes Mission spotting a camp of forest Ayoreoa, 201; the 2004 Cojãnone-Gari contact with Ayoreo by, 197–98, 201–3. *See also* Ayoreo people (Paraguay)

Pearl, Mrs. (Eastwood resident), 107

Pearl, Pete (Eastwood resident), 107

Pejei (Ayoreo people), 3, 208–9

People for Animals (India), 155

People for the Ethical Treatment of Animals (PETA), 153

perpetual war: distinguishing malleable from intractable aspects driving, 218; reparative "ecology of knowing" framing study of, 218; study of artifacts of death and Cyprus state of, 218–39. *See also* war

Pesquisa Nacional em Domicílios (PNAD) survey [Brazil], 183–90

Petryna, Adriana, 5, 27, 29, 243, 287, 294, 311–12, 313

pharmaceuticals. *See* medications

philosophy: Deleuze's exchanges between anthropology and, 7–10, 17, 47; ethnographic reclaiming of anthropology of becoming from, 212–13, 214n30; Foucault on displacement from accepted truth through, 30

Physicians for Human Rights, 221, 240n13, 308

Piketty, Thomas, 20

place (territory): assemblage as concretization of power, desire, and, 55–56, 79–80; BiH as assemblage of desire, peoples, hopes, grievances, and, 79; land rush over former Ayoreo habitation (Paraguay), 206–8, 301, 303. *See also* cartography; geographies of becomings

plasticity: anthropology of becoming on subjects and lifeworlds, 3–6, 22–23; anthropology of becoming's study of, 7; Butler's study of self-empowerment through experience and, 12, 28, 95, 122; consequences of disregarding in individual and collective struggles, 80–81; Deleuze's understanding of techno-capitalism and power's, 24; ethnographic peopling of critical theory through study of, 11–14; Freud on "allo-plastic" capacity to alter reality, 12 political sphere: animal activism relationship to India's, 153–56; becoming a subject path toward hopeful postgenocide, 235; challenges of using big data to predict the, 27; declining faith in liberal democratic, 18–19; entanglement with material objects, 16; ethnographic sensorium maintaining the space for engagement in, 22–23; Fanon on the "I" in the, 12; Metzl's argument on treatment of mental illness framed by, 99–100; reemergence of religion in public sphere of, 19; "switching points" moments of political maneuvers in, 13; the uncounted and ambiguous in the, 21–22. *See also* nation-states; social movements

Poniatowska, Elena, 115

poverty: Brazil's population living in, 52; Deleuze on capitalism's role in maintaining, 26; Eastwood neighborhood demographics and levels of, 96; evolving modes of control implications for, 26–27; literature on mental illness risk factors of racism and, 100. *See also* inequalities

Povinelli, Elizabeth, 17, 152, 160

power: Anthropocene geological era on global workings of, 13–14; assemblage concretization of desire and, 55–56, 79–80; becoming as style of noticing the dynamics of, 10; Deleuze's writing on totalizing forms of knowledge and, 7–9, 10; epigenetics understanding of evolution conditioned by, 14; ethnographic fieldwork revelations about, 17; ethnographic sensorium to demystify capitalism and, 22–23; Foucault on individual ethics vs. state, 137–38, 149n20; social reconfigurations of discipline, profit, and, 24–28; *Urstaat* (state power), 301, 305, 315n17

Precarious Life (Butler), 95

Prevention of Cruelty against Animals (PCA) Act [India, 1960], 154, 305

Princeton University, 250

Principle of Hope, The (Bloch), 111, 128n15

prisons and discipline, 25

projection modeling. *See* climate modeling

Project Mohole (1961), 311

Project Tiger conservation initiative (India), 154

Prometheus, 181

Protest Psychosis, The (Metzl), 99

Proust, Marcel, 84

psychiatric rationality: abandonment by Catarina's family excused through, 44–45, 46, 59; anthropological work to understand politics and ethics of, 46; Brazil's new regime of public health leading to condition of, 59–60; Catarina's narration of her abandonment through, 1, 10, 17, 30, 41, 44–45, 46, 51–55, 58–65; Deleuze's thoughts used to understand Sarajevo's "missing people," 47, 65–72, 80–81. *See also* anthropology of disability; humanitarian psychiatry (Sarajevo, BiH); medicalization; mental health care

PTSD (posttraumatic stress disorder): collective depression among Sarajevan lives along with, 79; "The War Is Over but Sarajevans Cannot Find the Peace They Seek" article on, 71; "Yugo-nostalgia" as symptom of, 73, 74, 78

Pupavac, Vanessa, 67

Purcell, Bridget, 10, 28, 133, 308, 309–10

question-machines (self), 17, 164

Quran: Kadir Gecesi (Night of Power) celebrating revelation of, 133, 140–41; treating wart by tying a string and reading verse of, 146; Zehra's story on reading the, 144, 310. *See also* Islam

Rabinow, Paul, 9, 49

race: Butler's theory of grief and systematic dehumanization role of, 12, 28, 95, 122; color (prejudice of mark) categorizing, 183; inequality of grievable and ungrievable lives and, 122; multiplicity reworking of classification schemas of, 29–30. *See also* skin color

racism: #BlackLivesMatter struggle against, 22, 98–99, 272, 298; literature on mental illness risk factors of poverty and, 100; progressive struggle against, 19. *See also* dehumanization

Rafa, Padrino (Grupo Centro founder), 119–20, 124, 125, 300

Ralph, Laurence, 5, 21, 29, 93, 294, 298, 299

Rancière, Jacques, 21, 22

Rapp, Rayna, 24

Raw and the Cooked, The (Lévi-Strauss), 179

realities: Catarina's creation of a new identity for more livable, 1, 45, 46, 57–58, 60, 63; ethnography revealing unfinished subjects and, 31–32, 60; Freud on "allo-plastic" capacity

to alter, 12; of Vita (Brazil) as one that kills, 278–79, 286
reason: denialism of climate change, 257, 261–62; detachment from accepted truth and, 30. *See also* scientific knowledge
Redfield, Peter, 270
religion: Christianity, 139–40, 204–8; European religious battles over the Eucharist, 304; gentrification of shrines across the world, 309; ISIS destruction of ancient ritual sites of, 134; Islam, 137, 141–43, 149n17, 309; Mexico's *anexos* folding together violence and, 25, 121–22, 126, 294; missionary ethnocide through, 204–8, 302; reemergence in public spheres of identity and politics, 19; Turkish "orthodoxization" of local religiosity and, 137–38; Zehra's story on her trajectory in belief and, 143–47, 148, 149n32, 310. *See also* ritual landscape; Urfa ritual space
Renshaw, Layla, 219
Republic of Cyprus, 226. *See also* Cyprus
revolutions: Deleuze on failures of, 273; Deleuze on how people become revolutionary, 273, 274; Iranian revolution (1979), 302; preconditions required for a, 273. *See also* social movements
Rice, Tamir, 298
Rieff, Philip, 67
Rimbaud, Arthur, 9
ritual landscape: anthropology of Islam's limited study of shifting, 134–35; examining how individuals orient themselves in shifting, 135–36; Zehra's story on her trajectory in the, 143–47, 148, 149n32, 310. *See also* religion; Urfa ritual space
Rogers, Crystal, 2, 151–52, 153, 157, 158, 160, 304, 306
Rohit (Indian animal activist), 163
Rorty, Richard, 18–19
Rosy (Ayoreo people), 210–11
Rousseau, Jean-Jacques, 193

Sacred City (Eastwood neighborhood, Chicago), 96
Sahlins, Marshal, 177
Said, Edward, 177
salafi Islam, 309
Sanal, Ashhan, 239
Santa Muerte (the Death Saint), 123
São Paulo (Brazil): Adriana Varejão's skin color ink project, 2, 182–92; drought in, 256; mutual appropriation and cannibalization in art of, 303
Sarajevo (Bosnia-Herzegovina, BiH): confronting the effects of international neoliberalism on, 30; continuing trauma of wartime rape victims living in, 65–66; examining becoming experience of, 75–77; failures of postwar governance of, 66–67; humanitarian psychiatry and psychologization of war's aftermath in, 45–47, 65–81; Koševo Hospital caring for traumatized war victims, 65; local NGOs left to help people of, 66, 67–70; Locke's observations on the continued struggles of, 274–76; the "missing people" of, 47, 65–72, 80–81; *New York Times* travel writer on condition of postwar, 72; outward evidence of normalcy hiding continued problems in, 274–75; residents longing for lost collectivities and solidarities, 71–72; revisiting Mirza, Milan, and Maja (2015 and 2016) in, 275–76; a subjectivity defined by collective struggles in, 80–81; subjectivity of a milieu, 72–74; using Deleuze's work to understand social transformation of, 45, 50, 63, 76; Wings of Hope's psychosocial services for youth of, 66, 69, 76–77, 78–79, 273–76; "Yugo-nostalgia" for prewar, 73, 74, 78. *See also* Bosnia-Herzegovina (BiH); former Yugoslavia
Sard, Ed, 218
Šarić, Marija (Maja) [Wings of Hope director], 69, 72, 76–77, 275–76
Satija, Carmelia, 158–60, 164, 165–67, 304, 306
Schmittian, Carol, 301
Schwarcz, Lilia M., 16, 29–30, 173, 303
scientific knowledge: denialism of climate change, 257, 261–62; horizoning work of climate scientists, 259–64, 295, 310–13; negotiating climate threat with imperfect, 27, 29. *See also* knowledge; reason
Scott, Pastor (Eastwood neighborhood), 106, 107
Sebald, W. G., 261
Sedgwick, Eve Kosofsky, 218, 220, 237
Segal, Judah, 149n28
Šehabović, Šejla, 271
self: Adriana Varejão's art representing parody of the, 174; alterity as discovery of Other and suspicion of, 193; existential improvisation for "out of time," 259; turned into a

self (continued)
  question-machine by becoming, 17, 164. *See also* individuals
self-empowerment: Butler's study of plasticity and experience role in, 12, 28, 95, 122; Eastwood's community-driven alternative framework of care, 104–8
Seremetakis, Nadia, 229, 230
sexuality: Catarina's narration on her own, 54, 64; Foucault's *History of Sexuality* on, 55
sexual minorities: lesbian activism in India, 165; progressive struggle for rights of, 19
sexual violence: Catarina's story on her ex-husband's, 53–54; Sarajevo's Koševo Hospital's care for wartime victims of, 65
"shadows of men," 206
Shakespeare, William, 281, 282
Shalins, Marshall, 301
Sibertin-Blanc, Guillaume, 302
Sierra Leone, 269–70
'68 (Taibo), 116–17
skin color: "Aquarela do Brasil" (Watercolor of Brazil) song on, 190; Brazil's Pesquisa Nacional em Domicílios (PNAD) on, 183–90; functioning as a language in Brazil, 183; "pigmentocracy" creating hierarchies based on, 183. *See also* race; *Tintas polvo* (Octopus ink) series [Varejão]
Small, Burton, 261
Smyrna (now Izmir) burning [1923], 233–34, 235
Snowden, Edward, 23
social bonds: Catarina/Catkine's story on mental health care remaking, 44–45, 46; psychologization of war aftermath in Sarajevo and remaking of, 46–47
social death of stasis, 12
social fields: Deleuze on potentials of desire, unfinishedness, and transformation of, 43, 55; Deleuze's theory of individuation and formation of, 8–9, 10; ethnographic fieldwork to understand plasticity of, 12
social justice: #BlackLivesMatter demands for, 22, 98–99, 272; Bosnian Spring legacy of hope and struggle for, 22, 271–73, 296. *See also* social movements
social media: Anonymous's political use of, 24; Bosnian Spring coverage on mass media and, 271–73; Cyprus Committee on Missing Persons (CMP) coverage by mass media and, 222, 237; Deleuze's failure to consider control societies and tools of, 25; dependence of forensic theatre on mass media and, 222, 237, 241n22; U.S. presidential election (2016) role of, 36n88. *See also* digital technologies; Internet
social movements: Arab Spring, 273; #BlackLivesMatter, 22, 98–99, 272, 298; as full of becomings, 164–65; moment of hope for better future created by, 271–73; Occupy Wall Street, 273; politics and antipolitics played out through, 22; witnessing by, 156–64; Zapatista social justice movements (Mexico), 300. *See also* political sphere; revolutions; social justice
social processes: entanglement with material objects, 16; ethnographic work on dynamism of everyday becomings and, 43–44; ethnography as way of staying connected to changing, 10–11
social roles: Catarina/Catkine's story on mental health care remaking, 44–45, 46; psychologization of war aftermath in Sarajevo and remaking of, 46–47
social theories. *See* theories
social transformations: anthropology of disability on, 24; cannibalization in art use to manage question about, 175; challenge of understanding through quantitative models, 26–28; Deleuze on shift toward "control societies," 23–25, 27; examining implications of Anonymous's political tools for, 24; experienced by Sarajevans through neoliberal rationalities, 30; general longing for, 2; Sarajevo's urban poor still waiting for, 2–3; using Deleuze's work to examine process of Sarajevo's, 46–47
social worlds: Adriana Varejão's art created from subjectivities of culture and, 177–78; becoming as style of noticing dynamics of power and flight in, 10; collaboration of individual narrators and unified voice to explore, 51; critical theory's focus on people's plasticity and experiences in, 11–18; examining how individuals orient themselves to overlapping multiple, 28–29; impact of neoliberalism encroachment into our, 19–20; inclusion and exclusion in, 27; multispecies ethnography on the human, animal, and material, 14–16; "poetic density"

of space shaping and reshaping, 139. *See also* worlds/worldliness

societies: of "anticipation-warding off," 301; Deleuze on monetarial and ideological flows of, 9; Deleuze on the shift to "control," 23–25, 27; Foucault on transition from sovereign to disciplinary, 23; "societies of refusal," 310, 315n18

Society against the State (Clastres), 301

Society for the Prevention of Cruelty to Animals (SPCA), 151

Socolow, Robert, 250, 312

Sofia Mosque (Istanbul), 309

South East Anatolia Development Project, 309

Soviet Union fall (1990s), 19

space: becoming through experiences of time, desire, and, 6; created by Turkish "orthodoxization" of local religiosity, 137–38; "poetic density" shaping social life, 139; Urfa's Balikligöl center as a ritual, 133–34, 137, 138–41; Urfa's "heterotopic," 138

Spanish civil war, 219

Spectacle of the Races, The (Schwarcz), 173, 177

Srebrenica genocide anniversary (BiH), 2, 275

stabilization wedges, 250–51, 312

standardized testing, 25

Stasch, Rupert, 139

Sterling, Alton, 298

Stewart, Kathleen, 10

Štiks, Igor, 272

Stockholm Water Prize, 252

stories: Aasi (Ayoreo people), 201–2, 203; Catarina's children sharing and continuing her, 290f, 290–91; crafted from instances of becoming, 29–33; Greenblatt on Genesis and Apocrypha's origin and human life, 281; how ethnographic subjects become part of the researcher's, 284; Iraci (Vita resident), 280–81; of life as also a story of death, 279–80; Pejei (Ayoreo), 3, 208–9; Rosy (Ayoreo people), 210–11; Tié (Ayoreo people), 197, 198–99, 200. *See also* Catarina's dictionary; lifeworlds; myths

subjectivities: Adriana Varejão's art created from social and cultural, 177–78; Catarina's writings and Sarajevo postwar struggles as defining kinds of, 80–81; Deleuze on desire as undoing forms of power and, 55; Fischer's *terrae incognitae* of, 57; how ethnographic analysis reveals unexpected findings through, 81–82; pieced together into new theories and relationships, 314; Sarajevo's subjectivity as a milieu, 72–74

subjects: anthropology of becoming on plasticity of lifeworlds and, 3–6, 22–23; archaeology versus cartographic approach to defining, 56–57, 62; becomings of the colonized, 12–13; Catarina's "dictionary" as ethnographic theory of herself as, 41, 44, 45, 51, 52–53, 57–58, 60–61, 62–65; Deleuze on the multiple construction of, 42; ethnographic theory as emerging from unfinishedness of, 31–32; how their stories become part of researcher's stories, 284; Tié as indigenous and bastardized, 200; witnessed animal as "spectacle for a specular," 157. *See also specific individuals*

substance abuse: Ayoreo Cojñone-Gari aftermath and increase in, 210–11; Mexican *anexos* residential treatment centers for, 25, 118–27, 129n35, 299–300; Mirza's loss of hope in Bosnia and life of, 275. *See also* Mexican drug war

Sunni Islam: espoused by modern Turkey, 137, 149n17; local reformer intermediaries between Urfa citizens and state-sanctioned, 142; Turkish politics of purification of, 141–43. *See also* Quran

su-vive (to live on), 314, 316n40

Sweig, Stefan, 304

Taibo, Paco Ignacio, 116–17

Taussig, Michael, 12, 212, 237

Telles, Edward, 183

"Tell My Story" (Greenblatt lecture), 281

temporalities: understanding people in different kind of, 82–83; value of research that is receptive to different, 83. *See also* Cyprus time machines

territory. *See* place (territory)

Testmunhas oculares, x, y, z (Eyewitnesses, x, y, z) [Varejão], 175–77

theories: balance of nature, 252–56; catastrophe, 253–54, 254f; contradictions in indigenous populations, 211–13; critical theory, 11–18; Deleuze's theory of individuation, 8–9; ecological nonequilibrium, 252–56; ethnographic, 30, 31–32; ethnography's capture of the implications and impact of, 30–32; Hirschman on long-term engagement with people as antidote to, 48; impact on becomings by anthropological,

theories (continued)
	30–31; as a multiplying "tool box" for action, 32, 294; new materialisms of contemporary social theories, 16; subjectivities pieced together into new, 314
theory of individuation (Deleuze): on becomings as the second line, 8, 55; on line of flight, 8–9, 55, 295; on segmentary line defining categories of people, 8, 55
Thirty Tyrants amnesty (Athens 403 BCE), 236, 307–8
Thom, René, 253
Thomas, Jo Jo (Mrs. Lana's son), 93–94, 98, 101–2, 105, 298
Thomas the Apostle, St., 140
Thompson, Officer, 96
Thousand Plateaus, A (Deleuze and Guattari), 111, 164, 301, 302
Three Mile Island nuclear accident, 302
Tié (Ayoreo people): as indigenous and bastardized subject, 200; on not having her own story, 197, 198–99
Tiko (Eastwood resident), 107
time machines. *See* Cyprus time machines
Tintas polvo (Octopus ink) series [Varejão]: background of the, 182–83; drawing from Brazil's PNAD survey, 183–90; English translation for NYC exhibition (2014), 192; as expression of cannibalization, 2, 182–92; social function of skin color in Brazil expressed in, 183. *See also* race; skin color
tipping points. *See* climate tipping points
Tito, Josip Broz, 73
Totobiegosode-Ayoreo. *See* Ayoreo people (Paraguay)
transformation. *See* social transformations
Travis (Mrs. Lana's son), 102, 103–4, 105, 106
Tristes Tropiques (Lévi-Strauss), 179
Trump, Donald J., 18
truth-and-reconciliation process: comparing Athens (203 BCE) and Cyprus potential for, 236–37, 307–38; question of possible Cyprus, 226
Tsing, Anna L., 15–16
Tswana people (southern Africa), 12
Tupinamba women cannibal feasting (sixteenth century), 303, 304
Turkey: Armenian genocide disputed by, 233–35; broad changes under President Erdoğan in, 310; cave of Abraham in, 138–39, 140, 144, 308; relationship between Urfa province and, 136–37; Smyrna (now Izmir) burning [1923] in, 233–34, 235; state secularism (*laiklik*) and regulation of religious life in, 137; Sunni Islam espoused by modern, 137, 141–43, 149n17. *See also* Urfa (Turkey)
Turkish Republic of Northern Cyprus, 226. *See also* Cyprus
Turkish Cypriots: CMP working to identify intercommunal conflict victims among, 220–30; conflict between Greek Cypriots and, 218–19, 221–22, 239–40n5; violence by Greek Cypriots (1974) against, 233, 307

Undoing the Demos (Brown), 19–20
unfinishedness: anthropology of becoming's study of, 5–7; Deleuze on potentials of desire, transformation of social fields, and, 43, 55; disposition for becoming driven by, 114–15; ethnographic theory as emerging from, 31–32; openness to knowledge of Others and ethos of, 33; power of art to invoke the human potential of, 84; zen elementary exercise on, 295, 313–14
United Kingdom Brexit (2016), 18
United Nations (UN): BiH international protectorate role of, 67; Cyprus's Committee on Missing Persons (CMP) established under auspices of, 220–39, 307; Cyprus Green Line (1958) cease-fire line established by, 218, 219, 221; reporting on "huge dependency syndrome" of BiH, 73–74
United States: backlash against progressive inclusion in the, 18–19; changing dynamics of wildfires in the, 247–48; election of Trump to presidency of the, 18; institutional transformations going on in, 25; shift in diagnosis of schizophrenia in the, 99; social media role in 2016 presidential election of the, 36n88
University of Sarajevo (BiH), 69, 71
University of Wisconsin's Center for Limnology, 251, 252
Urfa (Turkey): description and population of, 136; early history of "Orhay" or, 139–40; Güneydoğu Anadolu Projesi (GAP) in, 148n14; "heterotopia" space of, 138; Kadir Gecesi (Night of Power) celebrated in, 133, 140–41, 148n1; relationship between Turkey

and province of, 136–37; rise of Islamic revival in, 141–42; state "orthodoxization" of local religiosity in, 137–38; state-sponsored Sunni Islam in, 137, 141–43, 149n17; zen elementary exercise on becoming of, 295, 308–10. *See also* Turkey

Urfa ritual space: Christianity adopted into, 130–40; layered nature of, 140–41; Mother Mary Church, 140; "poetic density" of the, 139; politics of purification in the, 141–43, 149n28; state "orthodoxization" of local religiosity and, 137–38; Zehra's story on her trajectory in, 143–47, 148, 149n32, 310. *See also* Balikligöl ritual center (Urfa, Turkey); religion; ritual landscape

Urstaat (state power), 301, 305, 315n17

urusoi (madness), 208–10

U.S. Department of Labor, 245

U.S. Forest Service, 247

utopia: Bloch on central function of, 115, 127; societies of "anticipation-warding off" and figures of, 301; suggested by *anexos* as potential reality, 127

Valmir (Catarina's dictionary), 62

Vaquinha (João Paulo Nestore Soares) [Vita resident], 285–86

Varejão, Adriana: cannibalization and colonization in art of, 174–75, 182–94, 303; exploring multiple meanings of art with, 16, 174–78; "Eyewitnesses" by, 303–4; incorporating idea of cartography in art of, 176; learning about art from, 173–78; *Testmunhas oculares, x, y, z* (Eyewitnesses, x, y, z) by, 175–77; *Tintas polvo* (Octopus ink) series by, 2, 182–92; understanding her art as parody, 174

"Varejar, ladrilhar: uma cartografia ladrilhada da obra da artista" (Schwarcz), 175

Venizelos, Eleftherios, 233

Venus study (Hansen), 258, 313

Vera (adoptive mother of Catarina's child), 279, 280, 282, 288

Vibrant Matter (Bennett), 16

viciosos (Puyedie, or Prohibited Ones) [Ayoreo people], 210–11

Vidal, Gore, 218

Villegaignon, chevalier de (Nicolas Durand), 303–4

Vilma (Vita resident), 286

violence: Ayoreo people living in postcolonial and neocolonial, 26, 31; Bloch on construction of better future and role of, 31, 111, 113–15, 117, 120, 126, 127, 128n15; cow protection (*gauseva*) association with caste, 153–54; as force for annihilation and also hope, 127; Idgah slaughterhouse (New Delhi) animal, 159–60; increase of Mexico City kidnappings and, 123–24; Mexican darkness manifested by, 115–16; of Mexico City demonstration (2014), 112; Mexico's *anexos* folding together religion and, 25, 121–22, 126; stalking small indigenous populations, 211; witnessing of, 156–60. *See also* genocide; war

Vita (Biehl), 41, 59, 291, 295. *See also* Catarina/Catkine (Catarina Inês Gomes Moraes)

Vita (Brazil): Clóvis and Luis Carlos residents of, 62, 64; death of Catarina at, 278–79; emergence as part of institutional transformation, 25, 59; Iraci's story, 280–81, 295; Jorge's work as infirmary caregiver at, 288; mentally impaired Vaquinha and Caminhãozinho who live at, 285–86; origins and description of, 51, 52; Oscar, chief caretaker at, 278, 279; as a reality that kills, 278–79, 286; return trip (2011) to, 285–88; society of bodies of the abandoned living at, 52–53; visiting Lili at, 286–88; visiting Vilma at, 286; as zone of abandonment, 52, 53. *See also* anthropology of disability; Brazil; Catarina/Catkine (Catarina Inês Gomes Moraes)

Viveiros de Castro, Eduardo, 175

war: Bosnia-Herzegovina (BiH) deaths and population displacements during, 67; Cyprus inter-communal conflict, 217–39; Locke's work on postwar psychologization of, 45–47, 65–81; "permanent war economy" of, 218; Spanish civil war, 219; World War II, 234, 243, 261. *See also* genocide; perpetual war; violence

"The War Is Over but Sarajevans Cannot Find the Peace They Seek" (*Daily Telegraph* article), 71

War on Drugs. *See* Mexican drug war

Way of the Masks, The (Lévi-Strauss), 179

wedge stabilization, 250–51, 312

Welfare for Stray Dogs (India), 156

West Africa: Ebola epidemic and revelations of global health deficits in, 19, 270; global health's "minimal biopolitics" operations in, 270; Sierra Leone, 269–70
"What Children Say" (Deleuze), 56
white flight, cities reshaped through, 25
Whitehead, George, 222
wildfires: California (2015), 247; Cerro Grande wildfire (2000), 248; changing dynamics of, 247–48; Dome Fire (1996), 247, 248; Las Conchas fire (2011), 247–48
Wings of Hope (Sarajevo, BiH): evolution from "psychodetraumatization" to family support services, 69, 76–77, 78–79; Locke's fieldwork at, 66, 69, 76–77, 78–79; Maja's work as executive director of, 69, 72, 76–77, 275–76; multisystemic approach to psychosocial support now used at, 276; observations of small and marginal becomings in, 273–74
witnessing: Carmelia Satija on her, 159–60, 166–67; Crystal Rogers's on the event of her, 151–52, 153, 158, 160; Derrida's cautions about, 157; Erika Abrams-Meyers's experience with death, 163–64, 166; as intimate event followed by becoming animal, 152, 160–64; obligation to live after, 158; significance and implications of, 157; three elements of, 156–57; time machine function of Cyprus death artifacts form of, 217, 219–20, 226–32. *See also* Cyprus Committee on Missing Persons (CMP); death
women: association of death with, 241n29–42n29, 308; CMP image of caring for bones by careful, 231, 308; how the dead are adorned by the Inner Maniat, 229, 230; images of mourning, 222, 241n22; Mexican drug war image of *encobijado* (murdered body), 126; Mexican femicide pandemic, 126; progressive struggle for rights of, 19; Tupinamba women cannibal feasting (sixteenth century), 303, 304
World Health Organization, 19
worlds/worldliness: ethnography sensorium providing a way back into, 17–18, 21–23; historic roots of crisis over our humanity and, 19–20; political sphere of the uncounted and ambiguous in the, 21–22. *See also* lifeworlds; social worlds

World War II: allies' bombings of German cities during, 261; carbon dioxide (CO_2) and toxic gases released during, 243; Holocaust of, 234
wounded horse encounter (India): Crystal Rogers's activism triggered by, 2, 151–52, 153, 158, 160, 306; description of the, 151–52
writing: becoming the Other through, 193; Deleuze on benefits for missing people, 45, 50, 63, 76, 200; *ekphrasis* (images in words), 192; reconciling art and, 178; for Sarajevo's missing people, 47, 65–72, 80–81. *See also* Catarina's dictionary; literature
Writing Culture (Marcus and Clifford), 48–49

"Yugo-nostalgia" (Sarajevo, BiH), 73, 74, 78
Yugoslavia. *See* former Yugoslavia

Zapatista social justice movements (Mexico), 300
Zehra (Urfa citizen), 143–47, 148, 149n32, 310
zen exercises: catching moments of becomings, 293; examples of powerful affective anthropological, 294–95; New Delhi (animal rights activists) example of, 304–7; restaging zen moments of becoming through, 293; São Paulo (cannibalized art) example of, 303–4. *See also* anthropology of becoming; becomings
zen exercises list: calligraphies (Eastwood neighborhood, Chicago), 298–99; calligraphies (Mexico City *anexos*), 295, 299–300; camaraderies and trajectories (Brazil and Bosnia-Herzegovina), 295–97; cannibalizing and indie-gestion (Ayoreo people, Paraguay), 295, 301–3; horizoning and emergent forms of life (climate change), 295, 310–13; poisoned histories, divided cities (Cyprus), 295, 307–8; poisoned histories, divided cities (Urfa, Turkey), 295, 308–10; swinging the pendulum (affective-material shifts or movements), 295, 297–98; unfinished exercises and lifelines, 295, 313–14
Zimmerman, George, 98
Žižek, Slavoj, 271, 272
Zuhal (Islamic theology student), 2, 134, 135